The Price of Dissent

The publisher gratefully acknowledges the generous contribution to this book provided by the General Endowment Fund of the Associates of the University of California Press.

The Price of Dissent

*Testimonies to Political
Repression in America*

Bud Schultz
Ruth Schultz

UNIVERSITY OF CALIFORNIA PRESS
Berkeley · Los Angeles · London

University of California Press
Berkeley and Los Angeles, California

University of California Press, Ltd.
London, England

© 2001 by the Regents of the University of
California

Library of Congress Cataloging-in-Publication Data

Schultz, Bud.

   The price of dissent : testimonies to political
repression in America / Bud Schultz, Ruth Schultz.
      p.   cm.
   Includes bibliographical references (p.   ) and
index.
   ISBN 0-520-22401-9 (cloth : alk. paper)—
ISBN 0-520-22402-7 (pbk. : alk. paper)
   1. Political persecution—United States—
History—20th century.   I. Schultz, Ruth.
II. Title.

JC599.U5 S393   2001
323'.044'0973—dc21   00-051166

Manufactured in Canada

10   09   08   07   06   05   04   03   02   01
10   9   8   7   6   5   4   3   2   1

The paper used in this publication meets
the minimum requirements of ANSI/NISO
Z39.48-1992 (R 1997) (Permanence of Paper). ∞

To Paul, Steve, Dan, Susan, and David

Contents

Acknowledgments

We are grateful to the persons whose stories appear in this book, and to many other dissenters, for so generously sharing their experiences with us. To Edith Tiger, former Director of the National Emergency Civil Liberties Committee and now Vice President of the Center for Constitutional Rights, whose help with this and the previous volume was so necessary when we were just beginning our work, and to Naomi Schneider, executive editor at the University of California Press, whose patience and guidance were especially helpful at the end of this effort, we are deeply appreciative. We are indebted as well to Ronald Schatz and Cheryl Greenberg, who read and thoughtfully critiqued portions of the manuscript, and to Jonah Raskin and Robert Goldstein for their detailed and important corrections and suggestions for improvement. We were delighted that Mary Renaud was able to work with us again. Her keen eye and precise editing were of immense help in making what we did more accurate, consistent, and readable. And we want to thank Dan Schultz, who developed the cover design that we believe captures so well the point of the book.

Targets of Political Repression in Twentieth-Century America

The Chicago Police Department contained a unit . . . entitled the Subversive Activities Section from 1968 to 1971, the Subversive Activities Unit from 1971 to 1973, and the Security Section from 1973 to 1975 [that] systematically carried out the following actions: investigated and maintained, without reasonable suspicion of criminal conduct, dossiers on, among other things, the lawful First Amendment activities of individuals and organizations; collected information on thousands of organizations and individuals of various political persuasions who were not the subject of any criminal investigation; used infiltrators who became involved in the targeted groups, sometimes as leaders; targeted for neutralization peaceful civic organizations . . .

> *Stipulation of facts agreed to*
> *by the Chicago police department, 1985*

There is a special irony in the existence of political repression in America. We Americans—and others—justly consider our country to be a sanctuary for, if not the birthplace of, modern-day political liberties. Yet our government has often gone to great lengths to silence those who exercise such liberties—and it has even done so in the name of protecting democratic rights.

Although, clearly, a price has not been attached to all dissent, a stiff price indeed was exacted for some of the most important protests of the twentieth century. Dissenters who sought relief from the effects of skewed power relationships in order to realize the elemental human rights of economic security or political justice have often done so at the risk of attacks by local, state, or federal government agencies. In America, the gun and the lynch rope have been used to defeat the efforts of workers to secure nothing more than a living wage and the efforts of African Americans to secure nothing more than voting rights. At other times, repression has been more circumspect but just as effective: local ordinances and court injunctions crippled workers' attempts to represent themselves collectively to their employers, and southern Jim Crow laws disenfranchised and stigmatized African Americans and created the political context for decades of near peonage, when resistance to oppression was all but unthinkable. Those who opposed foreign policy in times of war or impending war also risked government action against them for their dissent. The well-cultivated belief that criticism in the face of real or imagined foreign enemies would weaken the nation's resolve reduced free expression from an inalienable right to a rescindable privilege. With "patriotism" thus cast in opposition to constitutional rights, critics of war faced disruption from secretive police agencies, brutalization by local police forces, and prosecution under laws that curbed dissent.

Our first book, *It Did Happen Here: Recollections of Political Repression in America,* is a collection of firsthand accounts of activists from a wide variety of social movements, ethnic backgrounds, and sectors of American society. In this second book, in contrast, we focus in more depth on three of the most dramatic, sustained social movements of the twentieth century. Labor, African American, and antiwar activists mounted popular upheavals, powerful crusades that repeatedly filled the streets of the nation with protesters—and that drew the full force of government repression. Despite the daunting obstacles they encountered, they succeeded in limiting the absolute control of employers and improving abysmal conditions of work; they overturned deeply embedded codes of white supremacy that had deprived African Americans of full citizenship; and they broke through "patriotic" strictures against opposing war. The effects of these movements continue to be felt today, notwithstanding any recent erosion in the gains that were made.

In examining the repression directed against these three movements, we also consider, as we must, the attempts to silence radical dissenters among them. Radical groups that sought to transform capitalism as well as to win labor, civil rights, and foreign policy reforms were not only attacked directly to eradicate their influence. In addition, those in power attributed the radicals' stigmatized beliefs to labor, Black freedom, and peace groups that were seeking only limited policy changes, thereby providing a rationalization for launching assaults against this broader range of activists. The extraordinary admission of the Subversive Activities Section of the Chicago police department that it "targeted for neutralization peaceful civic organizations" (noted at the beginning of this introduction) is but one case in point.

Inevitably, each progressive movement experienced sharp internal differences, even fierce battles, among contending advocates over its policy and direction. Divisive and frustrating as these ruptures may have been, they are not our primary concern here. Factional disputes do become relevant to the subject of political repression, however, when the government weighs in on the side it favors, as it did decisively with the labor movement, or when it secretly exacerbates existing differences, as it did with the Black freedom and peace movements, thereby weakening them from within. By "political repression," then, we mean actions by government—both its frontal assaults and its divisive tactics—that try to silence challenges to its policies or suppress efforts to redress grievances and thereby violate the basic tenet of a democratic society: the right of free expression.

The first three parts of this book examine the repression directed against these three historic social movements. Each part focuses on a crucial period of this history: the red-baiting attacks on labor during the Cold War era, the assault on the modern civil rights and Black Power movements, and the suppression of those opposed to the Vietnam war. But repression transcends specific historical periods. As the prologues and epilogues in each part demonstrate, it is a pervasive thread in the American experience, reaching back in our history and continuing into more recent years. The final part is an account of how one group of insistent civil libertarians succeeded in rolling back repressive measures that had been in place for most of the past century and winning protections against their recurrence.

We have tried to tap both recent and older memories, some of which stretch back across the better part of the twentieth century. For this book and its predecessor, *It Did Happen Here*, more than one hundred persons were interviewed. We photographed these individuals, tape-recorded and then edited their stories (sometimes reducing transcripts of more than one hundred pages to a fraction of their original size), and returned the edited versions to the interviewees for their approval. In a few cases—the Austin meatpackers story, the Kent State recollections, and the account of the Chicago red squad—we combined interviews that were conducted separately. In several instances, interviewees supplied us with documents that we included in the book, together with their reactions. In all cases, we tried to be as faithful as we could to the original meaning and spirit of what was told to us.

This, then, is fundamentally a book by and about extraordinary Americans who acted on their beliefs despite the sacrifices their actions entailed—Americans who paid the price of their dissent. Agree with them or not—and they would certainly find great disagreement among themselves—it is clear that by dissenting when it was unpopular or dangerous to do so, they were insisting on and preserving the precious American right of free expression for the next century's dissenters, whoever they may be.

PART ONE

Subverting the Organization of Labor

The right of labor to organize without interference, coercion, and intimidation derives from the exercise of the rights of free speech, peaceable assembly, and freedom of the press enumerated in the Constitution of the United States.

La Follette Committee, U.S. Senate, 1939

The man was lying on the ground, defenseless. The policemen stood over him, beating his limp body with long clubs while fellow officers watched. This scene, captured on film, was one among many in South Chicago on Memorial Day 1937. The beatings—along with a barrage of tear gas and a hail of bullets—were part of an unprovoked police attack on workers who were striking against the Republic Steel Corporation.

Union members and their families and supporters had come that day to picnic and then to demonstrate before the struck plant. As the strikers and their wives and children marched, Chicago police began to advance toward them. "Then suddenly, without apparent warning, there is a terrific roar of pistol shots, and men in the front ranks of the marchers go down like grass before a scythe," the *St. Louis Post Dispatch* reported, describing a Paramount newsreel of the event that was not released to the public at the time.[1] "Instantly police charge on the marchers with riot sticks flying. At the same time tear gas grenades are seen sailing into the mass of demonstrators, and clouds of gas rise over them." The police are "appallingly businesslike" in their attack; one strikes a marcher "horizontally across the face, using his club as he would wield a baseball bat. Another crashes it down on the top of his head, and still another is whipping him across the back." Ten workers were killed and ninety or more were wounded that day, in what came to be known as the Memorial Day Massacre. Within weeks, more strikers were killed by police at Republic Steel plants in Ohio and Michigan.

Two years later, the House Committee on Un-American Activities, then chaired by Congressman Martin Dies, held hearings in Chicago to investigate Communist influence in the labor movement.* The unwarranted police violence against strikers and the hearings of the congressional investigating committee stand as examples of two facets of the government's attack on labor. The Memorial Day Massacre was the culmination of sixty years of assaults by the armed forces of the government, a campaign conducted on behalf of employers in their disputes with workers over the right to representation and the often grievous conditions of work. The Dies Committee hearings were the renewal of an assault by the legislative and executive branches of the federal government on those within the labor movement who were said to harbor forbidden radical visions of America—an assault that would last another twenty years.

THE CLASS WAR AGAINST LABOR

Whether they were lumberjacks of the Pacific Northwest; coal miners of Pennsylvania, Illinois, and Colorado; migrant farm laborers of Wheatland, California; or needle trades workers of New York City, their work early in the twentieth century was grueling and life-threatening. In the textile factories of Lawrence, Massachusetts, "thirty-six out of every hundred of all men and women who worked in the mills died before they were twenty-five years of age."[2] At the Pressed Steel Car Company in McKees Rocks, Pennsylvania, one man a day on average was killed by the brutalizing pace of a giant, newly designed production line. To improve their conditions—indeed, to reclaim their humanity—American workers had no option but to act collectively, to unionize.

Success in attaining the right to union representation depended squarely on the efficacy of the workers' primary weapon: the strike. Undercutting strikes meant condemning workers to the absolute control of employers and to insufferable conditions on the job. Yet that was the practice of government in America for decades before the turn of the century and for at least three decades afterward. "The existing attitude of the courts and government officials," the congressional Commission on Industrial Relations wrote in 1916, "generally is that the entire machinery

---

*The House Committee on Un-American Activities (HCUA) has also been known as the House Un-American Activities Committee (HUAC) and, after 1969, as the House Internal Security Committee (HISC). We have used the more common designation HUAC throughout.

of the State should be put behind the strike breaker."[3] Because that machinery included the various armed forces of the state, which the government was quick to deploy, violent conflict often broke out. In what could rightfully and literally be called a "class war," the government's alignment with one side doomed the other to defeat.

Louisiana timber workers, South Carolina textile workers, West Virginia coal miners, Pittsburgh steel workers, San Francisco dock workers, Minneapolis teamsters, Detroit auto workers, Chicago packinghouse workers were gunned down by local police, state constabularies, National Guardsmen, and federal troops. From 1877, the year of labor's Great Upheaval, when more than one hundred railway strikers and their supporters were killed by police, state militia, and the U.S. Army, to 1937, the year of the Memorial Day Massacre, the employers' privileged access to the power of the state was most dramatically evident in the form of military force.

But it was also evident in judicial decisions and legislative enactments. "During strikes," the Commission on Industrial Relations said, "innocent men are in many cases arrested without just cause, charged with fictitious crimes, held under excessive bail, and treated frequently with unexampled brutality for the purpose of injuring the strikers and breaking the strike." Employer groups such as the National Association of Manufacturers had succeeded, the commission reported, "in preventing the enactment of practically all legislation intended to improve the conditions or advance the interests of workers." The "economic bias" of the courts in labor disputes was evident in the "long list of statutes, city ordinances, and military orders abridging freedom of speech and press" that have "almost uniformly been upheld" and in the "injunctions [that] have in many cases inflicted grievous injury upon workmen."[4]

In extreme cases, employers enjoyed more than the privileged access to state power—they usurped state power. "We unearthed a system of despotic tyranny reminiscent of Czar-ridden Siberia at its worst," the *New York Daily News* wrote of Pennsylvania's coal patches and steel towns in 1925. "We found police brutality and industrial slavery."[5] This assessment was confirmed by the La Follette Committee of the U.S. Senate a decade later. In company-owned and company-controlled towns, workers lived in conditions that approximated "industrial peonage." The police, paid by the companies but "vested with the authority of the State," were "used to abridge the constitutional rights of free speech and assembly and freedom of the press," the La Follette Committee added. "In times of strike these private armies have often assumed the attitude of the State toward a foreign enemy at war, or the attitude of public police toward criminals, shooting and killing union people in an effort to compel submission to the wishes of employers."[6]

In 1935, however, under Franklin Roosevelt's New Deal, the passage of the Wagner Act shifted government away from its uncritical support of industry. This legislation guaranteed collective bargaining; barred unfair labor practices that interfered with workers' rights; outlawed industrial espionage, yellow-dog contracts,* blacklists, provocateurs, private police, and arms stockpiles—all powerful weapons in the employers' arsenal— and established the National Labor Relations Board (NLRB) to enforce the law's provisions and carry out the election of union representatives.

Corporations denounced the law and "recognized it only after a near-revolutionary wave of sit-down strikes rolled through mills and plants in 1936 and 1937."[7] First at Goodyear Tire Company in Akron, Ohio, and then at General Motors in Flint, Michigan, workers put down their tools and occupied the stilled factories. They won a significant victory— union recognition—that energized spontaneous strikes elsewhere. Six thousand at Chrysler, twenty thousand at Hudson sat down. During two weeks in March 1937, Chicago experienced almost sixty sit-downs: motormen, waitresses, candy makers, cab drivers, clerks, peanut baggers, stenographers, tailors, truck drivers, and factory hands. In St. Louis, it was electrical and furniture workers; in Tennessee, shirt workers; in Philadelphia, silk hosiery workers; in Pueblo, Colorado, broom makers; and in Seminole, Oklahoma, oil workers.

These strikes, which the American Federation of Labor (AFL) largely ignored or denounced, took place amid the ferment of building a different kind of union organization—the Congress of Industrial Organizations (CIO). The older craft unions of the AFL typically restricted membership to skilled workers in a particular occupation, leaving great numbers of unskilled workers in the expanding mass-production industries unrepresented. The CIO's new industrial unions, in contrast, aimed to organize all workers in a particular industry: all workers in the auto, steel, or electrical industry, for example. The CIO's drive to organize the unorganized industrial workers brought great numbers into the union movement as the 1930s drew to a close.

---

*Under a yellow-dog contract, workers, in order to be hired, were required to sign a statement swearing that they would not join a union. After a Supreme Court decision in 1917 legalized yellow-dog contracts, all strikes by employees who had signed such statements became illegal, and employers could get injunctions forbidding union organizers from even speaking to those workers.

Many employers grudgingly accepted union recognition as a fact of life. And the emphasis on physical brutality and deadly force as ways of suppressing the right to organize lessened. It was a significant if bittersweet victory. "Lifting the suffocating burden of absolute managerial control from the working lives of Americans," labor historian David Montgomery writes, "was one of the greatest chapters in the historic struggle for human liberties in this country." But, he adds, "the government's intervention also opened a new avenue through which the rank-and-file could in time be tamed and the newly powerful unions be subjected to tight legal and political control."[8]

To maintain industrial production during World War II, unions agreed to a no-strike pledge and a virtual wage freeze. In return, the Roosevelt administration, through the War Labor Board, assured unions of support for a modified union shop, one with an escape clause that allowed workers to withdraw from the union during the first fifteen days of an agreement, and a dues check-off system that swelled union rolls.[*] But these reforms, together with other measures such as the ability to take disputes over grievances and contracts before government agencies, reduced union officials' dependence on rank-and-file support. Leaders also became distanced from, and opposed to, their memberships by having to discipline workers who rebelled against shop-floor conditions. Thus government intervention fostered a change in the character of unions, shifting them away from democratic participation and rank-and-file action.[9] The Taft-Hartley Act, passed after the war, subjected union leaders to fines and arrest for failing to break wildcat strikes and made forms of union militancy and solidarity that had been potent weapons against management illegal. The conditions were taking shape for a low-intensity class war that would continue for three more decades.

THE IDEOLOGICAL WAR AGAINST LABOR

Historically, the government's hostile actions against unions had an ideological quality about them. The revolutionary character of workers' movements was often wildly exaggerated in order to lay them open to

---

[*]In a union shop, all workers must join the union after working on the job for a specified time. In a closed shop, the employer can hire only persons who are already members of a union. The concept dates back to 1794, when the shoemakers of Philadelphia demanded that their employers hire only union workers. An open shop is one in which there is no union security. Early in the twentieth century, for example, the National Association of Manufacturers led a drive to impose open shops where unions had previously existed.

attack from courts, legislatures, and troops. In 1877, the Great Upheaval, a strike of railway workers, was quickly labeled "Communistic." In its aftermath, attempts to reform the conditions of labor were termed "un-American" and, as political scientist Robert Goldstein notes, "the myth of attributing the disturbances to an international communist conspiracy was firmly enshrined in contemporary American histories."[10]

A surge of strikes after World War I fed into and was affected by the rising tide of postwar hysteria. Referring to the 1919 general strike in support of higher wages for shipyard workers, Seattle mayor Ole Hansen charged: "The sympathetic revolution was called in the exact manner as the revolution in Petrograd." It threatened, he said, to "spread all over the United States," unless the "traitors and anarchists" understood that "death will be their portion if they start anything."[11] To oppose business was to oppose Americanism; to support unions was to support Bolshevism. Even as unlikely a group as the Boston police force was branded as "Soviet!" "Bolshevist!" when officers struck to demand representation by the conservative American Federation of Labor. On the heels of the police strike, thousands of steel workers struck for the right to be represented by the AFL and to bargain over wages and hours. But employers, the press, and the government made the strike turn on ideology, not on the bona fide grievances of steel workers. The U.S. Justice Department conducted "red raids" against immigrant steel workers, while a young J. Edgar Hoover slipped "proof" of the red conspiracy to the press and began accumulating a centralized file of "radicals," two habits that he used successfully for more than half a century.[12]

For their part, radicals in the labor movement felt the special repression reserved for them. Troops in St. Louis raided the headquarters of Socialists who supported strikers during the Great Upheaval. Socialist gatherings were attacked violently in Philadelphia, New York, and Chicago, where police killed at least one person attending such a political meeting. Sheriff's deputies abducted members of the radical Industrial Workers of the World (IWW) during a strike in Bisbee, Arizona, in 1917 and shipped them deep into the desert. Earlier, in Everett, Washington, IWW members were killed in a hail of bullets fired by deputies. The Wilson administration marshaled the departments of War, Labor, and Justice against the IWW, setting up a competing union under the auspices of the U.S. Army, undercutting the radical union in negotiations with employers, and imprisoning hundreds of its leaders. The nation's first red scare climaxed with the Palmer raids of 1920, when up to ten thousand suspected alien radicals—many of them members of workers' groups—were seized simultaneously in cities across the nation and held for deportation. The country was riding high on a wave of political intolerance that would be equaled only in the McCarthy era.[13]

Although this red scare subsided, its grip on the national consciousness was lasting. It resurfaced in the years before World War II, notably in the form of the House Committee on Un-American Activities, chaired by Texas Congressman Martin Dies. Established in 1938, partly in response to the sit-down strikes by automobile workers, much of the Dies Committee's first year of hearings was directed at the newly formed Congress of Industrial Organizations and at radicals in the labor movement.

As World War II ended, workers across the country, pressed by inflation, the loss of overtime, and the burden of accumulated unresolved grievances, began to walk off their jobs in spontaneous actions. The year 1946 also brought a historic wave of sanctioned strikes in the auto, steel, electrical, packinghouse, and other industries by more than a million and a half workers, amid corporate calls for the repeal of the Wagner Act. President Harry Truman, who had proposed legislation for the selective use of military conscription against strikes, seized the oil refineries, the railroads, and the packinghouses to break strikes of workers in those industries. Thirty states passed anti-labor laws, and sixty bills to curb labor were before a Congress that eventually passed the Taft-Hartley Act. It was a crucial reversal.

Standing before the AFL convention, John L. Lewis, leader of the United Mine Workers Union, thundered against Taft-Hartley: The statute contained "only two lines that say labor has the right to organize and thirty-three pages of other additional restrictions that dare labor to organize."[14] It outlawed the closed shop, sympathetic strikes, and secondary boycotts; it held union leaders liable for fines and arrests if their memberships engaged in wildcat strikes; it allowed strikebreakers to call for the decertification of striking unions and then vote in the subsequent NLRB elections; and it required all elected union officials to sign an affidavit swearing that they were not members of the Communist Party or any organization that believed in or taught the overthrow of the government by force and violence.

"We would not merit the name of free Americans if we acquiesced in a law which makes it a crime to exercise rights of freedom of speech, freedom of press, and freedom of assembly," the CIO executive board stated. The board then pledged: "We will not comply with the unconstitutional limitations on political activity which are written into the Taft-Hartley Act."[15] But Taft-Hartley's anti-Communist provision both wielded a stick (threatening to deny unions access to the NLRB) and dangled a carrot (offering union leaders an opportunity to squelch opposition within their own ranks), and the resolve of CIO and AFL leaders collapsed quickly.

Few could resist being swept up in the mounting hysteria that took hold of the nation in the Cold War era. Truman's loyalty program empowered the attorney general to designate any American organization as "subversive," without allowing the group an opportunity to defend itself; the FBI was unleashed to ferret out from among the millions in government employ those who might in the future perform a disloyal act; Dies's old House Un-American Activities Committee (HUAC), rejuvenated and made permanent, debuted in Hollywood; and Communist Party leaders were indicted under the Smith Act on the basis of beliefs the government ascribed to them.[16] States moved to protect themselves from the now imminent threat of subversion: Texas outlawed any party that "entertained any thought" contrary to the Constitution; Tennessee enacted the death penalty for advocating the unlawful overthrow of the government; and loyalty oaths were required to fish in New York City reservoirs, to get unemployment compensation in Ohio, or to box, wrestle, barber, or sell junk in Indiana. As John Henry Faulk, the blacklisted radio personality and leader of the American Federation of Radio and Television Artists, said of the moment, "Hysteria took the form of a frothing insanity."[17]

It became a Cold War crusade that the CIO joined with a passion. From 1946 to 1949, the CIO formulated what amounted to a "party line," a strict litmus test of orthodoxy, the centerpiece of which was support for the Truman Doctrine and the Marshall Plan and opposition to the third-party presidential bid of former vice president Henry Wallace. Then came the climax: The CIO, whose founding unions had been expelled from the AFL, itself expelled eleven dissident, left-wing unions in 1950, including two that had been among its founders. In all, close to one million workers were affected.

Many of the remaining unions, as well as others from the AFL, set upon the banished unions in bitterly fought jurisdictional battles. These raids were given credence and sustenance by government intrusions. Officers of ousted unions were indicted for perjuring themselves when they signed Taft-Hartley oaths; unions whose leaders refused to sign the oath were denied a place on certifying ballots by the NLRB; leaders of expelled unions were indicted under the Smith Act; foreign-born leaders and members were threatened with deportation. FBI harassment added to the intimidation; and congressional committees, especially HUAC, timed their investigations of the expelled unions to coincide with NLRB elections, placing the weight of government emphatically on the side of the raiders. Many of the ousted unions were unable to survive the ordeal, and those that did were left with their resources and leadership depleted, their memberships decimated.

Purged of its radical element and much of its militant presence and bound by the Taft-Hartley Act's restrictive provisions, American labor faced the second half of the twentieth century shorn of important forces and forms of struggle that had brought significant victories in the past. "Business unionism," while acclimating to the provisions of the Taft-Hartley Act, sought partnerships with employers in the period of relative prosperity that followed, and the government's actions against labor abated. But its iron hand, whether gloved or not, made its presence felt again in the closing decades of the century, after business once again assumed its aggressive anti-union stance and after a new generation of rank-and-file militants arose to press labor's age-old demands against speedup, wage cutbacks, and dangerous work conditions.

Attacks on Labor Before the Triumph of Industrial Unions

THE UNRELENTING CAMPAIGN AGAINST
THE INDUSTRIAL WORKERS OF THE WORLD

The nation had never before seen such a sustained, concerted attack against a legal, if dissident, organization as the attack that was directed against the Industrial Workers of the World (commonly known as the "Wobblies"). Nor would the nation again see, across the course of the twentieth century, a union that advocated a fundamental restructuring of the social relations of industry to create an industrial democracy controlled by workers. The limits of acceptable debate by labor were set in large measure by the denial of constitutional rights to these early dissenters.

The IWW and the workers it organized were assaulted by police, company gunmen, and vigilantes.[18] As the organization grew in strength, and as the patriotic fervor of World War I mounted, attacks by the government became coordinated and national, aimed at no less than the eradication of the radical union. Federal troops patrolled the timberlands of the Northwest, raiding and occupying Wobbly halls, breaking up the Wobblies' street meetings, holding Wobblies in bull pens beyond the reach of civil authority, and even setting up a competing union, the Loyal Legion of Loggers and Lumbermen, that workers were forced to join in order to be hired. One hundred sixty-six IWW leaders were indicted under the Espionage and Selective Service Acts in September 1917. "The Justice Department was indeed fortunate that public hysteria convicted the Wobblies before the jury heard the prosecution's evidence," historian Melvyn Dubofsky writes, "for the prosecution, in fact, had no evidence."[19] A Chicago jury took less than an hour to convict more than one hundred Wobblies on four separate, complex counts, amounting altogether to over ten thousand offenses.

The attempts to suppress the IWW continued. By 1920, twenty states, at the behest of employers, had enacted criminal syndicalism laws. Criminal syndicalism was defined as the commission of a crime in order to effect any change in industrial ownership or control or any political change. Persons who became members of an organization that advocated criminal syndicalism or who themselves spoke, published, or circulated such ideas were held liable for heavy jail terms. The laws attached harsh penalties to what the Supreme Court fifty years later described as "mere advocacy not distinguished from incitement to imminent lawless action."[20] In 1922 and 1923, in California alone, 265 people were arrested under such a law. It was then that Fred Thompson was tried for criminal syndicalism. His imprisonment in San Quentin only strengthened his commitment to the Wobbly cause. He went on to edit the IWW newspaper, *Industrial Worker,* and became the union's official historian.

FRED THOMPSON

My early years were spent in Canada. My father died when I was three. There were seven of us kids, but my mother always managed somehow to have something for us to eat. She had to do a lot of planning to make sure of that. Those were very rough times, when many of my friends went hungry.

I came home one night in 1913, took off my shoes, which were wet, with holes in the bottom, put my feet by the coal stove, and picked up the paper. It told about this wonderful harvest all over Canada. I thought that everything was going to be better now. When my feet got warmed, I went upstairs to ask my mother about it. "No," she told me, "it doesn't quite work that way." I couldn't figure that. When my brother came home, I asked him about it. "She's right," he said. "Having lots of big crops doesn't mean that people will eat." He said it was economics.

We had a small encyclopedia in the house, and there I read about economics for the first time. My father had a few books, and Adam Smith's *Wealth of Nations* was one of them. That's where I got my radicalism, by the way—from Adam Smith. He described what I could see going on around town. Pretty soon I was reading John Stuart Mill and Malthus.

FRED THOMPSON

I tried to figure things out. Then I got to know a family that introduced me to Marx's writings. But I think my economics came from the fact that my mother made good use of the available resources. Now, here is a planet with resources; people could live comfortably. Why don't they? That question has been the focus of my life.

I was active in the labor movement in Halifax and out west in 1919, so I was familiar with the IWW. From the beginning, the IWW championed the idea of one union for all in the same work. Then when I came down here in the spring of 1922, I heard some cockeyed stories that the

IWW went around burning barns and haystacks. I figured, if they're that nutty, I don't want to belong to them. But I traveled around on a number of jobs where Wobblies worked. I found that they were sensible people, so I joined them in San Francisco later that year. And I've been paying my dues ever since.

In the development of industrial life in America, there were certain areas where it didn't seem strange to have a union. At first, that was confined to the railroads and to machine shops and to a few places where the hired hands were mostly English-speaking skilled craftsmen. We Wobblies were ordinarily working in territory—either geographic or occupational territory—where unionism was not taken for granted. That's why we experienced more hostility than other unions did. When other unions got into similar situations, they experienced the same type of repression. So it wasn't simply our radical philosophy that provided the excuse for going after the Wobblies, but rather that we organized in territories where a union was an alien thing.

In the western logging industry, the IWW made a transformation in conditions. I don't think most people appreciate what we did there. As of 1916, the West Coast logger was a guy who carried his worldly possessions, including his bedding, on his back. He had no facilities for washing his clothes. The "timber beast," they called him. And he *was* the timber beast. He wore calked shoes that were good for walking along a fallen tree but would wreck a floor. The old saying was that when the logger came into town, you could smell him before you could hear him, and you could hear him before you could see him. He was viewed as a subhuman being, and he felt such. We changed all that to where about the best-paid, best-dressed, best-liked workers on the West Coast were the lumber workers. That was a human transformation the IWW made. I'd say that was one of our major achievements.

Much the same thing happened in metal mining and tunnel work. A lot of the early drilling machinery was very dangerous. The miners drilled with a dry machine, so they inhaled all that powder from the rock. We demanded that be changed by using wet drills. Even after the IWW was gone, replaced by another union, certain habits like that remained. I don't think any miner has changed from dry drilling to wet drilling and then reverted. And all those other safety devices are still there. You institute something that lasts long after you're gone.

Those were the days before radio, before television. Outdoor speaking wasn't an unusual thing. Single tax, women's suffrage, socialism, all kinds of things were promoted. Vegetarianism. You name it. All these heretical ideas were advocated from soapboxes. For example, the IWW objected to workers having to pay a fee to the employment shark to get a job. Ordinarily, the employment sharks had a deal with the foremen about how many days a guy was going to work before he would be canned. They had a system between them so that you wouldn't last too long. We wanted to be able to hire out at a company without having to pay a fee. The place we did our soapboxing about that was right in the skid road area, where working stiffs came into town, spent their money, and got another job.

The Salvation Army was in that area, too, saving souls. Old General Booth, who was a humanitarian, would have been shocked had he been around to see how the Salvation Army he started was in cahoots with the employment sharks. They'd come along with their big bass drum and try to drown out the Wobbly speakers. That's how the Wobbly songbook really got going. We made parodies of all the songs the Salvation Army played. When they played their hymn "In the Sweet Bye and Bye," we'd sing back, "You'll get pie in the sky when you die. That's a lie!"

The fact is that a large number of these free speech fighters were people who had just recently joined the IWW.* You have to realize that we were usually organizing migratory workers who hoboed, rode trains through the country. Well, I've done that. On a warm day, you come into the east end of a town and get off the freight train. You walk through town in the hot summer's sun with a heavy coat over your arm. You describe yourself with that coat: a drifting worker who has no place to sleep. Everybody knows that you are not "one of us." But if the IWW could win free speech in those towns, if the IWW could state its aims as a champion of those workers, it meant that they might be considered real human beings, the same as those who slept under a roof every night. I think that's why it was largely the migratory workers who furnished the manpower for the free speech fights, even though they were beaten and jailed for it.

The IWW encountered one or another form of repression from its very beginning. In the early days, one was far more likely to meet up with plug-uglies who beat up organizers. I've been knocked down more than once in my life when I passed out handbills. But it was really during the

---

*When Wobblies were trying to organize and spoke on public streets, western and midwestern cities and towns would often pass ordinances that forbade such speech making. In response, hundreds of other Wobblies would converge on the forbidden street corner to speak and to be arrested, one after the other, until the jails were overflowing.

First World War that the IWW faced its worst repression. I think the motivation is fairly clear. Here the IWW was stepping on the toes of very powerful people: the lumber barons and the copper kings. The IWW was making them spend more money on workers, and that's exactly what they didn't want to do. And these were people who had clout in Washington. In September 1917, federal agents raided the IWW offices all over the country and arrested several hundred people. They charged them with interfering with the war. The motive was evidently not to stop us from interfering with the war effort; it was to discourage us from getting workers to demand better working conditions.

I was arrested in April of 1923. I had been working up on the project that supplies water to San Francisco. If you ever get a drink of water there, remember I helped dig the hole that it comes through. I got fired on that job for distributing Wobbly papers. Then I heard that there was a free press fight in Oroville. That's in the Feather River Canyon in California. So I and a couple of others headed up there. I had been a member of the IWW for only a few months, and this was my first experience with anything of that sort. I went up to the jungles, the places where hoboes cooked and slept under the trees. There must have been about a hundred of us who came; we had heard that the people who were selling IWW papers were getting arrested. Our feeling was that if they were going to arrest people for selling our papers, they would have to arrest a lot of us. So we sent a committee to the sheriff, and he agreed that we could peddle our papers if we weren't too "objectionable." That was a little victory.

Then one of the people there said, "Somebody ought to distribute papers in Marysville." I figured, okay, I'd stop off in Marysville. I went down to the skid road there and passed out a few papers. I was arrested right away. When I got to jail, somebody said, "Don't you know this is the town where they killed the sheriff?" There had been a strike up at a nearby hop ranch in 1913. During the strike, some unknown person shot the sheriff when he disrupted a meeting. That sheriff's son was now the district attorney.

The first charge against me was having in my possession papers that advocated illegal ideas according to the state criminal syndicalism law. Well, they couldn't find anything in those papers to fit that description, so they changed the charge. When they arrested me, I had in my hip pocket membership cards and stamps to bring people up to date in their dues books. Now they charged me with being an organizer for a union that did in secret teach doctrines in violation of the state syndicalism law.

"Syndicalism" is simply French for unionism. But the word has been used, even by historians and sociologists in this country, to mean the type of unionism practiced by major labor unions in France from the 1890s up to World War I. That was a unionism that relied on direct job action. If you were working in a restaurant and you couldn't win an increase in wages, you told customers the truth about what happened in the kitchen. I think there was a sense of humor that went along with it.

Even the word "sabotage" is a French term. A *sabot* is a wooden shoe. An odd misconception grew out of this: that French weavers wore wooden shoes, and if they wanted to spoil the product, they would throw their wooden shoe into the loom. Well, that is about as incredible a story as I can think of. The use of the term actually came about when the workers in a town went on strike. The boss would get people from the countryside to replace them, people who hadn't absorbed the work ethic that it's wrong to scab on a guy who's gone on strike. The wooden shoes marked the peasants, who wore those clumsy shoes that were not suitable for the factory floor. To act like those country-bred scabs who didn't know the work—that's what "sabotage" originally meant. It meant slowing down, creating an inferior product, or going against the big brass.

But World War I, of course, changed the meaning of "sabotage" altogether. It became associated with dynamiting and blowing up ships. Sabotage was something the army engaged in, not something the labor movement did. So we quit using the word.

Now here was our old literature that mentioned that sabotage, as a job action, was not too bad an idea to use at times. And here was the jury that thought in terms of sabotage in the sense that they had read about it in the newspapers during the war years. That helped stack the case against us.

At the trial, they used two paid informers, Coutts and Townsend. Just those two were all they could find, despicable characters altogether. They went around from trial to trial telling the same damn lies, that we advocated burning barns and so forth. Well, the IWW certainly did not. You don't win improved conditions by burning barns. You win them by getting people organized who will demand, "Either you raise our wages or nobody's going to do the work here."

I think I made that clear to the jury. You know, you read a juror's face when you're on the stand. I talked about how I'd worked as a building laborer putting up foundations for houses. In a hurry-up job, the concrete wasn't completely mixed and it wasn't tamped down thoroughly. We'd see all kinds of defects that we had to cover over with cement slurry. I said to the jury: As working people, we'd much prefer to do good work.

But the contractors' motives were to make as much money as possible. And making as much money as possible for the contractors and providing people with good foundations for their homes weren't consistent. I think I made a fairly convincing presentation, for I could tell that I had won some of the jury over.

The first trial ended with a hung jury. The second trial included two more Wobblies they had arrested. They brought Coutts and Townsend in again to give their lies. Then I went on the stand to explain, just as I did in the first trial, what we were trying to do and how we were trying to do it. This time, the jury convicted two of us and freed one of us. I happened to be one of the two convicted. I heard the jury stood four for acquittal, eight to convict, so they settled it among themselves that way.

I don't know why juries convict in one case and not in another. I think a little detail may have made the jury more inclined in the first trial to acquit me. The prosecuting attorney was the crux of this thing. Everybody knew he was the son of the man who'd been shot in the Wheatland riot some years earlier. He was really venomous. He ended his last speech to the jury dramatically, sort of crouching down, and because I came from Canada he said: "This man from foreign shores comes into this country and gnaws at the foundations of our society like a rat." Well, it struck me so funny that I burst out laughing, and the jury started laughing, too. It was self-defeating for the prosecutor.

At the second trial, the prosecutor didn't make the long-winded speech he had at the first. Instead he said, "It's a hot day. Let's let the jury go out and get some refreshments." I was told that when they went outside, newsboys, who didn't usually sell their papers there, were hollering, "IWW sets fire to the rice fields of California!" The jury came back rather quickly and convicted us. And there had been no rice field fires.

On November 7, they took us to San Quentin, Dawes and I. I was in that prison for three years and four months. I forget just how many, but there were well over a hundred IWW members like me in San Quentin at that time, all for no real offense.

My experience there made me reevaluate things. I had thought that there was a criminal class, a special species of wicked people who were different from the rest of us. I found that the people in prison were like people I had worked with on the jobs and met with in the towns. These certainly weren't the large successful crooks. Many were just young people who were broke and took something that didn't belong to them.

A prison is an ideal place for bureaucracy to foster. They had all kinds of petty rules. When some guards took a dislike to certain prisoners, they'd find one reason or other to give them a hard time. They had a dark hole under the ground, with no light, no mattress to sleep on, no nothing. They just had a floor there and a bucket for toilet facilities. They'd throw people inside and keep them there. They had me in there for thirty days. It was not really the physical discomfort that was the worst of it. The hardest part was to keep your mind operating. I always had an interest in geography as a kid. When I was in the hole, I tried to recall how all the rivers in North America flowed to the sea. I would construct maps in my mind, such things as that.

Ordinarily, we were thrown in the hole for going on strike about something. When some injustice was done to one of the Wobblies, we would take a vote: Do we want to go on strike or don't we? Because they added a month every time we did, we actually sentenced ourselves to extra time when we went on strike. But when they mistreated our fellow workers, we figured it was the only thing to do.

We had our gripes, and we dealt with them in an organized way. You had beans almost every meal. Somebody put me wise when I landed there: On Mondays, don't eat too many beans because they're not quite cooked and you're likely to have digestive disturbances. Tuesdays, eat lots of beans because that's the day they're done. Wednesdays, they're sour. And then it was Thursdays, beans are raw again. Sundays, we did get corn pone and gravy, with a little sample of meat to remind us what it used to be like. Of course, that meat always had the iridescence of a rainbow on it. But we ate it.

I figured that the cycle of beans was amusing, so I got it out into the newspapers through visitors. We found that the San Francisco papers made a hullabaloo of what went on in the big house if it was something amusing. So we made sure the newspapers were supplied with all the details of our life. They gave us oatmeal sometimes with maggots in it—that would get into the *Chronicle*. As a result of the publicity, they did improve our diet. We were even beginning to get a few vegetables toward the end.

I still think a great deal could be done to make prisons more humane places if the labor movement would get involved. It is working people who go to prison, not millionaires. And I think working-class organizations ought to be concerned with conditions there. Four people in a cell that's really a small place for one is an impossible situation. It isn't just the physical crowding, but four personalities clashing. When you lock these same people up day and night, even if they were four saints, they would sooner or later be after each other. It cultivates the worst that there is, the most unsociable traits. But the Wobs got along fairly well because we were people in the habit of organizing.

I had a bifocal view of things. I knew how unconstitutional the law against syndicalism was, how contrary it was to the Bill of Rights. But even as that law was written, it said that you should be convicted only when you do certain things. We hadn't done any of those things. According to the rules of their game, as they declared them, we shouldn't have been in jail. But the other part of my own attitude ran this way: Here is a minority of people who have grabbed this round ball we live on, and since I wanted you and me and the rest of us to take it back from them, I expected they were going to react. So it didn't surprise me that they threw me in jail.

I haven't changed my views. I look at the world today with unemployment and starvation, literally starvation. There are millions of people on this globe dying for the lack of enough food, and yet we don't know what to do with the food we grow. We told the farmers not to plant so much, and even at that, they're going to have crops that are "too big." Well, can I think of anything crazier than a world where people are dying for lack of food and farmers are worrying because their crops are going to be too big? It's institutionalized, organized, well-established insanity, isn't it? That's what the economic system is. And most people think that's the way it has to be. The whole thing is bizarre, ridiculous.

Well, there were all kinds of things done to discourage us from organizing. But we Wobs were sort of irrepressible. We had little regret that we stood our ground and spoke our mind rather than bow down to Mammon. On a San Quentin cell wall, I saw a line from the *Aeneid:* "Haec olim meminisse iuvabit." It brought to mind Aeneas cheering his fellows on in the shipwreck: "Perhaps it will give pleasure to remember even these things." Yes, it is more pleasant to remember that we resisted than that we didn't.

AFRICAN AMERICAN SHARECROPPERS: REPRESSION AS A WAY OF LIFE

On September 30, 1919, a group of African American sharecroppers, the Progressive Farmers Union, met in a church near Elaine, Arkansas. When a deputy sheriff and others shot into the church, fire was returned. In the exchange, many of the sharecroppers were wounded, and a white railroad agent was killed. The church was burned down the next day. The American Legion mobilized posses, and four hundred federal troops arrived to smash the "insurrection." In the ensuing terror, five white people were killed, while African Americans were "shot down like wild beasts in the Arkansas cane breaks" by machine gun–wielding troops and white posses. "Upwards of two hundred men, women and children were slaughtered," the National Association for the Advancement of Colored People (NAACP) reported.[21]

Not a single white person was arrested for those murders, but more than a thousand African Americans were taken into custody. In a series of trials that lasted no more than hours, before juries that deliberated no more than minutes, twelve Black sharecroppers were condemned to death. Four of them were leaders of the Progressive Farmers Union.

In Arkansas, as elsewhere in the South, sharecropping was a way of life in which the social mores of white supremacy, the economic leverage of the plantation owners, and their grip on local political power were so deeply embedded into the day-to-day lives of tenant farmers as to make any effort to resist dangerous.[22] Nevertheless, in July 1934, eighteen men, both white and African American, met in a small schoolhouse in Tyronza, Arkansas, to form the Southern Tenant Farmers Union (STFU) to seek redress of the same conditions that had prompted the church meeting in Elaine in 1919. Sharecropper George Stith joined the union and braved the terror to help organize the cotton pickers strike of 1935. He was later to become vice president of the STFU.

GEORGE STITH

I'm the seventh child of a family of thirteen. My father was named James Stith; my mother was named Mary. I was born in 1915 in Dermott, Arkansas, but I was raised over a great part of the United States. My father, when I was very young, went to work for the government as a detective. He was one of only three Blacks in service then. He traveled a lot. We stayed with my grandmother most of the time until I got school age.

Then he decided that he wanted to have the whole group together, so he came and got us, grandmother and all, and moved us up in Illinois, where he was stationed. He finally resigned, at mother's request, and went to work at a steam heat radiator plant in Edwardsville, Illinois. He got some kind of poisoning at the plant and couldn't work there any more. Then we went to Tiptonville, Tennessee, in 1926 to pick cotton. Cotton prices got so low till the seed wouldn't pay for the picking or ginning, so we came back to Cairo, Illinois. We stayed there till we got caught

GEORGE STITH

in the high water in '27 and everything shut down. We came to Steele, Missouri, where we started farming as sharecroppers. We stayed there awhile, and then we came to Arkansas.

When I was fourteen, my father got down with arthritis. He was on crutches. The farm supervisor came to the schoolhouse one day and called the teacher out. They talked awhile, and then she came back and told me: "Get your books, and go with your boss man. He has something for you to do." I never did finish eighth grade; I had to go home and plow. I was the oldest boy in the family.

Sharecropping was a way of life, not a money-making occupation. The owner furnished the seed and the land. The sharecropper did the work and the gathering. He got half, and the owner got half. The owner's half was in the clear. All the expenses of the crop was yours. At that time, we were farming with mules. He did furnish the mules. And he was supposed to furnish the corn and hay to feed them, but most of the time you fed the mules out of your half.

I wish you could have seen the sharecropper houses. They were built out of mill-run lumber, and mostly put up green. And when the walls dried, you had cracks in them. So you went and got what they called a batten, which was another small plank, and you nailed it over that crack. They were tin-top houses. If it started leaking, you did the best you could. I've slept with a tub sitting in my bed to catch the water when it was raining. At night, you could look up through the house and see the moon. Oh, yeah, it was cold. In the winter time, we fed the chickens through the cracks under the house.

The police were controlled by the landowners. Large plantations had their own police, who were also farm supervisors. They would have a deputy's commission from the county sheriff or the township constable. If you did something, the supervisor arrested you and sent you back to the field. When it came time, he went to court and answered for you. He paid your fine. Of course, that made you a prisoner of the plantation owner because you owed him.

They even had control over a murder case. If you killed somebody— killed a Black, because back in that time if a Black killed a white, he got lynched—and if they decided you were a good worker, you went back to work on the farm. "The other fellow is dead, he can't do us no good now." "Well, all right, we'll give him five years on probation, and we'll turn him over to you."

Whether you had committed a crime or not, you were indentured, almost. If you were on a man's plantation, you had to have his permission to move on or slip off. Now, these were the big plantation owners that were up around Marked Tree, Trumann, Tyronza, places like that. And if you left, you didn't carry a thing out with you. Even though they'd taken it out of your sharecrop pay, they'd say, "That's mine. You leave it here."

But you adjusted yourself. You knew how far you could go. You knew what you could do. And you lived with what was there.

They had a bell that rang at four A.M. Your mules had to be out of the lot not later than sunup. We picked cotton not by a machine, but in a cotton sack. A sack was seven, nine, or ten feet long. The seven was rather small and mostly for kids. The nine was for the average grown person. And a cotton picker that picked three and four hundred pounds of cotton used a ten-, ten-and-a-half-foot size. You picked your cotton, you carried it, weighed it, and you got up in the wagon and emptied it.

You didn't get furnished money. You got furnished coupon books. You got credit for one dollar an acre each month for all the cotton you had planted. If you had fifteen acres of cotton, you got fifteen dollars a month credit to take care of your family. You traded at a commissary store that was owned by the planter. You stayed in debt because the books were kept by him or his wife. You weren't allowed to sell your cotton—he sold it. He told you how much he got for it. He told you how much you owed. And then he told you how much you had coming. It was usually just enough to get by on, enough to buy you some overalls and some shoes for the kids to go to school and some groceries for the winter.

Back in the thirties, there was too much cotton, and prices were down. So under the Roosevelt administration, they started a program where you plowed up a certain percentage of what you planted. The government was to pay you so much per acre. But the sharecropper's check would come to the county agent's office. The county agent would bring that check down to the plantation owner. The owner would say, "Now, you know you have to live next year, and you didn't quite pay me out of debt. So I'm going to put this on your account. You sign your name here." He would turn the check face down, and you wouldn't know how much it was. The plantation owner got the money, while the sharecropper had to plant the cotton and had to go back to plow it up.

I wouldn't sign mine. He finally sent for me to come up one day, and he said, "You're one of them stubborn niggers." He said, "I'm going to give you this check, but you keep your mouth shut. And after you make this crop, you can find you a place to move." So I signed the check and got the money and made the next crop. He came down that fall anyway and asked me would I work. I was a good worker. I could pick three or four hundred pounds of cotton a day. If you were a good worker, they let you know they didn't like what you were doing, but you could get by with a little bit more.

We worked sun to sun. It just depended on how long the day was. There was no such thing as carrying the boss man's mule to the lot before sundown. There was the riding boss, an overseer, who saw to it that you stayed in the field. If you didn't, the plantation owner knew it, and you were penalized. If you were getting, say, fifteen dollars a month for your family, he'd say, "Well, you don't stay out on the fields and work long enough, so you'll only get ten dollars." It was bad then.

That's why I got involved in the union. I had gotten to be of age, and the family sort of split up. I was sharecropping in Cotton Plant on my own. One of my friends, who was much older than I was, came by my house one night and said, "Come go with me." I said, "Where you going?" He said, "The union meeting." I asked, "What's that?" He said, "Well, it's something to help make it better for the sharecroppers and the farmers. Don't you want to make it better?" I said, "Yeah." So we went on down to the union meeting.

You had to be a member to sit in the meetings, because they figured once you joined the union, you wouldn't go talk to the boss. Well, I didn't have a dime—that was a lot of money then—so he gave me a dime to join the union. After they held the meeting, he got up a motion that I be made secretary of the local because I could write better than he could. That's how I got started in the union.

The Southern Tenant Farmers Union began in 1934. Seven Blacks and eleven whites got together and talked over the conditions. They decided to do something about it. And that's when the plantation owners really got mad. They started arresting union organizers. Ward Rodgers was charged with calling a Black man "mister." He got up at a meeting and said, "I'd be glad to introduce you all to Mr. E. B. McKinney." It was an insult to the whites to call a "nigger" mister. Rodgers was arrested for that. Quite a few were arrested for "interfering with labor." They had a state law to that effect. They could arrest a person at that time on any charge they wanted, especially if he was poor or Black, or if he was a Southern Tenant Farmers Union organizer.

Up around Earle and Marked Tree, in northeast Arkansas, they beat the union workers up. They killed some. Some came up missing; we never did find them. It was worse there because Paul D. Peacher, being the sheriff, was very active against the union everywhere he had authority. He'd arrest union members, find something to fine them for—he didn't need too much—and take them out and put them on his plantation. And they would have to work for him. It was like a prison. It had guards and everything. Peacher's activities finally drew him a prison sentence. I believe he was prosecuted under federal law for peonage. The local government never would have indicted him then.

Organizing was pretty hard. There were some places where we couldn't send things through the mail. We had to find a way to get it there, maybe drop it off by hand, because some of the postmasters would cooperate with the plantation owners. In fact, in a lot of places, your mail went to the plantation owner's store. Either way, they would open the mail and read it. And it was dangerous to hold union meetings. You had to do it in secret because boss men made that clear: "We ain't going to have no damn union." We were afraid to meet at one place too long because they had been beating up and killing some members to try to break the union. So we would rotate our meetings. We'd have lookout guards around the house. And if anybody strange would come up, they'd let us know, and we'd turn the meeting into something else. Or we'd leave. We'd just split up and walk across the field.

We organized both white and Black. The bosses tried to keep the whites separated from the Blacks. They said: "You better stay away from the niggers down there because you're going to get in trouble fooling with them. You know, you're white. You can always come to me." Actually, the poor whites were sort of slaves themselves, in a way, but they were a little better off.

It was a violation of the state law for the Blacks and the whites to meet together. We usually started out with a white union and a Black union on the same plantation. We met secretly in the night. When the white union met, they would say to three or four Blacks: "Come over and be with us." We would do the same. Eventually, we decided to have one union. We started meeting in homes. You went in, pushed back chairs, and sat on beds and the floor. It didn't make any difference at union meetings—Black or white, you were welcomed in through the front door. Whatever was on your mind, you got up and said it to whoever it was necessary to say it to. It was always a matter of what we can do to make things better for all of us. I don't know anywhere else that happened. Once the union got started and they understood what was going on, we were all the same.

We'd go around and sign up the sharecroppers. We'd write up the head of the family, but the whole family was counted as members of the union. In 1935, we had a cotton pickers strike. It had taken us more than a year to organize to make sure it was effective. We called a meeting in Memphis, and a representative from all our areas went. We mapped our strategy. We set a strike date. We decided to have it in the middle of the cotton picking season.

We put out handbills: "Cotton Pickers! Strike! For $1 per 100 lbs." And we agreed that these would be distributed on a certain night. Each local got its handbills. A person from each area was responsible for distributing them. He'd leave Memphis with a big case of handbills, carry them home, and put them under his bed or hide them in a closet. When the time came, we put them out on foot, anywhere from ten o'clock at night until four in the morning.

We put them everywhere. They were on plantation stores, on people's porches, on posts. And the next day when the planters got up and saw them, they said, "Oh, this is just a prank. It's one of them local union fellows here." And, pretty much, I was named in the area where I was. But then in about three hours, word spread. Handbills were put out in southeast Missouri and all over the state of Arkansas and down in Mississippi, the delta area of Mississippi, and some parts of Tennessee and Alabama. Then they decided, "No, this couldn't be a local fellow. They must have put them out with an airplane."

One man from Clarksdale, Mississippi, didn't get to Memphis to pick his up, so I went myself to carry his papers. I got off the bus and I started down the street, walking. The police pulled up and said, "Don't you know we don't allow niggers on the streets at night?" I said, "No, sir, I didn't." I said, "Well, I'll go back to the bus station."

He asked, "Where you going?" I told him whose house I was going to. He said, "Oh, we know him." He saw my briefcase and said, "Get in, preacher. We'll carry you."

I got in, and they went driving on and talking: "You know one thing that's good? You're a preacher. If we thought you was one of them damn union fellows, we would have put you in the Mississippi River." And I was sitting there with a briefcase full of strike handbills. If they had looked in it, I guess I would have been gone.

I had become a volunteer organizer then. In some ways, it was more dangerous for the volunteer organizer than it was for the paid organizer. The volunteer worked locally, within a twenty-five- or thirty-mile range. The plantation owner knew you and resented your union work. The union did threaten his control. He'd blackball you. If you moved off a place because you and the boss had a disagreement, especially about something like a union, you couldn't find a place anywhere else. That's why it was so dangerous for a man and his family. Yet quite a few of us were taking the chance.

I've organized where I've had to swim lakes, hide in fields, and wade across canals. I went over to Mississippi one time, somewhere out from Greenville, to make a speech to some sharecroppers. That night, they took me to a Black church. Pretty soon, one of the lookout guards came in, caught me by the hand, and said, "Let's go. They're coming." So we went across the field, over to the canal. We waded that canal—it came up about waist deep—till we got to somebody's house. The plantation owner did come. When he got to the church, they were singing and praying. There was no union speaker there. I had been long gone. The boss man knew something was going on. He couldn't quite find out what.

The strike was effective. The strategy had been planned. The cotton pickers had all been informed as to what to do when the bosses came around. The plantation owner and his supervisor would come down and say, "Look, you all go to the fields and pick cotton. Don't pay this strike no attention." The sharecroppers would say, "Well, we want to go, but look at all those handbills out there. Them union folks will come burn our houses down, hurt our children. We can't go out there." They knew what they were about. They knew they were participating in a strike, but they had to participate by saying, "I'm scared," and it worked with the boss.

We won the strike. We got some wages. We got some houses, not all of them. No contract. Well, we didn't start a union for a contract. We started a union to make working conditions and living conditions better. That's what we were really asking for, and we got some of it. This was a big boost for the union. It really started to grow. People believed in it. They said, "Look, this organization can do things."

But we lost some people. They were caught and beaten and killed, either by the plantation owners or by the deputy sheriffs. And you couldn't prosecute anybody. Who was going to arrest them? We had more of it around Tyronza and between Memphis and Jonesboro. A lot of churches were burned. They figured burning the church down was a way of stopping the union. They said, "Yeah, if you hadn't been fooling with that union, maybe the church wouldn't have burnt down." Late at night, they would shoot into the homes of people who were active in the union. They were hard times, but we lived through them.

Anybody couldn't be a union organizer. It was scary. It was dangerous, but it was just like the Black man coming out of slavery. They would say: "You will never get free; you are always going to be a slave." But there was always somebody who had the hope that one day something could happen. There was always somebody willing to take the chance— like the Underground Railroad, where they got Black people out of here into Canada. Well, it was the same thing with the union. It was scary and it was dangerous, but you felt like it had to be done. I was a young man, brave. I wasn't scared of anybody, anything. And it was a pleasure to me just to do it, just to see I could do it.

Ideological Assaults

Labor at Mid-Century

PREWAR RED SCARE:
HOLDING MILITANT TEAMSTERS AT BAY

The 1930s was a time of revitalization for labor. Taking advantage of Section 7(a) of the New Deal's National Industrial Recovery Act, which established the right to collective bargaining, thousands of workers joined unions. They were shaking off the past effects of localized repression, a vast network of industrial spies that had sustained a system of black-listing and strikebreaking, and one of the most concentrated periods of anti-labor court activity in the nation's history, in which courts had con-tinually issued injunctions to inhibit unionization.

It was during this period of labor upsurge that rank-and-file leaders in the Minneapolis Teamsters Union, most of whom were Trotskyists, called a surprise strike of coal truck drivers, which was won in three days. The Teamsters struck again when trucking companies refused to bargain. Unarmed Teamster pickets in Minneapolis were lured into a police trap and severely beaten. The police and the Citizens Alliance, a front for the employers, recruited a thousand deputies, and violence escalated in sub-sequent encounters, with casualties on both sides.

Throughout the strike and beyond, the Minneapolis Teamsters had been in sharp conflict with the national leadership of the union, espe-cially with its president, Daniel Tobin. The local leaders' opposition to World War II exacerbated the dispute. Tobin, who had supported

Roosevelt in the 1940 election, urged action against "those disturbers who believe in the policies of foreign, radical governments."[23] The Justice Department moved swiftly. It indicted twenty-nine members of the Trotskyist Socialist Workers Party (SWP), most of whom were leaders of the Minneapolis Teamsters local, under the newly passed Alien Registration Act (the Smith Act), which made it illegal to "knowingly or wilfully advocate, abet, advise, or teach the duty, necessity, desirability or propriety of overthrowing or destroying any government in the United States by force and violence" or even to print, write, or circulate matter advocating such doctrines.[24] As it had in the trials of the Wobblies, the government relied heavily on the books, pamphlets, and ideas of the militant unionists to convict and sentence eighteen of them, including Harry DeBoer and Jake Cooper, to prison.

The American Civil Liberties Union, in a letter to the attorney general, charged that the government had "injected itself into an inter-union controversy in order to promote the interests of the one side which supported the administration's foreign and domestic policies."[25] It was a concise statement of the form repression against labor would later take.

HARRY DEBOER AND JAKE COOPER

HARRY DEBOER: In the early thirties, Minneapolis was known as an open-shop town. During the deep depression, wages in the coal yard were as low as a dollar a day, and you would work from seven o'clock in the morning till nine or ten at night, depending on the orders. I was working in the coal yards then and was also a member of Local 574 of the Teamsters Union. We started to organize the coal drivers in the fall of 1933. We took in all the workers in the coal yards: the drivers, helpers, and coal shovelers. It didn't take long. By February of '34, we had the majority of workers signed up.

The employers were represented by the powerful Citizens Alliance. As a matter of fact, they were so powerful that if some smaller companies paid more wages than what the Alliance prescribed, they found their bank accounts tied up.

JAKE COOPER: The primary hate of the Citizens Alliance was unions, and they would do anything to prevent the unionization of workers in the Minneapolis area.

HARRY: The Alliance assured the bosses that they wouldn't have to sign a union agreement. Not one of them did, and we were forced out on strike. The winter was cold; we had the streets so tied up they couldn't

HARRY DEBOER

deliver coal anywhere. The result was that after three days we won the strike, and Local 574 got an agreement to represent the workers. Of course, we asked Daniel Tobin, the president of the Teamsters international, for support. We got a wire back from him telling us to continue to arbitrate and stop the strike. But we had already gotten a contract.

This was the first strike that was won in practically sixteen years in Minneapolis, and it naturally got a lot of publicity. Workers from all over, including warehousemen and inside workers, came up to join the union that won the contract for the coal drivers. Farrell Dobbs and I took in

JAKE COOPER

dues at the union office every night after work. We signed up fifty, sixty, as high as a hundred workers a night. It was the union they wanted to join, and thousands did.

We sent notice to the employers that we now represented these new members. They refused to even sit with us to talk about recognizing the union. We called a meeting where the membership, about five thousand, voted almost unanimously to strike. A Committee of a Hundred was elected by the members to conduct it. We had a strike headquarters. We had a commissary to feed the people. Most of the strikers got their sandwiches and coffee there. We formed a women's auxiliary. We had a youth section. We had a doctor. We even sent nurses out to the homes of members. We helped everybody who needed help, including the unemployed.

JAKE: One of the problems the trade union leadership had was to unite the unemployed behind the unions. We were in the midst of a tremendous depression, twenty million people out of work. In Minneapolis, it was not much different from the rest of the country. Workers were wandering through the streets, looking for jobs, even looking for a bite to eat. The employers could have used them against the union. But our leadership unified the unemployed behind the strikers. They called for reducing workers' hours to make more jobs. They set up a welfare organization that helped both Local 574 strikers and any other unemployed member who was in dire need.

HARRY: Our policy was: You call a strike, you tie up the firm. And we did a good job on that, to the extent that they couldn't get anyone to work: no finks, no scabs.

JAKE: We had a committee that had to approve anything that moved. Emergency trucks were allowed to operate; they got permits. Farmers could come in to sell their produce but could not haul things out unless it was for themselves. The farmers became friendly and not only donated things to the commissary but actually helped with picket duty on the highways.

HARRY: And the public supported us. We'd get information through women who worked in the company offices. That's how we found out a thousand special deputies were being organized, with baseball bats and clubs and what-not to attack the strikers.

We'd already had a run-in with the police down at the market. There they attacked us with tear gas and guns and clubs, and we were unarmed. We had never let workers leave the headquarters with any kind of weapons, including clubs. That was absolutely, positively out. But when they found out the cops were moving a truck with armed deputies who were prepared to beat them up again, all hell couldn't have stopped those workers. Before you knew it, a free-for-all broke out. A lot of people were injured, and two of the special deputies got killed. The rest of them just threw their badges and clubs away and took off. That's how the day May 21, 1934, came to be called the Battle of Deputy Run.

We did win a contract that represented all the workers. But then Tobin attacked the leadership because, he said, according to his international constitution, they couldn't represent the inside workers.

JAKE: Tobin said, "We don't want all this riffraff in the union. All they'll do is cause trouble." He was talking about the workers we were organizing. Bureaucrats think that if new people come in, it will challenge their leadership, and that was something he didn't want.

HARRY: So, right off the bat, we were going against Tobin and his method of organizing. Bill Brown was president of Local 574, but the real leadership came from Carl Skoglund and Ray Dunne. In early 1933, they both worked in the coal yard. Skoglund and Dunne had once been members of the Communist Party but were expelled from it when they supported Trotsky against Stalin. They understood the labor movement, that the craft union was obsolete and that we needed a union that would represent all the workers in the plant, whatever their job, just like the Wobblies. Under no circumstances would they sell out to anybody.

JAKE: And the workers were solidly behind them. You show the workers you're honest and that you're for a democratic union, they're going to support you. But the bosses were quick to jump on anything that indicated a division in the ranks of labor. In the midst of our negotiations, Tobin wrote a red-baiting editorial attacking the 574 leadership. The Citizens Alliance reprinted it as leaflets and an ad.

HARRY: The employers, seeing that Tobin was against us, started to renege on their agreement to recognize the inside workers. So, after practically a month of arbitrating and trying to get the contract signed, as they had originally agreed, we were forced out on another strike. That was in July. Again, our policy was to stop all deliveries. We learned through the coal strike that cruising pickets were very effective. We had over a hundred cars with five pickets in each car. Whenever they saw a truck, they stopped it and sent it back to the yard. The employers couldn't deliver their product.

I had been appointed picket captain during the coal strike, and that followed on through. On July 20, 1934, I was called to go to a warehouse because a bunch of cops were surrounding a truck and were going to move it. When I got there, there were about a thousand policemen. I called back for more help. Around ten o'clock, the police captain came up to me and asked if I was in charge. I said, "Yes."

He said, "Look, we don't want a mess here. Tourists go through and see this. What can we do?" I said, "All you have to do is send these cops away and don't move any trucks, and that'll take care of it." He said, "I have to talk to my superior."

He came back: "It's a deal. We'll leave if you do. But we have to keep one squad car here." I said, "Good, we'll keep one picket car here, too."

It was a phony deal. They were just trying to break the morale of the strikers. At twelve-thirty, the police went back to the warehouse. We went back there, too, thousands of pickets, all unarmed. In about fifteen to twenty minutes, the police surrounded the truck and started moving it. Nine or ten of us in an open-bodied truck moved in front of it in order to stop them. Then the cops started shooting!

So help me, it was just like all hell broke loose. Police up on second-story roofs and on a third floor were shooting from all directions right into the workers. When the strikers ran for shelter, the cops kept firing at them. Many were shot in the back. About fifty were injured. I was one of them; I pretty near lost my leg. Two strikers got killed. One of them was Henry Ness, the driver of the truck I was in.

There was a special investigating committee appointed by the governor that put it this way: "Police took direct aim at the pickets and fired to kill." They said that "no weapons were in the possession of the pickets in the truck" and that "at no time did pickets attack the police, and it was obvious that pickets came unprepared for such an attack."[26]

Governor Olson had a perfect right to arrest the mayor and the chief of police for murder and firing on unarmed pickets. Instead he declared a state of insurrection and called out the National Guard. They surrounded the union headquarters, arrested most of our leadership—I was in the hospital then—and put them in the stockade.

JAKE: Governor Olson was a Farmer-Laborite and claimed he was a friend of labor. But when labor was in a life-and-death struggle, when they had already sapped some of the union's strength, the guy who was "a friend of labor" calls out the National Guard. And they escorted the trucks with nonunion labor. They came very close to breaking the strike. But the union found a way to stop that with the roving pickets.

HARRY: And the windup was we won that strike. It was finally agreed that we would represent all the workers. In the meantime, we were still at odds with Tobin. In 1935, Tobin expelled us from the international because he said we were violating the union constitution. He set up Local 500, hoping to take away the members from Local 574. But Local 500 never got to be anything more than a paper organization, while we kept growing. We not only won better conditions for the truck drivers, we supported every union in town. When they had a strike, our drivers would never cross their picket line. That was right in our contract.

JAKE: When I joined the union in 1934, I was seventeen years old. I was a young guy, looking at everything open-mouthed. I learned, after seeing some of the struggles that went on, after seeing the brutality on the picket line, that the employers would do anything to safeguard their profit system. But then I saw how tremendous our leadership was, and I've never changed my mind about that.

HARRY: A leader would get the same pay as the top driver. If the driver got sixty cents an hour, the leaders would get accordingly, plus their expenses. And we didn't have any secrets. We had open meetings. By that time, we had over seven, eight thousand members and had to use two halls with loudspeakers in the second hall. So kicking us out of the international didn't stop us. But we didn't want to split up the labor movement, so we fought for reinstatement. We said, "We want to be a part of the AFL Teamsters. It's Tobin that's kicked us out." That position led all the good fighters in the union to support us. Finally Tobin gave in, and we merged the two unions into Local 544.

JAKE: In 1939, the government issued an order that they would no longer pay union scale on WPA jobs,* and they cut the wages of the workers. Thousands of WPA workers went out on strike spontaneously. Then they came up to the union hall and insisted that Local 544 do something to help them. And the Teamsters did. They supported the strike through the union's Federal Workers Section. So the government indicted a whole group from the Federal Workers Section. A number of them went to prison for what was called "striking against the government."

HARRY: Then the war was coming on, and we naturally were opposed to it.

JAKE: We were opposed to our entrance into World War II because we didn't believe it was really a war to fight fascism. It was a war that was fighting for control of the world by the United States, Germany, and other countries. And that is the basic reason why the federal government attacked us when it did, because of our stand on the war.

HARRY: Tobin supported Roosevelt's foreign policy. When we didn't go along with him, we were red-baited. You see, in the constitution of the international, it said you couldn't belong to the Communist Party. Tobin said that included the Trotskyists and began attacking our local leadership. But it didn't have much effect because the workers already knew we had gotten them better conditions. So he tried to put Local 544 in the hands of the receivers.† That's when we went to John L. Lewis's

*The Works Progress Administration (WPA) was a New Deal work relief program that provided federally supported jobs to five million unemployed.

†A receiver is a person appointed to wind up the affairs of an organization or to manage it during a mandated reorganization.

organization and got a charter as the drivers' section of the CIO. Then Tobin sent in his group to take over our Teamster headquarters and to set up a counterorganization again.

JAKE: This time, the international brought goons in from all over the United States. I got beat up during that period. They came on the dock of Werner Transportation, where I was working. They busted my nose. My cheekbone was busted. My scalp was lacerated. I got beat up pretty severely and put in the hospital. That day, my picture was on the front page of the paper with a bandage across my face, and the caption on it was "This man talks too much."

HARRY: One time, three goons came into the office and asked, "Where is this Harry DeBoer?" They had guns and clubs and immediately started beating me up. I knew I didn't have a chance, so I purposely lay still as if I was hurt bad. In spite of that, they stomped on me. They obviously knew my leg had been shot during the strike because they jumped on it. At the time, I was negotiating the Waterman Waterbury contract.

JAKE: We had asked for elections. We demanded they give the workers the right to vote on which union—the AFL or the CIO—they wanted to represent them. We finally got an election at the Waterman Waterbury plant. When we won that, it was apparent they couldn't defeat us anywhere else if there was going to be a democratic vote of the workers.

HARRY: Tobin saw he was in real trouble, that he was going to lose his fight here again. So he went to Roosevelt and asked for help. It took Roosevelt only a matter of days to act. The FBI and U.S. marshals raided the Socialist Workers Party headquarters and took all kinds of literature. Then the *St. Paul Dispatch* came out with a headline: "U.S. to Prosecute 544."

Twenty-nine of us were indicted under the Smith Act for conspiring to advocate the overthrow of the government by force and violence. They used the literature they had taken from the SWP office at the trial. The newspapers tried to make it seem like secret evidence, but there was nothing clandestine about it. Anybody could have come up and asked for it and gotten it. The whole thing was a sham, just a subterfuge to break our union. They really couldn't attack us on a trade union basis. But they wanted to get us out of the union movement. So they used our ideology. It was red-baiting from beginning to end. And the Smith Act was just a perfect tool for them.

JAKE: They claimed that the SWP would say one thing in public but something else in private. That's a lot of bullshit. We looked forward to a new and better society that we thought could be built. But we'd been stating publicly that we were for that; we'd been shouting it from the rooftops. And our defense was based on that, that there was nothing in our ideas that was hidden. We said that socialism would never come into being in this country until we convinced the overwhelming majority of people of our ideas. It could not be done by a small minority. And we were a minority, and we recognized it and functioned that way. But they were saying it like we were preparing tomorrow for revolution.

HARRY: One witness testified during the trial that we'd have guns hidden in churches—that when the time was ripe, we'd grab these guns and take over.

JAKE: Well, those stories were absolutely manufactured.

HARRY: I'm sure the witnesses were coached to say what they did. They would twist everything—things that were democratically arrived at—to make it look like it was a conspiracy. Like the defense guards.

JAKE: The Union Defense Guard came into being because there was a fascist organization in this area called the Silver Shirts. Their leader was Gerald L. K. Smith. And the Silver Shirts, who were against minorities and were especially anti-Semitic, said they were going to attack the Teamster headquarters. When it looked like they were really serious about attacking us, we formed a group of about one hundred and fifty militants within the union. We held two meetings in a downtown parking lot, to show the Silver Shirts that we would stand for no monkey business. Once they saw we had this kind of strength, we never needed to use it.

HARRY: The testimony they had against us was all lies. But they were able to convict us regardless of the facts.

JAKE: The chance of winning against the government in a federal court is pretty slim. They have all the power to manufacture a case, to buy witnesses. And none of our peers were on the jury, not one single union person. They were mostly business people and a few farmers. This panel couldn't understand trade unionism; they couldn't understand radical political ideas. So even from that viewpoint, we didn't have a ghost of a chance.

HARRY: The judge threw out some of the cases, but eighteen of the twenty-nine were convicted in 1941. Twelve of us got sixteen months, and six got a year and a day. That extra day meant you lost your civil rights after you got out. We went through all the appeals and so on. We were sent to prison on New Year's Day of '44.

JAKE: I was sentenced to sixteen months. I had just started going with some young lady. And we were really serious, you know. Right in the middle of it, they whisked me off to prison. Of course, this was not easy. But then the police department in Chaska actually went to the extent of contacting both her parents and succeeded in breaking us up. When I found out, it really had a bad effect on me. I find this woman who I'm really in love with, and they break me up with her, and I'm in prison. I've got no way to fight back. I started getting sick. I was throwing up and couldn't stop, just from this nervous reaction. Finally they put me in the hospital.

HARRY: Then she started to find out that the police were giving her a bunch of goop. So they finally got together again. She's his wife now.

JAKE: Prison is no fun. Nobody wants their rights taken away. Nobody wants to eat the kind of food they have. Nobody likes that kind of situation. But for me, in spite of everything, it was a memorable period. I did more reading there than I did at any time in my life. I'm talking about good reading, like Darwin's *The Origin of Species* and *The Descent of Man*. And I read a lot of radical literature. Not only that, but I spent a whole year with Harry and guys like Vince Dunne and Carl Skoglund and Jim Cannon. I really got to know these people, like you get to know a member of the family. I got to know them for all their bad qualities and their good qualities, and I respected them for the kind of human beings that they were. So prison wasn't a total loss.

HARRY: Well, life is what you make it, you know. We had made up our minds that we were not going to be suckolds to the prison guards but we would do the work we were assigned. Actually, the way we got along in prison was with discipline. It was the same kind of discipline that built the union, the kind we had to have to organize workers.

JAKE: After prison, both of us can tell you that we couldn't get jobs in the Minneapolis area. We were blackballed in the city. And I'm sure the federal government played a role in that. I had to leave home to get a job at Swift and Company, in the meatpacking industry. I worked there about a year before they caught up with me. They called me in one day and notified me that I was discharged because I was a threat to the government. So then I came back home and went to work for Armour and Company until 1949. Then I went to Chaska, twenty-five miles from Minneapolis, and became a businessman.

HARRY: Carl Skoglund and I opened up our own little business, servicing appliances. We were able to make a living for several years, and then I went into selling trucks.

But I wouldn't have missed that period. Here was Minneapolis, an open-shop town; a bunch of bosses had it tied up. It took the Trotskyists and a militant union to break it. We had established ourselves so solid and proved that we would do anything to get better conditions, including going to jail. And the members knew this. It took the local, state, and federal governments to break our union.

JAKE: They destroyed probably the most marvelous union that this country has ever seen. It was genuinely a democratic organization that used all the talents of the workers and had them completely involved in what was taking place. I'm not saying that the Teamsters still don't get better conditions for the workers. They do. But now, to a lot of the workers, the union is like an insurance company, instead of an organization that belongs to them, one that they have something to say about. And so the union changed dramatically.

POSTWAR TESTS OF LOYALTY: ATTEMPTS
TO SILENCE AN AUTO WORKERS' SPOKESMAN

In 1936 and 1937, workers throughout the country were using a new tool of their own making—the sit-down strike—to demand higher wages, better working conditions, and union recognition. It was in that historic upsurge, which reshaped industrial relations in America, that Stanley Nowak became one of the original organizers of the United Auto Workers (UAW).

To gain access to Ford employees, who faced intimidation and terror from company police, Nowak ran for the Michigan state senate in 1938. In his role as a Democratic Party candidate, he could speak to those who were too fearful to listen to him as a UAW organizer. Once elected, he was "labor's senator," the *Detroit Free Press* wrote, "the unwelcome voice of the consumer, the employee, the welfare client."[27]

In 1942, Stanley Nowak was arrested, charged with disbelieving in organized government, and threatened with the loss of his citizenship. The roots of this action could be traced back to the beginning of the century, when ideological tests for the foreign-born were instituted by the Immigration Act of 1903, a law that barred anyone who "disbelieves in or is opposed to all organized government" from entering the country.[28] That statute was honed across the next two decades as its focus shifted from excluding anarchists to deporting foreign-born Wobblies. Eventually its progeny, including state criminal syndicalism laws and the federal Smith Act, came to be used against dissidents of another era.

Pressed to withdraw its action against Nowak in 1942, the federal government made a second attempt to deport him in 1952, this time under the newly enacted McCarran-Walter Act, which allowed foreign-born persons to be held for deportation if they had joined "subversive" organizations. In that more repressive time, almost one-third of the persons facing deportation as "subversives" were officials or active members of trade unions.[29]

STANLEY NOWAK

When I saw these two men walking into the restaurant, they stood out so different from the rest. Then, when a hand was put on my shoulder, I looked at the man. He was young and tall, sort of a university type. He showed me immediately his badge, his FBI badge, and said, "You've been indicted by a grand jury, and you have to come along with us." He said, "Don't make any commotion here. We don't want any trouble."

It was about seven o'clock when the FBI picked me up and took me to the federal building. A Mr. Gordon, the special agent, showed me the warrant for my arrest. It said that when I received my citizenship, I falsely answered the question, "Are you a member of an organization that disbelieves in organized government and advocates the violent overthrow of the government?"

It was 1942, and I had just been elected to my third term in the Michigan state senate. How could I not believe in organized government when I was in government? So first I laughed when they read these charges. But then I realized that they could take away my citizenship and put me in jail for five years.

They started to interrogate me about eight that night, and it went on until midnight. They questioned me continuously, over and over. I made one mistake: I didn't have to answer their questions at all. I could have simply said, "Look, if you allow me to have my attorney, I will answer questions. Otherwise, I don't." But I had this feeling: I wasn't disloyal in any sense. My entire activity was in the spirit of being helpful to the country, at least to the majority of the people in the country. So what did I have to hide?

Gordon came in with a written statement for me to sign. It wasn't anything like what I said when he questioned me. I refused to sign it and asked to see my lawyer. The whole time they kept me there, I was not allowed to make a phone call. Finally, at twelve midnight, he let me call my wife, Margaret. Then he put handcuffs on me and took me to jail. They kept me there overnight, and the next morning I appeared in court.

There was a general uproar over the whole thing. After all, I was a

STANLEY NOWAK

state senator. And before that I was one of the first five national organizers of the United Auto Workers. I was in at the very beginning of this trade
union movement and participated in organizing a number of shops. So
immediately labor unions had meetings and acted on it.

Congressman Sadowski came the next morning and arranged to bail
me out. The people of my district set up a defense committee for me.
They went with a number of union leaders to see Francis Biddle, the U.S.
attorney general under Roosevelt, and asked him to drop the charges.
Over five hundred people came to a conference on my behalf at the Statler

Hotel. I got support from the top officers of the United Automobile Workers and from community and religious leaders.

When the state legislature session started, the question was whether I should be sworn in because I was under indictment. Photographers were there waiting. A Republican senator, acting very friendly, advised me that I should decline to be seated until my case was cleared. I did not intend to do that. I went to Joseph Baldwin, another Republican, and told him what he said. Baldwin and I had argued many times on the floor of the senate. We were the two opposites. But now he said, "Don't you listen to that old fool. If anyone objects to your being seated, I'll be the first one to speak against it." Well, no one raised any objections. And before I knew it, the secretary of the senate called my name, and I was sworn in.

Every senator got a letter from Gerald L. K. Smith, smearing me. He was a reverend who preached extreme conservatism in the name of God. To him, a Communist, a liberal, a Democrat who was somewhat liberal were the same thing. He had a radio program here. The entire program was anti-labor, anti-Black, anti-Semitic. After the letter, he sent a petition protesting my seating, and he tried to appear before the senate. But they refused. Some of the senators would call me or Margaret over to their desk. "Have you seen this?" Then they would tear up the letter from Gerald L. K. Smith and toss it in the basket.

On the evening of February 9, 1943, when Margaret and I took a walk, we picked up a copy of the *Detroit Free Press*. There was the headline: "U.S. Drops Indictment Against Nowak." We learned from the article that John C. Lehr, U.S. district attorney, had refused the order of the Justice Department to quash my indictment. Attorney General Biddle had to act over Lehr's head to do it.

The next morning, I got up on the podium and thanked the senators for their support. They would never applaud in the senate—it's a dignified chamber—but they did on that day. I was naturally quite surprised to see such a reaction. These were conservative people like Baldwin. Some of them were former judges, prosecuting attorneys. When they supported me this way, particularly when the press made such a big thing out of my indictment, I was touched by it.

When I was first elected to the senate, the press pictured me as some sort of extreme radical. With that kind of reputation, when I walked into the senate with Margaret, it was like an icebox, very cold. It took some time before we broke the ice and they realized two things: First, I was not for sale. Everybody was supposed to have their price. Second, they had a conception that if you are a leftist, you're just a dumb cluck. I was a complete beginner, but I tried to learn as fast as I could. I kept on listening, watching, studying.

The first time I had to speak was when a bill was introduced by Senator Baldwin, completely outlawing sit-down strikes. They had waited a long time for me to speak, and then when I finally did, they thought they had their chance to expose me. But they overlooked the fact that labor problems were old things to me. Well, I spoke about fifteen minutes, very briefly, and answered their questions. They didn't get me excited because I'd answered those questions on the soapbox and at labor meetings I don't know how many times. The gallery was filled with university students. They started applauding me until the lieutenant governor threatened to throw them out of the senate.

I was born in Poland. My people were peasants. There were seven of us in the family. My mother died when I was just six; I hardly remember her. We came here in 1913 and located around the stockyards of Chicago. I went to Catholic school where the nuns spoke better Polish than English. During the war, I sold newspapers on the streets and went to school in the evening. By 1916, 1917, my brothers and sisters all worked in the packinghouses. They joined the union and dragged me to meetings with them.

Then as soon as the war was over, wages went down. My older brother worked twelve hours a day, seven days a week. That's how they worked then. A strike took place, a bloody strike. Union organizers were killed. One of them was a neighbor of mine. I was introduced as a kid into this bloody thing. I saw race riots that took place soon after that. I watched the Palmer raids. When neighbors were arrested over the New Year's Eve holiday, some women came and asked if I would go with them to the police headquarters. They were seeking their husbands, who were in there somewhere, and they couldn't speak English.

Later, a friend of mine got a job for me at Hart, Schaffner and Marx. I took an active part in the union and was very young when I was elected a shop chairman. Then the depression came. It got so bad, there was only one day's work in two weeks. I had some savings, so I thought to myself: I'll catch up on my education—I left school when I was fourteen—or I'll go and travel and see the country a little. So I quit. Thirty days later, there were huge headlines in the *Chicago Tribune:* "Seventeen Banks Closed in One Day." And one of the banks was where I had my savings. I was left with fifty dollars in cash.

There was no unemployment compensation, no Social Security, no relief of any kind. What did I do? I took an active part in the Unemployed

Councils. There I was often called to speak. Somehow, I didn't have the patience for academic studies, but I did a lot of reading. I wanted to answer these questions: Why is there unemployment? Why does the packinghouse industry take pigs and cows and destroy them, burn them, when people go hungry? Why is milk thrown into the river? A librarian took an interest in me and gave me the first volume of Marx's *Capital*. Oh, I sweated blood over it. But I learned.

I traveled between Chicago and Boston, back and forth, living with the unemployed. Finally I landed in Detroit and decided to stay here. I met an old acquaintance from the Amalgamated Clothing Workers, a Polish fellow. I told him I was making a few dollars selling paint. "Oh," he said, "to hell with you selling paint. Why don't you come with us in the United Auto Workers? We have a big problem here."

I came to a meeting of the UAW board the next day. The president, Homer Martin, was there. Walter Reuther was a member of the board. He said to me, "Every auto shop has Poles. How do we reach them?" There were actually, in Wayne County alone, three hundred thousand Poles. The union needed someone who spoke their language and who they had confidence in.

Well, two things came to my mind: first, that we should have a Polish committee in charge of organizing the Polish workers; second, that we should find a way to get time on one of the Polish-language radio programs. That wasn't so simple for the UAW at that time. Luckily, an announcer on one of the Polish programs was a fellow I knew from Chicago. He agreed to sell us time, ten minutes, twice a week. In a few weeks, I had an audience of thousands. We had meetings. We met in churches and in empty lots. We had a car with an amplifier on top of it, and we would go around the neighborhood talking to people.

Applications came in, and the union grew very rapidly. It was a complete surprise to all of us. Not only the auto workers responded to us, but the cigar workers, who were mostly Polish and Slav women. They would call us on the phone: "We are sitting down. Send us an organizer." I would say, "Who are you? Where?" We had no time to organize cigar workers. We had very little funds, and there were only five of us organizers in the whole UAW at the beginning. Once, they sent a delegation to our headquarters and asked for me specifically, because they heard me on the radio. George Addis, the secretary-treasurer, told them, "Look, we cannot go into cigar factories. We can't do that." They said, "All right, we'll sit down in *your* office."

Addis called me: "Stanley, please come and help me." So I came, and

I told George, "Look, let me go there, and I'll see what I can do." Okay. I walked into the cigar shop, and they all were there, sitting down. I got up on a bench and asked, "Do you have a committee?" No. They had no committee, so we had to organize one. We had to notify the families because, after all, these were married women with children. We had to organize a kitchen to bring food. They had to arrange sleeping accommodations. By the time I was through, there was a delegation from another cigar shop, just a couple blocks away, waiting for me to finish here. For three days I didn't get home. I just went from shop to shop.

There was one day here—and it was not an unusual day—when we had seventy-five strikes in Detroit. We organized a number of plants in Dearborn. We organized Chrysler. We were effective. Some of us were left-wingers, some were Communists, most were good, militant trade unionists.

There was this Ternstedt plant, the biggest GM plant in Detroit. Twelve thousand people worked there, mostly Polish and southern women. We would distribute leaflets every day to all three shifts, and I would speak through an amplifier to the workers. Their first reaction was cool; they were scared. But they became accustomed to us. I would go to restaurants and barrooms nearby, where I got to know them. We started holding meetings in the Slovenian Hall. There were times when I didn't go home, when I slept on benches, because I would have a morning meeting, an afternoon meeting, and a midnight meeting. Well, the union started growing. By then, we had a couple of thousand members.

A problem developed while this was going on. There had been a strike in some of the shops of General Motors, and the first agreement between General Motors and the UAW had taken place. Part of the agreement included a no-strike pledge for a year. It happened just when the Ternstedt workers started meeting with the management. The manager, Skinner, had the mentality of a lawyer and a military man. He realized he had to meet with us, but he did not have to grant us any concessions.

What did we want? We wanted to abolish piecework. We asked for a ten percent increase in wages and recognition of the union. But he would sit with a long cigarette holder at a beautiful big table in his office. He would smoke and he would smile, and his answer to every demand was "No."

The workers began to come to me. "Look, Stanley, what are you getting out of those meetings? What are you doing at those meetings?" So I went to Walter Reuther, and he immediately said, "Remember, we cannot strike." I said, "Yes, I'm aware of it. What do you suggest we do?"

He was sort of a politician. He said, "Look, Stanley, you have more experience than I do. You should know better what to do. Think it over." I went to Homer Martin, the international union president, and he said to me, "Stanley, you cannot strike."

The workers were not so conscious of legalities as the union officials were. They simply said, "To hell with that contract." Well, I knew that I couldn't say, "To hell with that contract." A contract is a contract, and it was the first one with General Motors. So I struggled in my mind over what to do. Finally I thought: We will act like this manager. He fulfilled his obligation by meeting with us but not negotiating. We'll fulfill our obligation. We'll come to work and go through the motions but put very little out.

I went to Homer Martin. He listened to me, and he got excited. "You know what? I think you've got something. Only go very carefully so they don't catch you." I got together the bargaining committee and the two hundred shop stewards. The idea went through overwhelmingly.

The action was to start Monday, the very day that we had our meeting with Skinner. When we came there, he, as usual, welcomed us. We looked at him and knew that he didn't know anything. As the discussion started, he received a call. As we continued, another call. Then a third. One after another. Finally, he turned to me with a sneer, "You son of a bitch. You dare to come to my office when the whole shop is on strike. Go on. Get out of here!" So fine. We left.

These women were very militant. They were getting a big kick out of it. They said to me, "We thought they had you over a barrel. Now they're over the barrel." They were proud of what the union had done. But Homer Martin fired me and notified Skinner that I didn't represent the union anymore. Skinner called me on the phone and told me, "I don't have to talk to you now."

I went to the membership. They said, "Who the devil is this Homer Martin anyway? The hell with him." They passed a motion that I be put on the local union payroll, and I continued to work.

Finally, the president of General Motors, William Knudsen, got hold of Wyndham Mortimer, a UAW national officer, and asked him to do something about this strike. When Mortimer came to me, I said, "Look, explain to Knudsen we only want the very things GM gave the workers at Flint. We don't ask for anything more. Let Skinner sit down and talk to us."

So I got a call from Skinner. That's the first time he called me by my first name: "Stanley, let's stop this fight. Bring your committee, and let's get down to work." Good. I brought my committee. Now it only took a couple hours to get practically everything we asked for. We had huge victory meetings when it was all over, and ninety percent of the shop was in the union.

We had another problem when we wanted to organize the Ford workers. Why? The Ford Motor Company completely dominated the government in Dearborn. They had city ordinances forbidding public meetings. You actually couldn't get to their gates to speak to workers. Furthermore, the Ford Motor Company had an undercover service of their own. They would penetrate into every meeting that was held. People who were seen at union meetings were fired immediately. So we went house to house. We held meetings in private homes outside of Dearborn but would only get half a dozen people. It was almost like underground work.

In the 1938 election campaign, we saw that these very Ford workers who were afraid to come to our union meetings went to the Democratic Party meetings. The idea came to us: If we had a candidate for public office, he could speak about the union at all these meetings. So I became a candidate for the state senate. The object was not that I would get elected—I didn't think I would—but to get to these Ford workers. When I went to these political meetings, I talked about the need for the workers to join the union: "Look what we did in General Motors. Look what we did in Chrysler. But Ford is not organized."

Before I realized it, a committee to elect me came into existence. There were three hundred precincts that we had to cover for the election. It required tremendous organization. But when the election was over, my Republican opponent came to congratulate me. My term began in 1939. I spent ten years in the senate.

In 1952, I ran for city council together with Reverend Charles Hill, a Black minister. Right in the middle of that campaign, I was called before the House Un-American Activities Committee. They called Reverend Hill, too. They obviously hoped to destroy us politically. They had me before that committee an entire day. It was on the radio, and most of the city stopped to listen to it. Five lawyers were hammering at me. They tried to picture me as being a Communist and therefore anti-American. Once in a while my lawyer, George Crockett, would kick me in the foot and say, "Stanley, don't answer that question." Naturally, he was concerned that I didn't get myself in prison. My concern was that the people who were listening would think, "Well, the man has something to hide if all he says is 'I will not answer.'" So I would first answer the question as much as I could. And then when it got to the possibility of entrapment or names of other people, I would refer to the Fifth Amendment.

On December 24, 1952, the most sweeping of all immigration laws in our history, the McCarran-Walter Law, went into effect. That very night, I was notified of new denaturalization proceedings against me. You see, Eisenhower's attorney general, Herbert Brownell, actually had a plan to denaturalize ten thousand citizens and prepare them for deportation and to deport another thirteen thousand noncitizens. He said that publicly.

That's when the Committee for the Protection of the Foreign Born became so important. The question was what case to use as a test to try to stop this drive of deportation and denaturalization. My case was chosen. We realized that we faced a serious fight. The circumstances that prevailed at that time were quite different from ten years before. The labor movement had changed quite a bit. The atmosphere was different. Even so, people would stop me on the street, shake hands, and leave me ten or twenty dollars. Or they would take me to a bar, buy me a drink, and leave some money with me. Some did not even tell me their names.

Finally, my case came up in a lower court here in Detroit. The prosecutor, Dwight Hamborsky, charged me with fraud. He said I had denied I was a member of the Communist Party before immigration examiners and that that was a lie. Then he said I had lied when I answered on my petition for citizenship that I didn't belong to any organization teaching or advocating anarchy or the violent overthrow of the government.

Their first witnesses were Harold Hart and Stanton Smiley, the naturalization examiners who had questioned me sixteen years earlier when I applied for my citizenship. Hart said he interviewed fifteen hundred people while he was a naturalization officer and that when he interviewed me, it was only for about twenty minutes. But he said he could remember asking me whether I was a member of the Communist Party and that I answered, "No."

Those examiners never asked me that question. It was not even on the questionnaire. Hart said, "We often asked questions that were not on the questionnaire." How could he remember that after all those years? My lawyer, Ernest Goodman, asked if he made notes of those questions. "Generally I did." "Well, did you make a note of this?" "No." Smiley said he had interviewed around thirty-five to forty thousand people over the years. The day he interviewed me, in 1938, I was one of fifty-four. He couldn't remember any of the others, yet he "remembered" that he asked me if I was a Communist and that I denied it.

The government must have been searching for witnesses all over. They came up with the usual professional stool pigeons, drunks, or somebody who was in their clutches. Kazimer Rataj named me as a Communist. When my attorney, Goodman, questioned him, he found that Rataj himself had falsely denied being a Communist when he made his application for citizenship. He said he was visited in 1950 or 1951 by two men from the Immigration Service. And he was called to the immigration office for further questioning, where he named other people as Communists. Then what happened? Shortly after he testified against me, they gave him his citizenship.

Professor William Hewitt said he had been sent from Chicago to see me, but he did not remember who sent him. Somebody brought him in a car to our home, but he did not remember who brought him. He did not remember in what part of the city of Detroit we lived. He said that he was in our apartment, but we didn't have an apartment at that time. I never met this man in my life. His story was fabricated from beginning to end. We gradually discovered why. Hewitt testified about a visit from FBI agents in 1949 regarding falsification of an application he had filed. He admitted that he had failed to list his membership in the Communist Party on a questionnaire. "So there was a question raised," asked Goodman, "as to whether you were guilty of violating the federal perjury laws at that time?" "They suggested that possibility." Suggested?? They had Hewitt just where they wanted him.

Another witness, Richard Eager, had worked in the Ternstedt shop and became one of the first chairmen of the shop committee. But because of his fondness for the bottle, he didn't do his job. When he wasn't re-elected, he became bitter. He was expelled from the local for his disruptive activities. Then he went before the FBI, the Dies Committee, and the Immigration Service to testify.

But now on the stand, he wasn't saying what the prosecutor wanted him to say about me. I stared at him, and he looked down. He said, "It is so long ago, I can't remember him passing any particular remarks that would leave any indelible mark in my memory." Hamborsky kept trying. "Did you ever see Stanley Nowak advocate such a revolution?" "I can't say as I did." Hamborsky didn't know what to do. He asked more and more leading questions. Even Judge Picard said, "If he doesn't recall, you certainly can't take the stand for him."

But after the lunch recess, Hamborsky finally got Eager to say, "He told us that we couldn't depend too much on the ballot to gain our objective, but that it would eventually resolve to bullets." What happened? Even Judge Picard wanted to know: "Mr. Eager, you were asked a question as to what Nowak had said. You never mentioned bullets until after the recess. Now, when did you get the idea of bullets?" "Well," Eager said, "that is my impression of it."

That was enough to "convince" Picard. On July 15, 1955, a year after the trial started, the judge ordered my citizenship canceled. The court of appeals upheld the verdict. When it went to the Supreme Court, their decision was a surprise to all of us. The Court said that the government failed to prove its case and even that "some of the testimony was elicited only after persistent prodding by counsel for the Government." And then they said, "We rule that the charge of fraud was not proved."

Once the Supreme Court made its decision, the attorney general's plan to deport thousands was just thrown out. It was something to celebrate. I recall we had a little victory party. And George Crockett, who became our congressman, spoke there. He said, "The trouble with Stan is that he never knows when he's licked."

IMPOSING COLD WAR ORTHODOXY:
A TEACHERS UNION UNDER ATTACK

By 1940, in the midst of a "little red scare," twenty-one states had imposed loyalty oaths for teachers; between 1942 and 1946, fifteen more joined them. Public school and college textbooks and curricula were inspected by HUAC and even by military authorities. Texas required publishers to file an affidavit that the deceased authors on their lists—among them Aristotle and Shakespeare—disclaimed Communism. Teachers who availed themselves of their constitutional privileges under the Fifth Amendment when HUAC descended on Philadelphia or Los Angeles were suspended or dismissed summarily.

New York had been especially vigilant. In 1940, State Senator Frederic Coudert launched a search for "subversives" in New York City colleges that led to the dismissal of professors without regard for the quality of their teaching. After the war, the loyalty purge in New York was aimed squarely at the left-wing leadership of the city's Teachers Union. The instrument of the purge was to be the state's 1949 Feinberg Law, which required every school district to report to the state every year on the loyalty of every teacher. Disloyalty was established by a teacher's membership in organizations that state officials designated as subversive. Evidence of subversion extended beyond membership: "The writing of articles, the distribution of pamphlets, endorsement of speeches made or articles written or acts performed by others," the state commissioner of education told school officials, "all may constitute subversive activity."[30]

In 1950, leaders of the New York City Teachers Union, people with records of outstanding performance, were dismissed under loyalty proceedings. The membership of the union dropped from 7,000 in 1946 to 2,000 after the purge.[31] By the end of the 1950 school year, the New York City Board of Education was able to withdraw recognition from the Teachers Union. By the end of the decade, 38 teachers, Mildred Grossman among them, had been dismissed after highly publicized "trials," and 283 others resigned or retired to escape the ordeal.

MILDRED GROSSMAN

Minnie Gutride was an elementary school teacher, a very gentle person. She was an active member of the Teachers Union. One day, the assistant superintendent, the counsel for the school board, and a stenographer came to her school in Staten Island to question her about meetings she might have attended years before. When she asked to consult her attorney, they threatened to charge her with conduct unbecoming a teacher. Evidently, she was very upset. I think it was around the holiday season, and she was alone. Her husband had been killed in Spain. That night, she committed suicide.

The inquisition was under way. Its purpose was to smash the Teachers Union. Several hundred teachers lost their jobs in the period that followed the enactment of the Feinberg Law in 1949. It got to the point where they were calling in everybody who had been an active member of the union. And for very good reason. Our union had conducted a campaign against the racist policies of the schools when nobody else did. We demanded more money for new schools when they were trying to spend less. We organized parents in the community to fight with us against substandard education. They didn't want the community involved in the schools. We wanted more money for teachers and smaller classes, and we challenged the authoritarian rule of school administrators. And they didn't want that.

But most of all, this was the period of the Cold War. This was the period of the Truman Doctrine, the anti-Soviet hysteria, the heyday of the "let's go to war, boys" mentality. In the attempt to build up a war psychosis, there had to be no opposition: The schools were to become an "instrument of national policy." Students would be taught not how to think but what to think—and especially what not to think. What teach-

MILDRED GROSSMAN

ers were being asked to do was train a generation of robots. As far as
the union was concerned, this was not education, and we did not want
the schools to be used to promote the war.

The Feinberg Law was a Cold War law. It required school officials to
certify the loyalty of each and every teacher annually. Did they belong
to any organizations that the board of regents had declared "subversive"?
Being a member was grounds for immediate suspension unless the
teacher could prove his or her "innocence." That's guilt by association.

The board of regents didn't get around to making up a list of subversive organizations as long as I was there, but that didn't stop the New York City Board of Education from going ahead with their interrogations. It was sort of like the chopping block: You came in. They asked you questions. You were suspended. You had a hearing. You were dismissed. And you never knew who your accusers were.

Our position in the Teachers Union was that a teacher should be judged only on his or her performance. You cannot ask people what their political opinions are and make their political opinions the basis for employment. That's where the total unconstitutionality of it comes in. Even some of the officialdom were uncomfortable with this type of interrogation—but they did it.

The assistant corporation counsel, Saul Moskoff, conducted the interviews. He would start with his standard question: "Are you a member of the Communist Party?" If you refused to answer, Moskoff probed further: Have you read this book? Do you know so-and-so? Have you ever been to any meetings sponsored by the Communist Party? Then, if you refused to answer, you were called in before the superintendent and questioned again. After that, you were suspended from teaching on grounds of insubordination and conduct unbecoming a teacher.

If you said you had been a member of the Communist Party, he would ask who else was a member. If you refused to give them names, you could answer all the other questions you wanted, but it wouldn't do you any good. You were still suspended.

I was teaching in Manhattan when I got a letter asking me to come down to answer questions. When you were active in the New York Teachers Union, as I was, you sort of expected that you were going to get a letter. But it was still quite a shock when it came.

The interviews were conducted in an old warehouse where Moskoff had his office. It was dirty. You felt surrounded by dirt while you were in there. That added insult to injury. I remember how intimidating their big tape recorders were. To make matters worse, you weren't permitted counsel, which I felt was unlawful. The longer I was there, the more angry I got.

Moskoff started out with his standard question. I answered it, "No, I am not a member of the Communist Party." But he wasn't satisfied. "When did you leave?" I said, "When did you stop beating your wife?" I didn't believe he had any right to ask me about the organizations I belonged to. But by that time, the Supreme Court had ruled that the Feinberg Law was constitutional. So I would do what the Court required, but do no more. I told Moskoff I'd answer questions only back to the date the Feinberg Law was enacted, but no earlier. One discussed one's civil liberties, but that didn't mean anything to him. This was 1952.

Moskoff sent his report and recommendations to the superintendent, William Jansen. Jansen never read them before he assigned my case to the associate superintendent from my division, somebody named Pertsch. Pertsch also interrogated me about my political opinions, although he hadn't read Moskoff's report either. Pertsch was a charming gentleman who was terribly embarrassed by what he was doing. But he wouldn't give in to his feelings. He sent his report to Jansen, and charges were preferred.

There was a meeting of the board of education where I had the opportunity to speak. People from superpatriotic groups in the city would come early to pack the board meetings before teachers could get there. You would look out there and see the hate on the faces of those people. When they got to me, the president of the board turned to Jansen and asked, "Did she answer the question?" He meant the question about Communist Party membership. Jansen didn't know. I indicated that I had, but by then I was uncertain whether I should have answered it at all. I believed the board was using its power to negate everything this country stood for, and I told them that.

Then they suspended me. It was on the front page of the *Journal American,* which, incidentally, got the information before I did. They not only printed my name, but they printed my address. Then the hate mail came. A lot of it was anti-Semitic: "You dirty red Jew."

I was living with my parents then, and I can remember one night when the phone rang every few minutes. I would pick it up and put it back down without saying anything. My mother asked, "Why don't you let me answer the phone?" I said, "No. This is my affair. I'll answer it."

Then it rang again. Before I could answer, she had the phone. She heard, "This is the voice of death." "This is the voice of death?" she repeated. "Then drop dead!"

My mother wasn't letting any calls come through after that. A friend of mine said, "What's the matter? When I call you, I have to give your mother my name and what I want to discuss with you. Doesn't she remember me?"

It got to be very unpleasant. It was very unpleasant to get poison pen letters. It was very unpleasant to know that your telephone calls were being monitored and that you were being followed by the FBI. It was certainly unpleasant to get a job and have your employer say, "I'm sorry. The FBI has been around, and I have government contracts. Much as I want to, I can't keep you." It was a "free" society where you had to be careful about what you said on the telephone and what you threw in the trash. The FBI actually asked the superintendent in my building to go through my rubbish for any photographs I threw out.

All this aroused a great deal of fear. People were afraid to touch anything that was controversial. Anything. They just kept quiet. And teachers skirted issues in the classroom. There were teachers who felt this was pressure they couldn't take, and they just resigned. And some people became informers.

Right in the midst of the proceedings against us, a Brooklyn teacher gave a congressional investigating committee a whole slew of names, including mine, which were published in the papers. She gave them a lot of information that was totally inaccurate. And she kept her job. I always regarded these people as professional informers. A professional informer is somebody who is paid to inform. Well, if the reason you are holding your job or getting a promotion is because you are an informer, that, to me, is being paid. I know someone who had become an informer, and when somebody asked him why, he said, "I have a wife and I have two children, and teaching is the only thing I know how to do." *His* wife? *His* two children? The only thing *he* knows how to do? What about our wives and husbands, our children, our jobs?

"The only names I gave them," he said, "were the names they already had." But that was another nail in the coffin of those who had been named. And naming them contributed to the atmosphere of fear. It would have been a terrible world for his children if there hadn't been resistance.

But there was another side to the story. Hundreds of New York teachers contributed money each month to those who had been suspended. And that continued for a goodly number of years. I remember my cleaner didn't want to take any money from me. Another suspended teacher went into her little grocery to buy some food, and the man said, "As long as I'm here, you'll never have to worry about anything to eat." The *New York Post* had never been a terribly good paper. But after the first suspensions, they had a critical editorial that said the trouble with our schools is not that they're red but that they're rotting. Nevertheless, the board of education was determined to go through with the dismissals.

At my final hearing, I was represented by Leonard Boudin. Our defense was simple: The record showed that I had answered their question, that I had not been "insubordinate" and had not conducted myself in a manner "unbecoming a teacher." That didn't mean anything to them. Arthur Levitt, who was a member of the board of education, acted as the trial examiner. He made his recommendations to the board and then went back to the same board to vote on his own recommendations. He didn't even bother to change jackets. It was pure *Alice in Wonderland*—"'I'll be judge, I'll be jury,' said cunning old Fury, 'I'll try the whole case and condemn you to death.'"

They never were able to produce any evidence to say that anybody did anything subversive, whatever that means. They never even made the attempt. In his report, Levitt had to admit that all the evidence showed we were good teachers. As a matter of fact, he said these were outstanding teachers. And then he recommended our dismissal.

I was finally dismissed in 1954. I appealed to the state commissioner of education, and it was denied. By that time, the union had run out of money. It was a terrific financial drain on our teachers. And going to court would have been very expensive, so we didn't follow it through. But five professors from the University of Buffalo did.

Then on January 23, 1967, the Supreme Court ruled that the Feinberg Law was unconstitutional and pointed out where their earlier decision, upholding the law, was in error. It was a remarkable document, a beautiful statement on academic freedom. It struck down guilt by association. Now membership in an organization was not enough reason to fire a teacher. They would have to prove that the individual had *acted* illegally.

A few days after the Court's decision, many of the teachers who had been dismissed met with one of our attorneys. We asked him to consider the possibility of our being reinstated. I must tell you, not everybody wanted to join us. Some people felt we didn't stand a hoot in hell. For others, it was very simple: They didn't want their lives upset again by the publicity.

The Supreme Court's decision seemed to set the stage for the board to talk seriously. But every time we started to get someplace, there was a different board with a different president. So we waited. And we waited. I think the full board was still quite nervous about the issue. They knew that in the past, when people were dismissed, board meetings had been jam-packed with the Knights of Columbus and the Catholic War Veterans. They weren't sure what would happen now. And they weren't exactly ready to offer themselves to be hung on the tree of liberty.

They had other qualms. Reinstatement costs money, and if they didn't have to do it, they weren't going to spend the millions of dollars it would take. Furthermore, by reinstating us, they would be admitting that everything they had done in the past was wrong.

Then the California Supreme Court issued a ruling on a similar case. A professor there, who had been dismissed for refusing to sign the loyalty oath, sued for reinstatement. The California Supreme Court voted him reinstated. He got back pay and his pension rights. That's when we said: Enough of this! We went into the courts with a suit charging that the board had been arbitrary and capricious. It created an excitement. After all these years, we hadn't stopped fighting.

And it worked. A few days later, the board passed a resolution laying the groundwork for reinstatement. Finally, they decided that they would reinstate us with credit toward our pensions from the date of the Supreme Court decision. They wouldn't give us any back pay. That was out. Even though they didn't make full recompense, it was a tremendous victory. It was a terrific statement of the fact that what they had done was wrong.

At a press conference announcing the reinstatement of the last group of teachers who had been dismissed, one of them was asked: Did he now feel that he had regained his honor? He very quietly said, "Madam, I never lost it." And he really spoke for all of us.

I went back to my old school. I just had a feeling that one of us should go back. And I wanted to see what would happen. Some of my former colleagues, who had not been very friendly before, were delighted: "Oh, I'm so glad you won." Now, away from the chill of the Cold War atmosphere, it was a human thing. When one of the teachers became ill and was going to be out for the rest of the semester, they asked me if I would cover. I agreed.

I think the most difficult job in the world is teaching. It's also terribly rewarding. It's a marvelous thing to watch a young mind grow and develop. But I had been forced out of it. Now I would have the feeling of real teaching again. You know, it was fantastic. It had been twenty years since I taught, but it rolled right out. It was still there. I call it the mark of the beast. I stayed for the rest of that semester. And the next semester.

THE PURGE OF THE LEFT:
EXPELLING INTERNATIONAL UNIONS FROM THE CIO

In 1946, Philip Murray, the president of the CIO, stated emphatically, "As a democratic union, we engage in no purges, no witch hunts. We do not dictate a man's thoughts or beliefs."[32] In 1949, however, the CIO convention, under Murray's leadership, adopted a resolution that empowered its executive council to expel any union whose policies were

"consistently directed toward the achievement of the program and purposes of the Communist Party."[33] The actual point of contention was
the council's support for the Truman administration's foreign policy and
its opposition to the presidential bid of third-party candidate Henry Wallace, positions with which left-led CIO unions disagreed. By 1950, eleven
unions had been expelled as "Communist-dominated." Most prominent
among them was the powerful United Electrical, Radio and Machine
Workers Union of America (UE), which represented every General Electric and Westinghouse plant in the United States and Canada. After the
expulsion, the CIO backed the newly formed International Union of Electrical Workers (IUE) in its drive to replace the UE.

"Government officials," labor historian Bert Cochran writes, "intervened on behalf of the CIO against the UE in what was probably the
most sustained barrage against a labor organization since the Wilson administration's attacks on the IWW."[34] The FBI infiltrated the UE's staff;
the Justice Department instituted denaturalization proceedings against
the union's leaders and cited them for contempt of Congress; the Atomic
Energy Commission ordered General Electric to withdraw recognition
from the UE in Schenectady; the War and Navy Departments directed
employers to fire persons they had identified as "security risks"; and President Truman, Secretary of the Air Force Stuart Symington, Secretary of
Labor Maurice Tobin, and, especially, Senator Hubert H. Humphrey put
the prestige of their offices forcefully behind the rival IUE.

But it was the Taft-Hartley Act and the House Un-American Activities Committee that were the mainstays of the government's attack on
the UE, as they were against the other unions expelled from the CIO.
The Taft-Hartley Act allowed rival unions extraordinary advantages. Employers forced strikes when contracts with the UE expired, and then other
unions would challenge the UE in NLRB elections. It was at those critical moments that HUAC subpoenaed the UE leadership to face the "often reckless denunciations by anti-Communists and FBI infiltrators" that
"provided newspapers the wherewithal for a Roman festival to inflame
the community and intimidate UE activists in the plants."[35] Their point,
Francis Walter, chairman of HUAC, allowed, was to put the UE out of
business.[36]

The UE's membership fell from a half million in the late 1940s to half
that in 1953, and then to one-tenth of its earlier size by 1960. Workers
in the electrical industry, once represented by a single union, were splin-
tered into eighty different jurisdictions as a result of raids by the IUE and
others. "The wonder," Bert Cochran observes about the UE, "is not that

it lost heavily, but that it survived at all, that it was able to win as many elections and hold the allegiance of as many members as it did."[37] Ernie DeMaio, who headed the UE's Midwest district, shows in his account the grit and devotion that effort took.

ERNEST DEMAIO

Hartford is my hometown. I was born in 1908 on Mechanic Street, in the Italian community, close to the Connecticut River. They used to have very heated arguments there. I was just a youngster then—I didn't know Bolshevism from rheumatism—but I can remember the heat of it. And all kinds of activities were going on. You had a kind of mass upsurge taking place. Well, that had to be destroyed, and it was destroyed. My father and my uncle were picked up in the dragnet of the Palmer raids in 1920—no charges—just thrown in jail with thousands of others up and down the seacoast.

Sacco and Vanzetti were first arrested in that same year.[*] I got involved in the latter stages of their defense. Do you realize what a trauma it was for Italians when they were executed? It created the impression that all was hopeless, all was lost. It happened on the 23rd of August, 1927. There was a huge gathering at Times Square, where the New Year's Eve ball would indicate whether they would be pardoned or executed. The place was jammed with hundreds of thousands of people. Then it happened—Sacco and Vanzetti were executed. Some of the fellows and I went to a speakeasy—there was Prohibition in those days—and we proceeded to get plastered.

When I had to work the next day, I wasn't in the best of moods. My foreman was only interested in one thing: production. "Get the lead out," he said. I told him to get off my back. He said, "What's the matter with you?" I said, "There's nothing the matter with me. Just get the hell off my back."

He asked, "Hey, were you at Times Square last night?" I said, "Yeah, why?" He looked at me: "I always knew you were a no-good, dago son of a bitch."

Well, I hit him once and broke his nose and jaw. And then it was all

---

[*]Nicola Sacco and Bartolomeo Vanzetti, Italian immigrants and anarchists, were convicted in 1920 of a double murder in Braintree, Massachusetts. Eventually, two Department of Justice officials swore that the government knew that the two anarchists were innocent but was prosecuting them for their political beliefs. A quarter of a million people marched in silent protest in Boston the day Sacco and Vanzetti were executed.

ERNEST DEMAIO

over. They fired me. But I didn't realize that they blacklisted me, too. I would get a job, give my reference, and each time it would catch up with me. I lost dozens of jobs.

Those guys were trying to grind me into the ground. I decided: Hell, I'm going to fight back. I didn't know how, but I was going to do it. By then, the crash of '29 had come, and nobody could get a job. I got active in the Unemployed Councils. Then the WPA came along. I organized there. When the general strike in textiles took place in 1934, I became active in that.

In 1935, I went into Bridgeport to organize the General Electric Company. At that time, it was the largest manufacturing plant in Connecticut. My heart sank when I saw the size of that huge plant, and I timidly asked the union if they had any contacts. "Contacts?" they said. "If we had any contacts, what would we need you for?"

GE didn't think we had a snowball's chance in hell to organize them. And the first committee of six that I set up, the company bought them off—offered them each a job at forty dollars a week. That may sound like chicken feed today, but, mind you, this was the sixth year of the depression. After what happened to the first committee, I wasn't taking another chance of having them buy off the next one. So quietly I built until we were ready to spring out into the open.

There was a group of GE workers who were Coughlinites. They were ordinary workers who were getting off their frustrations and were taken in by Father Coughlin.* I decided to go to their meeting. We had a free-for-all there. The telling point I made with them was, "Hey, so you're Catholics. It doesn't matter who you pray to. It's who preys on us that's important." I finally won them over, and they became the most active force in building the union. Eighteen months after GE bought off the first committee, that plant was organized.

While I was organizing GE, I met with John Brophy, who was an advance man for John L. Lewis, the leader of the United Mine Workers. The meeting was at the old Taft Hotel in New Haven. He spent an afternoon explaining to me what Lewis was up to. They had set up the Committee for Industrial Organizations within the AFL. I asked him, "Why are you telling me all this?" He said, "Because it's young men like you who are going to do the organizing." The bosses of the AFL opposed all this. The end result was that they expelled eight unions. The Committee of Industrial Organizations was changed to the Congress of Industrial Organizations, and the campaign to organize the unorganized was on.

In 1938, there was a series of Dies Committee hearings to discredit the CIO by red-baiting. It was the earliest days of the CIO, and the entire organization was charged with being Communist-dominated. Millions of pamphlets were put out by the National Association of Manufacturers: "Join the CIO and Help Build a Soviet America." It was written

---

*Father Charles Coughlin, a Detroit-based cleric, had an influential radio program during the 1930s. With an estimated thirty million listeners, it had the largest audience in the world at the time. Both his programs and his magazine, *Social Justice*, were noted for their anti-Semitic, anti-CIO, anti-Roosevelt, and anti-Communist messages.

by a guy named Joseph Kamp of the pro-fascist Constitutional Educational League. These guys were running around creating a lot of noise, but they didn't settle any of the problems of the people.

I went from Bridgeport to Pittsburgh. I kept moving westward, to Dayton, Ohio, where I was in charge of organizing the electrical division of General Motors. From there, in 1941, I went to Chicago, where I spent most of my time. I became the president of District Council 11 of the UE, which included Minnesota, Wisconsin, Illinois, and Indiana.

The local police, the Chicago red squad, tracked us. Sometimes they made it obvious to you that you were being shadowed. They wanted to let you know they were there. At other times, quiet surveillance might be going on simultaneously. You think you're getting rid of your tail, but the guy you're not aware of is watching you. And they had every hall in town bugged. Anything that was said in a meeting was recorded. Every time a strike took place, they were there. If there was a big meeting at the headquarters, they were on the outside, even if they had guys on the inside.

I would bait George Barnes, Captain Barnes. We'd have a strike meeting around the Honeywell plant, and I would point to him, just tear him up and down. He would never touch me. I figured that going on the offensive is probably what saved me. He finally got his just deserts. He was taking big payoffs from the companies. And because he wanted to be careful, he turned the money over to his wife. Then he announced that he was retiring and going down to Florida to enjoy life. Well, at the time he retired, his wife took off with the money and another man. And poor George had to get a job as a security guard. I would see him every now and then and say, "George, all your ill-gotten gains, all the money you squeezed out of these corporations to protect them against us—what the hell did it buy you?"

The CIO established the practice where all of the major contracts expired at the same time. John L. Lewis had set up this concept. It was a good idea. All the mass-production industries would have been confronted with their unions at one time. But that went down the drain. Walter Reuther jumped the gun. Instead of waiting until April 1, 1946, when all the contracts expired, he struck General Motors in November of 1945. It split the ranks. Today, the full power of the trade union movement is not felt. You have a highly fragmented union operation.

After the war, the CIO took the position that the executive board would set the policy on politics, and every union would have to toe the line. Phil Murray said, "This is the policy," and everybody there said: "Yes, yes, yes, yes." They all did, except our guys and maybe a few others: Harry Bridges of the Longshoremen's Union; the guys from Mine, Mill and Smelter Workers; the Office and Professional Workers; and some of the other smaller outfits. So we had sharp differences with the CIO.

We used to put out a little paper in the UE, *District 11 U.E. News,* and I would have a column in it all the time. In one of my columns, I started out by saying, "The theme of Phil Murray's marching song reminds me of the old hit tune 'I Surrender Dear.'" Murray screamed bloody murder about it. He got back at me in 1949. Just before the CIO convention, I met with him. The old man wagged a bony finger in my face and said, "Ernie, wipe that sneer off your face." "Sneering," he went on, "is a peculiar form of idiocy." And of course all of his henchmen went, "Yak, yak, yak, yak." He smiled. "Nothing personal, Ernie."

Well, we had to make a decision as to whether we would stand our ground and fight or whether to go like the rest of them: play the game, cover up, and get along with the boss. We made the decision to fight. We knew that if we took them on, we'd go through hell. We just didn't realize how much hell we'd go through. So you might say we were foolhardy. All we were doing was taking on the U.S. government, the employers, the officialdom of the trade union movement, and the Catholic Church, which was very active in the industrial areas.

The CIO was just about to expel us when we walked out. But that was a "you can't fire me, I quit" business. Then they set up their own outfit, the International Union of Electrical Workers, to raid us.

The IUE is given credit for splitting the UE, but it could never have done it without GE and Westinghouse and the attacks of the government through the House Un-American Activities Committee, the Senate Internal Security Subcommittee, et cetera. Let me give you an example of how GE used the Taft-Hartley Act and the House Un-American Activities Committee. If you're going to petition for a union election, you have to have signed cards from thirty percent of the eligible employees of the particular bargaining unit you're petitioning for. In this case, the IUE could not get that thirty percent. But the Taft-Hartley Act provided that companies could call for an election without getting the thirty percent. So GE called for an election to kick the UE out. Then GE adopted a rule that if any of their employees were called before governmental agencies and didn't answer all their questions, they would be fired. The House Un-American Activities Committee under J. Parnell Thomas—who later on went to jail himself for taking kickbacks from his staff—would announce publicly that they were coming to town. They would name the leading officers of the union and subpoena them.

When you were called before HUAC, the question would be: Are you now or were you ever a member of the Communist Party? We all decided not to answer it. We would take the First and Fifth Amendments. We had a legal and constitutional right to that protection. If you know the background of the Fifth Amendment, it comes out of the Inquisition. They would torture people to get them to say what they wanted. So the whole concept developed that no person should be forced to testify against himself or herself.

Besides, there was no way you could answer "Yes" without crawling and becoming an informer. They would want you to name names. You had to become a rat. If you answered "No," then someone could come out of the woodwork, a stool pigeon or a company plant or an FBI informer, to say that he or she was a member of the Communist Party and had collected the dues of the individual who was on the hot seat. They could charge you with perjury, and that meant a five-year rap. And since the certification of the union was involved when an officer was accused of perjury and fired under those circumstances, the company could call for an NLRB election—and the IUE, the UAW, the Teamsters, the Machinists Union, they all came like locusts to tear us apart. But here's the bind: If you took the First and Fifth Amendments, which you had every constitutional right to do, you were immediately fired by GE.

They were out to destroy the unions by gutting the leadership. They drove out all of the progressives and, yes, the Communists from the unions. Were there Communists? Sure. They helped organize the unorganized. But you see, the question was not whether you were a Communist or not. The important thing was that you would be called a Communist if you wanted to fight the company, even if you just tried to implement the resolutions adopted by the CIO itself. Their positions were there on paper just for the record. We in the UE were red-baited, and in the red-baiting, a hell of a lot of very good people got ground out.

On April 1, 1949, the Stewart-Warner Company, the Sunbeam Corporation, and Foot Brothers, three companies we had under contract, fired five hundred officers and stewards of our union on the grounds that they were security risks. The courts ruled that if an employer had a reasonable doubt regarding the security of an employee and he fired him, no law was violated. If I accuse you of being subversive, how do you prove you are not? Since there was no defense, they could charge anyone. That's what the whole red-baiting thing was.

We were in negotiations with Stewart-Warner then. The company said we had to accept the contract and extend it for another year with no changes. If we insisted on changes, then they would break off negotiations. We did. That's when they came out with their wholesale discharges. That company, alone, fired two hundred and fifty union officers as "security risks." You had those massive firings—and there was blacklisting, too—in bad economic times. We were heading into our first postwar recession, with the prewar depression fresh in our minds. Not being able to get a job is sometimes worse than death. Guys who did get work had miserable, menial jobs, jobs that were low-paying, long hours.

But the big scare was in 1952 in Chicago. On September 2, we struck the International Harvester chain. That's the day I was called by HUAC. The strike was set for midnight. At nine A.M., I'm in the House Un-American Activities Committee. Some three thousand of our guys took off from the picket line, surrounded the courthouse, and, as I was being sworn in, stormed the courthouse, singing, "We'll hang Chairman Wood on a sour apple tree." The next day, the newspapers had an eight-column spread, with scare headlines: "Reds Seize Courthouse."

The UE had the largest union in the city of Chicago at the time. And we were extremely active, not only on the basic economic issues but in the political life of the city. But the red-baiting turned the community against us. We were made to look like pariahs. In the Chicago Loop, if they saw me coming, they would scurry over to the other side of the street. They didn't want to even be seen saying hello to me. And many of those were people I had helped in the trade union movement: took them on the job, trained them, gave them staff positions.

Yes, the public was frightened. But those who stuck, why did they stick with us? Under the conditions that prevailed, we had nothing to hold them except what they saw as our integrity. Why would they demonstrate for me when I was under attack? Because they saw it as an attack against themselves. Those workers fought for me, and I fought for them. We had that kind of a relationship. Without it, I would have rotted in some federal prison a long time ago.

The day after they marched into my HUAC hearing, our guys said, "What'll we do for an encore?" I told them to stay home. The National Guard had been called out. They had sandbags, machine guns, the works. They were out to frighten us. I walked in there alone, and I'm whistling to myself, thinking, "You idiots."

They asked me if I knew a guy from Quad Cities who worked at the John Deere plant down there. He had already testified. I looked over at him and said, "Hey, I wouldn't know that guy if he crawled out of my living room rug." One guy testified that in Quad Cities he was collecting my Communist Party dues. Another guy said he was collecting my dues in Chicago at that time. This is at the same hearing. You would think that the only thing I did then was fly around the country paying dues to FBI agents. But you know, it didn't matter. It didn't have to be consistent. The important thing was that in the hysteria that prevailed, they could nail you to the wall.

On the third day, the chairman, John Wood, had a heart attack, and they had to call off the hearings.

Well, it wasn't a pleasant thing, but I'd made up my mind a long time ago, I was not going to cooperate in making myself a punching bag for somebody else—or let the organization that I represented be a punching bag. If they were going to hang me, they'd hang me for being a lion and not a lamb.

A PITTSBURGH STORY: TWO RANK-AND-FILE LABOR LEADERS AND A LABOR PRIEST

"The violent epicenter of the anti-Communist eruption in post-war America," David Caute, author of *The Great Fear,* asserts, "was the steel city of Pittsburgh in Western Pennsylvania."[38] There, a repressive complex of civic and patriotic organizations, employers, hostile unions, the press, and the church—with government at the core of the complex—inspired hysteria and marginalized the left. The *Pittsburgh Press* published the names of a thousand persons who had had the temerity to sign nominating petitions for Progressive Party presidential candidate Henry Wallace. One member of Americans Battling Communism (ABC), Judge Michael A. Musmanno, arranged for the arrest of Steve Nelson, a local Communist leader, who was then tried for sedition before another member of ABC, Judge Harry M. Montgomery. When FBI informant Matt Cvetic named three hundred people as "Communists," their names, addresses, and employers were printed in the papers. Almost one hundred lost their jobs, and "many workers were ostracized . . . saw their kids abused or attacked at school, were denied state welfare benefits, or were threatened with denaturalization or deportation."[39]

An important participant in Pittsburgh's anti-Communist crusade was Father Charles Owen Rice, the "guiding force" behind the Association of Catholic Trade Unionists (ACTU).[40] Rice and the ACTU became deeply engaged in bitter factional battles against the left-wing leadership of UE Local 601 at the huge East Pittsburgh Westinghouse plant.[41] "Father Rice was active in directing every detail of our activities," an opponent of the UE said. He "schooled [us] in the art of name-calling, red-baiting, and particularly how to rabble rouse a meeting at which we might be in the minority."[42] On the eve of a hotly contested UE election, the House Un-American Activities Committee, at Rice's request, called the leaders of the union before a hearing to pillory them there and in headlines for local consumption.[43]

After the expulsion of the UE from the CIO, the new International Union of Electrical Workers challenged the UE at Westinghouse. It was just prior to that critical election that Matt Cvetic appeared before HUAC to name leaders of Local 601 as Communists. Musmanno, in full military regalia and accompanied by a contingent of National Guardsmen, spoke against the UE at the plant gate, and Westinghouse workers heard their priests urge them to vote against the UE. With a voter turnout of 90 percent, IUE won by the narrowest of margins. More hearings by the Senate Internal Security Subcommittee and by Senator Joseph McCarthy were to follow. UE leaders who had helped to build the union lost their jobs and were forced out of the labor movement.

"One time I was organizing the union. Next I was selling eggs," Peg Stasik recalled. Stasik, a coil winder at Westinghouse, was the first woman to hold an office in any UE local. She was, labor historian Ronald Schatz says, "the outstanding female leader at the East Pittsburgh works, one of a trio of sisters who gave their lives to the labor movement."[44] Pittsburgh steel workers, too, including many left-wingers, were under attack by, among others, Father Rice and the ACTU. The rank-and-file union slate Sonny Robinson had helped to form at Crucible Steel was unable to withstand the many-sided assault once the hysteria in Pittsburgh reached a high pitch. "Fight like hell when we leave," Robinson told those who remained on the job, "because they're coming back to get you."

By the mid-1960s, however, Father Rice had undergone a remarkable conversion: "I lost my anti-Communism. I realized that's not where the menace was." Becoming an activist in the civil rights movement and an opponent of the Vietnam war, he was, ironically, red-baited profusely for his efforts.

MARGARET (PEG) STASIK

I started work on an assembly line at the huge Westinghouse plant in East Pittsburgh when I was sixteen. That was in 1924. The work was dull and repetitive. We tried to make the time go by talking to each other.

MARGARET (PEG) STASIK

Sometimes I would fantasize, making believe I was somewhere other than
at that long bench with the never-ending noise, the whining of machines.
Thirteen years of my life were spent there.

Hundreds of women worked at those benches. With prosperity, more
and more were added. But when the market crashed in 1929, the benches
were emptied almost overnight. I don't know how many were let go, but
my gosh, it was devastating. Those of us who were held on would work
maybe one day every two weeks. I can still remember coming home with
a pay envelope that only held fifty cents. My sister Evelyn was doing

housework just for her meals, so that fifty cents was the total extent of our income.

We felt the pinch at home, but, believe me, we had a lot of company in those days. We didn't have enough to own a house; we rented. But many people who had put their life's earnings in their homes lost them. In spite of those tough times, there was a feeling of solidarity. That sentiment was something special. If a family was put out of their house, people would gather there to stop the eviction. When gas and electricity were shut off, unemployed workers would go around and turn them back on. They fought for surplus food, then flour, oleo, and dry milk were distributed. There were kidney beans and canned meat, too. Not gourmet, but it was something to eat.

With the election of President Roosevelt, there were changes that began to benefit working men and women. Hoover's trickle-down theory was abandoned for the alphabet-soup agencies: CCC, NRA, WPA, NLRB.* A refreshing breeze stirred in the valley, and things were beginning to look up. By 1933, work at Westinghouse had improved, and it felt good to bring a full pay home.

I would stop at the library on my way from work to get books. The library was in a bank that had closed after the crash. That's where I met Dora Deight, who asked if I would like to come to classes held at the YWCA. Together with my sister Evelyn and a girlfriend, Helen Talder, we went two evenings a week. The professors who taught us were from the University of Pittsburgh and Pennsylvania College for Women. While we attended those classes, we learned that two girls would be selected to go to a Bryn Mawr summer school that was part of the WPA. My friend Helen and I were picked.

It was a six-week course, and that meant no pay coming home. But my family supported me. They wanted me to go. My sister Ella even made my "wardrobe" from material she got from the welfare department. I got a leave from Westinghouse and went on a trip that was the turning point in my life. This happened so many years ago, but the teachers, the students, the atmosphere, all are vivid in my mind. There were girls from the New York garment industries, from England, from Norway and Sweden, and one girl from Germany, a quiet, thoughtful girl, who spoke about what was happening in her country.

---

*These acronyms refer to various New Deal programs and legislation: the Civilian Conservation Corps, the National Recovery Act, the Works Progress Administration, and the National Labor Relations Board.

Before the crash of 1929, I accepted things without question. I was glad to get enough money to pay the rent and put food on the table. There was not much left for other things. The evening classes at the Y caused me to question, but I had no answers. Bryn Mawr was the turning point. The girls from the garment industry, from Sweden and other places talked of their unions and how they worked. That hit home. We at Westinghouse had nothing to say about our jobs, seniority, vacations, pensions, and medical payments. There was a company union, but we had no real power. The need for workers to band together for the good of all was the answer for me. I believed it then, and I believe it now.

When I came back home, the idea of a union of Westinghouse workers was strong. Evelyn, Helen, and I heard there was to be a meeting at Kidd's Hall in Turtle Creek to discuss the possibility of organizing at Westinghouse. We went there, and I was nominated recording secretary of Local 601 of the United Electrical and Radio Workers of America. This was an unaffiliated industrial union, independent from the AFL. We had a good, honest leadership; some were left-wing, and some were not.

The first thing we had to do was break down the fear that was so prevalent in the plant. Our object was to get as many people as possible to come out publicly and openly for the union. They were skeptical, and they had reason to be: They would be putting their jobs on the line. But men of courage, like Logan Burkhart, Frank Gasdik, and Bill Ebling, would hold meetings inside the plant at noontime.

To reach more people, we decided to hold meetings out of doors, at the shop gates. George Bush, a loved and respected union member, felt uncomfortable speaking at these outdoor meetings. We challenged each other. He finally said he'd speak if I would. I agreed, but I was scared, really scared. My sister Evelyn worked in the plant. How would she feel? When we were walking to work that morning, I said, "Evelyn, I'm going to make a speech today in front of the employment gate." Her first reaction was, "What if you lose your job?" But I had given my word, and I told her that I could not turn back now. Evelyn was a quiet and gentle soul. I can still hear her: "Well, Marge, if you are going to speak, I will be there." And she was.

The work of organizing went on. The executive board met weekly, and applications trickled in. William B. Simpson, president of the union, suggested at a meeting that I be put in charge of the union office on a full-time basis. It was felt that if someone was there, workers would have a place to come and talk. It would give them the feeling that the union was not temporary. We had, by then, enough money to rent a small storefront at 809 Braddock Avenue in East Pittsburgh. It was unheated except for a small gas stove.

Believe me, I did a lot of soul searching before I agreed. I had no profession. After eight years of school, I had to go to work. That was it. And I had a job in Westinghouse that was as good a job as I could get with my education. There was my mother and my brother Richard, whom I helped support. It wasn't easy for me to risk losing that job for something that was so uncertain. But I could remember my father in the coal mines. He fought to build that union, even with the coal and iron police there. My mother, a woman of great courage, said, "Take it, Margie." And I did.

Before quitting, I talked to the personnel manager, Johnny Schaffer. I can remember going up to him—I had more guts than brains—saying, "I'd like a leave of absence." When he asked me why, I told him the truth, that we were opening up a union office. He said, "You know we can't give you a leave of absence for that. It just isn't our policy. And you know you're never going to succeed. They've tried it before." Years ago there had been a strike at Westinghouse that was broken. There was bloodshed.

Trying to sound confident, I said, "Well, Mr. Schaffer, I disagree with you. I'd like it if you'd give me a leave, but if you won't, then I have no alternative but to quit." And I did. I quit my job, and all I could do was keep my fingers crossed and hope.

The fate of unionism in that plant was still very much up in the air. Dues were on a voluntary basis. But we managed to pay our bills and my salary, too. We had a monthly newspaper, *The Union Generator*. Some merchants supported us by putting in ads. That helped defray the cost. Our leaflets and the *Generator* were well received at the shop gates. Some were thrown away, but very few.

While we were in the process of organizing, there was no obvious attempt by Westinghouse to smear the leadership. What they tried to do was to deprive us of our most intelligent and forceful leaders. Sometimes they succeeded. They offered Frank Gasdik a job in Cleveland, and he accepted. This was most discouraging, since the workers remembered how they had been sold out in previous attempts to organize. Then the company sent Logan Burkhart on a "troubleshooting" trip to Texas. This turned out to be a prolonged business trip. But Burkhart saw through the company's scheme and, after some negotiations, returned to us. Organization continued, slow but steady.

After the Wagner Act came into being, workers all over seemed to come out of their shells. Those who had been reluctant to make themselves known were not so shy now. There was a nice "Hello" from workers who used to cross the street to avoid you. We were growing in numbers and growing financially as well. The organization of the CIO, the sit-downs, added to the electricity of the moment. You could sense it in the air. Finally, at Westinghouse, UE Local 601 was able to get recognition. It was very exciting.

We were certified by the National Labor Relations Board, and the company agreed to meet and negotiate. Since the law demanded that they recognize the union, they did. But there was nothing in the law that said they had to sign contracts. Instead, the company posted "articles of understanding," with only their signature, on the company bulletin boards. When the Supreme Court ruled in the *Heinz* case that a signed contract should result from negotiations and agreements, we negotiated our first local contract.

Then came national and international agreements with Westinghouse. A grievance procedure was established, seniority rights, wage increases, better vacation pay, and the elimination of the "Women's Key Sheet." They had what they called men's jobs and women's jobs, with separate pay rates. We raised the question: Why should there be this separation? I remember going in to negotiate that. It was a real struggle, but we were successful. Jobs were listed as jobs rather than men's or women's jobs. This was a beginning.

But as the benefits we gained grew, those of us in the forefront became targets of red-baiting. They red-baited me. They red-baited Charlie Newell and those who represented the left in our union. The only thing they had to throw at us was that we were "Communists" or that we were led around by the nose by Communists. The "red" label—people were frightened by it. From then on, I don't think there was ever a time when we weren't vilified by the press. It caused a real division in the union. That's just what the company wanted. You could not see the hand of the company openly, but somehow you knew it was a hidden force.

Admittedly, the progressives in the union made mistakes, and some of them were stupid. But the right wing couldn't say that we had done anything against the people in that shop. That wasn't true for some of those who opposed us. A right-wing steward in one of the shops didn't turn in the union dues he collected. I'd say, "Look, that isn't your money. Turn it back to the union." He hated me for being on his back, but that was okay. He was stealing from the workers, and there was nothing right about that.

This fellow was the one who pointed the finger at us. Isn't that the history of these hundred percenters? Who was the head of the Un-American Activities Committee? Parnell Thomas? He went to jail after he got caught stealing. You know these hundred percenters: Scratch them and you'll find someone who wants to advance themselves on the backs of others. They hide their misdeeds behind a facade of patriotism. I don't go for their crap.

Then all stops were pulled out in the smear campaign against the UE when a rival organization, the IUE, was established nationally. Churches preached and the press editorialized. Father Rice had organized the Association of Catholic Trade Unionists. They got into the red-baiting, too. You had Congressman McDowell of the *Wilkinsburg Gazette,* a little tabloid that carried articles, shouting "Red!" every week.

It was in that atmosphere that an election was ordered to determine who represented the workers at Westinghouse. The UE and the IUE were on the ballot. The hysteria mounted. The Un-American Activities Committee was going full blast against the UE. Even Hubert Humphrey, the great "liberal," sent a message to the workers of Westinghouse: If you vote for the UE, the question of national security comes into play, and we don't know whether the company will get any government contracts. Now, you know that was quite a threat to everyone's job.

But even with everything that was done against us, the election was so tight that we had to have a run-off. And then when we had the second election, we lost by just a few hundred votes out of many thousands. In spite of all the propaganda, all the lies and distortions, and the weight of the government, the church, and the press, we evidently had won the hearts and minds of a lot of people.

But Westinghouse succeeded in doing what they had to do: They eliminated the militant core of the union. The company really won that fight. When they attacked the UE, they broke up a good, honest union. I think Father Rice is a little ashamed now of the role he played then. My sister Evelyn was bitter to the end about what they did. She felt they had destroyed the thing she had really treasured—her union.

It was terrible even after the elections. My God, it was terrible. The fear was so thick you could cut it with a knife. My family was continually victimized. My sister Evelyn had worked at Westinghouse for more than twenty-five years. One day, a United States marshal came right up to her place of work. In front of her shopmates, they took her down for questioning. The FBI went to Evelyn's home. My sister Ella was hounded from one job to another. And the FBI had their eye on me, too. They checked on my activities with my neighbors, who later told me. My nieces and nephews of school age were pointed at by other children. Talk about a police state—we knew what that meant.

McCarthy called hearings in Washington, where people from Westinghouse were to testify. Evelyn had gotten a telegram that she was to appear. Well, it so happened that she had very high blood pressure. We worried that she could have a stroke. Our family doctor had her admitted to a hospital. Being hospitalized excused her from the hearings, but she was fired by the company as a poor "security risk" anyhow, without any supportive evidence. And this after twenty-five years of service.

My sister was one great gal, loyal and trustworthy. Her friends, however, completely deserted her after the red-baiting. When Evelyn went to visit one of her best friends, she took a basket of homegrown vegetables along. This "friend" told her that she didn't want to have anything to do with her and asked her to leave. Could you believe that people were so afraid of being associated with her? Evelyn never really recovered from the emotional shock of that period. She didn't have a job. She was shunned by friends. But no one who knew her or worked with her could say that she ever did an unkind act.

They even went to my nephew John. He was wounded in World War II. He got a job working for the veterans' hospital. Everyone he worked with thought he was just great. There was no problem of "security" involved in his job, but the FBI followed him there. They kept after him till he quit the VA. It was a treacherous thing, this happening.

My husband, Joe, died in 1953. I sold the house and took a job at Putney School in Vermont. My daughter, Cathy, was only three. I realized that institution was no home life for a little kid. We left there after one term and came back here and bought a farm. We had a thousand hens and an egg route. I worked so hard and didn't make anything. But I had a home for my little girl and me.

When I peddled eggs in East Pittsburgh, I'd meet up with many people who worked at Westinghouse. They greeted me like an old and trusted friend. They'd say, "Margaret, if you tell us those eggs are fresh, we know they're fresh." I thought: It's good to have that kind of reputation. It's good to be able to look people in the face, to shake a worker's hand with no need to apologize.

One time I was organizing the union. Next I was selling eggs. How did that happen? I think it happened because the left-wing movement contributed so much to the strength of the union. That strength had to be dissipated. Get rid of it. Get it out of there. If the left could be isolated out in the country somewhere, selling eggs, would there be any reason to worry? Would there?

MONSIGNOR CHARLES OWEN RICE

When I was ordained in 1934, the surge of unionism was beginning, the New Deal surge of unions. Even though I was a child of the bourgeoisie, I was influenced by Dorothy Day and read the *Commonweal.** The Dorothy Day philosophy was that you support the workers, you feed the poor, and you educate. So we started labor schools and something called the Catholic Radical Alliance.

There was a strike in 1937. I simply went over and joined the picketers and brought a group there, with signs saying "Catholic Radical Alliance Supports You." The steel workers, hearing about this, asked if we would join the Little Steel strike in Ohio, and we did. We walked scores of picket lines, spoke out in behalf of the workers. Then I had this little column I was writing in the *Pittsburgh Catholic,* where I would discuss what we were doing. Later I got a radio program, and I became very close to Phil Murray.

When the CIO was started, there were repressive people, like the Moral Majority. There were ministers like that then, and they joined with Father Coughlin, who was an anti-Semite. They were denouncing the CIO as Communist. I remember I went out to see Coughlin at Royal Oak and disagreed with him.

During World War II, there was a very friendly spirit in Pittsburgh toward Russia, and there were some people talking pan-Slav stuff. But after the war, when their countries were overtaken and became Communist, they changed. Many ethnics were turned off when they heard from people at home about deprivation of liberty. And of course, the priests and ministers got them worked up about it. The Communists had been too successful. They looked too powerful. And when they put down Cardinal Mindszenty,† it was a mistake. Communism's very success made people furious and fearful.

Our feeling then was that the Communists were an aggressive force.

---

*Dorothy Day was the founder of the Catholic Workers Movement, a group that sought to defend the rights of working people and to promote peace, charity, and nonviolent change. The *Commonweal* is a review of religion, politics, and culture, edited by Catholic laypeople since 1924.

†József Cardinal Mindszenty was sentenced to life in prison for crimes against the Communist state of Hungary.

MONSIGNOR CHARLES OWEN RICE

Many of us had the feeling—I did particularly—that the Communists were unbeatable, that once they won something they wouldn't lose it. And I actually felt they had a chance to take over the American labor movement. Well, I became very active in fighting the Communists in the unions. They rated me as one of their oppressors. They were very effective fighters and didn't always fight fair, any more than we did. What I wanted to do, actually, was fight them and their unions, fight them democratically, and remove them from leadership. But I was really not careful about their civil rights, because I had the feeling that they were a menace. The Communists here followed the Soviet line when it didn't make any sense to do so.

But I suppose they would not have been knocked out of the CIO if they hadn't endorsed Henry Wallace in 1948. Phil Murray and the others were so angry because the Communists and other progressives were going on the side of Wallace. We thought that by going for Wallace there was a good chance that they would split the Democratic vote and give Dewey the victory. We thought they would defeat Truman. That's one of the reasons it was so bitter.

I very much regret that I wasted so much time and energy on it. I think, in the aftermath, they were all good unionists. Everybody was idealistic and was all for the workers at that time. Everybody. I wish there was a stronger Communist presence in the trade unions today. I wouldn't want them to run the labor movement, but I wouldn't mind having them have a union or having strength here and there. They might do a better job running the steel workers union than the fellows who ran it afterward. The Communists did run democratic unions in the old days. And when they would say that, they were telling the truth. Their unions were the most democratic.

But I didn't defend Communists then. I would defend people who were just liberals and ordinary progressive people. I would fight for them, friends of mine, people who felt as I did but who were accused of Communism. Many of these non-Communists were fighting for their lives. When you were accused of Communism, you were out. I realize now that it would have been better and fairer if we had fought for everybody's civil rights.

I would have hated to have been a poor Communist in those days, or even a fellow traveler. It was miserable. Ziggy Paszkowski was a fellow that we treated unjustly, I thought, in the Crucible Steel local. I think he probably was a Stalinist. He got elected president of the Crucible local, and he was putting through those resolutions, whatever the line was. I organized a cabal to defeat Ziggy just because of the red thing. It alarmed me at the time. I thought: My goodness, where did he come from, and how did he take over that local from nothing? That's the way it appeared to me.

George Wuchenich, we red-baited him. And Wuchenich, a very famous fellow, had been decorated with a Silver Star for bravery in World War II. He had been dropped behind the lines in Yugoslavia. A great friend of Tito. Ziggy would produce him at meetings and stuff like that.

Many of the people who were wrongly accused of being Communists fought back. Tom Fitzpatrick was one. He was a big man in UE Local 601. When that local went to the IUE, there was nothing much left for him. I don't know what happened to Tom. But it's a shame. He was a good man, a good trade union leader. I liked him, although we fought each other.

In one of the UE unions, Local 610, they fought to the bitter end and won. They didn't give in, and they got a good contract. They would not repudiate the leadership of the UE because it was red-baited, and they wouldn't go IUE. The leadership just did a good trade union job. And they didn't do any talking and admitting to the Un-American Activities Committee.

I went down to see Congressman Francis Walter of the House Un-American Activities Committee on one occasion on something I wanted, on a very tough election. It was one of the key elections when it seemed that the Communists were very strong. I'm not very proud of it.

Oh, for a while there, I thought that me and my friends had done a great deal, that we had been largely responsible for clearing the Communists out of the unions. Later, we realized that what really did it was the McCarthy business. If it hadn't been for the McCarthy business, they wouldn't have been cleared out. I have since come to regret it because I think it would have been better to have this minority present in the labor movement.

All sorts of characters were riding the Communist thing. There was a judge in Pittsburgh, Michael A. Musmanno. He had been a congressman. He was an odd one. He had a squeaky voice, and he used to wear his hair long and had a string tie. Musmanno, in his young days, had actually been left-wingish. And he did something to protest Sacco and Vanzetti. He was a well-known writer and a popular orator, a good radio man. And he was an effective rabble-rouser. Mike decided that he would become a rabid anti-Communist. Now, whether he felt anti-Communism seriously or not, I don't know; but he was screaming about it all the time. Musmanno actually railroaded an attorney for the Communists, Hymie Schlesinger. Schlesinger was a very good attorney and one of the foremost experts on marine law. Musmanno tried to disbar him. That was prevented by the bar association because it was so outrageous.

Then it was the informants sounding off. These ex-Communists who had been FBI spies were surfacing all over the lot. We had several of them in Pittsburgh. There was Matt Cvetic. For years he was paid by the FBI. Poor Matt was a drunk. He would get drunk, and he'd have some girls someplace, and he'd be talking. And he'd spread all this stuff about the Communists. Then there was a fellow called Mazzei. Mazzei did put the hammer on a friend of mine, Harold Levine, and some others who were not Communists. Levine was a United States magistrate. He was a liberal, an innocuous, decent liberal. But Mazzei swore that he was a Communist. Although Levine survived, he was badly hurt by it. It was crazy. Even Phil Murray was accused of being a Communist.

There was a lawyer around called Harry Allen Sherman. He was always making a lot of noise, screaming about the Communists and accusing everyone of being a Communist. He would go around to Kiwanis and alumni meetings, and much of the stuff he would tell would be lies and nonsense. Occasionally I would have to fight him. I remember once Sherman said that Phil Murray was a Communist, a dedicated Communist. My brother was there, and he was a friend of Murray, and he said, "Mr. Sherman, you're a liar." My brother was a priest also. And Sherman said he didn't like to be called a liar by a priest in a place like this. And Pat said, "Where would you like me to call you a liar?"

After Phil Murray died, I was less active. And then I was out of it. Finally, the McCarthy period quieted down. You can't keep screaming all the time. They had run "The FBI in Peace and War" on TV ad nauseam. Stupid thing. And people rethought it. I have a feeling that what really helped it to run its course, what really ended it, was the uprisings of the sixties and the Vietnam stuff. The radicalization of the young really finished it. But by then the damage was done. The Communists were all out of the unions.

Some good unions were messed up in the process. I wish that the UE had survived in its old strength, over four hundred thousand strong, and in which Communists and non-Communists would fight and clash back and forth. The unions in which that went on were honest unions. Often, when the Communists were thrown out of a union, the crooks got in. That happened years ago in the butchers union. It happened in the fifties with Joe Curran when the seamen's union went corrupt.

In the 1960s, the shoe was on the other foot. I was red-baited to a fare-thee-well because of my stand on Blacks and on the Vietnam war. To tell you the truth, it felt great. It didn't bother me at all. My anti-Communist credentials are impeccable. The Communists used to have a joke: One fellow says, "But I'm an anti-Communist." And the other answers, "I don't care what kind of Communist you are." I used all the gags that the Communists had used against me. By then, the Communists and I made peace. I realized that they were a responsible element.

When they would be in a meeting where you would be discussing something very heavy, they were on the side of sensible action, not crazy action.

I don't accept all the dogmas of the Cold War period now. The sixties reradicalized me. I remember the thing that was very important to me was the invasion of the Dominican Republic. That really sent me up through the roof. And I began to find out about Vietnam. Then I lost my anti-Communism. I realized that was not where the menace was.

JOSEPH (SONNY) ROBINSON

The Taft-Hartley Bill was made a law in 1947. We could see that it was aimed at destroying the unions. That's why John L. Lewis said: You'd better fight now before it's too late. You kill a wolf while he's next door—you don't wait until he's on your doorstep.

There were coalitions springing up all over to save the unions. I was working at Crucible Steel at the time, and I had decided that I was going to run for union office. Then I met Steve Merges, and he said, "You know, I'd like to run for office, too." He said, "I got another friend up here I want you to meet, Ziggy Paszkowski." Ziggy came from an old-time socialist background. His father was a socialist and a union organizer. Ziggy had worked at Wards Bakery, where he did a lot of organizing. They got rid of him at Wards because he was too radical for them. Then he came to Crucible and got a job.

I asked, "Well, how do you feel about it, Ziggy?" He said, "Let's make a slate." So I said, "All right." A couple more friends of mine wanted to run, including Allen Thomas, who since has passed away. We got a slate of ten people. We had some guys who were middle of the road; some guys were left; some guys were right. There were Democrats, Republicans, and socialists, but they all agreed on one thing: Save the union. They agreed on another thing, too: The Taft-Hartley Act was aimed at destroying the union, and it left people helpless and powerless, without any defense.

We ran a slate, and we won by a landslide. The whole slate was swept in. They say a new broom sweeps clean. After we got into office, we wanted to clean up some of the injustices that had been heaped on the people. One of the injustices at Crucible Steel was that they had lily-white departments. For example, there was a general labor gang. Then they had another labor gang that got to do skilled jobs. The company made sure that Black people stayed on the general labor gang and never got to

JOSEPH (SONNY) ROBINSON

do the skilled work. We wanted Blacks, minorities, in every department, and we started putting them there.

It wasn't easy. We needed help from the outside. I was a deacon of a Baptist church, and I sang in the choir. So I made arrangements through our minister to speak to the Baptist Ministerial Alliance. They all went on record to support our fight at Crucible. We got two hundred and fifty ministers to support us. That represents a lot of Black churches, a lot of Black people.

When we approached contract negotiations, we did our homework and found out what Crucible Steel profits were and how much they were able to pay. When we asked for wage increases, we could prove that they were able to do it. We said it in leaflets that we put out every week. There was always something happening in the mill to write about.

Now that workers found they had someplace to go, they began to bring us plenty of grievances. Before we were elected, nothing had ever come of their complaints. We told them to bring all the complaints to us, no matter how insignificant they thought they were. There were many types of grievances, but safety was the biggest one. For example, in the pickling department, where they soak steel, fumes come up. If you're a pickler, you have to inhale those fumes. They get into your lungs. The workers there wanted safety devices. In the chipping department, they wanted goggles and shields and protective clothing.

Philip Murray said he never understood how in the world we could get so many people to a union meeting and it's not election time. They used to get twenty or thirty people, but now at every meeting we were getting hundreds. Once people came to the meetings, they saw who got up and spoke on behalf of the membership. There was hardly anyone on our entire slate who couldn't get up and express himself plainly and correctly. We were building. And we had Polish people, German people, Greek people, Black people, and Italian people. We built from the grassroots.

But the company had on the books little "laws" that they thought up years before so that some day they could use them for "incorrigibles." Now that the progressive forces were building and the union was getting stronger, the company reached back and used what we thought were old, harmless laws. One law said: If you gamble, you lose your job. But nobody had gotten fired for that. And another said: If you don't report in when you're off work three different times, the company can fire you. But nobody had lost their job for that either.

Now they began to use laws like that. They used the gambling law on me. I was just standing there watching others gamble, but the company said, "Oh, no, you were gambling." Well, on Allen Thomas, they said, "You were stealing paint." He said, "Stealing what paint?" They said, "Come up here and look in your locker." He looked up, and there were two brand-new gallons of paint in his locker! That's how they worked it.

We saw things beginning to fall apart. We fought as hard as we could, but we couldn't keep it up on so many fronts. We weren't fighting just the company. We were fighting the leaders in our own international union, too—Philip Murray and David McDonald. Then Father Rice set up the

Association of Catholic Trade Unionists. It was a union within a union. They would hold their own private meetings not far from the mill. They'd tell people that we were the main enemy, that we were trying to destroy the union, and that it was up to them to save it. They were very skillful. At union meetings, they would throw cold water on our proposals: "What you're doing is all right, but not yet. You're too early." "Not now." "You're shooting for pie in the sky." They'd say anything to throw us off, to deter us. But the biggest attack was red-baiting. They said we were Communists and that we had to go, that we were fighting for things we knew we couldn't get but were doing it for political reasons, to gain control. They made it seem as if it might even help Russia.

The McCarthy period was just beginning to take wing and get up off the ground. There were three or four bills put out, like the Mundt-Nixon and McCarran Acts.* The people were in trouble, the working people in general and especially the progressive people. There were hints about concentration camps. We'd pick up hints here and there that there were camps out in the West, camps out in the California area and in the Midwest area, but that they were keeping them on the back burner. If those guys did get desperate and if too many people woke up, they would open the concentration camps.

Murray had just put a measure into the union constitution to eliminate Communists. The leadership just inserted it. They were trying to get it in the rest of the steel workers' constitutions across the country, too. We fought like hell to try to get the loyalty oaths out. That gave the company a new weapon: "See, we're not doing it to you. Your own union doesn't want you." That made it double tough for us. And it threw a certain amount of fear into a lot of good people.

In 1949, 1950, they really turned on the heat. Screaming headlines in the *Pittsburgh Press*, the *Post Gazette,* and the *Sun Telegraph:* "The Commies Are Coming—They're in Crucible Steel," "We Got to Stop Them," "Everybody Has to Stop Them—Every True Red-Blooded American."

There was a lot of hysteria, and they were attacking us from all sides

---

*This refers primarily to the Internal Security Act of 1950, which made it virtually impossible for groups designated "Communist action" or "Communist front" organizations to function, and which authorized the attorney general to use concentration camps to detain alleged subversives without trial in the event of an "internal security emergency." President Truman warned that the bill was "so broad and vague in its terms as to endanger the freedoms of speech, press and assembly protected by the First Amendment" (Walter Goodman, *The Committee: The Extraordinary Career of the House Committee on Un-American Activities* [New York: Farrar, Straus and Giroux, 1968], p. 292).

now. Especially Ziggy. Ziggy was very well liked because he was a hard fighter, and he would display it when he took grievances into management. And he had a special way to handle words, more or less like John L. Lewis. He had that forceful delivery, that forceful disposition. Everyone had a lot of faith, a lot of confidence in him. That's why they made up their minds: We'll attack him and destroy the whole damn thing. You cut off the head, and the body will die. That was the idea. And they really put a war on him. They attacked him, and they attacked his family.

Ziggy's kids went to a Catholic school on Polish Hill. The people there were very religious. And if the church said it was so, well, it was so. When his kids went to school, the other kids would say, "Your father's a Commie. We don't want to play with you. And if you come up here, we're going to beat you up." And they did. Then they threw rocks through Ziggy's window. Ziggy started drinking pretty heavy, and I told Ziggy, I said, "That's what they want you to do."

The FBI came to my house on Perry Street. They do that to put a certain amount of fear in you and also to intimidate people you know. But when they came, my neighbors looked out of their windows and yelled, "Give 'em hell, Sonny, give 'em hell!" Oh, about fifteen windows went up. And they went to clapping their hands. "Give 'em hell." So the big agent, the big tall one, he said, "We better get the hell out of here. We'll come back another day." The little fellow said, "I don't give a damn if we don't ever come back here."

The FBI doesn't usually come to arrest you. They didn't arrest me. But I was arrested at other times. When that happened, I'd say, "What's the charge?" "Never mind what the charge is." And the next morning they'd turn me loose. When I was arrested, that was put on the front page. The newspapers would say I was using the Black people to trigger my political ambitions or that I was being misled. The next day when they turned me loose, it was on page fifty-three in the lefthand corner.

Then stool pigeons turned up at very opportune times. Each time they would name names. The *Pittsburgh Press* printed the names and sometimes the pictures on their front pages. In other words, "Fire these people. We don't want you to make no mistake." Oh, a number of people lost their jobs. It wasn't just at Crucible Steel. It was widespread.

The company finally fired me and some of the others, with the help of the international union. When we were fired, I told the people who were still there, "Don't be like an ostrich. Fight like hell when we leave, because they're coming back to get you, and you might as well go down fighting. At least you'll help somebody. At least you'll wake up somebody." Then, maybe two months later, they fired more, the ones who thought, "Well, I made it. I was lucky." This thing stunned a whole lot of the workers at Crucible Steel. They just couldn't put it all together: "I know these are good people that they're firing, and I know that they fought for us." It caught people off guard and weakened the union.

After I left out of Crucible Steel, I couldn't get a job in the mills. They blacklisted me there. So I got a job at Kaufmann's department store. One day the manager came up to me and said, "Your name is Sonny Robinson, not just Joseph Robinson." I said, "That's right." "Wasn't your name in the paper when they blackballed all the Communists at Crucible Steel?" I said, "You're exactly right." So I got fired again.

I went into construction, and the same thing happened. When they got rid of me, I'd go to another construction area where they didn't know me, and I'd get another job. Every time they'd find out, they'd say, "Ain't you Sonny Robinson?"

"Yeah."

"I think we're going to have to let you go."

Cracking Down on New Voices of Union Militancy

THE LOCAL P-9 MEATPACKERS STRIKE, AUSTIN, MINNESOTA

From 1950 into the 1960s, industrial unions won increases in wages and benefits more or less routinely, without the bitterly fought strikes that had occurred in the past. But by the 1980s, organized labor faced a crisis. Union membership had declined precipitously. Union strength had been sapped by plant closings and plant migrations out of the country or to low-wage, nonunion southern states, where employers used "right-to-work" laws outlawing union shops to fend off union organization. Threats to abandon remaining plants left industrial workers vulnerable to militant employer demands for concessions. Gains won over decades were eroding, where jobs themselves were not lost.

For the Hormel workers of Austin, Minnesota, the dislocation between a relatively serene, paternalistic past and a hostile present was as great or greater than for any other group in the country. In August 1985, Local P-9 of the United Food and Commercial Workers (UFCW), representing meatpackers at Hormel's flagship plant, struck against additional givebacks in wages and medical benefits and against dangerous speedup, initiating "one of the most important labor-management confrontations of the decade."[45]

To break the Local P-9 strike, the company had to secure a workforce adequate to maintain production. Thus, the plant gates, through which strikebreakers entered the workplace, became the focus of essential struggles; and it was in those struggles that the weight of government fell heavily on the side of the company: court injunctions limiting the union presence at the gates, assaults and arrests by police, resurrection of the ancient criminal syndicalism law, and occupation by the National Guard. The National Guard troops restricted the movements of everyone but the strikebreakers through sections of Austin, ensuring them access to the Hormel plant. The troops did more than that, however: The National Guard's logs indicate surveillance of the inner workings of the union, including monitoring of P-9's morale, current strength, base of support, tactical options, access to publicity, and fundraising ability. Local P-9 was portrayed as a radical conspiracy—indeed, as "the enemy."[46] It was the Austin police, with spies in Local P-9, that supplied the National Guard with names of "ultra-radicals" among the strikers. "They would really be burnt bad," one undercover officer reported, "if they knew that sitting right in front of them was a cop."[47]

Now, as in the past, the assumption was that the police, indeed "the entire machinery of the State should be put behind the strikebreaker," as the Commission on Industrial Relations described it in 1916. A critical component of the present-day "machinery" is the Taft-Hartley Act. Under the terms of that act, the NLRB won injunctions against secondary boycotts and mass picketing, which crippled P-9's strike efforts. The Taft-Hartley Act also has been interpreted to permit employers to use permanent replacement workers during a strike. Thus companies such as Hormel, prohibited from firing workers for union activity by the Wagner Act, can all but nullify the right to strike by replacing strikers permanently. Strikebreakers who took the jobs of Local P-9 workers on the Hormel shop floor eventually also replaced them on the UFCW union rolls, forcing the strikers to relinquish their demands about concessions and work conditions and to focus instead on demands to return to their old workplace. That the National Labor Relations Board, established to protect unions under the Wagner Act, ruled consistently against Local P-9 is not surprising. After Ronald Reagan was elected president in 1980, the board's members "were drawn from the ranks of lawyers engaged in fighting the unions," and the NLRB's rulings favoring employers more than doubled.[48]

In the end, the strikers failed to achieve their original objectives, but the struggle of the Local P-9 meatpackers represented the renewal of the tradition of union militancy. The story that follows incorporates accounts of the strike from the perspectives of strikers Cecil Cain and Denny Mealy; Local P-9 business agent Pete Winkels; Local P-9 president Jim Guyette;

CECIL CAIN

Ray Rogers, the local's labor consultant; Carol Kough, wife of Tom Kough, mayor of Austin and a P-9 striker; and Emily Bass, one of its volunteer attorneys.

LOCAL P-9 STRIKERS AND SUPPORTERS: CECIL CAIN, PETE WINKELS, JIM GUYETTE, DENNY MEALY, RAY ROGERS, CAROL KOUGH, AND EMILY BASS

CECIL CAIN: I was born and raised in Montana. We had our own small business there. In 1981, things started getting pretty bad. That whole country was based on agriculture, and the farmers and ranchers were having a hard time. Then that was all covered up by an oil boom. It turned our small town of five thousand people into fifteen thousand. And, God, for about eighteen months, you couldn't do anything wrong. You made money hand over fist. Then they left. Whoosh! The refineries are full. Oil in the ground, but no place to go with it. So they just sealed it all up and pulled out. We had to survive again on farmers and ranchers who didn't have any money. In '82, we had to sell out.

In our part of the country, we thought you could do just about anything you were big enough to do. I was taught to believe that it's a land of opportunity and freedom and the only thing that holds you back is your ambition. My business had worked for ten years. There was surely something I could have done when it didn't work the way it should. The problems, I thought, were due to me. And I was still trying to get over that. If it weren't for my experiences in Austin, I probably never would have.

I kept hearing from my in-laws how great Hormel was: a brand-new plant, they take care of you, good wages. I didn't realize until I came here what it was like. If I hadn't had a family—geez, I wouldn't have lasted five minutes in there. It was the worst job I ever had, absolutely the worst. And I don't mind work. It makes you feel good. You perspire a little, and you look back and see that you've got something done.

Well, I walked down in that kill floor. We were killing seven hundred and sixty hogs an hour, so there had to be seven hundred and sixty hogs hanging from a chain all around that floor. You put eight, nine, ten hours in there, and you see thousands of hogs. I just knew that this whole world was out of hogs after a week.

I worked on a line there, transferring guts. I would lift tons of guts a day with my one hand. You get so tired and so sore. Just before me, three guts snatchers took the guts out of the hogs. And you put them in pans. It's hot and it stinks. Every now and then, something would be defective or cut in the intestines. The stuff would splash in your face. There were days when I'd take a shower at work, a shower at night, and another shower the next morning. You could still smell it.

After I did that job for a while, I went up on the gambrel table. That wasn't so messy, so smelly. That's where the hogs are stunned, immobilized, and then stuck to bleed. They're put through tanks to loosen the hair up and then through a tumbler, probably fifty feet long. They just toss those hogs around like you would a washcloth inside a dryer. When they come on the table, you turn them one way so another guy can make four cuts in them. Then you put the gambrel sticks in them and hang them up so they go down the chain where people finish shaving, removing the ears, and removing the guts.

It was faster work on the gambrel table. It just keeps going and going and going—and at the same speed at the end as when you started. You start fresh, feeling good. By the end of the night, if you can't keep up, tough tootie. And then when they cut our wages in October 1984, they sped the line up. So here I am working at that speed, I'm sore, wore out, and I'm upside down because I work nights.

PETE WINKELS: We figured it out. I think between my dad, Uncle John, John's wife and their children, Uncle Tony, Aunt Mary, Aunt Martha, and Martha's husband, the whole family has something like three hundred and fifty years at Hormel. And that's nothing out of the ordinary. I think Jim's great-grandfather worked over there, so he's fourth generation. I worked with a couple of people whose great-great-grandparents were part of the nine originals who started with George Hormel here in 1891.

For years, Austin had been a complacent community. We were recession proof, depression proof. Anything that happened somewhere else didn't matter, because the company was going good. I used to race cars in the drag strip and had Hormel labels on the side of my car because I was so proud to work there. I didn't like the work itself. My God, who wants to kill pigs all day? But you were proud of what it enabled you to do. The majority of the people were able to own their own homes, get away for a two-week vacation, and maybe send their kids to college. Now that's gone.

JIM GUYETTE: I was born and raised here in Austin. This is my hometown. My father was raised here. I want to raise my family here. I'm as much a part of this community as the people who run the Hormel Company now. In fact, probably more so.

I started working at Hormel in July of 1968. In 1978, I got active in the union because they were negotiating a concessionary contract with the company. It was agreed that we would loan the company money to build a new plant, an interest-free loan, supposedly in return for never having our wages cut. I said, "The banks got more money than I do. Why are they coming to me for a loan?"

We were told we had to vote for the concessionary contract, but neither the company nor the union officials told us everything that was in it. It turned out to be open season for management to do whatever they wanted. It meant concessions in benefits. It meant concessions in every aspect of work. There was a no-strike clause for eight years and real speedup in production. At that speed, there were many injuries.

PETE WINKELS

DENNY MEALY: I can recall as clear as day Chuck Nyberg, then Hormel's executive vice president, saying over TV that the workers will never receive any less in the new plant than what they earned in the old plant. But when I transferred to the new plant, I lost my incentive pay, which cost me a hundred dollars a week. The reduction in medical benefits was retroactive. I personally was paying back to the company forty-three dollars a week for medical expenses I had incurred. Between the transfer to the new plant and the concessions, I lost about one hundred sixty dollars a week. The working conditions had changed. The attitude of

JIM GUYETTE

management to labor had changed. The injury rate was just phenomenal. It wasn't the same company.

JIM: The union meetings were held in the evenings. They would hold
one the next day for those of us who worked nights. The president and
one or two officers would sit up there and talk about what happened the
night before. If one of us tried to make a motion, they would say that
these meetings were simply a "courtesy," that all we could do was ask
questions. But when we asked questions they didn't like, they'd get up
and leave. Later, when I went to evening union meetings, they'd always

DENNY MEALY

rule me out of order. Finally, one of the older veterans said, "Look, I'm getting sick of all this 'out of order' stuff. He pays dues just like we do. Let's hear what the kid's got to say."

In 1981, I was on the executive board. We went to Chicago for a meeting before negotiations. What they did was booze you up, pound you on the back, and tell you what a great leader you were until your hat didn't fit. Then there was this big staged deal, that we had to take more concessions because everybody else was doing it.

Well, we had taken concession after concession. And I had pretty much stated where I was coming from in '78, '79, and '80. I mean, if the company wasn't making money, I could see the argument. But I couldn't see any rationale in offering new concessions to a profitable employer, one making more money than it ever had before. And I could see no rationale in beating the company to the punch. I just said, "Look, I'm going to tell you guys right up front, when we go home I ain't telling people to vote for this." They said, "We got to be united." I said, "Well, you be united all by yourselves—I want to give a minority report." I did, and we voted the contract down.

The international wasn't satisfied, so we had to vote again. Basically, it was "vote till you get it right." Well, the election was just a sham—I mean, there were ballots passed out wholesale. People were dropping in twenty-five at a time. I asked for a recount, but they destroyed all the ballots the next day. So it finally went through, and I was marked as a troublemaker.

Then I ran for president in '83. My opponent was John Ankor, who's now president of the scab union and was one of the first to cross the picket line. Before the election, I had made a motion that the rank and file choose an election committee from the membership itself. I asked the head of the committee if he would buy his own padlock to keep the ballot box from being stuffed. He did that. And, lo and behold, I won.

When I took over, we had friction within the union between the old leadership and the new folks coming up. The rumor through the plant was, "Guyette got elected, but nothing's going to get done because the executive board controls everything." But I went straight to the membership, and we started turning things around. What we said made sense to the rank and file. We were very upfront and honest with people and answered questions the best way we knew how. I think that's been the strength of what we've been able to do. I had confidence that if they were informed, if they knew the issues, they'd generally make the right decisions. And if they didn't, people had a right to be wrong.

Prior to my taking office, we'd be lucky to get a quorum of thirty-five people at the meetings. Our union hall held five hundred. Once we started communicating with everybody, we'd have to have four meetings a day to get them all in there. Issues got debated pro and con. Everybody got a chance to voice their opinions, whatever they were. That was just unheard-of.

CECIL: I came to Hormel about the time these rank and filers were taking over this local, Jim Guyette and Pete Winkels and a host of others. One of the first union meetings I recall was in July or August of 1984.

The union had already given a ton of concessions. Now the company was threatening to cut wages. Here I was, working for $10.69 an hour, and it still wasn't enough. So I went to that meeting. I remember Jim Guyette brought back a plan that the company wanted to offer us, paying $8.75 an hour. Good God, that's two dollars less! Here's a company, absolutely the most profitable meatpacker in the country, and they wanted more. And they didn't come after it nickel and dime.

I couldn't believe Jim was asking us what we thought. In my mind, he's the union president and he's supposed to take care of us. Why didn't he tell them to stick it? I walked right up to the podium and said, "I don't know why you even bother to come back and tell me this." But I found out that Jim Guyette doesn't make a move without coming to the rank and file. I got to appreciate it better. He would even present two or three aspects of a problem and say, "What do you want to do?" That's the way he always was: before the strike, during the strike, today.

JIM: Hormel had a tight control over everything. People in our community didn't see this complete domination so clearly before. Now they see how power corrupts, how power controls, how those who have so much money never seem to lose the desire for more and don't care how they get it or who they hurt. We could no longer stand by and watch people hurt to the tune of two hundred and two injuries per one hundred workers each year.

DENNY: My first five years with the company, I worked in the most dangerous area, the beef kill, doing the most dangerous job in the packinghouse industry. In that five-year span, I required a hundred and ninety-six sutures and ended up having two surgeries to realign my wrist. This injury rate was running rampant.

JIM: Young women, twenty-two years old, worked at the plant for less than two months and got carpal tunnel syndrome. They couldn't even pick up their kids anymore. People, thirty and thirty-two years old, big enough and mean enough to eat nails, couldn't lift a ten-pound box. Then the company retrains them to fry hamburgers at Hardee's and McDonald's and tells them to get on with their lives. After they've ruined people! We couldn't in good conscience stand by. We tried to approach the Hormel Company to create a safe place to work. They said to us: If you don't like it, there are plenty of others who will work under these conditions.

We saw the company's intent very early on. A year before the strike started, it became clear we were headed for confrontation. In order to avoid a war with Hormel, we said, "We'll gamble with you. We'll tie our wages to your profits. We'll guarantee you more money than you made a year ago or take a cut in pay." It took the company a minute and thirty-five seconds to tell us that wasn't enough. When we asked how much was enough, they didn't have an answer.

Well, if you're going to get into a fight, it only makes sense to train for it. Corporations think nothing of hiring consultants, professional union busters, like Hormel did, to put pressure on our families, to put pressure on working people. But Hormel cried foul when the union hired a strategist to help us. Ray Rogers, the head of Corporate Campaign, was instrumental in helping P-9 set up its fightback program.

RAY ROGERS: My partner, Ed Allen, and I started Corporate Campaign, Inc., in 1981. We were troubleshooters who would go into very difficult situations and represent the underdog. We'd try to help correct the tremendous imbalance that exists between those who have far too much power and abuse it and the people who have far too little power and suffer from that abuse. We know that workers' struggles are not simply against one entity, but against an integrated web of banks, insurance companies, investment companies, and other large corporations and institutions. We try to figure out how to pit one corporate and financial institution against the other, to divide and conquer them just as they divide and conquer poor and working people.

Our plan in Austin was to take on the financial power structure behind the Hormel Company. We researched Hormel, and all we saw was one thing: First Bank System. It was that simple. Three top policy makers of First Bank and Hormel were the same people.

JIM: First Bank had its fingers into ninety-two percent of the pork slaughtering and seventy-three percent of the beef slaughtering in this country. We talked about the relationship between Hormel and First Bank, with their interlocking directors, with direct stock control, and with First Bank providing the financial wherewithal for Hormel to make good on its threat to pick up and move unless workers agreed to concessions. We decided to inform the public that First Bank was very much behind Hormel in calling the shots that put people out of work. Twelve hundred of us surrounded First Bank and handed out leaflets. We said to people, "We'd like you to tell this bank you don't want your money being used in a way that hurts so many of us."

RAY: We wanted to raise the stakes so high that First Bank would use their enormous clout to come down on Hormel. People began taking money out of that bank; unions were withdrawing big funds. In Austin alone, First Bank lost fifteen million in deposits. Every week there were

RAY ROGERS

demonstrations about how they shaft the communities, how they shaft the workers. It was all over TV. We handed out literature in front of all the bank branches throughout the Midwest. Then Hormel filed charges with the National Labor Relations Board, and we were brought into federal court.

JIM: The NLRB said that was a secondary boycott and claimed we didn't have the right to demonstrate in front of the bank. Even if we were ten miles away, the NLRB said, we couldn't talk about the connection between the company and the bank. We did not have the right to identify large shareholders in First Bank System and ask them to question the bank. The NLRB has done everything possible to help Hormel. And I think they have superseded the Constitution. To them, people who belong to a labor organization do not have the same rights of free speech as those who do not.

RAY: We also wanted to activate and empower the rank-and-file workers. We set up the organization for every one of the sixteen hundred strikers to go door to door across the entire state of Minnesota with our campaign literature. All told, the rank-and-file workers and their spouses went to over half a million homes. We knew if we could build solidarity between the Hormel workers in Austin and the Hormel workers in other cities, we could shut down the entire operation.

DENNY: Hormel's work was still being accomplished by seven other plants within the Hormel chain. By law, whenever work is transferred out of a struck plant, you have a right to follow that struck work and ask people who are in the same union to honor your picket line. The executive boards from all Hormel locals met with the president of UFCW, Bill Wynn, to ask for a sanction of roving pickets, and he agreed. Then he flip-flopped. But things were already in motion. We had people in Ottumwa honoring our picket line, five hundred and fifty that first day.

RAY: When the strike started, the union hall cellar was full of junk and dirt. Strikers cleaned it out, repainted it, and opened a twenty-four-hour kitchen, seven days a week. We had huge caravans of trucks coming in with food that was donated to us. Farmers brought truckloads of potatoes. From the first week of that strike, every rank-and-file family could get their week's worth of groceries there. It was viciously cold, sometimes fifty degrees below zero. Every morning Mert DeBoer, with a lot of other people, made sure there was always a full stack of logs. Every family had firewood. People said they never saw anything like this, never saw such organization.

CECIL: When we first went on strike in August, Hormel's attitude was: They're going to get real tired and real hungry. The company "knew" that the strike would soon be ended. Only it didn't end in a couple or three months or four or five. We were real successful in staying out, and we were not going to buckle. But believe me, it's tough when you're getting forty bucks a week, now and then supplemented with twenty-five dollars. Then we started the Adopt-a-Family program that Corporate Campaign brought before us. We made an appeal to locals across the country at the end of November. By Christmas time, we started getting responses. Holy Christ, it was a way we were going to survive!

DENNY: By now, Hormel had been closed for five months, and their productivity had been cut because we were effective with the roving pickets. On January 13, 1986, Hormel reopened the Austin plant.

JIM: When they tried to fill the plant up with scabs, our people decided to show up for work the same time the scabs did. They drove around the plant about two miles an hour. There was a giant traffic jam in Austin, Minnesota! Nobody was really breaking the law, and the police were frustrated.

The company went to the judge and said, "It's Guyette's fault. He's ordering people to do this." I said, "Look, I am not." P-9 is not a one-man show and never has been. We have a lot of leaders in our rank and file. But the judge said he was going to hold me responsible if there were more than six P-9ers at a time on any one street surrounding the plant. I stood up and said, "Your Honor, people have a right to be on the street without me telling them they can or can't. What do you expect me to do, stand at the end of the block and ask if they're P-9 or not?" I said, "It's ridiculous." Well, he admitted this was a violation of First Amendment rights, but he said it was something that had to be done.

People were asking me what they should do. I said, "You didn't ask me what you should do yesterday. Why are you asking me today? You want to drive by the plant, you have every right to do so. And if necessary, I'll go sit in the pokey until this thing gets resolved."

DENNY: We decided on civil disobedience, a nonviolent protest. We would place ourselves strategically at the plant site, locked arm in arm. This was successful for several days until the company called the cops. The police would pull people out of the groups and immediately arrest them. Several times people were beaten to the ground. We went through a series of three arrests. On the day of the largest number, one hundred fifteen people were jailed. As our numbers increased, the police and the sheriff's department also increased their forces, calling in help from outlying communities. They used tear gas and riot dogs. For a situation we designed to be completely nonviolent, they employed force.

JIM: You see, they needed to use violence. So they had to try to make us into violent, crazy people. And that's something we've never become. The *only* violence in Austin was created by the company, the police, and by the National Guard. We preached nonviolence from the very beginning. We used ideas from Gandhi, from Martin Luther King Jr. And we took a tremendous amount of time and conducted a lot of meetings to talk about what it was we wanted to do and how we wanted to do it without violence.

CAROL KOUGH

CAROL KOUGH: I was at the picket line most of the time. Basically, what everybody did was link arms. They stayed peaceful, linking arms. Terry Arens was the first one arrested. He was just talking to an officer. He said, "We're not doing anything wrong. We're not violent. I hope you guys remain the same." That made the officers mad. They said, "Let's get him." The officers pulled so hard, Terry said he thought his arms were going to come out of their sockets. When they couldn't get him loose, the police put their fingers in his eyes and pulled him down that way. Terry's a big guy, but they pulled him down to the ground. He had injury to his eyes.

Then they started macing people. They had police dogs there that could rip you apart. It got to the point where they didn't care what happened to a P-9er. That's an awful feeling, but that's the feeling people had. They didn't really care if they hurt you.

CECIL: We were winning at first. We'd turn out four or five or six hundred people there. We were effective in keeping it shut down. If you go down there and you're *effective,* here comes an injunction: You can only have three pickets per gate. In effect, they were outlawing pickets. The same difference to me. Then they started hauling up people, arresting them. Here they come on radio: "Violence!" "Mobs!" In comes the Guard.

PETE: I was up in Duluth to talk with their central labor council. The governor was there that night. I went into a room with him, and we talked back and forth about the National Guard. He did it, he said, because the local officials told him that cars had been overturned in the streets. But a guy by the name of Joe Sutree, a writer for a Minneapolis or St. Paul paper, had come down because he wanted to investigate all the violence. He went to the hospital; nobody was there. He went to see the overturned cars; there were none. He looked for broken glass; there was no broken glass. He went to the law enforcement center; no one was in jail. He asked, "Where's the riot?"

CAROL: They had the nerve to claim that one of the reasons they needed the Guard was because there was a physical attack on the company photographer by one of the workers. I was out at the gate that morning. Traffic was circling both ways, plus people going into work. There was a mixture of strikers and scabs. The photographer from Hormel was purposely agitating. And if you read the police reports, they admit that this man was purposely agitating. Then he got out of his car and took a swing and a kick at one of the P-9 strikers. That's when the striker kicked him back. The photographer got in his car and drove over to the corporate office. All of a sudden, they take him away by ambulance, supposedly because he's been hurt. Yet he was able to drive over and walk into the office, no problem. I still feel it was a set-up—I really do—because of the way it happened. They said that was one of the reasons they called the Guard—a "physical altercation."

DENNY: The National Guard cut off every entrance except one, the very north gate. Then they formed a V, almost like a funnel, that led from Interstate 90 directly to the gate. Any way they could, they would get the replacement workers, scabs, into the plant. This "private security force" for Hormel cost the taxpayers of Minnesota over three million dollars.

We decided we would block that exit with cars and begin a bottleneck. Traffic started backing up. Now the Highway Patrol became involved. Hormel had the political power to get them to use their vehicles as tow trucks, pushing cars off the tops of bridges, down through the medians, through the intersections.

CECIL: I was in Fremont, Nebraska, with the roving pickets and freezing my tail off there. I came back here and heard that the National Guard had come. They were housed in St. Edward's Church; they just took it over. I drove in and went right to the interstate. I saw all those big National Guard trucks and the soldiers standing out there with shields on them. You see those things other places, you know, always on TV, but not where you live and not where your kids go to school and not against you. We didn't do anything. We didn't hurt anybody. We said, "They can't do that, can they?"

We used to say, "They can't do that, can they?" We don't say that anymore. When we hear somebody say it, we laugh, because they can do any damn thing they want to. Jesus Christ, I've worked all my life, paid all the goddamn taxes, did everything you're supposed to do, and these guys come in here. This was wrong, absolutely wrong.

PETE: You can't imagine what it's like until you go through it. The actual military, the National Guard, comes in, exerts its authority, and blocks off half the town. And they have got absolute control. For the first time, people in this town saw them: What in the hell is going on? I mean, it really heightened everyone's consciousness. They could understand what it was like in Korea or Central America or Poland when someone voiced their dissent.

RAY: Hormel had asked for injunctions limiting the number of people we could have picketing and how close they could be to the plant. Not only did the judge agree, but he applied that ruling to any demonstrations, the kind that anybody else under the Constitution would be allowed to hold. And he tried to get me to agree to that. He threatened to hold me in contempt of court. But there was no way I was going to commit myself to a ruling that would violate my First Amendment rights.

Thanks to the tremendous work of Peggy Winter, our attorney, we got the judge to back off. He finally said we had a right to have public demonstrations. To test his guidelines, we got about a hundred people early one morning to march peacefully down the side of the street toward the plant. The National Guard had cordoned off the whole area so only strikebreakers could get near there. We got down to where the Guard had a sort of barricade with their trucks. We weren't trying to block any entrance. We weren't trying to block any street. We followed every police order. We just wanted to stand alongside the road as the strikebreakers drove into the plant.

Then the police told us to disband and to get out of there. It was like the government was doing everything they could to make sure that the company's interests were protected and the strikebreakers would have free access in and out of the plant without being challenged in any way, even by people simply holding up signs. I asked why we were being given that order, and they wouldn't answer. They just said, "If you don't get out of here, we're going to arrest you." I told everyone, "We are only doing what the judge said we could. Let them arrest us. We have a right to be here." They grabbed me first. Then they put another twenty-seven people in paddy wagons.

I could have gotten out on bond, but I said, "I didn't do anything wrong, so there shouldn't have to be any bond." I didn't know what the heck they'd charge me with, but I figured they'd trump up something or drop it. I was in there for five days when they came across with the criminal syndicalism charge.

EMILY BASS: Ray was indicted on two counts of criminal syndicalism, each one carrying a possible five-year prison sentence. The criminal syndicalism law provides heavy penalties for committing a criminal offense or infraction in order to advance political or industrial ends. Under ordinary circumstances, the worst Ray could have been charged with—if he could have been charged with anything—was obstructing traffic or refusing to disperse. He probably would have gotten a small fine for that. But since he committed a traffic infraction or technical violation in order to advance political or industrial ends—that is, the strike—he was suddenly charged with a major felony.

That's the essence of criminal syndicalism. What would ordinarily be a misdemeanor becomes a felony because of the political beliefs, motivation, or philosophy of the person charged with the offense. In other words, someone's beliefs or statements become an "aggravating circumstance," and that is used as a justification for upgrading an offense. Not only is this a threat to civil liberties and freedom of speech, it violates equal protection principles because it subjects those who are political activists or union activists to a whole category of charges the ordinary citizen is not subject to. And it converts someone who would be at most a trespasser into a major felon.

RAY: I remember one TV reporter who some months earlier really did a hatchet job on me, a vicious series of pieces on the news out of the

EMILY BASS

Twin Cities. After he saw the way the police handled our peaceful demonstration, he was a different person. And then to see that I was arrested on a charge of criminal syndicalism—he found that outrageous. He went to court and spoke on my behalf.

EMILY: Luckily, in Ray's case, the judge took the bull by the horns and said that the law was unconstitutional. He agreed that it threatened and violated First Amendment rights and held that it couldn't be the basis for any more charges.

About half an hour before copies of his decision were first made avail-

able to the public and the police, there was another demonstration outside the plant. Although Ray wasn't at that demonstration, he was picked
up across town and rearrested. I think they did that in order to buttress
their criminal syndicalism charges, and that's what they were going to
book him on. They also picked up several members of the local's executive board, some outside the plant, others at home. It appeared, little
by little, that they were trying to create the image of a "syndicalist conspiracy." But by the time they got these folks to the law enforcement center, the judge's decision had been issued in our favor. It took them two
days before they came up with new charges.

RAY: It wasn't until I was being brought down to court that I found
out the new trumped-up charge was felony riot. The police chief was
quoted in the *Minneapolis Star and Tribune* saying that the police saw
me orchestrating the riot. It was a lie. They finally dropped the felony
riot charges.

EMILY: If in fact there was a riot, it was created by the police. The
demonstrators themselves were peaceful. Several hundred people, not
only strikers and supporters from the local area but people from unions
around the country, had come to show their support for the Hormel
workers. They locked arms so that replacement workers and strikebreakers couldn't get inside the plant, and they sang some of the songs
I recall having sung during civil rights days. Then the police charged the
group. They threw tear gas and started beating people. Among those who
were gassed was Tom Kough, the mayor of Austin.

Then something even more startling happened to Tom Kough. Although he was the person entrusted by the city charter with the responsibility for public safety, he was deprived of his jurisdiction at the demonstration. I think it was a sheriff from another county who said: "You
have no jurisdiction to act here." We checked the city charter and the
city ordinances. It seemed to us that that was absolutely unconstitutional,
that they had no right under any circumstances to come in and displace
the mayor, usurp his authority, and take control of the police. But that's
effectively what they did. I guess because Tom was a P-9er and a striker,
besides being mayor, they didn't trust him.

JIM: It was just crazy stuff that was going on. The company would
videotape people in front of the plant and get their license numbers. Then
police would go to their homes and arrest them at eleven o'clock at night.
They were charged with "blocking ingress and egress to the plant." "Wanton destruction of property" was another one. There was no property
destroyed. At times, people were arrested who weren't even at the picket

line. They arrested us on bogus charges to make the support group post
bail and bleed us dry of money that people needed to live on. The jails
were full in Austin, and they were full in both counties to the east and
to the west and full to the north. They can hold a person for thirty-six
hours without a charge. That's something the police have clearly
abused.

CAROL: The strikers were getting mad because "law and order" applied only to them. It did not apply to anybody who worked in the plant.
A guy came by the picket line with a gun. We hollered to the officers,
"He has a gun on the front seat of his car! Do something about it!" They
ignored it. Everybody was getting irritated: "How come the rules are just
for us? The law should be both ways." I went over to the police officer
in charge and asked, "Why isn't somebody doing something about the
gun?" He said, "I didn't see it."

Then another one of the scabs came through. He drove his car in and
hit people. He ran over a teenager's foot. He scraped one of the fellow's
legs. He hit a parked vehicle, one of the picketers' trucks. He continued
to drive into the plant, and the police did nothing. Everybody's standing there: "Wait a minute! He hit people! We took two of them to the
hospital. Nothing's being done. A man drives by with a gun. Nothing is
done." Then the picketers moved their protests from the gate over to the
corporate office. As they were walking over there, one of Hormel's head
security guards drove his car off the road, hit a fellow, and went back
up on the road. The police officers saw it happen. The tire tracks were
there. They said they'd pursue it later.

Then one of our fellows grabbed an aerial on one of the cars and let
it go so that it sprang back. *That's when the police went to make the arrest.* And that's why everybody surrounded the officers. They said, "Wait
a minute, all he did was grab an aerial! We had two assaults with cars,
plus the gun. Nobody did anything. So let him go." Everybody just
chanted: "Let him go! Let him go!"

See, the police didn't care about the strikers. That was the problem.
It's very obvious when you read the law enforcement books: They are
to remain neutral. But it was very far from it—and we could prove it all
the time, that it was anything but neutral.

JIM: There's no question that we've been under constant surveillance. I've been followed home by police and by private security people
from the Hormel Company. When the strike started, police officers
would come down here, wired for sound, and they would tip off the
company to what we were going to do. The police admitted under oath

that they called our members up and told them they were from the press, to get them to say things over the telephone, not knowing they were being tape-recorded.

One striker, a Vietnam vet, used to come into my office and tell me how he wanted to buy hand grenades and blow up Hormel's catfish ponds in Arkansas, Mississippi, and Alabama. I would tell him, "Look, that ain't what we want to do." It turned out he was an informant for both the local police department and the FBI. I have a copy of an affidavit he submitted, admitting that the whole time he'd been paid by them.

Once I walked into the local FBI office and asked if I could see my file. They said they didn't do that sort of thing and they weren't sure who I was. I said, "Look, you know who I am, and you know I've got a file. I want to see it." They finally admitted they knew who I was and that they probably had something there, but I couldn't look at it.

PETE: Things kept getting progressively worse. We'd read in newspapers about "outside agitators" and "Communists" coming into town. And, God, you can't have Communists in our town! Then if you were with the press and went into the union hall, the cops wanted you to register with them. Well, that's not freedom of the press. And look at the influence that the company has on governmental bodies. You've got a sheriff who's half nuts—he's carrying a gun and, by God, he's the law—who has openly made statements in favor of the company. The same with the chief of police and the majority of the city council. There's Kermit Holverstein, who sits on the Hormel Foundation board of directors. He's also the attorney for the city who was finding all these obscure laws, like criminal syndicalism, to restrain the union.

JIM: There's a lot of harassment you have to put up with just to do your daily business of trying to beat a Fortune 500 company. For many, this became a community that lived in fear, fear of what the corporate master could do. Those who refused to bow down were made examples of. A principal was fired for renting a gymnasium to us for a benefit basketball game. A Catholic priest who came to the support group meetings found himself running a church at the other end of the county. A high school social studies teacher was fired just because he wanted to talk, as he put it, about the most profound thing to impact our town since its inception—the strike. When the police saw a car with a "Boycott Hormel" sticker on it, they told the company. Then Hormel fired the striker.

DENNY: I wrote an article in a newsletter, inviting people to come to Austin for our April 12 rally. The editor placed the words "Boycott

Hormel Products" above my column. I was immediately fired—after eighteen years at Hormel.

We were constantly being defeated through the winter of 1985, 1986, and through the summer months that followed. Injunctions were placed against us. The unfair labor practice charges heard by the NLRB always went against the union. We had court hearings for fired workers that went completely against the evidence. Testimony by people who were in the plant outweighed testimony by people who were on strike.

JIM: We obviously were considered a threat by a lot of people. You know, you're only ignored if you're ineffective. And we weren't ignored by federal judges, the governor of the state of Minnesota, the National Guard, the local police and the FBI, the churches, the schools, the Hormel Company at its highest official level, and the international union at its highest official level.

But we have gotten a tremendous amount of support from other local unions. In fact, in April 1986, six thousand people came to rally here in Austin. Just before that, the authorities pressed charges against me. Obviously they wanted to remove me from the rally. So I went "underground" in Austin, Minnesota. Then, in front of the six thousand people, I showed up. After it was all over, I turned myself in.

They can get away with charging people with anything they want, and it's up to you to prove your innocence. I was incarcerated on four felony counts for aiding and abetting a riot. I was charged with giving speeches and inviting people to Austin. I was looking at ten to twenty years in prison, and I didn't do anything wrong, unless it's wrong to give speeches or invite people to your hometown. Fortunately, we had attorneys who worked very hard to get those charges overturned, as they had worked to get Ray Rogers acquitted of criminal syndicalism.

DENNY: We were confronted with obstacles that seemed insurmountable. But we didn't sit around stewing. Everyone had a job to do. We still met seven days a week. We still offered recreation in the basement of our labor temple and discussion groups for people who were bewildered as to what was happening to their lives. We had a communications group. We had a "tool box," an emergency service people could use for help with their problems. And Ron Yokum and I were in charge of a sign group. We could mass-produce signs with volunteer help on very short notice.

In the spring of 1986, a professional muralist and I and two others in the art field decided to produce a mural on the side of the Labor Center. We had over one hundred people volunteer to help paint it, and in a very short six days, through the winds and rains of April, we accomplished a mural sixteen feet tall and eighty feet long. It showed immigrants forced to support themselves in a work world controlled by corporate greed. The work world was a series of buildings surrounded by a large serpent, squeezing the life out of its workers. But on the other side of the factories, workers were exiting with smiles and banners, willing to stand up for what they believed in.

RAY: You've got to understand that we did all this with a lot of organized opposition from the top echelon of the UFCW and the AFL-CIO. I would say the UFCW had to have spent at least three million dollars to oppose us. They didn't send one person in to help P-9 out, but they sent thirty-five people to Austin, paid their hotel rooms, paid for their rent-a-cars, to try to bust us.

While the Hormel workers were out there fighting, Bill Wynn, the head of the UFCW, was telling them that they should take concessions. He was telling all the workers in his union, "We're in a controlled retreat program." But Bill Wynn raised his own salary fifty thousand dollars during the height of the Hormel dispute. So he was making two hundred thousand dollars a year. And that did not include his expenses; Bill Wynn had his own jet, his own chauffeur. So I made a statement in the *Milwaukee Journal,* saying that the union leadership dressed like, talked like, thought like the corporate leadership. They don't feel comfortable sitting down with the rank and file. Boy, I know that really hit home.

Why in the hell aren't there fightbacks by the AFL-CIO leaders like the ones we've been involved in? What would happen if, from the top down, they said, "We're going all out to support the strikers. Whether it's the paper workers in Jay, Maine; or in Lock Haven, Pennsylvania; in Mobile, Alabama; or DePere, Wisconsin; or the Hormel workers in Austin; or the Morrell workers who were getting the hell kicked out of them in Sioux City, Iowa; in Sioux Falls, South Dakota—we're going to send in the buses. We're going to mobilize rank-and-file members and union leaders across this country; we're going to go there and we're going to lay down in the street; we're going to block those gates, and they're not going to bring replacement workers in. Hey, we realize we're going to face fines, we're going to face jail sentences. But we'll do it in such masses, we'll break the system, the same way they did in the antiwar movement, the same way they did in the civil rights movement." Instead, the vice president of the UFCW was quoted in the University of Minnesota newspaper: "I'm fed up with the solidarity bullshit line that Jim Guyette puts out."

But this is what we were building. It was such a strong grassroots movement. It was the beginning of a civil rights movement for workers. And they couldn't let it happen.

DENNY: On May 9, 1986, trusteeship was imposed on us by the federal court. Our executive leadership was removed from office, and we were given a directive by our international union to unconditionally surrender and return to work. Democratically, again, we decided to continue our struggle, even with strike support cut off by our international union. Members who were receiving forty dollars a week now had to learn to live on nothing. Finally, by a judge's ruling on July 3, the UFCW came in and took over the Austin Labor Center, ejecting the retirees, ejecting the supporters, and ejecting the members. We were told never to return. On July 5, our mural was ruined. Paint bombs had been thrown against it. The word "abort" had been sprayed across it.

PETE: Originally, fifteen hundred workers went out. Then four hundred and five went back in. They crossed a sanctioned picket line in January. Five or six months before the trusteeship was imposed, these people were scabs. And what happened to them? Were they banished by the UFCW? No. They were passed off as heroes of the strike. But of course, this strike was different, you know. You could cross the picket line and still be a good union member. They just proved that yesterday when they elected a scab for president. If you're going to cross the picket line and be a scab one week and union president the next, what's the sense of having a union?

I've known the new president, John Ankor, for a long time. I used to run around with him, carry on and party with him. The new secretary-treasurer, who's a scab—I was at his wedding, he was at mine. We've been to Canada fishing and hunting. A town this size is not like a large metropolitan area where everyone goes their separate ways. I mean, if I go to the store, I'll probably run into a couple of scabs. If I go buy gas, I'll probably see a couple. If I want to see a whole bunch, I just drive by the plant.

Whether you stayed out or went in was a deep moral question that transcended any kind of political or ideological or any other descriptions you'd want to place on people. People felt that it was either right or wrong. You had some families where the father went back to work and the son stayed out. You had brothers who split up. I know one family in particular where a brother-in-law, a brother, and a sister and another brother-in-law stayed out. One brother went back to work, and then a younger brother got hired as a replacement worker. This is just in one family. It's even to the point where the mother sides with the ones who stayed out and the father says, "Well, they needed a job." They don't have too many family reunions at Christmas or Thanksgiving anymore.

CECIL: That whole scab business—you know, off the street scabs, old P-9 scabs—it was all wrong, but I understand why some of them thought they had to go back in. They've got families. They've got homes to take care of. But you go back to work over there, you lose everything three years down the road, five years down the road. You want to fight now? Or do you want to fight after you've tried to live on six dollars an hour, when everybody's a little poorer, everybody's a little more tired, everybody's a little more bruised? You'd better fight the first opportunity you have, or you're going to get beat on worse.

PETE: Like everybody else, I haven't drawn a paycheck in almost two years. That wears and tears on you. I'm your typical welfare recipient now, living on food stamps and AFDC. It's not anything I relish doing or enjoy being on. In fact, I put it off until last May. But you're really left with no choice. I'm a single parent, and I have custody of three kids: a daughter sixteen, a boy thirteen, and a boy who's going to be eleven next week. I needed medical coverage for them. I was borrowing money from my dad all the time. He's retired, eighty years old, and I was starting to cause him hardship.

I'm thirty-nine, and I've paid taxes since I was eleven years old. Now I go up to the welfare office, and I sit in this long line of chairs, waiting to go in there. And everybody who goes through the courthouse knows what I'm there for. Until you experience it, you really don't have a feeling for how demeaning it is. Like in the supermarket, if you'd see somebody with food stamps, you'd say, "Oh, them so-and-so's. Look at all that food they get that they don't have to pay for." It's very easy to be down on them until you've gone through it yourself. Then all of a sudden I find myself in a checkout line with food stamps. I don't hear people saying anything, but I know what they're thinking.

I started at Hormel in 1967. My dream was always to get the hell out of there. My ambition was to sell minnows and night crawlers to fishermen up in northern Minnesota, maybe Canada. I never had any intention of being a business agent. I wasn't even a grievance person until 1982, when we went into the new plant and nobody else would do it.

But there are very few times, if ever, in a person's life when you're actually able to do some good for people. And these people have given everything that they have to the strike and put a lot of trust and a lot of faith in us. There's nothing left to do but fight, and that's what you keep doing. I don't think anybody's given up. I know that I haven't really given up hope of getting the people back in. But it's not going to be back with a contract that would have been reflective of the worth of the company and the worth of the employees to the company. That things didn't turn out the way we had hoped or planned is something we'll probably have to live with.

CECIL: We wanted to get our jobs back, but it's changed a bunch. All those hundreds of years when people thought there was a difference between whites and Blacks, men and women, young and old—all that crap, it's changing. In a small town in the middle of no place in Minnesota— just a bunch of farmers, a bunch of white Caucasians, for cripe's sake, experience the same problems Black people have had trying to get a job and decent housing, the same problems Hispanics face getting jobs other than under-the-table dirt, or the same problems women have been facing, trying to get the same wage for the same job. Until you walk a mile in somebody else's moccasins, you really don't understand what they're talking about. The walls are coming down. These guys are looking at the country different, at the world different. We got a lot of people talking about their problems, talking about unionism, and a lot of people watching. We've got a lot of people holding hands together. And we've had quite an impact on the labor movement.

PART TWO

Suppressing the Black Freedom Struggle

The Constitution has been slain in the house of its friends. So far as colored people are concerned, the Constitution has been a stupendous sham, a rope of sand, a Dead Sea apple, fair without and foul within, keeping the promise to the eye and breaking it to the heart.

Frederick Douglass, 1886

Claude Neal was lynched in 1934 by a mob of white people in a sadistic frenzy. Parts of his body were sliced away while he was still alive. Red-hot irons were pressed into his flesh. For hour after hour, the unimaginable agony continued, until he was at last put to death. His lifeless form was mutilated and then dragged behind a car to the courthouse square, where it was hung on display from a tree.

Thousands from several states came to Greenwood, Florida, to celebrate the lynching of Claude Neal. Invitations to the "party," with a schedule of events for the torturing and final killing, had been sent out beforehand over radio and in the press. But no one would respond to the desperate pleas to stop it. Not the local police. Not the governor. And not the attorney general of the United States.

How many others had suffered Neal's fate? In 1899, Sam Holt was burned at the stake, silently watching flames lick his flesh. The same year, young Richard Coleman screamed as a crazed mob burned him alive. Men, women, and children roared and screamed, too, in approval, as each new, ghastly torture was inflicted. Among them were church women and men, professionals and business owners, persons of "distinguished ancestry" who made no effort to disguise themselves. But the coroner's inquest said that Richard Coleman—like the others so openly tortured and killed—had come to his death at the hands of "persons unknown." In 1899, an average of two African Americans a week were put to death in this way. By the 1950s, more than four thousand lynchings had occurred in the United States of America.

Lynching and other violence enforced fiercely guarded codes of white supremacy. Within a mutually reinforcing complex of economic and legal structures, such violence made resistance to the servitude imposed on African Americans life-threatening. After World War I, an expanding apparatus to combat "subversion" was added as another means of repressive control, exercised by southern and federal authorities alike. Although both forms of control were severe and lasting, resistance by African Americans was never extinguished. The first type of control—based on physical and economic terror—remained in force until it was overturned by the civil rights movement of the 1960s. The second—based on charges of subversion—was firmly established after two red scares before it was marshaled against the civil rights movement and against the subsequent movement for Black freedom in northern ghettos.

NEITHER SLAVE NOR FREE:
THE CONDITION OF PRIOR RESTRAINT

Although they were no longer the property of slaveholders following the Civil War, freedpersons still enjoyed few rights that white people were bound to respect—even the right to life. Indeed, lynchers often lynched capriciously: Any Black person would do. And lynchers committed their crimes confident that there would be no retribution. Even when sheriffs and jailers and courts and governors were not in direct collusion with lynchers, they gave license to lynching by their silence. U.S. presidents from William McKinley to Harry Truman were silent, too. African Americans in Boston minced no words in addressing President McKinley: "We have suffered, sir—God knows we have suffered—since your accession to office, at the hands of a country professing to be Christian, but which is not Christian; from the hate and violence of a people claiming to be civilized, but who are not civilized, and you have seen our sufferings, witnessed from your high place our awful wrongs and miseries, and yet you have at no time and on no occasion opened your lips on our behalf."[1] There was no federal response to stop the madness, and African Americans in the South had to live for generations with full knowledge of the dreadful possibility they faced.

A hundred years ago, Bishop Henry McNeal Turner said that the object of lynching was to "prevent blacks from speaking in their own defense."[2] That was the case when African Americans were put to death

for a subtle or direct word or deed that expressly defied the racial barriers white society had erected. But it was also the case when racial barriers were not explicitly challenged. More intolerable than any of the real
or imagined crimes that prompted most of the lynchings was the fact that
they had been directed toward a white person and were because of that
an implicit but impermissible defiance of the system of white supremacy.
The reprisal of lynching made clear that *no* challenge, neither explicit
nor implicit, neither grave nor petty, would be allowed. It was a drastic
prior restraint on dissent, exercised within a complex of economic, social, and legal suppression.

In the plantation system of the South, Black sharecroppers—men,
women, and children—toiled in an endless striving to subsist and to escape debt. The landowner ruled as lord of the manor, a paternal despot
who exerted sweeping control over those who worked the land: control
over the conditions of their work, the sale of their product, and the price
of their supplies, as well as control over courts and law enforcement agencies that prosecuted and judged them. This condition of servitude, which
brooked no complaint, was what most African Americans endured from
the 1870s to the 1930s—and well beyond that, for some.

This way of life was built on the betrayal of the post–Civil War Reconstruction, a period in which for the first time a half million Black children attended schools and newly enfranchised Black men voted and held
office in state legislatures and Congress. White supremacists responded
to the enfranchisement of African Americans both with election fraud
and with stark terror. "You are Anglo Saxons. You are armed and prepared, and you will do your duty," Colonel Alfred Waddell, of Wilmington, North Carolina, instructed white citizens on the eve of the 1898
election. "Go to the polls tomorrow, and if you find the Negro out voting, tell him to leave and if he refuses, kill him, shoot him down in his
tracks."[3] To eliminate the possibility of Black political power in that city,
white mobs raided the Black community in Wilmington, burned down
its only newspaper, and, with the Wilmington Light Infantry, shot down
African American citizens, as one witness said, "left and right in the most
unlawful way."[4] In an American coup d'état, white supremacists forcibly
removed Wilmington's sitting mayor and city council and launched a
dragnet for dissident Black leaders and their white Republican allies, ban-
ishing them from the city at the point of bayonets.

Across the South—in New Orleans, Louisiana; Eutaw, Alabama;
Danville, Virginia; Vicksburg, Mississippi; Atlanta, Georgia; Phoenix,
South Carolina; and Wilmington, North Carolina—the wanton murder

of African Americans in "riots" staged by marauding white people defined quite precisely the outline of prior restraint as the promise of Reconstruction faded. African Americans were not to express their views publicly and were not to vote, hold office, or form political alliances. These prohibitions were initially established outside the legal arena by force and violence, but they were made legitimate and lasting when they were encoded as Jim Crow laws: the poll tax, the literacy test, the white primary, the grandfather clause, and laws that relegated African Americans to separate and inferior facilities and accommodations. Precious little room remained to mount movements of opposition.

But in song, at prayer, in manifold social encounters, resistance, often subtle, was expressed and kept alive. A collective memory of the past, "a vision hidden or masked from the white world and oppositional to the core" lay beneath a sometimes placid surface.[5] At times and at great risk, African Americans abandoned deference in speech and conduct. The million-member Colored Farmers' National Alliance called for a general strike of Black cotton pickers at the end of the 1800s. Black soldiers and veterans of World War I and II, sent abroad in the name of democracy, insisted, at the cost of their lives, that they realize some measure of freedom here. At times, resistance flared up into powerful, even violent opposition, as African Americans resorted to arms in battles fought against invading mobs of whites. In southern cities, African Americans boycotted segregated transit systems long before the 1950s; in northern cities, they boycotted businesses that refused to employ them; and in urban ghettos, they withheld rent and blocked evictions.

CASTING THE FREEDOM STRUGGLE
AS A SUBVERSIVE FORCE

Whether Republican or Democrat, U.S. presidents and the U.S. Congress were all but oblivious to the outrages of repression in the South. In one hundred years, no anti-lynching legislation was passed by Congress or seriously put forth by a president. Silence by design or by deference to southern politicians was one federal response to white supremacy. Another was to undermine African American dissent directly.

The latter effort is illustrated by two intelligence-gathering agencies—Military Intelligence and the Bureau of Investigation, the parent of the FBI—that established their secret political missions during and after World War I. These agencies operated according to assumptions that fundamentally accepted and accommodated both white supremacist ideology and a security-state mentality. Unrest among Black citizens was considered the problem to be contained. These agencies saw dissent by African Americans not only as an affront to sacrosanct racial sensibilities but also as dangerous to the nation's security. "The head of Military Intelligence," according to Roy Talbert Jr., "firmly believed that complaints about lynching damaged the defense interests of the United States."[6] "For the director," Kenneth O'Reilly writes of the FBI, "the advocacy of racial justice was itself a subversive act."[7] Accordingly, protest by Black Americans, seen as a security threat in its own right or as being susceptible to Communist influence, had to be monitored and suppressed.

The first entry in the Military Intelligence file on "Negro Subversion," initiated shortly after America's entry into World War I, noted "several incidents of where colored men had attempted to make appointments with white women."[8] But of greater concern was the African American press. The NAACP's journal, *The Crisis*, decried "the hundreds of thousands of white murderers, rapists, and scoundrels who have oppressed, killed, ruined, robbed, and debased their black fellow men and fellow women" and then noted that those crimes had been "unrebuked by the President of the United States."[9] Military Intelligence, unable to tolerate such "carping and bitter utterances," banned *The Crisis* from army posts and sought successfully to censor its offensive message.[10] Concerned that the Black-owned St. Louis newspaper *Argus* was "exploiting stories on discrimination and lynching," Military Intelligence dispatched an agent to its offices to effect a "change of tone and character" in the paper's editorials.[11] Similar "warning talks" were held with the editors of the *Chicago Defender* and the *Baltimore Afro-American*.[12] Military Intelligence monitored Marcus Garvey's movements, opened his mail, and sent stenographers to record meetings held by Garvey, the charismatic leader of the largest African American organization in the nation's history, the Universal Negro Improvement Association (UNIA).

The Bureau of Investigation's covert operations against Garvey in the early 1920s foretold the abuse of the modern civil rights movement by the FBI. The bureau cooperated with local police to raid a UNIA meeting in New Orleans, seize its books and papers, and arrest its leaders on bogus charges. The bureau agent on the scene reported that in the future the police superintendent "intended to break up the meetings of GARVEY'S organization if possible, and lend any aid to this Department within his power."[13] Bureau Informant "800" became a confidant of both Garvey and another Black leader who was his most bitter rival at the time. In that doubly duplicitous role, the informant was able to play them off against each other to destabilize both groups, especially Garvey's, in a prelude to COINTELPRO, the FBI's later counterintelligence program.

During World War II, a nationwide FBI probe of "foreign inspired agitation" in "colored neighborhoods" included recruiting Black informants, instituting mail covers, transmitting derogatory information to prospective financial contributors to the NAACP and the Urban League, bugging the offices and tapping the telephones of the NAACP and the National Negro Congress, and investigating newspapers owned and run by African Americans.[14] The African American press's insistent demands that the war against race superiority abroad be accompanied by assaults on race superiority at home—its criticisms of Jim Crow America—were viewed as seditious by government officials. Under provisions of the Espionage Act of 1917, which was still in force during World War II, the Post Office and the Office of Censorship sought to cripple these newspapers by banning them from the mails. J. Edgar Hoover's FBI was the most tenacious, urging the suppression of African American newspapers for devoting too much space "to alleged instances of discrimination and mistreatment of Negroes."[15] In the bureau's 714-page wartime report on Black America, it contended that protest by African Americans was Communist-inspired, a view that pervaded the FBI from its director to the special agent in charge in Oklahoma City who complained that an issue of that city's Black newspaper was "sprinkled with such well-known Communistic phrases as 'Civil Liberties,' 'Inalienable Rights,' and 'Freedom of Speech and of the Press.'"[16]

Despite the measures taken to suppress African American dissent, the social ferment of the New Deal era also created opportunities. The CIO's organizing drives offered new hope for attacking the historic divisions between white and Black workers, for joining forces in the name of economic security and racial justice. The left-led unions, especially, confronted the deeply ingrained racism of southern white workers and the segregation of the southern workplace; they brought forth new militant African American leadership, defied segregationist rules to hold interracial meetings, attacked discriminatory practices on the job, and even organized voter registration drives. Yet it was precisely these unions that were called before the inquisitions held by HUAC and the Senate Internal Security Subcommittee (SISS), harassed by the FBI, vilified by the press, and expelled from the CIO. The Cold War purge of the left in labor, Michael Honey observes, eliminated "strong black leadership and integrationist forces almost wherever they existed."[17]

To no one's surprise, McCarthy-era witch-hunters, whose "leading figures . . . were also southern racists," produced accusations of Communism against prominent integrationist organizations: the Southern Conference for Human Welfare, the Highlander Folk School, and the Southern Conference Education Fund.[18] Also under siege was the Communist-led Civil Rights Congress, founded in 1946. If the CRC's use of mass appeals and direct action—marching, picketing, boycotting—distinguished it from its more conventional ally and frequent adversary, the NAACP, those tactics were harbingers of the civil rights movement that was on the verge of happening. The CRC became a textbook example of an organization decimated by repression in the Age of McCarthy. It was listed as "subversive" by the attorney general, investigated by the Internal Revenue Service and by grand juries, and monitored by FBI agents who spied on its meetings, tapped its phones, secured records of its bank accounts, and burglarized its offices before it finally succumbed.

The year 1956, when the federal government forced the left-wing CRC out of existence, was also the year a number of southern states banned the more conventional NAACP. That same year, too, the Mississippi Sovereignty Commission was founded as the state's official "watchdog of segregation," a political intelligence agency explicitly created to defend white supremacy laws against the gathering storm of protest that would finally overcome them.[19]

THE EVOLUTION OF REPRESSION: CONTINUITIES AND DISCONTINUITIES

In 1955, inspired by the actions of Rosa Parks, the African American citizens of Montgomery, Alabama, decided to walk rather than ride segregated buses. Their year-long boycott initiated the modern civil rights movement. In the extraordinary decade between 1955 and 1965, activists braved a violence that now, as in the past, was initiated or condoned by local law enforcement agencies. In Albany, Georgia; Birmingham, Alabama; McComb, Mississippi—across the South—African Americans who dared to assert their rights as citizens were murdered, shot at, and beaten; their homes and churches were bombed and burned; their livelihoods were destroyed.

The federal government did little to protect civil rights workers. Indeed, the FBI effectively parlayed the "myth of communism," as political scientist David Garrow puts it, into years of surveillance, especially into the affairs of Martin Luther King Jr. and the Southern Christian Leadership Conference (SCLC).[20] It didn't matter that the bureau's expanding network of wiretaps and bugs produced no evidence of Communist influence; the FBI's hyped-up projection of conspiracy would not yield to the benign reality. The March on Washington in August 1963 convinced Hoover that it was time for a frontal assault. The bureau laid out its campaign to "neutralize" Dr. King and, ultimately, to promote someone else of the FBI's choosing to be his successor as the new "national Negro leader."[21] The FBI attempted to cut off SCLC's sources of funds and block the group's publications. It tried to undermine Dr. King's reputation in other countries and discredit him with churches, universities, and the press in the United States. In a shockingly personalized campaign, it sought to destroy Dr. King's marriage and even to provoke his suicide.[22] "No holds were barred," the FBI's William Sullivan testified before a Senate committee, asserting that the tactics used against King were similar to those used against Soviet agents.[23]

The nature of the repression directed against African Americans was being transformed. The civil rights struggle that culminated in the passage of the Voting Rights Act in 1965 overturned the South's reliance on physical and economic terror as a prior restraint on dissent, just as it cleared away the legal obstacles to the enfranchisement of African Americans. That is not to say that violence had ended. It was in 1968 that Martin Luther King Jr. was assassinated in Memphis. And as late as 1979, five demonstrators were killed as they began an anti-Klan march in Greensboro, North Carolina, shot by a squad of white supremacists that included an informant for the FBI and local police.[24] Overall, however, the tactics used in attempts to subvert the Black freedom movement began to shift in emphasis from abject terror to legislative resistance to the Voting Rights Act in the South and to more intrusive covert operations by the federal government.

In August 1967, the FBI initiated a counterintelligence program, known as COINTELPRO, against African American organizations and leaders. Hoover secretly instructed his agents in the field "to expose, disrupt, misdirect, discredit, or otherwise neutralize the activities of black nationalist, hate-type organizations and groupings."[25] Among those he listed for "intensified attention" were SCLC, the Student Nonviolent Coordinating Committee (SNCC), the Congress of Racial Equality (CORE), and the Nation of Islam.[26] At that time, the Black Panther Party (BPP) was too new on the scene to be included, but it was soon to become the FBI's primary target. By September 1968, the Panthers were, according to J. Edgar Hoover, "the greatest threat to internal security in the country."[27] Field offices were instructed "to neutralize all organizational efforts of the BPP."[28] In the three short years after its founding, the Black Panther Party was disabled by the arrests of its leaders, heavily infiltrated with FBI informants and provocateurs, subjected to damaging police raids, attacked by rival groups at the instigation of the FBI, and sabotaged by a campaign of disinformation and disruption designed to split the party from within and isolate it from its outside supporters.

While the FBI conducted its covert operations against the Panthers in the North, the southern establishment responded to the passage of the Voting Rights Act of 1965 with a campaign of massive resistance. The counterinsurgency was led by white state legislators who instituted racial gerrymandering and at-large elections to dilute Black-majority districts, effectively delaying African American representation into the 1980s. Nevertheless, inroads were made, especially at the local level. As the number of African Americans holding elected office rose, a third wave of attacks against the right of Black citizens to political representation gathered force. First denied the vote by terror, then denied representation by white-dominated legislatures, African Americans, once elected, were targeted by federal law enforcement agencies, especially during the administrations of Ronald Reagan and George Bush. This was the case for Richard Arrington, the first Black mayor of Birmingham, Alabama. "It is now readily apparent to the City and others," stated a 1990 complaint to the Senate Judiciary Committee on behalf of Birmingham, "that the IRS, FBI, and U.S. Attorney's office have converted the grand jury process into a vehicle of convenience for circumventing the political fruit enjoyed by blacks under the Voting Rights Act of 1965."[29] A century after the promise of full enfranchisement under Reconstruction had been broken in the South, it was yet to be realized either there or in northern and western states, where similar attacks on Black elected officials effectively compromised the African American vote.

Cold War Constraints on African Americans' Demands for Freedom

ERADICATING A POWERFUL, DEFIANT VOICE FROM THE AMERICAN CONSCIOUSNESS

Paul Robeson's innovative rendition of "Old Man River"—"I must keep fightin' until I'm dyin'"—spoke of his uncompromising commitment to the cause of African American freedom. That, and his opposition to Cold War policies, brought severe reprisals. Prohibited from traveling outside his country during the McCarthy era and blacklisted within the United States, he found his brilliant career as an actor and concert artist under assault. In the panic of the moment, rife with congressional investigations, loyalty oaths, and witch-hunts, all who advanced the cause of equality were suspect. "Have you ever had Negroes in your home?" a government employee was asked by a loyalty board established by President Harry S. Truman.[30] Interspersed with questions about Communist beliefs and affiliations were other questions that asked employees their views on racism or whether they enjoyed Paul Robeson's records.

Militant spokespersons for the freedom movement such as Paul Robeson and W. E. B. Du Bois were attacked and isolated from the mainstream civil rights movement to which they had contributed so much. Dr. Du Bois, a distinguished scholar, had been a founder of the NAACP and an outspoken editor of its journal, *The Crisis*. Although the U.S. government issued a postage stamp in his honor in the 1990s, it was a different story in 1951. In the early '50s, Du Bois was denied a passport and put on trial for being a foreign agent because of his work in the Peace Information Center, which opposed the Truman administration's Cold War policies. "The secret police swarmed in my neighborhood asking about my visitors," he wrote in his autobiography. "My mail was tampered with or withheld." Although the government's case against him collapsed, it successfully cast him as a pariah. "Negro papers were warned not to carry my writings nor mention prominently my name. Colleges ceased to invite my lectures," he recalled. "From being a person whom every Negro in the nation knew by name at least and hastened always to entertain or praise, churches and Negro conferences refused to mention my past or present existence."[31] The "unpersoning" of a legendary figure had begun.

Paul Robeson's transgression was his thundering denunciation of America's treatment of Black people and his refusal to bend before the force of the Cold War. Pointing to the "swelling wave of lynch murders," he demanded of President Truman at a 1946 Madison Square Garden rally: "Why have you failed to speak out against this evil?"[32] In Paris, Robeson declared that it would be unthinkable for African Americans to participate in a war against the Soviet Union by fighting for a nation that had oppressed them for generations. "There is hardly a Negro in the South," a Black newspaper in North Carolina responded, "who, at some time or other, has not felt as Robeson expressed himself, as unwilling to lay down his life for a country that insults, lynches and restricts him to second-class citizenship."[33]

But, coming at a moment when the Cold War was particularly heated, Robeson's words ignited furious denunciations and even attempts on his life. He became the target of a many-sided attack aimed not only at punishing him but also at eradicating him from the American consciousness. Only recently, in 1998, on the hundredth anniversary of his birth, has his stature in American life begun to be recognized.

PAUL ROBESON JR.

A Welsh choir came to this country to perform after my father, Paul Robeson, died. It had been twenty-five years since dad was there in 1958. Some of them had sung with him, and some of them had seen him come to the mining valleys when they were kids. They talked about him like it was yesterday. To everybody in the choir, he was "our Paul." It was as if they could touch him, see him. It was really very moving. Few of us get to experience that much love and affection.

PAUL ROBESON JR.

Dad went to Rutgers from 1915 to 1919, the third Black student ever there. He made Phi Beta Kappa as a junior, which is unusual in itself. He was inducted into the Cap and Skull Society, an exclusive group for the most outstanding students. He was a champion debater and the valedictorian of his graduating class. As a college football player, dad was the prototype middle linebacker. Walter Camp, the most famous of All-American team selectors, called him the greatest defensive football player of all time. He was an offensive player, too, the first tight-end type. Above all, he was a blocker, knocking everything down for the running end.

In 1917, 1918, he was the number one football player in the nation. He just dominated the game. For a Black person to be on the lips of everyone who talked about football was doubly extraordinary during one of the most racist interludes of the twentieth century. People had seen *Birth of a Nation*,* whose caricatures became folklore. It was vicious everywhere. The football players at Rutgers threatened to strike when dad first came. They weren't going to have a "nigger" on their team. The coach supported dad, but it was tough to break that kind of barrier. Dad was pretty well brutalized—his nose was broken, his shoulder sprained—by his own team!

Dad became expert at sitting on his anger. He learned from his father that he couldn't afford the luxury of spontaneously expressing it in a white racist society. It was a Black male rule because we were the ones who got lynched. Dad taught me the same thing: "Don't act out your anger"—just like "Don't run across the street." It was something your parents beat into you psychologically—physically if necessary. It meant your survival. Of course, you still had the rage, but you transformed and transcended it.

All dad's college friends remember: "Robey never got angry. He took all that stuff and never complained." But when a certain threshold is crossed, your fury overrides everything. Dad spent ten days in the infirmary after his nose was broken. The day he came back for practice, they kept running at him. Finally, after one play, he was resting on the ground for a moment, getting his breath. The guy who had been carrying the ball, on his way back, stomped on dad's hand with all his might. It wasn't just a personal insult; it was going to any length to stop a Black person from playing. The next play, when they came at dad again, he just knocked everybody else aside and picked up this one guy. He later said he was so furious he was actually prepared to break his spine across his legs. And he would have if the coach hadn't stopped him.

I had somewhat the same welcome when I first went to Cornell—I was like cannon fodder. The first team would run at me, then the second team, then the third. Guys were beating on me all day. I kept trying to get tougher. I would stay an hour longer than everyone, train harder.

---

*The film *Birth of a Nation*, directed by D. W. Griffith, glorified the Ku Klux Klan. It had its premiere at the White House during Woodrow Wilson's presidency, the first motion picture to be shown there.

Well before the season, I was a hundred and eighty pounds of whipcord muscle. Finally, they put me on the second team, and by the beginning of the season I started the game. I had been so toughened by the sheer initiation of just making my own team, I was an absolute terror.

Frankly, I would have preferred soccer, because I didn't particularly like this game of butting heads and knocking everybody around. I would not have bothered if I hadn't felt this tremendous responsibility: You're the third Black player ever at Cornell; it's your duty to prepare the way for others. It was almost like betraying your people if you had the ability and then chose not to use it. Or grades. Having gotten into this Ivy League school, whose quota had been more or less zero for Blacks, you'd read yourself out of the human race if you didn't make the dean's list.

Dad was tough enough on me, but his father, born into slavery and self-taught, must have been far tougher on him. The drive to accomplish, not just for oneself but for the race, was in dad's case enormous. Now, it helped that he was that talented, that handsome, had a wonderful singing voice and an outgoing, easy-going personality. The point was, when you get there after all the sacrifice, it isn't just to enrich yourself; you've got to bring everybody else along.

My father was hailed as one of America's greatest actors. His serious stage career began when Eugene O'Neill offered him the lead in two of his plays, *The Emperor Jones* and *All God's Chillun Got Wings*. *Emperor Jones* was both a play and a film. The film was considered a classic because it was the first time a Black man was portrayed as a human being, not a total caricature. In that sense it was a watershed for a different portrayal of Blacks, overcoming Stepin Fetchit and *Birth of a Nation*.

Dad's crowning achievement as an actor was his role in *Othello*. It ran longer than any Shakespearean play on Broadway. The reason *Othello* was so great in 1943, 1944 is that dad had been studying it for twenty years. He learned the role in four languages. And he studied in the ancient Anglo-Saxon of Chaucer, the Elizabethan of Shakespeare, which came from Chaucer's English. On top of that, he studied the Moorish and medieval Venetian cultures. He incorporated it all into his portrayal of Othello and won the Donaldson Award for best male performer on Broadway in 1944. He received the Gold Medal for best diction in American theater from the National Institute of Arts and Letters, only the ninth given in twenty years.

At a time when the minstrel show was a cultural fixture, *Othello* had an impact on race relations that was quite extraordinary. I remember seeing the play in New Haven when I was sixteen. I'll never forget how dad strode onto the stage, totally dominating the atmosphere. His effect on the audience was absolutely shattering. Both Black and white were deprived of every stereotype they had about themselves or the other for two and a half hours. It took away the Blacks' inferiority complexes. People eighty years old still talk about it. And for the whites, not only was this African equal, he was superior.

They performed across the country, everywhere but in the South and in Washington, D.C., where theaters were segregated. There was some concern about a play showing a Black man kissing a white woman: "Will there be riots in the theater?" Even dad was a little nervous when they opened in Cincinnati, which was almost like the South. Well, the audience may have been disturbed about it before the play started, but dad's Othello so disarmed them that by the time he kissed Desdemona, it seemed totally natural. It was amazing to me. One reviewer said, "Even those with the greatest sensitivity"—meaning those most racist white folks—"didn't turn a hair."

Dad began his singing career in 1925 with the first concert ever given that consisted solely of Negro spirituals and secular songs. He had this wonderful singing instrument with an extraordinarily rich sound. His rendition of the spirituals was so compelling that it launched him on a concert career. He expanded to other folk songs. He was unusual in his sensitivity to all the many different groups. He learned their languages and cultures as well as their music. The effect of it on audiences was enormous. They felt he sang to them from his heart. For most of the 1930s and 1940s, dad was the leading concert singer in the world.

He had more than a magnificent singing voice. His speaking voice was naturally a rich one. He'd come out on the stage and just say, "Hello," and it would reach down and make an intimate room out of a huge auditorium. It was almost like a caress of the whole audience. There was something electric about his personality, about his communication, a personal connection that people felt. He could win over even a hostile audience with a reading and a song.

But I've never seen dad, even at his peak, when he wasn't scared to death before he walked on the stage. He felt he always had to deliver a thousand percent. I learned as a little kid never to come near him right before a concert, because he was impossible then. But what could one expect? He was just a human being like you and me. He could be wonderful, nasty, and everything in between. The character you saw singing "Old Man River" on a concert stage or playing Othello with total confidence was him and wasn't him. At times he was fearful, indecisive, felt inferior, didn't know whether he could get through the first song. Yet he had this great command once he was on stage.

Dad went from football player to law school graduate and then in just a few years—between 1923 and 1926—to leading actor and concert singer. He was catapulted into a public appreciation that was quite spectacular. Bang! All of a sudden, he's a major cultural personality from nowhere, a role my mother, Eslanda, helped him cope with, as a manager and as a buffer. In his early career, she was a critical factor in helping him anchor himself. She was more pragmatic, more scientific, more philosophical. He would hone his ideas on her, fantasizing here and there. She'd make him come down to earth. It was an important interaction that enriched them both. That partnership continued throughout their lives and overrode a lot of the personal conflict, which later got quite acute.

Mother was an outstanding person on her own. She had a very good job in the pathology lab at the Presbyterian hospital. She was the first Black technician to become head of a lab in town here. When dad was out of work, she supported him. They had a common purpose, to advance Black people and humanity as a whole. Although they shared broad goals, she was a bit more elitist, but she surely never forgot where she came from. On the other hand, he may have been more plebeian in one way, but he liked to live well, too. They both had their contradictions.

Dad's cultural and political consciousness came together during a twelve-year stay in Europe, from 1927 to 1939. In England, he became part of the British labor movement and met such figures as George Bernard Shaw, Aldous Huxley, and H. G. Wells. It was there, too, that he became political in the sense of making a commitment as an artist to the principles that motivated him. By the time of the Spanish civil war, when he risked his life to sing for the Republicans in their struggle against Franco's fascism, he said—and this quotation is inscribed on the plaque that is on his grave: "The artist must elect to fight for freedom or for slavery. I have made my choice. I had no alternative."

It was in England that dad came to know the leaders of the colonial freedom movement, like Jomo Kenyatta of Kenya, Kwame Nkrumah of Ghana, Nnamdi Azikiwe of Nigeria, and an extraordinary man named Jawaharlal Nehru of India. In 1934, 1935, British intelligence started keeping tabs on dad. By 1936, the British government would not let him travel to Africa. They warned him about radicalizing the Africans he was talking to. Actually, a lot of dad's political radicalization came from the colonial freedom movement leaders, who introduced him to African culture and anti-colonialism. Dad wrote: "I've discovered this magnificent, virile African culture. And now I think Black, not white."

Kenyatta and others were the ones who urged dad to go to the Soviet Union, because of the Soviet nationalities policy. Then Soviet filmmaker Sergei Eisenstein invited dad there. Eisenstein wanted to do a movie called *Black Majesty,* with dad playing Jean Jacques Dessalines from Haiti. Marie Seton, an English writer who was a very good friend of Eisenstein's, arranged the trip. The visit was marked by top-level government-cultural gatherings for dad and mother, where they were accepted completely as equals. What a contrast with other places.

Dad was treated as a full human being, not "less than" because he was Black. There was curiosity, not hostility. Once, he was walking down a main street from Pushkin Square. A bunch of mothers were out with their little kids, who were playing in the snow, and here comes this huge Black man. The kids were totally taken with him. They called him "Black Father Frost." When he squatted down, they came from all directions and swarmed over him. What struck him was, "These kids weren't frightened. And the mothers were perfectly happy for them to be climbing all over me." The kids had no feeling they had to "watch out for Black people." Just the opposite: "Gee, this big guy looks different, wonderful." That was one of his most memorable images.

When dad came back to the USA in 1939, he was very much involved with NAACP benefits and was good friends with Walter White.* He was key in helping recruit Blacks into the CIO, the auto workers union, the packinghouse workers union. He was on the picket lines in '40 and '41, during the great auto strikes in Detroit. He sang to a hundred thousand in Cadillac Square. He went around to the churches, urging Black workers to join the union and not break the strike.

His involvement in cases like the Martinsville Seven came mostly as a result of his association with William Patterson and the Civil Rights Congress.† The CRC defended many victims of police brutality and rape

---

*Walter White was the secretary of the NAACP from 1931 until 1955, the year of his death.

†The Martinsville Seven were African American youths who, despite protesting their innocence, were executed in Richmond, Virginia, in 1951 for the rape of a white woman. At that time, no white man had ever been executed for the crime of rape. William L. Patterson was the executive secretary of the Civil Rights Congress, which is discussed on p. 127.

frame-ups, which were common in the postwar period. Dad was active in publicizing and building support to break these frame-ups. They were a backlash against Blacks who came home from World War II and claimed their democratic rights. In Columbia, Tennessee, there was a rebellion led by Black GIs over the brutalization of a veteran and his mother. A couple of thousand National Guard troops descended on the Black community, which fought them for a while. Black GIs in another Tennessee town were denied the vote. They stormed the city hall with machine guns—and voted.

There were many lynchings in '46, '47, '48, and even '49, mainly to prevent voting rights from being established in southern states. There was a general increase of violence against Blacks, often shootings by police. In 1946, dad and Albert Einstein and others sponsored the Anti-Lynch Crusade. Dad led a delegation to President Truman, asking him to initiate anti-lynch legislation in Congress. Truman said it was a political, not a moral, issue, and he didn't think it was the opportune time for him to get behind an anti-lynch bill. Dad replied, "If the government does not do something about lynching, then Negroes will have to defend themselves." Truman got red in the face, jumped up, and shook his finger at dad: "That sounds like a threat." Dad calmly stood up: "Mr. President, it was not a threat, but merely a statement of fact about the temper of the Negro people, ten percent of the population of the United States." Well, it was headlines across the nation: "Robeson Collides with Truman."

In '46–'47, dad had his most successful tour ever. He was the number one draw in the country, making twenty-five hundred dollars a concert. But he decided that there was too big a gap between his doing that and what was happening to Black Americans. He announced that he was going to take a year off and do nothing but benefits supporting Black freedom and union struggles. That led to his campaigning for the Progressive Party ticket in 1948. He saw it as a way to roll back reaction not only in the South but nationwide.

In the summer of that year, dad toured the islands of Jamaica and Trinidad, where he was received with an unprecedented welcome. He sang to sixty thousand in a stadium in Jamaica. Then he sang a free concert in the city square. His impact on the West Indian population frightened the powers that be. They alerted British intelligence: "Can't you keep him out?" He went to Hawaii and sang for Harry Bridges's union, the longshoremen's union. Huge crowds. He also stopped off to sing for the striking workers of the Panama Canal. There was a progression in that he spoke out on political issues while at the same time being a leading artist-singer-actor. Outside of Joe Louis, he was probably the most revered and well-known Black American in the Black community, even though very few could afford a ticket to his concerts at Carnegie Hall.

With all this, you have to ask: Why is Paul Robeson so little known today in his own land, the United States, while he is so well known to the rest of the world? Several generations of Americans, Black as well as white, either do not know his name at all or have only the vaguest inkling of who he was. His entire record of achievement has been all but eradicated in the attempt to make Paul Robeson a nonperson. The 1950 issue of *College Football,* the most complete record of the sport, listed a *ten-man* All-American team for 1918, the only one in its history. The missing name was Paul Robeson. It was deliberate censorship of a person's existence, exactly the same use of suppression as occurred under Stalinism. My father was the only two-time Walter Camp All-American who is not in the College Football Hall of Fame. During World War II, he was the most popular concert artist in America. Yet in any book on concert singers published after 1949, he is barely mentioned. He was one of the initial hundred members inducted into the Theater Hall of Fame, but in any reference book published after 1949, his acting career is almost completely ignored.

Why? One piece of the answer is that my father refused to let his extraordinary success be used to explain away the oppression of millions of Black Americans. More than that, he used his success and his immense prestige and talents as weapons in an all-out struggle against the oppression. What the top elite of the United States couldn't forgive dad for was that "their Black man" turned down a place among them and turned on them just because he had to bring the rest of his people with him. They were hostile not only to Robeson but to the cultural independence and diversity he represented. Dad, as much as any single person in American history, represented Black America, a distinct culture: a different way of thinking, different worldview, different artistic expression. Not better, not worse—different. And yet very much a part of the mainstream on the most important levels of Western culture.

The other piece was that in 1946, when the Cold War began and the political winds shifted one hundred and eighty degrees, dad wasn't about to readjust his principles. They went after him not just because of his friendship with the Soviet Union but because he believed in curbing American imperialism, if you will. If the U.S. wanted to launch a third world war, he, Paul Robeson, was prepared to challenge it in every way possible. What he did was totally legal, and it was totally illegal for them to persecute him against the rules of their own Constitution. But his thoughts, his ideas, were clearly "subversive" to those who wanted a Pax Americana.

For over twenty-five years, my father was investigated by the Federal Bureau of Investigation, the Central Intelligence Agency, the State Department, the Criminal Division of the Justice Department, the Internal Revenue Service, the U.S. Immigration Service, Naval Intelligence, Army Intelligence, Air Force Intelligence, the National Security Council, the White House, the office of the attorney general, the Secret Service, and quite a few more.

After dad's death, Michael B. Standard from the firm of Rabinowitz, Boudin and Standard obtained material from the FBI and CIA on my behalf through the Freedom of Information Act. My file was relatively small—six hundred pages. But on my parents, I got over thirty-five hundred. I found out there are twenty thousand more pages on Paul and Eslanda Robeson in the New York field office alone. In addition, other field offices have files. FBI personnel attached to consulates or embassies have many reports on dad's activities abroad. A lot of those files in Paris, Bonn, et cetera, and many field office files in Oklahoma City, Philadelphia, and so on, on dad and mother and myself were destroyed within a year of my father's death—in toto. And it's in the field offices where the dirty tricks are specified.

From the files I received, it was obvious there were agents who did nothing but follow every public event of my father, or even of me. You'd think that after they got a thousand and nine examples of Paul Robeson being friendly to the Soviet Union, they're not going to send a guy to record the thousand and tenth time he speaks for Soviet-American friendship. But no, it took on a life of its own. They clipped everything written about it. Meticulously. They have reams of stuff on what Paul Robeson said at Carnegie Hall from the *New York Times* or the *Daily World* or wherever. Then there's a report on what he said. And then an analysis of the report. You know, paper, paper.

The FBI targeted him as early as 1940. In 1943, they put dad on the custodial detention list, contrary to existing law then. They added mother to the list in late '43, early '44. That meant that in the event of a "national emergency," the FBI or any security agency or the police were authorized to pick them up within twenty-four hours. In 1958, Hoover still wanted dad listed for detention: "Robeson continues to be of sufficient importance and potential dangerousness from an internal security standpoint to require his immediate apprehension in the event of an emergency."[34]

I think Truman never forgave my father for challenging him, and he had it in for dad personally. The gauntlet was thrown then, and I'm sure Truman gave the green light to the FBI and everybody else: "Whatever you can do to this guy, go ahead." Certainly J. Edgar Hoover went all out beginning in 1946. The documents show that the FBI was determined to "prove" Paul Robeson was a member of the Communist Party. They got dad's Social Security records, his law school records; they monitored his IRS records—everything under the sun. Hoover finally had to admit in 1949: "No open documentary evidence to prove subject's Communist Party affiliation available at Bureau."[35]

But that didn't stop them from coming up with the total fabrication that he was a Communist under the assumed name of John Thomas. Their FBI informant testified that he'd seen dad at secret meetings. Can you imagine dad, with his stature, trying to sneak into a meeting with a pseudonym!? But that's what they kept using. He was personal friends with Earl Browder, Ben Davis, and others in the Communist Party. He was also personal friends with a lot of Democrats, including Mrs. Roosevelt, and some Republicans, for that matter, but they only focused on "the guy who hangs out with Ben Davis." We found records of phone surveillance in the files. They'd tap my phone, mom's phone in Connecticut, dad's friends' phones, his lawyer's phone, every phone they could think of. They logged everything, including a conversation between my mother and her grandchildren or my mother and my wife talking about going up to Connecticut to look at some property next Tuesday. The FBI bugged the premises of a lot of people dad went to see in various cities.

They tried to intimidate people around dad. They would threaten them where they were vulnerable, like on the job. Nine times out of ten, our friends, even conservative ones, told them to go to hell. But not always. A very good friend of mine wanted a career in the service. We grew up like brothers from when we were twelve till we were twenty-two, the time of the Korean war. I got married. He went off to California. After the FBI visited him, he cut me off dead. He knew they would ruin his career. He sent word through his sister: "Don't write. Don't call. You never heard of me."

By the mid-1950s, I got used to being followed. Sometimes it was on the subway. Sometimes a car was outside the house. It was random, but consistent enough, as if they were saying, "We're always watching you."

Our greatest fear, my wife Marilyn's and mine, was for our children. We were really anxious about them being stopped by FBI types. At the same time, we didn't want to terrify them. We managed by saying, "Don't speak to strangers." We told them, "Grandpa is very famous, so all kinds of people want to find out where we live, where he lives." We let the kids know that there was such a thing as racism and that there was considerable danger for Blacks in certain areas of New York City. We didn't expand it very much beyond that until they could handle it, when they were past ten, eleven. Even then, the vulnerability of our children was our biggest concern.

Fortunately, we lived in Harlem, in a place that was very much a community. Many times when the FBI was in the neighborhood, somebody would tell me. One day, I went to my local post office, and a guy behind the counter, obviously some sort of supervisor, called me aside. He leaned over and said very softly, "By the way, you know your mail goes downstairs and comes up." He went like this, meaning they steam it open. It was interesting to me that people retained a certain decency even inside the system. Indeed, a Black policeman tipped off a friend of mine that they had put my picture up in the precinct as someone who was to be automatically picked up for detention within twenty-four hours of a so-called national emergency.

As far as dad was concerned, they tried everything under the sun. The government tried to discourage any contact with him. People lost jobs for having Paul Robeson records in their home or attending a Robeson concert. Such cases are recorded in the District Court in Washington, D.C. In 1947, at a hearing of the House Un-American Activities Committee, a young congressman from California, Richard Nixon, asked actor Adolph Menjou how he identified a Communist. Menjou replied, "Well, I think attending any meeting at which Mr. Paul Robeson appeared, and applauding and listening to his Communist songs."[36]

By 1949, my father's concerts were being canceled all over the country; his records were taken out of stores; he had no access to radio or television. But he went on his most successful tour ever abroad. It was in Paris where he said he believed it was unthinkable that American Negroes should support an aggressive war against the Russians on behalf of an America that had oppressed Negroes for generations. This statement caused an uproar back in the United States. He had touched a very deep and painful nerve. But he absolutely struck a common chord in the Black community. Many said: "Why should we fight those guys who are not doing anything to us for these guys who are?"

When he came back to the U.S., a Black leader whom dad knew well approached him, as an emissary from the highest level of the State Department, with a deal. If he signed an agreement not to make any more political speeches, everything would be forgiven. He didn't have to take anything back or say he was sorry. When the commotion died down, he could resume his concerts and acting. Even television would be open to him. This friend begged dad, "Just lay low, because if you don't, you'll need *life* insurance, not career insurance." The *New York Times* came out simultaneously with an editorial saying the same thing in more guarded language: "We hope Robeson will reconsider. We'd much rather hear him sing than make these speeches." Dad knew it was really the State Department talking.

He gave his answer at Rockland Palace, in that famous Harlem hall, to thirty-five hundred people: "At the Paris Peace Conference, I said it was unthinkable that the Negro people of America or elsewhere in the world could be drawn into a war with the Soviet Union. I repeat it with a hundredfold emphasis. They will not. We do not want to die in vain anymore on foreign battlefields for Wall Street and the greedy supporters of domestic fascism. If we must die, let it be in Mississippi or Georgia. Let it be wherever we are lynched and deprived of our rights as human beings."

I think he knew what he was getting into. I don't believe he just did it on an impulse. He was very much in the position that King was in when he made his speech: "I've been to the mountaintop." I think dad was consciously aware that he could be gunned down any minute. He figured, "Well, I've had a full life. I've done more than most people do in several lifetimes. If it's time for me to go, so be it."

The government branded Paul Robeson "Enemy Number One" and declared open season on him. The House Un-American Activities Committee tried to get Blacks to denounce him. But nine out of ten witnesses did not testify the way the committee wanted. It undercut HUAC when witnesses demanded: "What about discrimination in the U.S.?" It reflected the mood of Black America, responding to the years of persecution. Jackie Robinson testified, "I'm patriotic; I'll fight for my country." But then he went on to say, "We're not going to stop fighting race discrimination in this country until we've got it licked."

The HUAC hearings had a different effect in the white community. As part of a nationwide campaign by the government and the mass media against my father, they helped create the climate for the riot at the Peekskill concert, in New York state. The riot was in fact a police riot.

Many of the two thousand state and local police officers assigned to "keep order" joined the rioters in attacking those who came peacefully to attend a Paul Robeson concert. The rioters used fascist slogans: vicious anti-Semitic epithets, anti-Communist epithets, and their rallying cry "Wake up, America!" was reminiscent of the Nazis' "Germany awake!" They were violently anti-Black, not just in their slogans but in the vicious beatings of any Black person even seen in the vicinity of the concert grounds. The environment at Peekskill was set up so that dad could have been killed, but a lot of very brave people guaranteed that he would have some reasonable protection.[37]

Dad went on a concert tour from city to city after Peekskill. I think one of the reasons he was not killed then was explained in a column by James Hicks in the *Afro-American*. Hicks described him as a stick of dynamite swinging back and forth like a pendulum between the Black and white communities—a stick of dynamite that would explode if he should be maimed or killed. There would have been riots and bloodshed if something had happened to him. The "Black Mafia" in New York and elsewhere made it known that nothing better happen to Robeson in their town, or the cops might not want to walk the streets in the Black community. These guys were armed to the teeth, and they made it plain they'd use it all to defend Robeson.

The city governments reacted to the threat of arms and agreed to assign him a contingent of Black detectives as a guard during his tour. There was correspondence back and forth between them and the Justice Department saying, "Let's do that rather than have these freelancers around." On top of that, many off-duty Black policemen showed up on their own time, ready to give their lives to protect him from an assassination attempt.

The pullman porters at a railroad station, the skycaps at any airport became a flying wedge for dad. They'd find out what flight he was on. When he got off the plane, twenty guys were there: "Okay, Paul, give me your bags." They put him in a cab with a Black driver. And he couldn't pay them. No way. He was safe in any airport, any train station, and any Black community in this land. And it wasn't only Blacks. The same kind of thing happened in some of the unions: District 65, Fur and Leather Workers, Packinghouse in Chicago, Harry Bridges's ILWU. "That's our Paul." It was one of the things that kept him alive and going.

Dad denounced the Korean war right after it broke out in August of 1950. Almost simultaneously, the State Department took his passport away, saying it was not in the interests of the United States for him to travel abroad. But even that wasn't enough. The U.S. vice consul in Accra, Ghana, Roger P. Ross, worried about the African press's support of Paul Robeson. He wrote to the State Department in 1951: "There is no way the Communists score on us more easily and more effectively, out here, than on the U.S. Negro problem in general and on the Robeson case in particular."[38] He suggested that an article be written, "preferably by an American Negro," that "must pay genuine homage to the man's remarkable talents" and treat dad's political views as an "illness of mind and heart." The "story must tell of a few of the other instances where gifted and sensitive Negroes . . . have not broken under the strain, but have risen above it—the Marion Andersons, the Todd Duncans, the Jackie Robinsons, the Joe Louises, the Ralph Bunches." The memo was stamped "Action taken," along with the handwritten words "article on Robeson, *The Crisis*, 11–51."

Sure enough, the November 1951 issue of *The Crisis*, the NAACP journal, carried an article written under the pseudonym "Robert Allen," called "Paul Robeson: The Lost Shepherd." It matched Ross's proposals, even to the point of saying, "Nothing that Mr. Robeson can say will be half as important as the very fact of the existence of Roland Hayes and Ralph Bunche, or Joe Louis and Jackie Robinson, of Marian Anderson and Dorothy Maynor." Ross ordered thousands of copies for distribution in Africa. The State Department paid for it; John Foster Dulles himself initialed it; and they shipped the copies over there.

In 1952, the Mine, Mill and Smelter Workers in Canada sponsored a concert for Paul Robeson. The State Department stepped in again. As far as I know, dad's the first American citizen in modern history, and perhaps in the entire history of the U.S., for whom a special presidential order was issued preventing him from traveling outside the mainland to places where a passport is not required. That included Canada, Alaska, Hawaii, the Virgin Islands, and Mexico. Truman's special order was read to dad at the border. Instructions given to immigration agents, who carried sidearms, were that his entry into Canada should be prevented by any means necessary, which meant they were authorized to shoot him if he tried. Yet he was not accused of any violation of law.

The Mine, Mill and Smelter Workers held the concert for him anyway. It was at Peace Arch Park, on the border of Blaine, Washington, and Canada. People assembled on both sides. Some Americans came, and a huge Canadian crowd, something like thirty thousand, was there. They set up the microphone just a few feet on the American side. He sang from there and said, "I want everybody in the range of my voice to hear, official or otherwise, that there is no force on earth that will make me go backward one-thousandth part of one little inch."[39]

Dad felt an enormous responsibility, and he stood up to it. But it would be a mistake to think it was not a burden. He was human like the rest of us, bled like the rest of us. And he couldn't but know that everybody close to him was carrying a load. I mean, mother wasn't going to say anything; my wife wasn't going to say anything; my friends weren't going to say anything; but we caught hell, too. He had to be aware of that. And he felt he couldn't really protect his own family. What do you do if they call you up and say, "You got these two grandchildren you love, huh? We know where they live." What do you do? I had to ask myself that question: What if they come after our kids? It so happens they didn't. But you obviously think about it. You live with it.

And it's true that over time, even for someone as powerful and with as many resources as dad had, intellectual resources in particular, the attrition got to him. They nibble at you by inches—'49, '50, '51, '52, '53—and on and on. I worked with him through those years. As far as he knew, it could go on for the rest of his life. In a certain sense, compared to that, Peekskill is easy. You take your chances, and twenty thousand other people are taking the same chances. There's a certain exhilaration because you're doing something worthwhile. After Peekskill, everybody rallies around for a year or two. But that wears off. People still love you, but you can't mobilize every Tuesday forever. The spectacular things have come and gone. That's when you're all alone: Back in your own apartment, or out on the street, you're all alone.

At the same time, dad couldn't go anywhere for thirty seconds and not be a walking bull's-eye. For him, it was twenty-four hours a day, three hundred sixty-five days a year. You can't run, can't hide, can't even get away by joining a crowd. I could go to Jones Beach. He couldn't go anywhere except to a friend's house. And then the "guys" are sitting outside. So if he does go to a friend's house, he brings the FBI with him. Well, there's a limit to how many people you want to subject to that. Those are, from my point of view, some of the burdens people aren't normally aware of.

But it wasn't all unrelieved nightmare. Bless his heart, his brother, Reverend B. C. Robeson, who was a staunch Republican, a conservative, said, "Paul, come live in the parsonage." That was a hell of a thing to do. My uncle wasn't a stupid man. He knew that when Paul Robeson came to live with him, he and the church would be liable to attack. But he said, "We're family, Paul. You come here." And those friends who said, "Come up and stay with us anytime," knowing what they were letting themselves in for—that meant an enormous amount. So there were those personal redeeming things, very moving things, very warm things that canceled out some of the other.

When dad was called before the House Un-American Activities Committee, it was a difficult point for him. After Peekskill, concert halls and public meeting halls were closed to him; any organization that sponsored a Paul Robeson appearance was threatened. Dad would sing at small meetings and at Black churches, but if you're a great artist and aren't in Carnegie Hall and aren't in the theater, you lose your craft in a certain way. You begin to die as a major performer.

Dad had requests to perform worldwide, but he had lost his appeal on the passport case. The State Department didn't want him wandering around the world talking about colonial independence. And they complained, "During the concert tours of foreign countries he repeatedly criticized the conditions of Negroes in the United States."[40] As far as dad was concerned, he could have been confined here for the next twenty years. In 1956, he was fifty-eight. Suppose it's another five years, and he's sixty-three before he gets to sing again. Or seven years. Each year that goes by, you know your instrument will lose a little more. You're looking only downhill.

Right about then, it was a real downer for dad. That's when HUAC went after him. What was interesting is the way he rose to the occasion. He took them by storm: "I am being tried for fighting for the rights of my people, who are still second-class citizens in this United States of America. My mother was born in your state, Mr. Walter,* and my mother was a Quaker . . . and my own father was a slave. I stand here struggling for the rights of my people to be full citizens in this country. And they are not. They are not in Mississippi. And they are not in Montgomery, Alabama. And they are not in Washington. They are nowhere, and that is why I am here today. You want to shut up every Negro who has the courage to stand up and fight for the rights of his people."[41]

Dad made that place his stage and beat their brains out. Congressman Gordon Scherer said to him, "You are here because you are promoting the Communist cause." And dad replied, "I am here because I

---

*Francis E. Walter, a chairman of HUAC, was a congressman from Pennsylvania.

am opposing the neo-fascist cause which I see arising in these committees. You are like the Alien Sedition Act, and Jefferson could be sitting here, and Frederick Douglass could be sitting here, and Eugene Debs could be here."

It was one of his finest hours. I mean, when he sat down in the chair, in effect he demanded, Who the hell are you to question me? *Who are you!?* He raised his voice, "You are the nonpatriots, and you are the un-Americans, and you ought to be ashamed of yourselves." Walter tried to end it: "Just a minute, the hearing is now adjourned." But dad came back: "I should think it would be . . . and you should adjourn this forever."

That's when I was most proud of him. I mean, "proud" is not even enough of a word. That he could do that from down in the pits, from a low point to come up and take them on—to me, that was one of the most impressive things he ever did.

It's true, the "Communist" label was a problem for dad in the Black community in this sense: "It's bad enough you're Black, but if you're mixed up with the reds, it's too much to bear. I mean, we can't carry that thing." But most of them didn't believe he was a Communist, and the fact is he wasn't. He was an African American who chose radical allies because he thought it was in the interests of Black people, the oppressed. He saw the unity between radicals and Black people here as two separate fists that come together, not both integrated in one. He understood that anywhere—and he taught me this—anywhere you are like one fist with white people in America, without exception, the whites will use you and the Blacks will be weak.

But dad wasn't about to come out and say, "No, I'm not a Communist"; it would betray his principles. He stated in his book *Here I Stand*: "In 1946, at a legislative hearing in California, I testified under oath that I was not a member of the Communist Party, but since then I have refused to give testimony or to sign affidavits as to that fact. There is no mystery involved in this refusal. . . . I have made it a matter of principle, as many others have done, to refuse to comply with any demand of legislative committees or departmental officials that infringes upon the constitutional rights of all Americans."[42]

In 1958, Prime Minister Nehru and his daughter, Indira Gandhi, proposed to honor dad on his sixtieth birthday with an all-India Paul Robeson celebration. The State Department had a whole project afoot to try to head it off. They called in the Indian ambassador to Washington. They implied that if India carried out its plans, they'd have problems with aid. The State Department did everything possible to squelch it. Quite extraordinary, but it failed. Nehru and Indira went ahead with it. Of course, dad couldn't attend.

Dad's isolation in the U.S. was like a quarantine: You cut off access to the media, cut off access to artistic outlets, cut off access to everything—hoping he'll die on the vine. Then you work on him psychologically. Dad had arteriosclerosis, which at a certain point began to affect the flow of blood to his brain. When he started not recalling, there was a certain element of extreme anxiety. If someone in that condition were subjected to psychological warfare, it would be devastating.

By the sixties, the FBI had refined their psychological profiles of individual activists. "Let's see. What's his history? Oh, financial problems? Let's get him through the bank." "This one's got a marriage problem; that one's got a kid who's in trouble; we can use that." Then things begin to happen. You get funny phone calls. You start looking at your friends with suspicion. The system encourages that. It's a paranoia producer, quite consciously. And I'm sure they tried it on dad. I'm sure they had psychological profiles running out of their ears, with all those buggings alone. How many years of phone conversations? They could play a whole organ full of stuff on you, and unless you are in condition to pay it no mind, in a way they've got you. When dad had good days, he would shrug it off. But when he had bad days, he was very vulnerable.

I think they used all the psychological and psychopharmaceutical techniques against the left, against activists. They had a project in the CIA called MK-ULTRA, concerned with how you drug, poison, and eliminate the mental capacities of domestic and foreign "enemies." LSD was developed in the late 1950s by the CIA as just such a weapon, under the name "BZ." It was designed to produce extreme paranoia and suicidal tendencies. CIA agents would practice on each other first by putting a little LSD in somebody's coffee. They found one guy cowering and naked in some fountain across town. Another guy went out of a twelfth-story window. He committed suicide. Then they practiced in bars on unsuspecting derelicts or prostitutes. They could keep it in a matchbox. They could spray it out of a pen. People walked out stoned on LSD. You don't know whether they went over a cliff or not.

Nobody would have believed it all, if the Senate Select Committee that investigated intelligence agencies hadn't brought the whole thing out. But Richard Helms, who was in charge of the CIA, shredded most of the documents. So you wonder about all kinds of things.

In 1958, dad finally got his passport back and went to London. He performed there and in Prague, Berlin, Moscow, Australia, and New Zealand. By 1961, he was anxious to go home to join the civil rights movement. I'm quite sure the government knew that and wanted to keep him out of the public consciousness. Also, my father had planned to go to Cuba on his way home, but he was nervous about arranging it from London. He felt like a sitting duck there because the MI-5, British intelligence, kept track of him very carefully. And the FBI was all over the place. There's a memo from the FBI resident in the London consulate: "Have Paul Robeson's travel plans to Cuba."

Dad decided to arrange the trip from the Soviet Union. During his first seven, eight days in Moscow, he was in quite a whirlwind of activities and seemed to be in mighty good shape. There weren't any qualitative changes from his last medical reports. Then all of a sudden, on March 27, at a "wild party" that invaded his hotel suite, he has this "breakdown," with some bizarre side effects, such as extreme hallucinations and paranoia. My theory is that he was drugged at the party. I don't have a smoking gun—the evidence is all circumstantial—but obviously their track record shows that they were capable of doing it.

If you recall, the Bay of Pigs invasion of Cuba was April 17, three weeks later. Richard Bissell was the CIA operations chief for the Bay of Pigs. Bissell, who had engineered the assassination of Patrice Lumumba in the Congo, and James Angleton, notorious for dirty tricks, were also responsible for the Robeson case. Were they thinking: "Do we want Paul Robeson in Havana with Castro when we hit the beaches?" Obviously the U.S. government had a strong motive to prevent dad from going there then. It's at least a possible reason for them to have tried to head it off. What's really strange is that in its documents on my father in that period, the CIA deleted any information on his health status because they said revealing it would be injurious to national security.

I arrived in Moscow a few days after dad's "breakdown" and saw him in the hospital. What he told me tallied with what I had heard about some strange people being at the party. I began an investigation of my own. I retraced dad's steps. I tried to find out what had happened to his luggage at the hotel—it had vanished. I traced down a number of people who had been at the party and asked them what was going on. I talked to some top officials as to who had been at the party, and they turned ashen. There was no doubt in their minds that anyone could have walked in off the street, including FBI or CIA agents. It was an ideal milieu for somebody to do a hit like that.

In the middle of my investigation, I had a similar experience to dad's. It started after I had dinner with a lot of people who seemed to be friends and acquaintances. I came upstairs, and about an hour later, I hear Lenin talking over the radio. I mean, he's long dead, so I've got a clue I'm not doing too well. I turn on the television set and see Chinese heads on Europeans. I'm clearly hallucinating. I start writing down notes systematically, counting backward from a thousand—anything I can think of to stay sane. It lasts through the night. I can't stay inside. Outside, I'm weightless. Then I weigh a ton. I see halos around people's heads. They finally gathered me up with the white coats and took me away. The symptoms were those of an LSD trip, from beginning to end. In about thirty-six hours I was clean, about the time it takes a drug like that to complete its trip. I've never had an episode like that before or since. Strange.

I think the FBI and the CIA played games in the media, too. There would be major headlines like "Has Robeson Turned Against the Soviets?" or "Are They Going to Kidnap Him Behind the Iron Curtain to Keep Him Quiet?" They floated rumors that his son and wife were plotting against him. It's all garbage, but what are you going to do? Then there it was, in 1963 in the *National Insider*, a complete fabrication: "Paul Robeson Speaks—This Is My Story." They had him saying, "I've been a Communist, Socialist and a Fascist, all three. I'm a little ashamed about being a fascist but the other two weren't so bad at the time." That's ridiculous! And they put racist stuff in there. When you see the way he supposedly describes his own father, a Black preacher, it's an insulting caricature. The interesting thing was that although the article appeared in two sections, on January 6 and January 13, an FBI memo dated the previous December 21 discussed the contents of it. Fascinating. They knew before it came out.

Dad felt at the end of his life that it was worth it, despite all the travail. There's no question about that. In one of his last public statements, during the Freedom Summer of 1964, my father spoke hopefully of the civil rights movement he had anticipated: "The 'power of Negro action,' of which I wrote, has changed from an idea to a reality that is manifesting itself throughout our land. The concept of mass militancy, or mass action, is no longer deemed 'too radical . . . ' Today it is the Negro artist who does *not* speak who is considered to be out-of-line, and even the white audiences have largely come around to accepting the fact that the Negro artist is, and has every right to be, quite 'controversial.'"[43]

My father died in 1976. He was, and he remains, the symbol of the Black American who uncompromisingly insists on full equality. He said, "I am looking for freedom, full freedom, not an inferior brand." His example and his fate strike to the very heart of American racism. That's why the American establishment and its media tried to make Paul Robeson a nonperson while he was alive and have attempted to distort his image after his death.

The Black Freedom
Movement Under Siege

FACING UP TO SOUTHERN TERROR

On December 21, 1956, Martin Luther King Jr. boarded a Montgomery municipal bus to ride in a front seat. His act signaled the end of the 382-day bus boycott, which had been directed against the humiliating treatment of African Americans in public transportation, and the beginning of a movement that would finally do away with the system of American apartheid. However, the reign of terror that had instituted the codes of white supremacy at the turn of the century was now being directed full force against those who were attempting to dismantle those codes.

Shortly after African American citizens had stopped riding the Montgomery buses, a bomb was thrown into Dr. King's home, and other homes and churches were bombed with impunity. Black college students who sat down to eat at "white" lunch counters, first in Greensboro, North Carolina, in 1960 and then across the South, were beaten and jailed. Freedom Riders, under the auspices of the Congress of Racial Equality and the Student Nonviolent Coordinating Committee, were also greeted with beatings and arrests. In Birmingham, the movement led by the Southern Christian Leadership Conference withstood the arrest of thousands, the crack of nightsticks, the ferocity of police dogs, the force of fire hoses turned against children. In 1964, Freedom Summer brought a thousand young, northern volunteers to Mississippi to help SNCC register African American voters and conduct Freedom Schools. Within two and a half months, four people were dead, eighty had been beaten, one thousand had been arrested, and sixty-seven churches, homes, and businesses had been burned or bombed. "The Mississippi experience was almost like being in a war zone," SNCC organizer Cleveland Sellers remembered. "You were constantly under attack."[44]

In Selma, efforts by African Americans to secure the right to vote were met with outbursts of violence. During a peaceful march in nearby Marion in February 1965, Jimmie Lee Jackson was murdered by rioting state troopers. The subsequent protest against Jackson's murder was so brutally assaulted by Alabama troopers and mounted posses that the nationally televised rampage became known as "Bloody Sunday." The effect of the widespread media coverage was galvanizing: Demonstrations erupted nationwide, and in a matter of days a historic march began from Selma to Montgomery—the site of the beginning of the modern civil rights movement. That march, with the passage of the 1965 Voting Rights Act that immediately followed, signaled a significant victory in the Black freedom struggle. But even in triumph, volunteer Viola Liuzzo would be shot to death as she transported demonstrators home from Montgomery.

There was, of course, no relief to be had from local or state law enforcement agencies, legislatures, or courts. Indeed, these governmental bodies were among the worst offenders. To prevent protesters from providing alternative transportation during the Montgomery bus boycott, a state court issued an injunction banning their carpools. To undercut the movement's capacity for protest, state and federal injunctions were issued in Albany, Birmingham, and Selma that forbade mass demonstrations or public gatherings. To drain the movement's bail funds and keep thousands in prison, the state legislature of Alabama drafted a bill that applied only to the city of Birmingham, raising the maximum bond there on misdemeanors from $300 to $2,500. To quell student demonstrations in Americus, Georgia, four SNCC workers were charged with seditious conspiracy, which carried the death penalty. And to secretly disrupt civil rights organizations by using undercover operatives and informants, to promote segregation, and to channel public monies to the White Citizens Council, the Mississippi state legislature established the Mississippi Sovereignty Commission.

There were occasions when the federal government aided civil rights activists. Yet its sporadic response could not be relied on. Indeed, at times it invoked a double standard for dispensing justice. When civil rights activists of Albany, Georgia, were beaten by local sheriffs, the Department of Justice found no reason to act. But the Justice Department aggressively pursued federal indictments against leaders of the Albany Movement on spurious charges of obstruction of justice: Upward of eighty-six FBI agents combed Albany searching for evidence, and a corps of federal marshals invaded the African American community to serve nearly sixty subpoenas.[45] FBI agents failed to even warn activists when the agents had prior knowledge of a planned Klan attack. And yet, as Kenneth O'Reilly notes, "the Bureau routinely forwarded intelligence regarding movement strategies to police departments across the Jim Crow South," sometimes with the full knowledge that the information would find its way into the hands of the Klan.[46] In Mississippi, the FBI cooperated and shared information with the Jackson police, the Mississippi Highway Patrol, the Mississippi Sovereignty Commission, and even J. B. Stoner's National States Rights Party—all hostile to the Black freedom movement.[47]

The struggle nevertheless endured and at long last touched the conscience of America. The story of it is told here by three participants. Walter Bergman, a member of CORE and a Freedom Rider, who was beaten by Klansmen with the foreknowledge of the FBI, spent the remainder of his life in a wheelchair. John Lewis—once a divinity student, then chairman of SNCC, and now a member of the U.S. Congress—weathered the most brutal assaults without relinquishing his deeply felt belief in nonviolence and the possibility of a beloved community. Fred Shuttlesworth, a Baptist minister and a leader of SCLC, withstood beatings, arrests, and the dynamiting of his home to lead efforts to desegregate Birmingham even before the city was propelled into the nation's headlines.

WALTER BERGMAN

I had been the director of research in the Detroit public schools for many years. I was considered the oddball there. I was the first person to employ a Jewish secretary. And I had to do it over my boss's objections: "You don't want to do that. She won't get along with the other secretaries. She'll be shunned by everybody." I said, "Now, do I have the right to pick my secretary or not?" "Of course you do." "Well, this is who I want." That was 1929. Later on, I hired the first Black secretary at the board of education. Again I had quite a problem because the other people didn't want me to bring a Black person into the building.

By the late thirties, they had a Black man working in the employment office. I decided that I would take him out to lunch. I had gone to a rather modest restaurant fairly regularly for a couple of months, and I had gotten to know everybody on the staff. I took him over there one day, and

WALTER BERGMAN

they served us very pleasantly. I had scarcely gotten back to the office when the restaurant manager walked in. He said, "Now, didn't I serve you nicely when you and your Black friend were in my restaurant?" I said, "Yes, you certainly did, and I appreciate that. Of course, that's what I would expect one human being to do for another human being." He said, "But please don't do it again!"

After I retired in 1958, I spent a lot of my time working with CORE, the Congress of Racial Equality. We did a great deal of picketing to break down segregation. We picketed the international headquarters of the

Kresge Corporation, which was close to downtown Detroit. We picketed a swimming pool, and some of us got arrested for that. Then in February 1961, CORE had a conference down in Kentucky. My late wife
and I both went. While we were there, one of the field secretaries of CORE
came back with information about a Supreme Court decision. Not only
were interstate buses and coaches open to people regardless of race, but
now the public facilities, such as rest rooms and restaurants and waiting rooms were to be open as well. We decided right there, in Lexington, Kentucky, that we would see how far south the Supreme Court's decisions actually did run.

That was the birth of the Freedom Rides. I don't think any of us
thought we would accomplish as much as we did. At that time, Black
people in the South had been living in a kind of serfdom to whites. Many
of them were forced into inhuman conditions. What the Freedom Rides
did was to give a stimulus to the freedom movement, which already had
two big boosts: the Montgomery bus boycott in 1955 and the sit-ins at
the Greensboro lunch counters and elsewhere in 1960.

We decided that we would get a group with the same number of Blacks
and whites. Fourteen of us went into training for three days in nonviolent techniques, Gandhi- and Martin Luther King Jr.–type techniques.
We had to be absolutely nonviolent, no matter what happened to us. On
the last day, the leader, James Farmer, asked, "Will each of you under all
circumstances, no matter what the provocation, refrain from reacting violently?" I was sixty at the time, and it wasn't too difficult for me to say
I'd be nonviolent. But there was one young man, a big football player,
who said, "I don't know. If some southern sheriff comes up and tells me
that I've got to move along and starts to shove me, I just can't say that
I won't shove back." So James Farmer said, "Well, we'll have to leave
you behind." That made only thirteen of us, six whites and seven Blacks.

We started our trip south from Washington in two buses. We went
through Virginia with very few problems. When we got to Rock Hill,
South Carolina, we did have a little trouble. A group of whites—I don't
know whether they were Klansmen, but they were Klan-like in their
actions—attempted to prevent the people on the other bus from going
into the station. And they did knock one or two people down, but no
one was badly hurt.

We went further into South Carolina. Our bus had been diverted from
the place it regularly stopped, to a different town. Apparently, it was a
set-up. There in Winnsboro, South Carolina, Jim Peck, who was white,
and Hank Thomas, who was Black, sat down to eat their sandwiches to-

gether. They were sitting on the white side of the lunch counter. Someone told Hank, "You sit over there." He said, "I want to sit beside my friend." They must have had a policeman secreted in the woodshed or somewhere. He came out in no time at all and took them both to jail. My wife was the person who was supposed to watch what happened in case of an arrest. She did, of course, and notified CORE headquarters in New York. Hank Thomas was turned loose about midnight, but Peck was kept all night in jail. In the morning they let him go.

Then we went on to Georgia. In Atlanta, we had dinner with Martin Luther King Jr. The next morning, we boarded two buses and left for Birmingham. I did not go on the first one, the Greyhound. That bus got as far as Anniston, which is the only town of any size between Atlanta and Birmingham. There, the Greyhound was to have a luncheon stop. And there a crowd attacked the bus. They cut the tires, but the bus went on.

Our Trailways bus got to Anniston about an hour later. There was a very peculiar stillness in the town. The bus station had handmade signs in the windows that said "Closed." So I went out to a civilian restaurant and bought sandwiches and drinks for the people on the bus. When I got back, there were three policemen, and later they were joined by a fourth, who stood outside the bus. One of the men, who apparently was in charge of the detachment, came in and talked to the bus driver and then went out. The driver turned around and said, "Before we go any farther, we'll have to rearrange the seating." It was the custom in the deep South to have the Blacks sitting in the back of the bus and the whites sitting in the front. So we knew what the driver meant.

Then eight or ten Ku Kluxers stood up. Some of them had ridden from Atlanta with us, and others had jumped on the bus here in Anniston. When the bus driver told us we had to change our seats, nobody moved. The Ku Kluxers picked up the Black Freedom Riders and tossed them to the back of the bus. Peck and I went up and tried to talk to the leader of the group. They attacked us, hammered us to the floor of the bus. And then they kicked us again and again, until we lost consciousness. That was where I got the injury that has kept me in this wheelchair.

During the entire attack, the four policemen were there, outside. We were less than six inches—how thick are the sheet metal walls of the bus?—well, we were that far from the majesty of the law. But they stood there flat-footed and did nothing.[48]

After we came to and got into our seats, the bus started out for Birmingham. The Ku Kluxers who beat us up stayed on the bus, too. They didn't say a word. But they had coke bottles in their hands, and they were constantly waving them. It was quite an unusual experience. I had crossed the ocean once in a convoy during World War II and was attacked by a submarine. That was a scary situation, too. But I guess this was probably the scariest situation that I have had in my life.

Meanwhile, the first bus had gotten about three or four miles out of the city when the tires that had been slashed in Anniston gave way. The bus had to stop. There was a crowd that followed in cars and trucks. They knocked in the windows, and one of them had an incendiary bomb and threw it inside. The bus was soon filled with black smoke. The mob held the doors closed so people couldn't get out. After a bit, someone said, "Hey, this thing is going to blow up!" Then an Alabama state trooper did his duty. We found some very decent white southerners. And now here was one. He opened the doors and held them open to let everyone off the bus. All the Freedom Riders had to go to the hospital for smoke inhalation. One of them was there for several weeks.

We didn't see this from our bus because we took a different route. When we got to Birmingham, there was not a policeman on the street. Bull Connor, the commissioner of public safety, had said that it was Mother's Day, and he sent all his policemen home to have dinner with their mothers. Actually, we learned later that there were police, a crowd of them, opposite the Greyhound bus station. But the police had assured the Klan that they would stay out of the affair for fifteen minutes, and that's what they did.

When we landed in Birmingham, there was a mob of several hundred people waiting. A great many of them had brown paper bags, but the shape of them was such that it was obvious they had something much more substantial than sandwiches in them—probably hammers or pipe lengths. They attacked us on the loading platform. A Black man was there on his honeymoon and had no connection with us at all. He was rather badly beaten up.

The two people who were supposed to be the test team in Birmingham were an eighteen-year-old freshman from Atlanta University and Jim Peck. They tried to go into the dining room, but never got there. The younger fellow, Arthur Person, was just a teenager, fleet of limb. He got a cut on the back of his head, but he escaped. Jim Peck didn't.

My job was to be the outside man. After waiting a bit, I went down the covered corridor that connected the loading platform with the dining room. There I found Peck, half sitting, half lying, with a great deal of blood on his face. I got him to his feet, and I almost carried him out to the street and then tried to get a taxi. Probably a dozen taxis slowed down and were obviously empty, but when they saw Jim Peck's bloody face and my two beautiful black eyes and swollen jaw, they sped away.

Finally, a taxi did stop, and we went out to Reverend Fred Shuttlesworth's parsonage. We immediately took Jim to the hospital. They sewed him up with fifty-odd stitches in his face. Then they told him he had to get out of the hospital: "It isn't safe for you, and it isn't safe for our hospital." A crowd had begun to gather outside. Reverend Shuttlesworth sent a pair of cars for Peck. Down there, when Black people exercised their civil rights, they went in pairs, never in one car alone.

That night, we had a meeting in Shuttlesworth's church. The people from the Greyhound bus were still in the hospital in Anniston, and others were pretty badly shaken up. There was no one else to speak, so I told them our story. Afterward, there was a great deal of singing. It was a glorious meeting, one of the most exciting evenings I've ever spent in my life. Then someone looked out and said there was a mob outside the church, Ku Kluxers and their friends. So we kept singing until after eleven o'clock, when the crowd outside began to break up and go home.

We stayed at Reverend Shuttlesworth's, sleeping all over his house. As the senior members of the group, my wife and I got a bed. There were constant telephone calls all night long. If a Black person answered, the callers would shout, "Nigger, nigger." And if a white person answered, they'd say, "Nigger lover." Shuttlesworth took it all calmly: "I'm used to this from years of experience." He is a wonderful man, Fred Shuttlesworth. And his wife is equally dedicated. She has been through everything with him.

At that time, Howard K. Smith was in town making a TV documentary, "Who Speaks for Birmingham?" He told us he was across the street when our bus landed in Birmingham and saw the absence of any policemen. Later that evening, he set up his cameras in a motel in a remote part of the city. Four of us went out there, and we were interviewed. When we got out to his motel, the men who were driving us said, "Let's sit still for a minute and see if the coast is clear." Then they told us, "Now you run to that door as fast as you can." When we got back to our cars after a couple of hours, one of our drivers looked under the hood, and another looked underneath the car. I said, "What are you doing there?" "Normal operating procedure. We always check for bombs." It took brave, brave people to live the life that those Black southerners lived.

The next morning, we met to decide what to do. All of us felt there was only one thing we could do. That was to go on to Montgomery, which was our next stop. We went down to the station and lined up for the bus.

The driver refused to take the Freedom Riders, so we waited for the next one. He, too, refused. We decided that since we couldn't go on to Montgomery, there was nothing to do but fly to New Orleans. Reverend Shuttlesworth organized a caravan of cars that took us out to the airport. We got there before the crowd showed up. This time, the police kept the Ku Kluxers from coming into the airport. We got on the plane, but then we had to get off because of a bomb threat. The next flight to New Orleans was canceled, too. We called Bobby Kennedy's office. An assistant attorney general flew down with an airplane that took us to New Orleans. We had a wonderful meeting there. The place was just crowded with thousands of Black and white people.

In 1975, the Senate Select Committee that was investigating intelligence agencies, under the late Frank Church, held hearings on the FBI. A paid undercover agent named Gary Rowe testified that he had been working in the Birmingham Klan for the FBI. Rowe told the committee that he got a message about the Freedom Riders that was meant for the Klan from a Birmingham police sergeant. He passed it on to the FBI. An FBI memo actually quoted that sergeant: "We're going to allow you fifteen minutes. You can beat 'em, maim 'em, kill 'em—I don't give a damn. . . . There will be absolutely no arrests. You can assure every Klansman in the county that no one will be arrested in Alabama for that fifteen minutes."[49]

The FBI had this information. They knew there was an illegal conspiracy between the police and the Klan, but they did nothing to protect American citizens or even warn them of the danger to their lives. In fact, the FBI told Rowe to continue his Klan activities. Apparently, he was more than a messenger. We have a picture of him taken at the Birmingham station on that first Freedom Ride. People identified him by his size and the kind of garment he wore. They said there's no question that he was there and took part in the beatings on the loading platform.[50]

The American Civil Liberties Union helped my late wife and me to file a suit against the FBI in 1977. We charged that they participated in activities that resulted in the attack on the Freedom Riders and the injuries they received. Peck had started a similar suit in New York City, backed by the Emergency Civil Liberties Committee. I went to New York City and testified for him. He was awarded twenty-five thousand dollars in damages, a minuscule sum for his injuries.

Before my trial started, I had to give a deposition. When I told them about the angry mob armed with weapons, the beatings, the missing police in Birmingham, the U.S. attorney had the nerve to ask, "Did you think about making a citizen's arrest when you saw this riot?" What a preposterous question!

The trial itself was held before Judge Enslen in Michigan. The government had produced some of the documents our lawyers requested. Volunteers went over them with a fine-tooth comb to get to the bottom of the whole thing. They would find that one document led to others and that there was more information to be uncovered in documents we didn't have. So we requested them. We wanted to learn what else Rowe might have done and what other FBI agents were in on it.

When the government attorneys refused our request, we asked the judge to order them to turn over those documents. This time, the deputy attorney general of the United States sent the judge a letter in which he refused to comply. The judge was indignant. He said that he had never received such an arrogant letter. A few months later, he announced his verdict. It was that the FBI was liable for our injuries, that they had known about the events in Anniston as well as in Birmingham, and that they could have prevented it if they had wanted to. In fact, he ruled that the FBI had a duty to prevent it.

The judge awarded fifty thousand dollars to us. We had sued for much more, but money wasn't the important thing. It was a principle we won: that the FBI was responsible for protecting citizens and had no right to cooperate with vigilantes by giving them a free hand for mayhem as they did in Anniston and Birmingham.

JOHN LEWIS

I'd grown up in a very segregated community. Signs saying "White" and "Colored" were everywhere. When I would visit the variety stores in the tiny town of Troy, there would be a fountain marked "Colored" in one corner, just a little spigot. In another corner, there would be a fountain marked "White," all shiny and beautiful. Sometimes they were both located in the same corner. I would go downtown to the theater with my sisters and brothers and my first cousins. All of the white children went downstairs. We had to go up to what we called the "buzzard's roost." At a very early age I resented that. I literally stopped going to the movies.

It was strictly a Black world and a white world. As a young child growing up in rural Alabama, I felt that the system was so evil, so vicious, so extreme that it would take some type of extreme good to counteract it. But there was a great sense of hopelessness, a great sense of despair in those days. You couldn't see a way out. It was the Montgomery

JOHN LEWIS

bus boycott, with Martin Luther King Jr., that provided the instrument, the philosophy, and a way to protest, a way to say no. To see fifty thousand people walk the streets for over a year with pride, with dignity, rather than ride segregated buses was a great inspiration. Maybe we could create a better way of life that would respect the dignity of all humankind, where people wouldn't be discriminated against, even in the heart of Alabama.

I came under the influence of the philosophy of nonviolence. I believed in it, not simply as a technique or tactic but as a way of life. I believed in the possibility of change, of the creation of a beloved community. In 1960, I took part in the Nashville sit-ins and was jailed five times during those weeks. And when I was a twenty-one-year-old theology student and a member of SNCC, the Student Nonviolent Coordinating Committee, I signed up to go on the first Freedom Ride.

We met here in Washington, D.C., at some place called the Fellowship House, thirteen of us, both whites and Blacks. We went through a period of training in nonviolence. On the night of May 3, 1961, we all went to a Chinese restaurant. I had never eaten Chinese food before, and this was one of the most unbelievable meals. We were served at a huge table, family style. I remember someone saying, "You should eat well tonight because this may be like the last supper."

We left the next morning, six of us by Greyhound and seven by Trailways, to test the facilities between Washington, D.C., and New Orleans. I was a part of the Greyhound group. We would stop in the evenings in different places, like Richmond and Lynchburg, Virginia, and hold rallies to explain the Freedom Ride to the local people. We continued through North Carolina. In Charlotte, at the Greyhound station, a young Black Freedom Rider went into the so-called "white" barber shop to get a shoe shine. He was arrested and taken to jail. The next day, our Greyhound group arrived at Rock Hill, South Carolina. I tried to enter a waiting room with Albert Bigelow, who was white. The moment we went through the door marked "White Only," some men came up and began to beat us. They knocked me down and attacked Albert Bigelow. That was the first violence we experienced.

I got off the Freedom Ride the next day. I had applied to go with the American Friends Service Committee to East Africa, and they had called me to Philadelphia for an interview. I was going to rejoin the others the following Sunday in Montgomery, but they never got there. Right outside of Anniston, Alabama, the Klan and the White Citizens Council attacked the bus I would have been on. They threw smoke bombs and Molotov cocktails, and the bus caught on fire. The other bus went into Birmingham, where Jim Peck and several others were beaten unbelievably. Bobby Kennedy, who was the attorney general, suggested a cooling-off period. The ride was finally called off when no bus would take them to Montgomery.

That Sunday evening, I flew back to Nashville, Tennessee, where I had been in school, and suggested that the Freedom Ride should continue. The Nashville student movement, made up of deeply committed people, felt we just had to go on. We couldn't allow the violence in Anniston and

Birmingham to stop the Freedom Ride. It was risky. There was a possibility of death. But in a sense we didn't have a choice. We had to go. I will never forget that Sunday evening when we literally begged the SCLC local chapter to provide us with the necessary money to buy tickets for the Freedom Ride. Late that night, we convinced them, and I was selected as the spokesperson from that group. We left Nashville at 6:30 A.M., on Wednesday, May 17, and rode down the highway to Birmingham.

Bull Connor and several members of the Birmingham police department stopped our bus right outside the city limits: "You have a group of Freedom Riders on here." He directed the driver to take the bus on to the Birmingham station. When we arrived, he put us all in the paddy wagon and took us to jail. We went on a hunger strike as part of our noncooperation with the city of Birmingham and with the police.

Around 4:00 A.M. on Friday, Bull Connor took us from our jail cells. It was an eerie feeling, really, because we didn't know where we were going. He drove us about one hundred and twenty miles out of the city and dropped us off in a little place on the state line. It was Klan territory and very frightening. One of the guys had the right mind to say, "Let's try to find the home of a Black family." It was still dark when we came upon a weather-beaten old house. An elderly Black man opened the door. We said, "We're the Freedom Riders." It was dangerous to harbor "outside agitators," but his wife called out, "Honey, let them in, let those poor children in." That probably saved our lives.

We called Diane Nash, head of the Nashville student movement, and told her we wanted to continue the ride. She sent a car to pick us up. We drove back to Birmingham as fast as we could, eight of us. Going down the road, we heard a news bulletin say, "The Freedom Riders were dropped off by Police Commissioner Bull Connor, and now they're back in Nashville." An hour later, another bulletin said, "The UPI is now reporting that the Freedom Riders are on their way by private car back to Birmingham." That scared us, because they knew what was going on. That meant there was close communication between the different police departments and all of our telephones had been tapped.

We got back to Birmingham Friday evening about five o'clock and went directly to the Greyhound bus station. We were greeted by Reverend Shuttlesworth and several other people. Eleven more riders were there, waiting to join us. We were refused passage on every bus and were forced to stay in the waiting room all night. The Klan was outside the bus station. We tried to get a little sleep on those hard wooden benches, but most of us couldn't because we were so excited and tense.

Late that night, Attorney General Robert Kennedy and the Department of Justice worked out an arrangement with the Greyhound Bus Company and officials of Alabama for us to get to Montgomery. We got assurances that we would have protection: a patrol car every fifteen miles and a plane flying overhead. And we did see them along the way. But as soon as we got thirty-five or forty miles outside of Montgomery, all signs of them disappeared.

When we arrived at the bus station Saturday morning, it was eerie. You knew something was about to happen, but you didn't know what. The moment we stepped off the bus, a group of media people came up to us. In a split second, hundreds and hundreds of people gathered, a mob that grew to about two thousand. They had baseball bats, clubs, chains, every conceivable weapon. First they went after members of the press. Anybody who had a camera or notepad was a target. They demolished all of the equipment and beat them up.

You didn't see any police, but you could see the precinct from the bus station. They knew we were coming. They knew, but it was a conspiracy on the part of the officials in Birmingham and the police officials in Montgomery to allow the mob to gather and to beat us.

After they had beaten the press people, they turned on us. Four young women, two Blacks and two whites, tried to get in a cab, but the Black cab driver said, "I can't drive you. It's against the law." Two of the young women who were trying to get away from the angry mob started walking very fast, in a sort of trot. John Seigenthaler, the personal representative of President Kennedy, got between the mob and the two women. He was hit in the back of his head and left lying in the street.

Several people were able to jump over a rail and escape into the post office at the federal building. Some of us were caught by the mob and severely beaten. I was hit in the head and left lying unconscious. While I was still there in the street, the state attorney general came up and read me an injunction from an Alabama circuit court. It enjoined any group from traveling together in an interracial fashion in the state of Alabama.

We were scattered all over the place. There were those who had to be hospitalized. I went to a local doctor's office with a concussion and a big gash in my head. Later we gathered in a little church on the outskirts of Montgomery. Reverend Ralph Abernathy and Dr. Martin Luther King Jr. heard about what had happened and met with us late that Saturday night. They suggested that we have a mass rally at Reverend Abernathy's church on Sunday.

By four or five o'clock, the church was full. You couldn't even find standing room. People wanted to be there in support of the Freedom Riders. The Klan rallied across the street and then marched on the church. You could hear threats of bombing, shooting, and everything. It was so tense and dangerous. We were forced to stay in the church all night. Outside, federal marshals' cars were being burned. Dr. King appealed to people to be calm and cool. President Kennedy threatened to federalize the National Guard, so the governor finally put the city of Montgomery under martial law.

We had a press conference the next afternoon, Reverend Abernathy, Dr. King, Diane Nash, and myself. From the backyard of Reverend Abernathy's home, we announced to the nation that the Freedom Ride would continue, that we would not stop. On Wednesday morning, we left in two groups, one on a Trailways bus, the other on a Greyhound. Some of the National Guard got on our bus and rode with their guns and bayonets. They had jeeps in front and behind the bus. They took us as fast as they could down Highway 80, through Selma, to the Mississippi state line. There, the Mississippi National Guard took over and drove like there was no tomorrow.

We arrived in the city of Jackson and went straight to the bus station. When we attempted to test the facilities there, the police captain arrested all of us, white and Black. We filled the Jackson city jail in two or three days. It was no longer just the twenty-one of us. People were joining the Freedom Ride from all around the country. Then we were transferred to Hinds County jail. And we filled that prison.

They couldn't deal with these Freedom Riders. In spite of our situation, we could still sing songs of joy. We would sing and sing, and the man would threaten to take our blankets, our mattresses, our toothbrushes. They couldn't deal with the sense of faith and hope we expressed when we sang "We Shall Overcome," and "Paul and Silas bound in jail / Had no money to go their bail / Keep your eyes on the prize." You would hear somebody four or five cells down or in another cell block sing. And you would sing back: "I woke up this morning with my mind on freedom." They just couldn't deal with it.*

One morning, the jailer came to our cell: "We're taking you all to Parchment." Parchment is the state penitentiary in Mississippi. Between 1960 and 1966, I was arrested forty times, but this was probably the

---

*Lyrics from "Hold On," by Alice Wine (originally "Keep Your Hand on the Plow"); and from "Woke Up This Morning," by Rev. Osby, additional lyrics by Robert Zellner, copyright 1960, 1963, Fall River Music, Inc. Used by permission.

worst period I ever spent in jail. I was there for thirty-seven days. When we got to Parchment, this guy came up with a rifle and said, "Sing your jitty freedom song, sing your freedom song. We have niggers here who will eat you up." I guess these were the trustees they told to beat up on people. Then they told us, "Take off all your clothes." We had to stand in front of them without any clothing. If you had a mustache, a beard, or sideburns, you had to shave them off. They took us in twos into the shower. While we were there nude, this guy had his gun drawn on us. They tried to dehumanize us by destroying our dignity. I thought about World War II, the concentration camps. I thought about the Jewish community, really. A lot of that went through my mind.

Some of us were literally forced to grow up overnight. Sometimes I feel like I never had a childhood because I had to take on those responsibilities. I was nineteen or twenty, but some were younger than that when they started sitting in. There were kids in grade school, in middle school, in junior high. And we had to overcome the fear of something happening to us, the fear of going to jail. My mother and father and relatives had embedded in us: "Don't get in trouble with the law." They weren't talking about the law, really, but the high sheriff, the white establishment that had become the law and meant bad things for Black folks. But I felt proud of my arrests because I was participating in something that could bring about change in the South.

All through June, July, and August, the Freedom Riders kept coming. In November, the Interstate Commerce Commission issued a ruling banning segregation on all facilities dealing with public transportation. They ordered all bus stations and airports to put up signs that said, "Seating on this vehicle or in this waiting room is regardless of race, creed, or color." You saw the "White" and "Colored" signs coming down all across the South.

We used to refer to ourselves in SNCC as being a band of brothers and sisters, a circle of trust. And there was a sense of community. I felt during those early years, during those high days, that the only true integration that existed in American society was the integration within the movement itself. It didn't matter whether you went to Morehouse or to Harvard or whether you were the daughter or son of a sharecropper— you had been beaten together, you had been jailed together, and you were all in the same boat. You had a cadre of people who were willing to march into hell, really.

After the Freedom Rides, SNCC initiated a voter registration drive. We had to really fight for certain basic civil liberties: the right to assembly, the right to protest, the right to organize. In Selma, Alabama, the sheriff issued an order that no more than three or four Black people could assemble on the street. People were told that they couldn't pass out leaflets or come to a voter registration workshop. They tried to ban mass meetings. They wouldn't actually arrest us for trying to register to vote. They would use one of their trumped-up charges like parading without a permit, disorderly conduct, or disturbing the peace. Most of the charges were eventually thrown out on appeal, but you would need lawyers and money to bail people out. That would take us away from our efforts to organize.

Many of us tended to look to the federal government as a sympathetic referee in our struggle for civil rights. We became disillusioned. In the midst of our effort to desegregate Albany and to win the right to vote in southwest Georgia, the Department of Justice served indictments against peaceful picketers. Yet they never indicted those who were preventing us from exercising our constitutional rights. The question was asked over and over again: "Why?" For the federal government to come along in the middle of our movement, when we had mobilized the whole city of Albany, and return indictments against a group of people fighting for freedom—that sent a message. It incurred great fear and misgivings on the part of those we were trying to organize. And we had the strange feeling it had been sanctioned at the very highest level of government, that it was a political decision.

The FBI also played a very strange role then. On a great many occasions, they catered to the local officials and seemed partisan toward the existing segregationist customs. J. Edgar Hoover, who had such a hatred for Dr. King, saw our movement as a conspiracy. We assumed he was watching us. Instead of the FBI spending their time finding the bombers, the midnight assassins, the brutal racists who denied us our rights, they were out looking for "Communist" influence in the civil rights movement.

The press and media types accused SNCC of being leftist. As a matter of fact, once Rowland Evans and Robert Novak, the political columnists, did a piece on me, saying that I might not be a Communist but I had Communist leanings. I felt that charges like these were made to divert our attention, to take us off of our main focus, to try to get us not to keep our eyes on the prize. And also to confuse our supporters. SNCC had a fantastic network. We had Friends of SNCC around the country—in New York, California, Boston, Connecticut—and on college campuses. They didn't want these people providing resources and money. They didn't want us recruiting college students to come South to work. So it was an attempt to say to a lot of our supporters: You're working with a bad group of people, people who may not really be loyal to the American dream. I think it was a deliberate, systematic attempt to divert our attention and to try to get us to fight among ourselves, to fight some other battle.

Even within the movement itself, even in some of the Black organizations, you had people saying: Maybe you shouldn't be so identified with some of these groups, like the Lawyers Guild. They said there must be something wrong with us because of our associations, that we would elevate Anne Braden and people like her.* But during that period, SNCC took a position that I think was the principled position to take and the right position. We said: Whosoever would, let him come. If you believed in the discipline of nonviolence, if you wanted to end segregation and racial discrimination and create what many of us called interracial democracy, then you were welcome. We didn't get hung up on somebody's past political ideology or leanings.

In 1963, we went through a terrible summer. Medgar Evers had been shot in Mississippi. We witnessed the violence of Birmingham, the police dogs, and the firehoses knocking people down when they were demonstrating. When the local authorities beat us or jailed us in the hundreds, they thought it would stop the movement. But the civil rights movement had been so effective and so forceful that it created widespread support in large urban centers of the North. There was all kinds of support coming from church groups, the academic community, the unions, and the entertainment world. Stars like Harry Belafonte, Barbra Streisand, and Lena Horne raised money for the movement.

I think President Kennedy and Congress saw that something had to be done, that if they didn't act, we'd be headed for a major clash. A civil rights bill was introduced in Congress. Around the same time, the leaders of the civil rights movement decided to have a march on Washington. We met with President Kennedy and informed him of our plans. He was not open to the whole idea of a march. But it was A. Philip Randolph who said, "Mr. President, we will march; we *will* march on Washington."† Of course, we had no idea, those of us sitting in the White House on June 21, that by August 28 we would see two hundred fifty thousand people at the Capitol.

I was the speaker representing SNCC at the march. First, I expressed our dissatisfaction with the civil rights bill as it stood:

---

*For information about Anne Braden and her work, see pp. 184–200.
†A. Philip Randolph, founder of the Brotherhood of Sleeping Car Porters, was the veteran civil rights leader who proposed the 1963 March on Washington.

"There is nothing to protect young children and old women engaging in peaceful demonstrations. This bill will not protect the citizens of Danville, Virginia, who must live in constant fear in a police state. It will not protect the hundreds of people who have been arrested on phony charges. What about the three young men, SNCC field secretaries, in Americus, Georgia, who face the death penalty for engaging in peaceful protest?"

We wanted to know which side the federal government was really on:

"Do you know that in Albany, Georgia, nine of our leaders have been indicted, not by Dixiecrats but by the federal government for peaceful protest? But what did the federal government do when Albany's deputy sheriff beat Attorney C. B. King and left him half dead? What did the federal government do when local officials kicked and assaulted the pregnant wife of Slater King, and she lost her baby?"

They did absolutely nothing! Then I appealed to the people there:

"All of us must get into this great social revolution sweeping our nation. Get in and stay in the streets of every city, every village, and every hamlet of this nation, until true freedom comes, until the unfinished revolution of 1776 is complete."

As I spoke, I looked out at the crowd, at that sea of humanity, and got a great feeling. It was a coming together of America, really. I saw Black and white; young and old; there were Protestants, Catholics, Jews. I saw America at its best: people from Syracuse, Buffalo, Iowa, Hawaii, Alaska, Detroit, Philadelphia, from all over. And there were people from the heart of the deep South. I knew we had won a moral victory, and it was just a matter of time until civil rights legislation would be passed.

The March on Washington, in my estimation, was one of the finest hours for the civil rights movement. But less than a month later, this good feeling was just dashed; we had that terrible bombing of the church in Birmingham that killed four little girls on a Sunday morning. Our work had just begun.

Conditions that existed in the Delta were semislavery. Mississippi, more than any other state in the South, kept people isolated, divided, and suppressed. Counties with fifty to sixty percent Black people had very few, if any, Black registered voters. An NAACP leader had been shot down on the courthouse steps in Belzonia, Mississippi, because he had encouraged people to register to vote. Black people had been shot, killed, dropped in the Mississippi and Pearl Rivers for attempting to register. We felt we had an obligation to bring the nation to Mississippi.

In Selma, Alabama, SNCC's main goal was also to register voters. I'll never forget one march we had as long as I live. On January 18, 1965, it fell to my lot to lead a group of about a hundred people to the Dallas County Courthouse. When we got to the courthouse steps, Sheriff Jim Clark met us. He was a big man, very mean and vicious. And in his hand he had an electric cattle prodder. He would go up and down the line sticking this prodder into people, shocking them in very sensitive areas, men and women. It was very frightening and painful. He came up to me just shaking: "John Lewis, you're an outside agitator. And an agitator is the lowest form of humanity." Then he arrested all of us, pushing us into the paddy wagon and burning us again with the electric cattle prodder.

On March 7, 1965, we planned to march from Selma to Montgomery. One of the reasons was that in neighboring Perry County a young Black man, Jimmie Lee Jackson, had been shot in the stomach and killed by a group of state troopers while he was on a peaceful march. We felt it was necessary to dramatize to the state of Alabama, to the nation, to the world, that Black people wanted the right to vote, the right to participate in the democratic process without being beaten and killed. So about six hundred people, primarily elderly Black women and young children, set out on that march. Hosea Williams and myself were selected to lead it. It was a beautiful Sunday afternoon. We walked in twos from Brown Chapel AME Church. We had no idea that we would be beaten or tear-gassed or bullwhipped.

We started onto the Edmund Pettus Bridge, which crosses the Alabama River. When we got to the other side, we saw a sea of blue—Alabama state troopers. The sheriff of Dallas County, Jim Clark, had deputized all white men over twenty-one who showed up. They were on horseback with bullwhips and clubs. The moment we got across the bridge onto a little grassy area, the commander of the state troopers said, "This is an unlawful march. I'm giving you three minutes to disperse." Only about a minute and a half elapsed when he shouted, "Troopers, advance!"

They put on their masks and began to throw tear gas. Then they waded into the crowd and beat us. I was hit in the head with a club. I remember so well when I was hit and later choking from tear gas and feeling awful. The horses were trampling over people, and I could hear them yelling. I could barely see because of the fog from the tear gas. At one point, I said, "Just let me be here." I just wanted to get it over with.

I don't know how I got back. In some film footage, I saw myself falling down. I turned around after I got up and was knocked down again. But to this day I don't know how I got from the foot of the bridge, across the bridge, back to downtown Selma and the Brown Chapel AME

Church. I do remember standing up in the pulpit there and saying, "I don't understand how President Johnson can send troops to Vietnam, to the Congo, to Santo Domingo, and cannot send troops to protect people who want the right to vote in Selma, Alabama." I do remember saying that that afternoon. And later I was in the Good Samaritan Hospital.

The event became known as "Bloody Sunday." It was the worst form of violence I witnessed in my entire involvement in the civil rights movement. And I think it was a turning point.

Eight days following Bloody Sunday, President Johnson spoke on nationwide television. It was one of the best speeches any president ever made on the question of civil rights. But you must keep in mind that the week before his speech, the American people literally took to the streets. They were angry. There were demonstrations in more than eighty cities. They picketed the White House. People got inside the Department of Justice and got arrested. People were singing in Lafayette Park and by the lawn of the White House. President Johnson complained his daughters couldn't sleep from all that singing. In Europe and Africa and Central and South America, people didn't like what they saw at Selma. So Johnson was forced, almost, to go on television.

In that speech, several times President Johnson said: "And I say tonight we shall overcome." I was sitting with Dr. King, and tears came down his eyes. And the others of us cried. And Lyndon Johnson said again: "We shall overcome." When we heard the president of the United States cite the theme song of our movement, we knew it was just a matter of time until the Voting Rights Act would be passed. And it was passed and signed into law a few weeks later.

When I look back on it, sometimes I wonder why we did it, why we went on in spite of the dangers. Some people died. Some of us came close to death. I remember that occasion in Selma, on Bloody Sunday, when the tear gas was choking me and I thought I was taking my last breath, that maybe this was the last demonstration. But somehow you had to bear witness to what you felt was right and true. It was necessary for somebody, for some group of people during the sixties, to take the stand, to make the move. And we had that sense of obligation, that sense of mission. I think Black people and white people in the South are better because of it.

REVEREND FRED SHUTTLESWORTH

I was born in 1922, so in the thirties I was just a kid. I was raised by my mother and stepfather, and I wound up with six sisters and two brothers. I recognized well that conditions were bad; my family was on welfare. And, of course, I came up under segregation. Everything I knew was segregated. Segregation was the system so decreed and so ruled and, basically, so accepted. And discrimination had no end of intimidative acts, acts of viciousness by the police or the officials. The Black man didn't have too many rights that a white man was bound to respect. There were repeated incidents that, legally or otherwise, you could do nothing about, except catalog them in your mind. They formed a basis for what later brought people out and made them rebel against the past. As Martin Luther King used to say: "There comes a time when the cup of endurance runs over, and men are no longer willing to be plunged into the abyss of despair."

Well, I grew up in Birmingham and finished high school in 1940. I got married in '41 and went to work at the Brookley air force base in Mobile. While there, I was encouraged to register to vote by a person in the NAACP who was very outspoken. A few of those people were tolerated. They were called "crazy niggers" or "biggety, uppity niggers." So long as there weren't too many of them, the system could roll on anyhow. But you had to appreciate those brave people.

I guess the church was the basic thing that Black folk had back then. Even now, the church is the only thing you've got that you can call your own. It can't be taken from you. Property, your status, your freedom—everything else in a system like this can be taken from you. Without the Black church, a Black man could never be fully cognizant of his possibilities. And I'm a product of that church.

While I worked at the air force base, I had an opportunity to read and study the Bible. Even before I went to Mobile, I had felt the call to preach. I was in the Methodist Church then. When we moved, I became friendly with some people who were Baptists, and I went to church with them. I loved their spirit of fellowship. I was baptized in the Corinthian Baptist Church in 1944. I acknowledged my calling to the ministry and was licensed and started preaching. Everybody was good to me. And God made ways, to the extent that I always had somewhere to preach.

My reading of the Bible and what little seminary training I could get made me feel the need of further study, deeper study. I felt this drive so strongly that even though I had built my own house, I gave that up, and my permanent job with the government, and we moved to Selma, Alabama. I was the first married student to live on the campus of Selma University. I got friendly with some people at the First Baptist Church, the oldest Black church in Dallas County. In May of '51, they asked me

REVEREND FRED SHUTTLESWORTH

to become their pastor. I was a young man full of zeal, and people took to me.

But I had difficulties there that made me understand life was no bed of roses, in or out of church. Two or three men would lead the others to sell church property without the congregation voting on it. I was the pastor, but I was supposed to sit in the chair like some kid, while the deacons did what they wanted. Then when I got a job teaching, they didn't want me to do it because I'd be too independent. At our meeting, one of them had nerve enough to say, "We have decided that you're going to stop teaching or else." Well, that got to me. I said, "I'll take the 'else,' whatever that is." To this day, I don't let people threaten me.

But it got to where I was just a bundle of nervous energy. I might have been close to a breakdown. We were going to have a Baptist convention in Oklahoma City at the time. On the train going there, people talked and joked until they fell asleep. I couldn't sleep. It must have been two, three in the morning when I got up and started walking. I went between the cars where they had these half doors. The train was moving so swiftly, you couldn't see what was passing. I just stood there and began talking to God. I said: "Now, I didn't ask you to bring me into the First Baptist. Whatever your motive was, I'm here. I'm willing to suffer, but I just want you to fix it so I don't worry so much." It seemed to me I was talking face to face with God in that blackness. Suddenly I felt a burden being lifted off me. I went back and fell sound asleep for the first time in weeks.

When I look back, that was one of the most moving experiences in my life. I guess God was preparing me for the rigors and the frustrations and the darkness in the civil rights movement, because it was then, as a young man, that I learned the capacity for standing for truth, being willing to suffer for it, and defying anybody to move me from it.

Then, in February of '53, I was called to the Bethel Baptist Church in Birmingham. At Bethel, I got involved in civic duties: getting ditches covered, fixing streets and street lights, and getting rid of dives and vice dens in the Black community, where police openly got their cut. I simultaneously began working with the NAACP. We were getting people to register to vote and instilling civic pride. Later, I was made membership chairman.

In May 1956, Alabama outlawed the NAACP. It was part of a conspiracy between the southern states. The Montgomery bus boycott that had started in 1955 became a massive type of thing, which threatened to overthrow the segregated system. Although the NAACP didn't start the protest, the state officials thought if they outlawed that group, they could kill the drive for freedom.

I was presiding over an NAACP committee meeting when a policeman came in carrying a pistol with the longest barrel I ever saw and a sheaf of papers that reached down to the floor. He said, "You're all enjoined." When he left, nobody knew what to do. One of the members on the board said, "An injunction means that you can't do anything." But I knew, injunction or not, we had to do something. Lucinda B. Robey, who was the only public school teacher with the NAACP, agreed with me. Someone else said, "You could go to jail." I said, "Well, some of us may have to be in jail. Some of us may have to die. We'll let the people say whether they want to fight for freedom or not."

People phoned me from all over: "What can we do?" I knew it would be a daring thing for anybody to call a mass meeting, living in a town with Bull Connor and the Ku Klux Klan. A few preachers warned me not to do it. The lawyers advised against it. But I felt we had to. When they served that injunction, I knew they were trying to kill hope. I called Reverend Lane and Reverend Pruit, friends of mine, and said, "I want you to go along with me in calling this meeting." And I called Reverend Alfred and asked if we could hold it at his church. He said yes.

So we called a mass meeting for Tuesday night, June 5. And boy, from Saturday noon, when I announced it, to the next Tuesday, it must have been on the air and TV hundreds of times: "Reverend F. L. Shuttlesworth, 3191 North 29th Avenue, called a mass meeting of Negroes." Every hour on the hour, it was blasting out my address—telling the Klan where to put the bomb, I guess. It was so upsetting to one minister that he called me Sunday night and said the Lord told him to tell me to call it off. I knew he was nervous, but I was getting a little vexed. I said, "I don't understand. The Lord told me to call a meeting. You go back and tell the Lord that if he wants me to call it off, he'll have to tell me himself."

And, of course, the meeting went on that Tuesday night. There were so many people, a lot of them couldn't get into the church. I gave one of those rip-roaring speeches, and we went on from there. It was the beginning of the Alabama Christian Movement for Human Rights. The people had an insatiable desire to meet for freedom. Every Monday night, we'd meet in a different part of the city. The police would harass people. They would arrest them and accuse them of running through red lights and so on. They'd go into a church and put people out. They did all sorts of things. But people would keep coming. The movement was one of the greatest things that happened in Birmingham. We sang and prayed and organized for freedom.

When the Supreme Court ruled in November 1956 that segregated buses were unconstitutional, we decided we would ask our city commission to voluntarily rescind the segregation law. We were going to integrate the buses ourselves if they didn't. The threat had to be there. And we were ready to carry it out the day after Christmas. I remember preaching that Christmas Eve service about wonderful Jesus. I made a prophetic statement that any day I expected Klansmen to throw a stick of dynamite at my house. A stick!?! On Christmas night, twelve to fifteen sticks of dynamite were put at the corner of the church, where it met the house.

And the head of my bed was right there. It blew the corner of the house off. It blew the front porch columns into the street. It blew the wall between my head and the dynamite away for about twenty feet. The floor was blown out from under my bed, and the spring was shattered. But I was still on the mattress, and I didn't get a scratch.

I was able to get up and shake all that dynamite dust off me. I felt like David: "The Lord is my light and my salvation, the strength of my life." A crowd started gathering. Everybody thought I was dead. The police were keeping people from the house. Finally, a policeman and a trustee, James Revis, who lived across the street, came around. I learned that my wife and the others had gone out through the back. Then Mr. Revis went out to tell the people I was alive. The officer, a Klansman, lingered behind. He wiped his face with a handkerchief. "I didn't think they would go this far. I know some of these people. They're really mean. Reverend, if I were you, I'd get out of town as quick as possible." I said, "Officer, you're not me. You can tell your Klan brothers that if God kept me through this, I'm here for the duration. The fight is just beginning."

And, of course, the next day we went downtown, intent on integrating the buses. We told people not to go to the back: "Sit up front, but don't sit together. Leave space for the white folks." It was a great successful thing. Over two hundred and fifty rode that day. I got on the bus myself and went to the hospital on the south side to visit my daughter. Twenty-one people were arrested, and we filed suit in federal court. These things just kept the mass meetings filled up every Monday night. When things were really hot, we would meet several times during the week, sometimes every night.

In March of '57, my wife and I went down to help integrate the railroad station. The white terminal area was so full of thugs and people, we couldn't get in the door. But when the policemen were going in, we just went right on in behind them and took a seat. LaMar Weaver, a white man, sat down beside me. He was run out into the mob. As it was, my wife and I did get on the train, and that day we integrated the station.

Then, in early September, a few days after the 1957 civil rights bill was passed, my wife and I decided to enroll our kids in the all-white Phillips High School. We were mobbed right in front of it. The police could have prevented that, but they didn't. My wife was stabbed in the hip. My daughter had her foot hurt in the car door by one of the men. And the mob intended to kill me. It was the first time I saw brass knuckles; I was being struck with them. And bicycle chains. I have pictures of the man with the bicycle chain. I don't think they ever did anything to him. Anyway, I was kicked, knocked down, stomped, and had most of my skin scraped off my face and ears. Things were becoming hazy. I began to realize that I had to get to the car if I was going to live. As I staggered back, one guy was so gung-ho to hit me again that he got caught off balance. I just stumbled over him and against the car. My friends dragged me in and drove to the hospital.

When the doctor saw me, I was lying there like a raw pig. He examined my head, and he just knew that I had to have a concussion or something. Finally he said to me, "It's amazing, the many licks and blows you've taken, and I can't find any sign of a concussion or fracture." I said, "Doctor, the Lord knew I lived in a hard town, so he gave me a hard skull."

We had a mass meeting scheduled for that night. I knew the people would be up in arms over this. Some were ready to do violence and tear up white people's homes. I had to be there. I remember the people were lined up almost a block around that little church. I went in and sat at the corner of the pulpit and said, "I guess you're mad." Everyone said, "Hell, yes!" I said, "I'm not mad, and it happened to me. Now Martin Luther King tells us that unearned suffering is redemptive. I recognize the price we pay for freedom, and I'm perfectly willing. So I don't want any violence, don't want anybody to attack a white person." I couldn't stay because I was really ill. I told the same thing to the people on the outside and went back home.

In 1961, we had the Freedom Rides. The group from the Congress of Racial Equality came first. Walter Bergman and Jim Peck were on those buses. One bus was burned by a mob. On the other bus, the riders were beaten up badly. Bull Connor's police were conveniently "sent home for Mother's Day," while the mobs kicked, stomped, and beat the riders to bloody pulps. We were just about to dismiss our service, when somebody came in and said, "There's a man outside asking for you. He's all bloody." Before I could get out and talk to him, in came James Peck. It was the first time I'd seen the human skull. Part of Peck's forehead was hanging open. We sent him to the hospital, and it took over fifty stitches to close it. The riders stayed at my house that night.

Bull Connor and the Klan thought they had stopped the Freedom Rides, but then the kids from Nashville came. Diane Nash of the Student Nonviolent Coordinating Committee called me and said they wanted to continue the rides. I asked her, "Do you know that the Freedom Riders were almost killed here and were given no police protection?" She said, "Their violence must not be allowed to stop us." Well, I was determined to ride with them. But the police came to my house and arrested me. They kept me in jail till the buses left.

To a segregationist, any Black person who would be for freedom, or any white person who would dare to work with Blacks in the struggle for freedom, had to be a "Communist." Anne and Carl Braden and Jim Dombrowski from SCEF, the Southern Conference Education Fund, were some of the bravest people in the world, because they were white southerners who dared to work with Blacks. They were harassed and persecuted. The word "Communist" was used against SCEF to scare people away. But it didn't bother me too much. You see, we didn't need to fear the word "Communist" to the extent that we couldn't work with good folks. And I knew I was too American Black to be Russian Red anyhow.

I appreciated Anne and Carl and Jim and the other people who would lay themselves open, make themselves liable to make things happen. We planned joint activities with SCEF to challenge the system of segregation. Anne and Carl had a whole communications network and somehow were able to get stories to the AP and other wire services. Lots of times, I would write news releases that the Birmingham papers would black out. I would call Anne and Carl, and they would get the news out all over. Everything that they could do to work with and help us, they did.

In 1958, Anne, Carl, and Jim asked me to join the board of the Southern Conference Education Fund. I told them I'd be glad to. I stayed on the board for years, and I could observe among these people no clandestine efforts to overthrow the government. It gave me an opportunity to see how the system tried to destroy the best minds and brains and run them out. So in the spring of 1963, when they asked me to be president of SCEF, I accepted. Right after I was elected, the *Jackson Daily News* had a headline: "Negro Pastor Heads Red Front."

Gloster Current, one of Roy Wilkins's assistants in the NAACP, was in town just then. We were both flying out that evening on the same plane. He saw the paper and was nervous as hell. I knew the word "Communist" just killed the NAACP, and they wouldn't touch anything with SCEF in it. When we got to Atlanta, he went right to the phone to call Roy Wilkins. I asked to speak to him. I said, "Roy, I was with your man when he saw the headline, and I know it might be a source of embarrassment to the NAACP." This was when they had all my cases on appeal—at one time I had between thirty and forty cases pending; my neck was always in the rope. But I told Roy, "If the NAACP finds it unfeasible to take my cases, I will understand." I said, "I fully knew what I was doing, and I'm not going to back out of it." He said, "Reverend, if the *Jackson Daily News* says it's wrong, I know it's right."

Shortly thereafter, I talked to King and Abernathy. At a lot of SCLC meetings, we had spent time discussing this idea of Communism, who to associate with, and so forth. So I took the bull by the horns and said, "Martin and Ralph, I want you to know that I've accepted the position as president of SCEF." Ralph said, "Yeah, and you get out of there." I said, "No, I'm not going to get out of there. In fact, I'm going to get more in it. I think Anne and Carl and Jim Dombrowski are some of the greatest Americans, white or Black, that I've ever met."

I knew the system divided people on the idea of civil rights and civil liberties. I took the position that without civil liberties there would be no civil rights. I told them, "I've decided we have to work together with SCEF. If it's going to be an embarrassment to SCLC, I'm prepared to offer my resignation as secretary." Martin said, "Oh, no, we won't accept it." It never was broached again. And Anne will tell you, it was because of my stand that we got SCEF and these other organizations to begin working together. So, you know, God uses you for different things.

We kept on fighting all of the facets of segregation legally. We sued to desegregate the parks. But when we won the parks case, it was a pyrrhic victory. The city closed all the parks and playgrounds. So I began to think we needed a different type of struggle, a nonviolent confrontation with segregation. It was time to ask Martin Luther King and Ralph Abernathy down. They would bring the spotlight to Birmingham and to Bull Connor, the symbol of police brutality in the South. It would shake the whole country. The SCLC needed Birmingham because their campaign in Albany had been no more than a standoff. And in Birmingham, we had already laid the basis for the last seven years with the Alabama Christian Movement for Human Rights. "We've been talking about filling the jails for freedom," I told them. "Now's the chance to do it. You've got people here who will follow me." It was on that basis that they came. And as God would have it, the time was right for the movement.

Our demands were the desegregation of all store facilities, nondiscriminatory hiring and the upgrading of people from domestics and sweepers to clerks and other better-paying jobs, and the establishment of a biracial committee to work out a timetable for desegregating other areas. Our idea was to boycott the downtown stores for the Easter shopping season, picket, demonstrate, and do whatever else needed to be done to attack segregation. Any nonviolent strategy that would work would be used. We agreed that Martin, Ralph, and I would meet every morning to discuss plans. And we made an agreement that all public statements would be issued jointly.

Along with Martin, Ralph, Wyatt Tee Walker, and myself, we had people like James Bevel and James Orange to help organize. Reverend Charles Billups and I led the first wave of demonstrators. Forty-two of us were jailed. Some people in prison were there two, three, and four times. You must remember that there was so much intimidation; many Black people worked for whites who would fire them if they were identified with the movement. And some people were saying that Martin hadn't marched, hadn't gone to jail. But he was more than just a local leader. He had to speak all over to help raise money for bail and other things. It wasn't intended that he would go. Then he himself decided to march on Good Friday. That was his way of dramatizing it.

But we were a long way from getting enough people to fill the jails. That's when we made the decision to let the schoolchildren come in. They were our salvation, actually. The young people left their classes to major in "Learning Freedom." They tried to keep them in school, but the kids would break over the fence and come. We held workshops to teach them nonviolent discipline. Dr. King would preach about unearned suffering being redemptive. We told people that they must not have any weapons at all—I used to say, "Don't even carry a toothpick."

It's amazing how people can discipline themselves when they get caught up in a movement. Those kids had such a discipline as you'd never seen before. They'd be in these workshops, and then they'd just begin moving out. First they headed for city hall and the county courthouse. Then the various stores and so forth. They were sitting in, demonstrating. They kept on marching in disciplined arrays until for the first time Birmingham's jails were filled up. We had to be down there in the courthouse almost daily because so many people were arrested, so many children were processed. I knew we were winning when I went to court and the judge couldn't sentence me. He said, "Mr. Shuttlesworth, I regret that because of the overcrowded condition at the jail, we have no place to put you." I said, "Your honor, we're making progress."

When there was nowhere to put us, they turned the dogs and the fire hoses on us. That stream of water would knock the bark off of trees at seventy-five feet. It would just wash kids down the street, knock grown folks off their feet, even tear the clothes off people. I was struck with a fire hose the day three thousand children and adults demonstrated. The streets themselves were filled with kids. The police tried to stop them, but you can't stop thousands of people. They'd expect us to start downtown one way, and we'd go another way. But one group of kids was driven back to the Sixteenth Street Church by firemen with high-powered water. I helped get all the kids off the street and into the church. I was just going to go down in the basement when I heard a fireman say, "Let's put some water on the Reverend." I turned around, and a powerful stream of water was already arching toward me. I threw my hands up and turned my face to the wall. The force of water slammed me against the concrete. My chest ached, my head pounded, and my heart felt like it would burst. I really thought I was dying. They rushed me to the hospital.

The next day, my wife and Reverend Gardner took me on back to the motel. Before I could get into bed good, Andy Young came in and said that Martin wanted to see me, that it was important. When I got there, Martin was saying, "Fred, we've got to call the demonstrations off." I said, "No, sir. We promised to demonstrate until we get something." We had told the folks, "You go to jail for freedom, and we are not going to call it off till we have a victory." That was our agreement. Martin said, "Well, the merchants claim they can't negotiate while there are demonstrations." I said, "The hell, they've been negotiating with demonstrations going on all this time!"

Burke Marshall and John Doar from the Justice Department were there. I found out Kennedy was planning to have a press conference in Washington and King was going to have one in Birmingham to announce a truce. I said, "Go ahead and have it. As soon as you have yours, I'll have one and announce the demonstrations are not over."

Martin told Burke, "We've got to have unity." I said, "We won't have it like this." And Burke said, "Well, we made promises to these people." I said, "Burke, any promise you made that I have not agreed to is not a promise. In fact, I never liked the idea of you talking to the merchants and then talking to us. We should be talking directly." Then I told Martin, "I'm going back home and get into bed. If I see on television that you have called it off, I'm going to get up and with what little strength I have, get those three thousand kids and go back on the street."

I don't mean this as a mark of deprecation to Martin Luther King. I would never want to detract from what he was, because King was the man for the age. But a man is a man and not God and is subject to human frailties. King had so much pressure on him. Then John Doar had Bobby Kennedy on the line. I heard John say that they had developed a hitch, "the frail one." I said, "I presume you're talking about me. Tell him I'm not so frail as to go back on an agreement I made with people who have been jailed and beaten up."

I know now why the Lord had me come, sick as I was. If we had called the demonstrations off, we never would have gotten an agreement. The merchants would later say: "We didn't promise you anything." In '62, they had given me their hand across the table that they were going to come up with something, and they didn't. The system is never prepared to give in. They always want you to give in. But we didn't have anything to back down for. So I wouldn't have cared if hell had frozen over. Burke went right on back and got the merchants to agree to our demands. The next day, Martin and I held a press conference and announced the decision.

Birmingham was the crucial point. And Birmingham was the toughest. I was prepared to give my life. In fact, I thought that I would be the first one to get killed. Everyone thought that. My church was bombed twice, I was beaten bloody and knocked unconscious with a fire hose. The city had me on so many charges: trespass, trespass after warning, conspiracy to violate a city ordinance, violation of a city ordinance, et cetera. And then they'd get me with breach of peace. I never was part of the sit-ins, but I got four convictions out of that.

Yeah, I went to jail so many times, I quit counting. Several times, they put a vagrancy warrant against me to keep me in jail. But I was a full-time pastor, so after two or three days, they would drop that and charge me with violating a city ordinance for trespass or something. Every time I went to court, I knew the judge was going to give me as much as he could. And many times when I was in a lower court on one charge, the state appellate court or state supreme court would affirm some previous decision that same day. I was involved in more than forty lawsuits. I knew what they were doing, and it wasn't going to stop me. When the city sued me, I sued the city.

I'm invariably asked: Would I do it all over again? I look back and try to find something that I might have done differently. I had to come up with this answer: Given the same circumstances, the same motivation, the same level of understanding, the same fearlessness I had then, and the same feeling that God was with me, I would do the very same thing over and over again, just like I did then, without any difference.

IN THE MIDST OF THE STORM

When Anne and Carl Braden bought a home on behalf of a Black family in an all-white community in Louisville, Kentucky, in 1954, the house was firebombed. In the perverse logic of southern justice at the time, the grand jury investigating the bombing charged the Bradens with sedition.

The trial, conducted with the assistance of HUAC and the FBI, incited racist and anti-Communist passions against the couple.[51] It was an object lesson for whites who dared to act in unity with African Americans.

Three years later, the Bradens were asked to join the staff of the Southern Conference Education Fund, which in the late 1940s had become "probably the most militantly anti-segregationist force in southern life."[52] By the mid-fifties, SCEF had to contend with the red scare at its height as well as with the rage that swept the white South in response to the Supreme Court's school desegregation decision in *Brown v. Board of Education.* "Like the McCarthy era," Kim Lacy Rogers writes, "the era of Massive Resistance stifled dissent and civil liberties in the South, subjected Black activists to terrorism, and destroyed southern liberalism as a political force for nearly a decade."[53] SCEF and the Bradens were indeed in the midst of the storm.

In 1958, HUAC called Carl Braden to appear at its hearings in Atlanta.[54] Meanwhile, legislatures in southern states such as Florida, Tennessee, and Kentucky established their own un-American activities committees. In 1963, the Louisiana Un-American Activities Committee raided SCEF offices in New Orleans and arrested its officers for operating a subversive organization. Although Black civil rights organizations and white liberal groups protested the arrests, the red-baiting of SCEF made any close association too uncomfortable. "Local activists found the 'communist' smear simply too controversial to contest," Rogers says in her study of the New Orleans civil rights movement. It "confirmed the lingering power of McCarthyism* in the changing South."[55] But if the civil rights movement was susceptible to the "lingering power of McCarthyism," it was also, more significantly, instrumental in dispelling its effects. The massive demonstrations of the Black freedom struggle, in the face of historic restraints, became a moral force that legitimized dissent for others.

A small but persistent band of white southerners was part of the movement to end segregation. In 1989, Anne Braden, a lifelong opponent of white supremacy, was honored by the American Civil Liberties Union "for distinguished lifetime contributions to civil liberties in the United States."

---

*The term "McCarthyism" is something of a misnomer. Political repression associated with the onset of the Cold War began before Senator Joseph McCarthy came on the scene and continued after he left, and it assumed more forms than the hearings of congressional investigating committees. "McCarthyism" has, however, become a generally accepted term for the political hysteria of that era.

ANNE BRADEN

Looking back, the sedition case my husband and I were involved in was certainly a turning point in our lives. We were living here in Louisville, in this house. Both of us were newspaper people by profession. Carl worked at the *Courier Journal*. I wasn't working at a paying job then because I had two babies, but I was doing an awful lot of work. I was secretary of the women's auxiliary at church. I was active in the NAACP membership drive. Carl and I were both part of a statewide committee to repeal the Kentucky school segregation law. We were also involved in trying to break down discrimination in hospitals.

In the spring of 1954, a Black friend, Andrew Wade, asked us if we would buy a house and transfer it to him. He and his wife had one child, two and a half years old, and another on the way. They were crowded into a small apartment and were anxious to move out of the city. Andrew had tried, but as soon as sellers found out he was Black, he wouldn't get the house. He decided the only way left was to have a white person buy it for him. Before he came to us, he had asked several others. For one reason or another, they refused. But we felt he had a right to a new house and never thought twice about doing it.

The section Andrew Wade picked turned out to be one of the places whites had moved to get away from Blacks. And the Wades moved into their new house the weekend before May 17, 1954, the day the Supreme Court decided that segregated schools were illegal. We caught some of the first fury people felt as a result of that decision. All hell broke loose immediately. Shots were fired into the Wade house, a cross was burned nearby, and a rock was thrown through their window with a note: "Nigger, get out." Threatening calls came all hours of the night, and hate-filled groups milled around.

A Wade Defense Committee was formed that had strong support in the Black community, but not a lot of whites. We got the police to put up a guard, which we never really trusted. Some people volunteered to stay all night to help the Wades keep watch. By the end of June, just as things seemed to be quieting down, somebody blew up their house. Dynamite was set under their little girl's bedroom. Luckily, she had gone to spend the night with her grandmother. Mr. and Mrs. Wade happened to be talking to a friend on the other side of the house. It was just by the grace of God nobody was killed.

The Wades moved back with relatives. Things worried along all summer. We and other concerned people kept up an agitation for the police

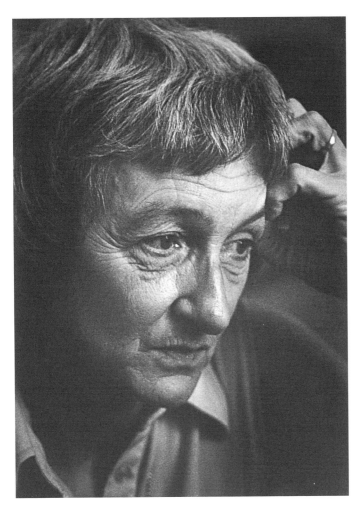

ANNE BRADEN

to catch the persons who blew up the house. At one point, we really thought they were going to do it. The police chief, whom Carl had known from way back, called him down to his office. They had a report that our house was going to be blown up next, and he wanted to put a guard out here. He told Carl they had a confession from the man who set the dynamite and there'd be an arrest in a few days.

There never was. They knew who blew up the house. It became public knowledge eventually—he was an ex-county policeman—but there weren't any arrests. We kept sending delegations to the commonwealth's attorney, the sheriff's office, the county judge, the mayor, the city police, to everybody. Finally the county prosecutor submitted the matter to a grand jury.

The day they met, September 15, was my son's third birthday. I was the first one called. I'd only been there a few minutes when I realized it was not the bombing that was under investigation. It was me! They began asking what organizations I belonged to and what books I had in my house. I'd heard that questions like those were being asked by the House Un-American Activities Committee, but I didn't expect them from a grand jury. I told them, "It's none of your business what my affiliations or reading habits are. It doesn't have a thing to do with who blew up this house."

The same thing happened when Carl went there. We called the newspapers because we didn't think they should be able to get away with this sort of thing in secret. The next day, the prosecutor made a statement that there were *two* theories about the bombing. One was that the neighbors blew it up to get the Wades out of the area. The other was that it was a Communist plot to stir up trouble between the races and bring about the overthrow of the governments of Kentucky and the United States.

The prosecutor was developing the theory that Wade would never have thought of moving there on his own, because Black people are really happy with things as they are until white radicals stir them up. And a lot of people really went for that. I think it's one of the psychological defense mechanisms many whites use to keep from facing the fact that their society is wrong. If those "dirty Braden radicals" stirred this up, then you don't have to worry about whether your society is depriving Black people of housing. By the beginning of October, instead of the grand jury producing indictments against the people who blew up the house, those of us who had been openly supportive of the Wades were charged with sedition.

The Kentucky sedition law was passed during the Palmer raids after World War I. It carried a twenty-one-year jail term and a ten-thousand-dollar fine. The only other time it had been used was against Theodore Dreiser and some others who came down to investigate conditions in the coal fields during the thirties. But it never came to trial then. Now they indicted seven of us, including Carl and me and Vernon Bown, a young white man who stayed with Mrs. Wade during the day while Mr. Wade worked. The grand jury never could understand why a white man would move in with a Black family. It was beyond their comprehension.

Two weeks later, they brought a second charge against five of us for conspiring to blow up the house. They also indicted Vernon on a plain bombing charge. He told the prosecutor: "Since the issue in this case is who bombed the house, try me first." Of course, they wouldn't do it because they didn't have a bit of evidence for that ridiculous charge. In fact, Vernon was in Minnesota the night it was blown up.

Then they raided our house and took all of our files. We'd been in touch with many different groups, and we had folders on left-wing organizations. They took a lot of our books. Carl had grown up in a socialist home, and he had a Marxist and left-wing library. They took anything with a Russian name: books by Tolstoy, Dostoyevsky, and Turgenev from a Russian literature course I had in college. The commonwealth detective who went through them testified that he didn't really know too much about books. When he was in school, he said, they made him read, and it turned him against books, and he hadn't read much since.

It would have been funny except that it was such a hysterical time. In the midst of the fifties atmosphere, the combination of anti-Black and anti-red mania gripped this community. If you haven't lived through a community hysteria, it's hard to imagine. It's still hard for me, looking back, to believe it. There was talk on the streets about how Carl and I should be lynched. People were so scared. Some Black women told us that the whites they worked for in the East End were going through their libraries and getting rid of books. In a couple of instances, they bundled them up in sheets, weighted them down with rocks, and threw them into the Ohio River. People would call up on the phone and disguise their voice and say, "I'm really with you, but I can't say so publicly." Friends we had known for years were afraid to speak to us, afraid of guilt by association.

Carl was tried first. It was December. The courtroom was so tense that if you struck a match, I think it would have exploded. Every once in a while, they'd imply that we blew up the house, that Vernon Bown's radio was used to set off the dynamite. They introduced our books; tables of them were on trial. But the main testimony came from nine "expert" witnesses, gotten from the House Un-American Activities Committee. They were there to create atmosphere. None of them claimed to know Carl, but they testified that anybody who read those books was probably a Communist. They said that the purchase and resale of the Wade house fit in with the Communist program for the South, of taking land away from white people and giving it to Black people. They actually got on the witness stand and said that.

Carl told the jury why we bought the house for the Wades, how that was related to his ideas about segregation. He testified that he was not a Communist. Then they put on in rebuttal a woman who testified that he was, and there wasn't any doubt who the jury was going to believe. Carl and I later agreed it had been a mistake to respond to the Communist issue.

The trial lasted thirteen days, the longest one ever held in Louisville. Carl was convicted and sentenced to fifteen years in prison and a five-thousand-dollar fine. The hysteria had gotten everybody's mind off the real issue, whether a Black family has a right to live in their house. The fact is, the Wades were never able to move back, and the real dynamiter was never punished.

Carl's bail was forty thousand dollars, the highest ever set in Kentucky. We didn't have access to any money, so he stayed in jail till summer. My trial was set for February 14, but for some reason that I never understood, they postponed it to the 28th, and then again and again until April, when they agreed to put off all our trials until the higher courts ruled on Carl's case. If they had gone ahead and tried me at that point, I'd also probably have been sentenced to fifteen years.

There were a number of state sedition cases going on at that time. There was one in Florida, there were Dirk Struik and others in Massachusetts, and Steve Nelson in Pennsylvania. In the Nelson case, the Pennsylvania court threw out the state sedition law. When the state of Pennsylvania appealed to the U.S. Supreme Court, Frank Donner got us to file an amicus brief.* Carl later heard from reporters he knew that our case had influenced the justices. They saw it as a horrible example of what happens when you turn every local prosecutor loose with a state sedition law.

The crux of the Supreme Court decision was that the federal government had preempted the field of sedition with the Smith Act. The decision came down in the spring of '56, but the Kentucky court took its time before it finally threw out Carl's conviction. It was obvious that they'd have to drop the sedition charges against the rest of us, but the bombing charge against Vernon Bown had nothing to do with the sedition law. We went into court and asked that Vernon be tried. There was no excuse left for them not to. Whereupon the prosecutor got himself up on the witness stand and read a long statement, asking that all the charges

---

*Frank Donner was a labor lawyer, civil libertarian, and author of books on federal, state, and local secret police agencies in America.

be dropped. He said everyone knew Vernon had blown up the house, but he couldn't prove it, so that charge should be dropped, too.

As I look back, it really seemed bad at the time. We had two little children, and we thought we would be in prison for years and years. But later on, I realized it was the best thing that ever happened to us. Between 1954 and 1957, Carl and I crisscrossed the country several times, talking about our case. People all over were losing their jobs and going to jail. Our case was so blatant and made it so clear what all this witch-hunting led to that it provided a weapon for those who were resisting. We became part of that resistance movement, a small group of people who were scared but not intimidated and were still fighting. They were the soul of America. And it was a wonderful experience to meet them. From there, we were propelled into working full time for the Southern Conference Education Fund while the tremendous civil rights movement was building up. If I die tomorrow, that was worth living for and being part of.

When you get involved in trying to change society, the people who run things don't just let you do it without hitting back in some way. That's a given. There's always the temptation, when things get rough, to withdraw. And to a certain extent, we whites usually can. I was lucky, in a way, that I never had to withstand that temptation. After the sedition case, life burned my bridges behind me. And looking back on it, I'm glad it did.

I was born in Kentucky, a descendant of the first white child born there—white as compared to Indian. My family saw it as a mark of distinction. The white southern mentality was literally a Nazi, fascist sort of thing. The attitudes of people I grew up with were not just that Blacks were inferior. To them, the South was the last haven of pure Anglo-Saxon culture, and the rest of the country was corrupted by all sorts of unpure strains. New York was so bad because it was filled with a lower breed of humanity from southern Europe.

It was agonizing to me when I had to face how wrong all this was. I thought of the people I grew up with as good people—and they *were* good people in so many ways. But their lives were distorted by the racism they absorbed from the cradle. It seemed tragic to me then and still does.

We moved to Mississippi when I was a baby and to Anniston, Alabama, when I was seven. I don't know when my ideas about segregation began to develop. I've never known any white southerners in the civil rights movement who could point to the one moment they saw a blazing light. You always felt something was wrong. It's like photography: The image is there the whole time, but it only takes shape and becomes clear in the developing fluid. That's sort of what happened to me. Nothing jived with what I had been taught in church about the brotherhood of man. And nothing jived with what I was taught about democracy and what a great country this was.

My college years exactly coincided with World War II. I was part of a generation affected by a spillover of thirties liberalism and a revulsion to the racist philosophy of Nazism during the war. I wasn't that unusual then. Many of my friends in college were not in favor of segregation. We rejected our parents' ideas about race, just as we rejected them about sex. But I don't think any of the people I went to college with ended up getting thrown in jail for sedition by the time they were thirty. And what makes the difference, what makes some get involved while others fade back into the scenery—which is what most people did—is accident. I think it's who you meet in certain times of your life, what your experiences are.

When I left school, I started working for newspapers. Covering the police courts in Anniston and the courthouse in Birmingham taught me that there were two kinds of justice, one for whites and one for Blacks. I saw long lines of Blacks, mostly young war veterans, who tried to register to vote. And they wouldn't register any of them. I came up against brutal injustice. I saw a Black man convicted of assault with intent to ravish, because a white woman testified that he passed her on the other side of the road and looked at her in an insulting way. I mean, literally that's all she could say. He was sentenced to twenty years in prison.

I felt all alone in my outrage and began to wonder if I was crazy. I had to get away from there. I came to Louisville, thinking that if I worked on the newspapers a couple of years—the *Courier Journal* or the *Times*—I'd be able to get a job in New York or Chicago. I'd get away from the South and advance my career as a reporter at the same time. But when I got to Louisville, I found a movement here; people were doing things. Then I found Carl. He was a labor reporter and came from a very different background. Carl grew up in a poor, working-class family. His mother was a devout Catholic. His father, a railroad worker, got fired during a strike when Carl was eight, and many days all they had to eat was beans. His father was a follower of Eugene Debs and used to take him to meetings. Carl combined his mother's and father's influences into a need to do something about the injustice he encountered.

I guess the most important year in my life was that first year in Louisville. I realized the people I had grown up with—my family, my friends, the people I loved and still love today—were just plain wrong on how they treated Blacks and bettered themselves by taking advantage of them. The hardest thing for any of us to come to grips with is that our own society is wrong because we project our ego onto our society. You really have to turn yourself inside out. But once you can do that, everything begins to fall into place.

My personal values changed. Up to then, I'd been very ambitious, wanting to get ahead and be a big reporter. Now I decided I didn't want to work for an establishment paper and just be an observer of life, to sit on a mountaintop and watch the Lilliputians down below. I had been against segregation but had never done anything about it. Now I wanted to be part of this movement for change. I got head over heels involved, not only in the civil rights movement but in the peace movement.

I became active in the Henry Wallace campaign. At a national Progressive Party meeting, I learned about Willie McGee, a Black man about to be executed for rape in Mississippi on what was clearly a frame-up. I got very interested because the myth of white womanhood had been used for years to murder Black men. On the last weekend before he was killed, the Civil Rights Congress asked people to go to Jackson and talk to the governor. I went with a group of twenty women. On our way, the cops stopped us and took us to jail for "protective custody." One of them was going on about people who come from New York and don't know anything about the South. I said, "I think I know a little bit. I've lived in Mississippi, and I'm ashamed of this state today." He got absolutely furious and threatened to kill me. You see, I was a "traitor."

Carl and I went to work for a group of trade unions. We set up an information center for them, put out publications, and trained some of them to put out their own newspapers. During the Korean war, we circulated peace petitions. It's interesting to compare the two movements, the lonely few who opposed the Korean war and the mass protest against the Vietnam war. What had happened in between was the civil rights movement. So we were involved in all these things. At one point, Carl went back to the *Courier Journal* because it was a way of making a living. That's what he was doing when Andrew Wade asked us to buy the house for him.

The *Courier Journal* fired Carl right after the trial. It had taken us about three years to win the sedition case, and then we had to figure out what we were going to do. It wasn't just a matter of economic survival. There didn't seem to be anything political we could do in Louisville. People were so afraid of us here, we couldn't call a meeting in a phone booth. Our out-of-town friends were pressuring us to move some place where we could be more effective. Yet I had the feeling we shouldn't go. I couldn't give a rational explanation, but something told me you just don't leave where you've been under attack, that he also serves who only stays. And I was looking for someone to support my position.

I wrote to Aubrey Williams, a great southern liberal in the best sense of the word. He'd been involved in the New Deal and had become a close associate of Franklin Roosevelt. He was active in the Southern Conference for Human Welfare and then became president of the Southern Conference Education Fund, SCEF. He was a haven in a storm, supporting anyone who got in trouble. During our sedition case, Aubrey became friendly to us. So when I was going through this turmoil about whether to leave Louisville, I sent him a letter. Aubrey, always dramatic, wrote back: "You have shed your blood on the streets of that city. The only way you should leave Louisville is in a coffin." We stayed.

Aubrey spoke to Jim Dombrowski about getting us to work for SCEF. It had started, actually, as the educational wing of the Southern Conference. By the time the Southern Conference had voted itself out of existence, in 1948, SCEF was developing a life of its own. Jim Dombrowski, the architect of the ongoing SCEF, was one of the greatest people who ever lived in the South. He was a founder, with Myles Horton and Don West, of Highlander Folk School.[56] He'd been involved in various struggles for social justice since the early 1930s. He saw the need for a group of Blacks and whites working together with a one-point program: End segregation in the South.

Everyone involved in civil rights activities in 1954 knew the Supreme Court decision on the schools was coming that year. They were pretty sure it would be favorable. SCEF began planning a series of conferences to bring people together in different communities for compliance. I think Senator James Eastland got wind of it and decided to attack SCEF. As head of the Senate Internal Security Subcommittee, he called hearings in New Orleans in March 1954, the same year our case started in Louisville. They were flamboyant hearings with a lot of publicity that played on the very same syndrome of whites stirring up Blacks. The white leadership of SCEF was called. I think Aubrey was subpoenaed. Jim was, as were Myles Horton, Virginia Durr, and others.* That moment in history was

---

*Virginia Durr, a native of Montgomery, Alabama, was a founding member of the Southern Conference for Human Welfare in 1938. The SCHW called for anti-lynching legislation; federal funds for education, recreation, and housing; and an end to segregation. Virginia Durr led the group's effort to abolish the poll tax in the South.

tremendously important. Up to then, there had been growing support for school desegregation. But Eastland was able to cripple the plans for regional conferences with his red-baiting.

When Rosa Parks sat down in that bus in Montgomery on December 1, 1955, it was a turning point in history. Yet nobody can tell why the Montgomery bus boycott happened then and there. It spread like wildfire. There were bus boycotts in Shreveport, Louisiana, and Tallahassee, Florida, and all over the place. It turned into a mass movement, and it was the beginning of the end of the pall of the fifties.

That was the period Carl and I went to work for SCEF. They didn't have much money, so we worked for practically nothing at first. Our main job was to reach white people and help them see that civil rights was their battle, too. We didn't have many resources, and we were fighting against a lot of fear. We traveled around, linking up with college professors, students, teachers, professional people, and ministers—many of whom lost their churches when they took a stand for equal rights. SCEF didn't make any mass breakthroughs in the white South, but we opened some doors and got a few white people on the picket lines, so it was not always white versus Black. We set an example, raised the issue, and provided a way for people to participate.

SCEF was always under attack. HUAC came south in 1958 and subpoenaed a whole bunch of people, all of whom had been active in something. Modjeska Simpkins, vice president of SCEF, had been looking for a way to tell HUAC to stay out of the South. The first thing you know, we had a letter going, and two hundred Black leaders signed it. In essence, it said: We've got enough problems down here. Our churches are being bombed. Our kids are being attacked as they go to school. The last thing we need is the House Un-American Activities Committee coming here to attack white people who are supporting justice. So don't come here unless you're planning to investigate who's blowing up the churches and who's conspiring against our rights.

That letter was the first mass protest against HUAC. We published it as an ad in the *Washington Post*. I always figured Carl's and my subpoenas to testify before HUAC were for that. HUAC's mistake was coming South at a time when the Black movement was unfolding, and people saw that they were really attacking those who were for civil rights. To a certain extent, there was a coming together of the Black civil rights movement and the white civil libertarian movement. It had a tremendous impact.

HUAC was still able to do its damage in 1958, though. My subpoena was postponed, but Carl was cited and convicted for contempt when he took the First Amendment. Carl told them, "My beliefs and my associations are none of the business of this Committee." I wrote a pamphlet with that title. Carl used to say that he always went to jail and I wrote the pamphlets.

A lot of the attacks on SCEF were attempts to scare people away from us. When the Student Nonviolent Coordinating Committee came along, a lot of people in it were afraid of SCEF. Those fears that divided people began to erode by the mid-sixties. By then, they weren't going to let anybody tell them they couldn't associate with SCEF or whoever else they wanted to. Earlier, when the Southern Christian Leadership Conference formed, many people also were afraid to associate with SCEF. They knew that groups had been destroyed by the witch-hunt, and they wanted to protect their organization. Martin Luther King was always under those pressures. We got to know Martin and Coretta pretty well when they were still in Montgomery. We'd sometimes stay at their house when they moved to Atlanta. So we talked to him a lot. There were a few times when SCEF was trying to work on certain things, and we'd ask SCLC to co-sponsor it.

For example, we were involved quite early in voting rights. Blacks who tried to register were put off their land in Fayette and Haywood Counties in Tennessee. We set up a tent city to dramatize the lengths they'd go to to keep people from voting. We got Bishop G. Bromley Oxnam to head up a people's civil rights commission to hear voting rights violations. But we really wanted to make a big thing of it, and we knew we couldn't do it by ourselves. We asked SCLC to co-sponsor it with us. The board had a tremendous debate on whether they should associate with SCEF. They finally voted to do it.

In 1962, Martin asked me to speak at an SCLC convention. Carl was just out of jail, and things were still pretty scary. After I spoke, Dr. King thanked me and introduced Carl and Jim. I think it was his way of defying the witch-hunt, of saying, "We're going to work with these people. We don't care who knows it." Somebody took a picture of Martin at the microphone with Jim, Carl, and me in the background. It was plastered all over a Louisiana Un-American Activities Committee report. Whoever conducted the hearings for LUAC said that they had asked Dr. King to repudiate this association and clear his name but hadn't heard one word from him.

States had set up their own committees: LUAC, FUAC—the Florida Un-American Activities Committee—TUAC in Tennessee. Mississippi had a committee and also something called the Mississippi Sovereignty Commission. When SCEF moved to Kentucky, they set up KUAC. We called it "QUACK." These committees did a lot of harm. Three Black ministers in Florida were indicted when they refused to turn over the NAACP membership lists. In Virginia, a state legislative committee, with local police, burst into the office of a Black lawyer who represented local branches of SCLC, demanding that he turn over his records to them. In many cases, they were even more blatant than HUAC.

The crescendo of the attacks on SCEF came in early fall of '63. Working in conjunction with Senator Eastland and the Internal Security Subcommittee, the state and city police and LUAC raided the SCEF office in New Orleans. They took everything: all the files, the lists of contacts and contributors, and even a picture of Eleanor Roosevelt inscribed to Jim Dombrowski. They arrested Jim and raided his home. They also arrested two lawyers who belonged to the Lawyers Guild. One of them, Ben Smith, was treasurer of SCEF and one of the few white lawyers who took civil rights cases in New Orleans. They confiscated their legal files and charged them with violating Louisiana's subversive law.

Jim was sitting in the jail cell when Ben came in. Jim thought Ben had come to get him out. And Jim was such a courteous man, he wouldn't say, "Okay, let's go." So they sat there and talked a little while. They talked about this, that, and the other. Finally Jim said, "Well, when do we leave?" Ben said, "We're not leaving. I'm here, too."

The South was a closed society. In order to maintain the segregated system, the people who ran it had to instill a police state for everybody. What the civil rights movement was about was not only to eliminate segregation but also to establish the right to organize. Everything Blacks did opened the way for everybody: the peace movement, the women's movement, the organization of handicapped people. It's not because Black people are especially virtuous and better than anybody, but because they were at the bottom, and when they pushed, things happened. Finally, in the sixties, this country began to acknowledge that it had been wrong on race. It was the same sort of thing that we, as individuals, went through. Once that began to happen on a national scale, for just a little while, we really did move in a more humane direction, and everybody benefited, whites as well as Blacks.

Desegregating public accommodations, which had been the big battle, was won in the streets long before it was written into law in the 1964 Civil Rights Act. By 1963, in big cities like Nashville, Atlanta, and even Birmingham, segregation had been broken down. That same year,

Fred Shuttlesworth, a leader of SCLC, became president of SCEF. Then Jim Dombrowski, crippled with arthritis, retired. Their board asked Carl and me to take his place. It was just a time in history that you couldn't miss.

We had two main organizing projects. One was GROW, the Grass Roots Organizing Work, which did some pioneering work in Mississippi and Alabama with Black and white woodcutters. The Mississippi Sovereignty Commission had people spying on our meetings and watching very carefully the work of our GROW group. They had one report about SCEF supporting the strike of the woodcutters and how we'd successfully recruited a number of former members of the Ku Klux Klan. They reported it as something very dangerous. I don't think we were as successful as they said, but just that little bit we did, of bringing Black and white workers together, scared them to death.

The other project was in Appalachia, where we were organizing against strip mining. The mine owners of Pike County, the biggest coal mining county in the country, got very upset. One fine night in 1967, the phone rang here in the SCEF office. The two people who were working on the SCEF staff in Pike County, Alan and Margaret McSurely, said they had been arrested and charged with sedition.[57] I couldn't believe it—the same Kentucky law we were indicted under in 1954 was still on the books.

When Carl went there to see about bail, they indicted both of us for sedition, again. This time, we were thrown in for window dressing. We'd become so notorious in Kentucky that it served the political purposes of the prosecutor, Thomas Ratliff, who was running for lieutenant governor. Our bail was ten thousand dollars each. We told the newspapers we were tired of having to scramble around and raise bond every time some ambitious politician wanted to get elected. "We've lived in Kentucky for years. A lot of people may not like us, but we're established citizens, and we want to be released on our own recognizance." They refused, and we went to jail.

But there were things you could do by then. Our attorneys, Bill Kunstler and Arthur Kinoy, asked for a ruling on the constitutionality of the sedition law on the basis of the Dombrowski case. The Supreme Court had established that when an issue of First Amendment rights is involved, the federal courts had the obligation to stop an injustice before it happened. Kunstler got a hearing before a three-judge federal court in Lexington. What a difference in atmosphere between the fifties and sixties! The courtroom was filled—not with people wanting to lynch us but with university students.

When Ratliff cross-examined me, he swelled up like a toad: "Mrs. Braden, are you now or have you ever been . . ." The courtroom exploded with laughter. One young woman told me later, "I'd heard about that phrase, but I didn't know anybody actually used it." Then he asked, "Have you ever been a Communist, by which I mean do you subscribe to the teachings of Marx, Lenin, Castro, Trotsky, Mao Tse-tung?" He included a few other names. Again there was laughter.

I waited a minute and said, "Mr. Ratliff, you have covered a broad range of political and economic thought in that question. I don't see how anybody can give an intelligent answer." One of the judges said, "I don't either. Ask her something else."

Another one of his questions was, "Is it true you have a printing press in your basement?" Here I was, charged with sedition. It was not "Do you have a bomb? Do you have an arsenal?" but "Do you have a printing press?" They had asked the same question in 1954. I remember the highly impassioned argument the assistant prosecutor made to the jury in Carl's case: "These people are dangerous. While you sleep, they run their mimeograph machines." But this was another time. The judges came back after an hour and declared the sedition law unconstitutional. It was a dramatic moment for Carl and me.

The last real overt attack on SCEF was the Kentucky sedition case. But I think it was replaced with covert operations. They managed to destroy SCEF, just as they did SNCC, by playing on internal dissensions. This was obviously a part of the COINTELPRO operation the FBI carried out at that time. It was a period when people were groping, and SCEF became a battleground between different political factions that were trying to figure out what to do. There were some important differences, but I'm convinced we could have resolved them, except that people were in there to see that this didn't happen. I don't know who they were, but I believe the government had people in every faction. And SCEF finally broke up.

Years before, I had written William Patterson, head of the Civil Rights Congress, about our trip to Jackson, Mississippi, to stop Willie McGee's execution. He didn't know me from a hole in the road, but I got a long letter back from him. One thing he said just stuck with me all these years: "You don't have to be part of the world of the lynchers. You have a choice. There is another America, the America of people who have from the beginning struggled for justice. It started before we came and will go on after we leave. That's what you can belong to." It was just what I needed to hear then. I've been in a lot of different organizations. Organizations come and go. But what I really joined then, and still am part of, is that other America.

THE CRUCIBLE OF LOWNDES COUNTY, ALABAMA, AND EMERGENT BLACK POWER

Lowndes County historically had been an area where landless African Americans had been held subservient to a small white elite by the force of terror. Then, in 1965, Stokely Carmichael and other organizers from the Student Nonviolent Coordinating Committee set in motion a movement that changed Lowndes County profoundly. Along with the African American residents—among them high school student Johnny Jackson—the SNCC activists formed the Lowndes County Freedom Organization, an independent Black political party. It ran candidates to challenge the ruling Democrats, whose motto was "White Supremacy." Despite the loss of jobs, evictions from plantations, church burnings, and shootings, political participation by African American citizens grew. In 1966, the Freedom Organization narrowly lost a contested election, but it forever changed the face of county politics, forcing Democrats to accept Black candidates on party tickets for county offices.

As African Americans entered Democratic Party politics, the opportunity for an independent, grassroots Black political movement in the county was lost—but the idea survived in SNCC. Many young civil rights activists, who had given so much in the fight against segregation, had become disillusioned with the possibility of integration, with Lyndon Johnson's Democratic Party, and even with the viability of nonviolence as a response to the attacks they had sustained. The very existence of the short-lived Freedom Organization gave impetus to a different goal: Black Power.

The most outspoken proponent of Black Power, Stokely Carmichael—later Kwame Ture—became a lightning rod, attracting the enmity of the FBI, Congress, and President Johnson. Johnson pressed the Justice Department to find some pretext to put Stokely Carmichael in jail, but the department could find fault only in his speeches. In the FBI's attempt to "neutralize" Kwame Ture, Kenneth O'Reilly writes, "no technique, no matter how ruthless was rejected outright." Ture was subjected to intense physical surveillance. The bureau tried to plant dissension among Ture and other SNCC leaders, to discredit him in the press, and to falsely implicate him as a CIA agent.[58] A phony FBI "pretext" call was made to his mother from "a friend," warning her that "it was absolutely necessary for CARMICHAEL to 'hide out'" because the Black Panthers "were out to kill him and it would probably be done some time this week."[59] J. Edgar Hoover sought to "prevent the rise of a 'messiah' who could unify, and electrify the militant black nationalist movement." "King," the director worried, "could be a very real contender for this position," and "Carmichael has the necessary charisma to be a real threat."[60]

When the Black movement not only broke seemingly impenetrable barriers in Lowndes County but also took on a new direction and developed on a national scale, the repression directed against it shifted in emphasis. The old-fashioned southern brutality visited on Johnny Jackson and other Lowndes County civil rights activists gave way to federal covert operations of the sort used against Kwame Ture: COINTELPRO.

JOHNNY JACKSON

Anybody who tells you that the Student Nonviolent Coordinating Committee died—they're wrong. I think all those grassroots workers back in their own states and counties still carry SNCC with them. SNCC challenged us to dream of a community full of love instead of hate. It challenged us to dream of people who were concerned about the human race. And SNCC taught me that time does not change things. People change things. When you act, something will happen. If you don't, nothing will happen.

There were civil rights workers in Lowndes County before the 1965 march from Selma to Montgomery, but people were afraid to talk to them or do anything. Nobody would go down and register to vote; they were getting killed all across the South for that. You had a few strong people who would slip into meetings in Selma or Montgomery, but they would come back here and wouldn't do anything because of the threat of death. They hadn't built up their courage yet.

Then the SNCC workers came, young men who looked approximately my age: Bob Mants, Stokely Carmichael, Scott B. Smith, and several others. They were different. They came in asking what the problems were and what they could do to help. They began to pull two or three people together to get them ready to register. They came out to my school to send leaflets home with the children. The principal didn't want us taking anything from civil rights workers. And at first everybody ran from them: "The white folks will kill you." But I wanted to talk to them to see what was going on. I guess it was just the spirit in me. We shook

JOHNNY JACKSON

hands, and we laughed. I had just begun to drive a school bus, so we drivers got together and put the leaflets on the buses. SNCC had challenged us to get involved.

I was born and raised here, the son of a sharecropper, the seventh child out of thirteen. I saw a lot of discrimination. There were separate water fountains for us to drink from, certain doors we had to go in. And I noticed that the courthouse had no Black people in political positions. I was about eight or nine years old during the Montgomery bus boycott. Then we read about the bombing of the children in Birmingham. I remember vividly that we were afraid. Anybody who was Black in Alabama who says they were not afraid is not telling the truth. But I came out of a very Christian home. And we thought that through faith things could be changed.

I talked to my father about the SNCC workers. He had a house that my brother had just left. I said, "Daddy, the house is vacant over there. Those boys are going to get killed going back and forth to Selma." They had already been shot at. I said, "Why don't you let them stay with us?" When my father met those fellows, he kind of liked them. And he was very courageous. He was a master mason and a Christian, and he did not blink. He said, "Hey, boys, you all could take this house over here. There's nobody staying in it." And they began to call it the Freedom House.

It got out that the Jacksons were messing with civil rights workers. I got fired for taking the leaflets. Then the whites in that county called my father in and said, "Hey, you don't need those folks staying there." It was leading up to the time for my daddy to borrow money for his next farming. The man told him, "We can't help you. You're fooling with those civil rights workers." So we didn't have any money to plant the crop. To make matters worse, my sister was a school teacher, and she was fired. None of us could get a job anywhere in that county or in that state because of our activities.

When the march came from Selma to Montgomery, they were trying to drum up support for it in Lowndes County. You had maybe forty, fifty people who just stood up and joined the march. My family did. After the march, more people got courage. Then SNCC began pointing out to us: "Why are you all riding on raggedy buses?" Students at my high school began to talk. Our schools were terrible. We didn't even have a library. No science equipment. No cafeteria. The students began to meet in April. We boycotted the lunch room. We turned the school out. We raised hell, and the superintendent came and promised us a cafeteria and buses with heat in them.

That summer, SNCC brought in a lot of college students and spread them across the county to help get people registered to vote. At first, just a few went down to register, those who owned their own place. We had to convince the people who lived on plantations. When the white man saw a civil rights worker, he'd warn the people on his plantation, "Don't you talk to them." And a lot of people wouldn't. But some of them started taking a chance. They met the civil rights workers and began to trust them. We told those sharecroppers, "You're working from sunup to sun-

down for two dollars a day. You don't have anything where you're staying, no inside bathroom. You can do better. Come on. If you get kicked
off, we'll try to help you." Every day we pulled somebody in.

All the while, we saw terrible things happening. Jimmie Lee Jackson
got beaten up and killed by troopers at a march in Marion. Viola Liuzzo
was killed two miles from where I lived. Viola was hauling people back
and forth on the march from Selma to Montgomery. Jonathan Daniels,
a civil rights worker, had dinner with my family right before he got killed
in cold blood by a deputy sheriff. Then when Samuel Younge Jr. was murdered at Tuskegee because he wanted to use the rest room, that tore me
up. And all their killers walked scot free!

They had been burning crosses and burning churches all over. And
they had already put out that they were going to burn my daddy's house
and kill him. The Ku Klux Klan came by and shot into it. There wasn't
anybody there but me and my sister. I ran out of the house with a little
pistol my daddy had and got in the car. I wanted to go and see about my
oldest sister, the teacher who got fired. I thought they were going to burn
her house down. I pulled up on the dirt road where she lived and saw a
truck. When I drove up near it, they started firing at my car. I fell to the
floor and closed my eyes. They kept firing. I heard them say, "We got the
nigger," and they pulled off.

I liked Martin Luther King. I could just feel the warmth and the spirit
of the man, but his nonviolent philosophy was not a favorite of mine. It
wasn't that I didn't cater to nonviolence. I've always been nonviolent.
But I felt we had a right to protect ourselves. We had a person come over
here from the Deacons for Defense, people who were working in Mississippi, and we began to set up our own defense.* We said that if they
came at us with guns, we would use force to stop them. It seemed like
white folks put out the word: "Look, they done got together. They organized. They've got guns." And I think that stopped a lot of them from
jumping on Black people in this county.

We were determined to exercise our constitutional rights as U.S. citizens by registering and voting. But when sharecroppers went down to
register, the registrar would call the plantation owner and say, "Get those
niggers off your place." People were evicted from the plantations. Pretty
soon, we had over thirty families come to my daddy's house and say,

---

*The Deacons for Defense and Justice, founded in 1965 in Bogalusa, Louisiana, was
an armed self-defense unit of African Americans that protected marches, rallies, and voter
registration drives in the South.

"You all told us to go down to register to vote, and now we don't have anywhere to stay." So SNCC put together a network to get the material to construct tents. That's how Tent City started, right there on Highway 80. More than thirty-seven families stayed in those tents for over two years.

In the meantime, we came together and formed a Poor People's Land Fund, to buy people an acre of land and build them houses. My daddy spearheaded the Poor People's Land Fund, and it was organized by SNCC. When the first family got their home built, that encouraged others: "If they did it, we can do it."

The Voting Rights Act was passed in August of 1965. They had been using the literacy test against Black people who went down to register, but now they couldn't do it. The federal registrars came in. Some Blacks became registrars. Everybody was excited, and everybody started going down to register. The number of Black registered voters was climbing toward the number of registered whites. And they couldn't stop it. We were meeting twenty and thirty at a time in churches in different communities, and every month it looked like ten or fifteen more would join. People started reading about what was happening in other places in our little newspaper, *SNCC Voice*. That gave them more courage. They started meeting statewide, regionwide, electing officers.

In September, they fired teachers who they heard were going to those meetings. Three of my sisters didn't get placed. They got rid of my oldest sister after she'd been on the job more than fifteen years. She was one of the two people from this county who had the audacity to file a suit against the state of Alabama and the board of education for violating her civil rights. In 1967, Judge Frank Johnson ruled that teachers could not be fired for their political activities. Johnson was a white federal judge who continually ruled according to what the Constitution says. His house was bombed, but his ruling brought about the teacher tenure law.

We gained a little at a time, just enough to give us strength to keep fighting for more. In September of '65, they gave new buses to the Black students. That fall, my brother Cliff tried to go to the all-white school. He and McGill and John Hulett's son—there were four of them—tried to enter, but they wouldn't let them come in. But people were encouraged when they saw those four students with that nerve. In the middle of September, the National Guard made the school admit them. Of course, by the time the school year was half over, all the white children pulled out and went to their own private academies. They still have them.

There were so many things going on: dealing with registration, running for office, education, housing. We started talking about credit unions to help farmers grow their stuff. Across the country, folks sent food and money. Doctors came into the community. Lawyers came in. Then SNCC brought teachers in, volunteers from Berkeley and Harvard. They came and lived in the community and had church schools, teaching people what their rights were.

A lot of Black students were much brighter than what they were getting in grades. When I was a senior, I didn't know what a biology lab was about, didn't even know what a library was about. The kids in our family were able to go to school, but we couldn't start until the last of October—we were picking cotton—and we had to come out around April to farm for the summer. Then SNCC put out a call for colleges to take these young people and let them go to school for a summer to see how they'd do on a college level. I went to Tuskegee in the summer of '65, and I did so well they offered me a scholarship.

For the 1966 elections, we had more Black people registered than whites, so they tried to keep us off the ballot. The Republican Party wasn't letting us in at all. And the Democratic Party's executive committee said, "Let's raise the fees. Instead of fifty dollars to run for sheriff, let's go to five hundred dollars." I mean, a Black man didn't have that much money. If he had five hundred dollars, he could run his farm. There was just no way a Black person could qualify for office as a Democrat.

We decided if they didn't want us in their party, we'd organize our own. We just had to call a meeting at a church, nominate our candidates, pick our emblem, and we'd be on the November ballot. It was that simple. That's when we organized the Lowndes County Freedom Organization. They had the elephant for an emblem in the Republican Party. The rooster was for the Democratic Party, and their slogan was "White Supremacy." Somebody came up with the idea of the black panther for our emblem. At that time, we were dealing with our image as Black people. We said we ought to be proud of being who we are. And we loved that cat. We even made a "cabbage patch" panther way before the Cabbage Patch dolls came out. I still have one.

We got on the ballot, and Black people came out overwhelmingly to vote. A lot of them could not read or write, but all they had to do was look at the panther and pull the top lever to vote for all Black candidates from the independent party. We gave that rooster hell, and we gave that elephant hell, even though we lost. But the most important thing is that we Blacks joined hands together as a people to make things work for everybody. And that was all done through SNCC and its organizers like

Courtland Cox, Stokely Carmichael, Rap Brown, Bob Mants, who is still here, Gloria House—people who were dedicated to helping us get to where we needed to be.

SNCC would send me to other counties to work, in order to give young people encouragement. I worked in Dallas County, Montgomery County, and Macon County. I helped get the first Black sheriff elected in Macon County, Lucius Amerson. We went over to help in Greene County, and they won the second Black sheriff in the state. I would be arrested everywhere I'd go. I think I was arrested more than twenty times during that whole struggle. They'd charge you with anything: speeding, resisting arrest. They'd put you in jail to hinder you and scare you, to see if they could stop you from doing what you were doing.

After '65, after all those murders, knowing that my own life was on the line, I had made a choice. In Demopolis, when I was organizing folks to register to vote, the police threw me in jail. They struck me, but I wouldn't strike back. I knew they wanted me to do that so they could kill me. They'd kick me and hit me, and I'd just talk right on: "Go ahead and kill me. Somebody else will take my place." You were afraid, but you could not show it. And whenever you were arrested, SNCC people from around the country would start calling that jail. Stokely called. Other folks called and said, "You'd better not put your hands on him. If you do, we're going to burn it down." Most of the time, they would let you go, but they wanted me in Demopolis, so they put me on a peace bond.

In the summer of '67, I was called out of school to appear at the induction center. I didn't feel that I had to fight in Vietnam, when Jonathan Daniels had been killed in Lowndes County and nothing was done about it. I told them, "I am not treated like a citizen of the United States, so I don't have to fight." I was willing to go to jail. I think I was seventeenth in the country and first in Alabama to refuse to be drafted. I joined Cleve Sellers, Muhammad Ali, and those other folks.[61] Ali had just refused to take the step forward. He was out on appeal. As a matter of fact, he called my induction center that day to let them know that whatever money it took to get me out of jail, he would raise it.

When they saw I was determined and I wasn't going to take that step forward, they called me into a back room with a psychiatrist and tried to cut a deal. They told me, "If you don't say nothing about it, we're going to let you go." They said they would classify me 4-F: "You can go home now if you don't talk to the press." So the only thing I told those reporters was that my fight was in Lowndes County. But the people at the induction center, *they* talked to the press. They told them I was mentally unfit, and that's what hit the news. I had to deal with that for the next two years.

I started having other problems. My father was in an accident that was never explained. His truck overturned and caught fire. I think something was tampered with. He was burned on thirty percent of his body, and we lost him my second year in college.

By 1968, white people saw that we were determined to have some Black elected officials. They met with us and said, "Hey, we got to work together now. We don't dislike y'all. Y'all just never asked for anything." I'm telling it like it was. They wanted to make sure that we were not going to treat them like they treated us. I think that was their greatest fear. By then, the slogan "Black Power" had come out, and the biggest myth about it was that Black folks wanted to do the same thing to white folks that they had done to us. The majority, including Kwame Ture, wanted the same justice and the same rights that other citizens had. That's all we were after.

The white folks sent in some Uncle Toms they could control, who said, "Well, you'll never win as long as you've got your own party." So we changed the name from the Lowndes County Freedom Organization to the National Democratic Party of Alabama. And a few whites joined. They said, "Y'all need to get rid of that panther." They said the cat was too arrogant and too vicious. So the cat changed into an eagle. That hurt my heart. But that's all right. It was still a symbol people could identify with. All of our candidates won in '68, but the white man stole it with "absentee" ballots. They were voting for dead white folks and stuff. They had about two hundred votes already in before the polls opened.

In 1971, I said, "We need more folks who can speak up." I had just come of age to vote, and I decided to run on the slate for tax assessor of Lowndes County. I was well known because I had been actively involved in getting folks registered to vote. I won in every precinct, but they took it from me with their "absentee" ballots. That year, we did get one position on the county commission. Of course, he had to go to court to win it.

Next time, I got a friend of mine to run for tax assessor, and he won. Then John Hulett became the first Black sheriff of Lowndes County. That stopped police brutality, because he treated everyone right. We got a Black superintendent of education. She was a thirty-year veteran in the school system. She had made up her mind that when she got in office, she was going to take a stand. The first thing she did was hire my sister who had been fired. We won four positions on the county commission, which meant we had control. And that's when they started respecting us. Then we won majority control on the board of education. I just wish my daddy had been living to see the kinds of changes we made.

That was the impact on Lowndes County of a ten-year struggle, from 1965 up until 1976. Through the people who got killed, through the total struggle, there was some improvement. It was those poor people, oppressed people, in the Lowndes County Freedom Organization who made those changes. It was not the educated people in that county.

In 1978, I got a lawyer, Hank Sanders, to file for my FBI papers. In 1980, I got three hundred sixty-four pages. They marked out the names, but it might have been some civil rights workers right with me who were government informers. In the files, they said I was on marijuana and stuff, which was untrue. I was called one of the most dangerous civil rights workers in the country. The FBI had followed me from the time I joined SNCC in 1965. They harassed me. They caused me to have problems in my schools. They cut me off from jobs, because everywhere I'd go, they'd be investigating me. I was just amazed that the federal government was spending that kind of money following and harassing people who wanted justice, just what the Constitution was based on.

I became mayor of the town of White Hall in Lowndes County in 1981. White Hall takes in Highway 80, where Tent City was. That's where Martin Luther King camped on the Selma to Montgomery march. And one mile from there is where Viola Liuzzo got killed. When I won the election, they challenged it. They said I stole it, but it was just because of my civil rights activity. We went into federal court, and the judge had to rule that I was mayor.

I do not make a lucrative twenty-five or thirty thousand dollars a year. I only make about five hundred dollars a month from the day care center my son and I started, and I'm paid about three hundred a month, plus expenses, as mayor. But we're able to live off of it. I am very conservative: I don't drive a big car; I don't wear a lot of fancy clothes; I don't run around to the clubs. I don't run around. I have a house. My wife works. And I'm proud of our efforts.

The city began to move forward. It went from having seven dollars and fifty cents in the bank to having a half-million-dollar city hall, a half-million-dollar water system. We started having immediate police protection. We created an ambulance service. Black people saw that we could manage cities and we could build towns. At that time, we had about eight or nine Black mayors in Alabama. Now we've got thirty-three.

But it looks like things are turning backward. Do you know what they're doing now? They took about a thousand people off the voting list because they didn't vote in the last election. They call that "reidentification." It's the same game they played twenty-five years ago, just a different tactic. It's a mess because they're trying to get Black officials out of office. Any leader they cannot control, any person who's becoming a role model and who's building prominence in the Black community, they try to set them up. Albert Turner is a good example of that.* It's almost as bad as it was in '65. People don't need to forget what happened.

KWAME TURE (STOKELY CARMICHAEL)

I was just with my mother, and she was reminding me of the terrible things the FBI used to do. They would call her up around three o'clock in the morning: "Have you heard from him recently?" Or, "We got him." Or, "He's going to be killed." Each time, they'd say they were someone else, from the Ku Klux Klan to the Black Panther Party. I told her, "Listen, don't worry. It's the FBI. Just ask them where their mama is." After a while, she began to recognize the voice of the FBI. But if I hadn't been able to detect it early, it would have had a devastating effect on her.

There was constant harassment. Constant. When I was married to Miriam Makeba, they cut her out of jobs everywhere.† The FBI would sit in front of my house in their car. Every four hours, there would be a new shift. They followed me twenty-four hours a day. And they didn't hide it. The FBI must have started with me a long time ago.

I had been a student at the Bronx High School of Science. My name was Stokely Carmichael then. We were seated alphabetically. The person next to me was Dennis. He happened to be Eugene Dennis Jr., the son of the general secretary of the Communist Party. We were co-captains of the soccer team. He lived in Harlem, so Dennis and I went along very well. In my senior year, we came to Washington, D.C., to picket the House Un-American Activities Committee. On the picket line, I met some other Africans. They said, "We go to Howard University, and we work with SNCC." "You're with SNCC!" "Yes. We work in the Nonviolent Action Group." I said, "Wow! I'm going to Howard."

*For information about Albert Turner, see pp. 250–251, in the introduction to Mervyn Dymally's story.
†Miriam Makeba, a South African singer and opponent of apartheid, rose to prominence in Africa, Europe, and the United States in the late 1950s.

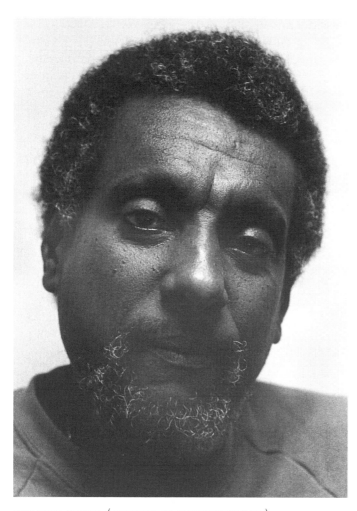

KWAME TURE (STOKELY CARMICHAEL)

In Washington, it felt as if I were in both the South and the North. Theoretically, Washington was the North. It was not segregated. But ten minutes outside of Howard University, I touched Maryland. I touched Virginia. I'd be segregated there. Even when I took a bus in D.C., as soon as we came to Virginia, I had to go to the back of the bus. So we fought segregation right there. We also picketed Senator James Eastland's house and the houses of other southern congressmen. And we were the ones who would picket the FBI offices when they wouldn't act on the atrocities in the South.

I began to understand the really close interrelationships among police networks during the Cambridge movement, in Maryland. Gloria Richardson was the leader there. What nonsense when they say that women didn't play an important role in the movement. And Cambridge was crucial, really, a turning point in the struggle. The issues were segregation, bad housing, and unemployment. There had been sustained violence against the African people, even shootouts between the National Guard and the community. For months, the National Guard was stationed there. As the nonviolent protest spread, we SNCC people around Washington were quite frequently in Cambridge. We would come up on weekends or on nights when there were mass meetings or extra problems.

The night George Wallace was to speak in Cambridge, we were going to hold a big demonstration. Gloria didn't want to plan it there because she was afraid they'd have listening devices everywhere. She came to D.C., and we made all the plans. Since they knew Gloria, we knew they would arrest her at the demonstration. We were going to have Cleve Sellers, Charlie Cobb, Courtland Cox, Ed Brown (Rap Brown's older brother), and Stanley Wise—a strong contingent of SNCC people from Howard—up front. We told her, "When you are taken, we'll be able to keep the march going."

Just as we thought, the National Guard arrested Gloria as soon as it started. After they put her in the paddy wagon, the head of the National Guard, General Gelston, came at us with about four of his soldiers with bayonets fixed. He said, "This one. This one. This one. This one." He was pointing at every one of us. In that instant, I realized: How could they know who the students at Howard were unless they had a strong connection?

When we saw that he was picking out every one of us, we said, "All right. Resist arrest." We piled on each other. He stepped back: "Okay, teargas them all." I'll never forget that night. I was overcome with tear gas at the front of the line. We couldn't move back because there were so many people behind us, and I fell unconscious.

At Cambridge, I became quite aware of how information was shared by police, how they acted like one body. Later, when I was an organizer in Greenwood, Mississippi, Bob Moses informed me that I should report the beatings, the shootings, and the burnings to the FBI. But I didn't want to waste my time going to them. I'd have to go report it; they'd have to come write it up; I'd have to sit there with them—*and they never did anything with the report*. Besides, we knew they didn't like us from the beginning. It was easy to detect their racism. Once that came out, for me, there was no more discussion. It got through to Moses that I refused to go to the FBI, and he called me. I said, "Look, I'm not wasting my time. I could be out there organizing." He said, "Well, unfortunately, we need affidavits from them in the cases we're building. So you'll have to do it." I said, "I will, but it's just paperwork."

They used to have this program on TV, "The FBI in Peace and War." And like most unthinking people in America, I thought the FBI did nothing but solve crimes. That's the image they projected. Our contact with them demystified the myth of their infallibility, that every individual FBI agent knows everything. I remember one night when whites shot into the Freedom House in Greenwood. After the shooting, a congressman must have called the FBI, so they had to come out to investigate. And were they mad! I sat on the steps to watch the whole process. Some bullets were up high, so they had to use a ladder to pull them out to get a tracing.

I waited until one FBI agent got up on the ladder. Then I said, "You know, those guys have been driving by here. They might shoot again." Just then I saw a pickup truck. I said, "Hey, here comes one now!" The FBI guy, the one on the bottom who was holding the ladder, he ducked. The guy on the top was trying to duck. Then he ran down, saying he'd be back tomorrow to get the bullet out.

We saw them exactly for what they were, not the way television presented them. We saw what cowards they were. We saw their racism, their defense of segregated policies. When somebody's house was burnt up, we knew who did it. The people always knew. At first, we would even present the facts to the FBI. But we learned that it would endanger the local person who had seen it. The FBI office was right next to the local police. They were chummy, chummy pals. They were sharing information. Whatever we told the FBI, they told the local police. You remember the Herbert Lee incident and the FBI's role.* But nothing they did stopped us from organizing.

When students from SNCC went to work in the South, it was the combination of African intelligentsia and African peasants—the sharecrop-

*In 1961, Herbert Lee, a fifty-two-year-old father of ten and a worker in the Voter Registration Project, was killed by E. H. Hurst, a Mississippi state representative. Lewis Allen, who was a witness to the murder, said that he would testify as to Hurst's guilt if he could be promised protection. According to Robert Moses, Allen was beaten by a deputy sheriff who had been told about him by the FBI. Several years later, Allen was killed in front of his house. See James Forman, *The Making of Black Revolutionaries* (Washington, D.C.: Open Hand Publishing, 1985), p. 231; Clayborne Carson, *In Struggle: SNCC and the Black Awakening of the 1960s* (Cambridge: Harvard University Press, 1981), pp. 48–49.

pers—that eventually gave the world the idea of "Black Power." SNCC had Black Power in mind long before the phrase was used. It emerged after the Mississippi Freedom Democratic Party was refused seating at the Democratic Party Convention in 1964. The "regular" Mississippi Democratic Party, which was seated there, had seen to it that Black people never entered the political arena. SNCC had helped create the MFDP to build a parallel political structure to challenge that stranglehold. The MFDP representatives came to the convention in Atlantic City to be seated as the legitimate Mississippi delegation. The Democratic Party's racist response was that they would pick two MFDP people to be delegates-at-large—a purely symbolic gesture.

SNCC refused to accept it. But the betrayal was swept under the rug quickly by those who had made their compromises with the Democratic Party. And, of course, King supported the Democratic Party. Oh, yes, I remember. He was ill at the time, on crutches, but he came to urge the MFDP people to accept the "compromise." The entire so-called civil rights coalition said, "How can you go against the Democratic Party? Are you crazy?" But Freedom Democrats had gone to Atlantic City to *replace* the racist Mississippi party, not to join it!

The SNCC people were boiling mad. That the Democratic Party was a racist party, of that there wasn't the slightest doubt. That it was a corrupt party, there wasn't the slightest doubt. And this was the party that was to be our savior! The question was raised: Do we continue to ask our oppressors to stop oppressing us, or do we speak to the masses of the people, organize them, and let their strength turn against the wrath of the enemy? This was precisely what Black Power represented. Those in SNCC who had previously assured us that we could easily melt into the Democratic Party now had nowhere else to go but to independent political action. That led us to Lowndes County, Alabama.

The population in Lowndes County was more than eighty percent African. Yet it had no registered African voters. Maybe five percent of Africans owned any land. The rest were sharecroppers, very impoverished and very threatened. Lowndes, which lies between Montgomery and Selma, was the most dangerous county. Montgomery had had a movement since 1956. And Selma had a movement. But between those two cities, nothing was going on. So you can imagine the terror that had to be there. Serious terror. If SNCC people could help crack Lowndes County, we could organize anywhere.

SNCC and SCLC had clashed publicly in Albany, Georgia. But by the time of the Selma to Montgomery march, I disagreed with having a public confrontation. People loved King. They'd climb over each other just to touch him. My position was simple: Take the momentum created by King to develop the Lowndes County Freedom Organization. And that's exactly what we did. Bob Mants and I didn't march from Selma to Montgomery, but we followed along to keep track of the people who came out to greet the marchers. We saw who was the strongest, who was ready to move. By the time King crossed Lowndes County, we had a place to stay, contacts, and three churches.

Lowndes County was organized in a year and a half, but it wasn't easy. They began to use direct terror against the local population: mass expulsions from plantations, shooting into houses, burning churches. There was physical intimidation on the streets, stopping people, slapping them, you know, to put them back "in their place." At first, we were just in a defensive position. There would be one incident; we'd go cool it. Before we'd turn around, there would be another one. Each one seemed to be a little more grave.

But we had had enough practice in how to break their tactics. You're talking about SNCC, which had the experience of southwest Georgia, Mississippi, and Alabama. You're talking about people who moved from one campaign to another without letup: "Where's the next battle? I'll get some rest there." And they brought that world of experience with them. While you saw only two or three SNCC organizers in Lowndes County, we had a whole organization behind us: research on legal issues, raising bail, knowledge of how to cope with intimidation.

When people began to be expelled from the plantations, we set up a tent city out on Highway 80. We informed everybody, starting with the sheriff, that we had guns. Every night, people guarded it. If anybody rode by and shot at us, we were going to shoot back. They rode by the first night. They shot. We returned fire. After that, there were no shootings. And we stayed right there.

Not one African was registered to vote in March 1965. Over the next twenty months, close to thirty-nine hundred Africans had not only registered but had formed the Lowndes County Freedom Organization, held a nominating convention, and put up seven people to run for county office. We spoke about winning, but we knew we wouldn't win the first election. *But the fact that the people of Lowndes County had formed an independent political party—we knew they had won.* That represented the break with the Democratic Party and an understanding of their power, Black Power. Our work had really been finished then.

After the Selma to Montgomery march, we swore off all marches. But the Meredith March in 1966 was to go through SNCC territory.* It would start at the Memphis line and go all the way down to Greenwood, Mississippi, through Yazoo, Belzoni, and then to Jackson. That meant it would go through the second congressional district, and I had been the SNCC director of that district. I had opened every project in the Delta myself. I knew every jail in the line of the march. No SCLC people had ever worked there, only SNCC people had. So the march was really our march.

In Greenwood, Mississippi, I decided to raise the slogan of "Black Power." Black Power was the call for Africans to unite, to recognize their heritage, to build a sense of community. It was the call for them to define their own goals, lead their own organizations, and create their own power bases from which they could change the patterns of oppression. Black Power rested on this premise: Before a group can enter the larger society, it must first close ranks.

I had worked in Greenwood for years. Everyone knew me there. I had canvassed the town. I'd been arrested there so many times. And I was arrested again the day we marched into Greenwood. They got me out of jail, and we went to a rally at the Broad Street Park. I told those people: "This is the twenty-seventh time I have been arrested, and I ain't going to jail no more! The only way we're going to stop the white men from whuppin' us is to take over. We've been saying freedom for six years, and we ain't got nothing. What we're going to start saying now is BLACK POWER!"

But when Black Power did come, SNCC was no longer able to carry out the struggle to ensure it. While all of us were against the brutal exploitation of the oppressed masses in this country, we never came to agree on exactly what we were fighting for. By the 1968 election, I recognized that, with all the pressure against them, the Lowndes County Freedom Organization would compromise with the Democratic Party. King was against them. The labor movement was against them. This was real pressure. The compromise reflected the weakness of SNCC, too. Most of those in SNCC were not prepared to sustain independent political action. They themselves did not want to go against the Democratic Party, once they

---

*In 1962, James Meredith enrolled at the University of Mississippi, the first African American to do so. That act precipitated a federal-state confrontation that climaxed with mob violence and, ultimately, with Meredith's admission to the university. In 1966, Meredith set out on a march across Mississippi, hoping to demonstrate that African Americans could exercise their right to vote without fear. He was shot in the early days of the march, however, and was hospitalized. Civil rights leaders were determined to continue the march Meredith had begun.

saw that concessions were being made. "They're going to integrate, and you say, 'Turn your back on it,' man. You must be crazy, Ture." The Lowndes County Freedom Organization died.

But we could have done it! If SNCC had truly been ideologically prepared, we could have done it, because we had organizers throughout the Black Belt, from Alabama all the way to Mississippi, down into southwest Georgia. Once the idea of independent political parties caught on, SCLC would have been forced to go along with it. But the SNCC people were not prepared for this. This was revolution, not reform.

I realized I had contradictions with SNCC, but the FBI manipulated them to wreak havoc on us. Many of us were aware of internal sabotage, but we just couldn't put our finger on it. I can remember when they spread three rumors about me at the same time: I had bought a seventy-thousand-dollar house; I had run away to Africa because I was afraid; and I was a CIA agent.

They had informers in every city and every organization. All they had to do was send out one memorandum—and overnight, a rumor was dropped everywhere, and it appeared to be the truth. The same rumor, and singularly effective: "It is also suggested that we inform a certain percentage of reliable criminal and racial informants that 'we heard from reliable sources that CARMICHAEL is a CIA agent.' It is hoped that these informants would spread the rumor in various large Negro communities across the land."[62]

You really cannot fight this. How can you go in every city and say, "It's not true. The FBI said it." You can't. There's no possible way. It's the same way they spread rumors about Dr. King. Somebody would just come down and say, "Ah . . ." and give you some "inside dirt." Then you go somewhere else and hear the exact same thing, cities away: "You know what I heard about King?"

When they did the seventy-thousand-dollar house thing, they put it on TV. Miriam Makeba had a song called "Piece of Ground." It showed that the white man came to Azania, South Africa, and took the land. It showed all the brutality. At the end of the song, she sang: "White man, don't sleep too long and don't sleep deep / Because I heard a rumor that's running around / The Black man's demanding his own piece of ground."[*] They played this revolutionary song on television while they showed the seventy-thousand-dollar house I was supposed to be buying.

*Lyrics from "A Piece of Ground," by Jeremy Taylor. Copyright 1964, Burlington Music Co., Ltd., London. Used by permission.

Some people in SNCC actually believed all that. They said, "Where does he get the money from?" "Oh, he's gone bourgeois." In 1968, I was expelled from SNCC. One of the reasons listed for my expulsion was ownership of the seventy-thousand-dollar house, which I never owned. I told the people in SNCC, "I can't understand you. We talked all the time about what the white man's newspaper and TV did to SNCC. Now when the white man's newspaper and TV attack me, you don't even check with me."

We were a unified force against the local southern sheriffs with their guns and the Ku Klux Klan. But the FBI was able to split us on every conceivable issue with their channels to the press and their informants inside our organization. That's where the real danger was—you were fighting an invisible man.

Everywhere, the Black Power movement has been derailed. In spite of the number of added representatives and elected officials, we are still a powerless people. We are still the victims of racist attack, not only in Mississippi but in New York City. It is clear that Black Power, with all the former emphasis of depending on no one except the oppressed masses, remains the correct line for the liberation of our people, not only in this country but throughout the world. In no way must you think that the struggle is not continuing. It is continuing everywhere.

THE ASSAULT ON THE BLACK PANTHER PARTY: THE MURDER OF FRED HAMPTON

Although the civil rights movement overturned legally enforced segregation in the South, African Americans in the North continued to live under de facto segregation. There, the National Advisory Commission on Civil Disorders observed, "segregation and poverty have intersected to destroy opportunity and hope and to enforce failure."[63] These volatile forces were ignited in Watts, an area of Los Angeles, during the summer of 1965 and in other northern cities in subsequent summers by arbitrary and abusive police behavior. Indeed, the National Commission on the Causes and Prevention of Violence, chaired by Milton S. Eisenhower, found that "many ghetto blacks see the police as an occupying army."[64]

Sensing the desperation and militancy of ghetto youth in Oakland, California, Huey Newton and Bobby Seale founded the Black Panther Party for Self Defense. They hoped to prevent the kind of spontaneous violence that had erupted in Watts by channeling the rage and rebellion of African Americans into an organized expression of opposition. When the city failed to place a traffic light on a corner where children had been seriously injured, Panthers stopped the flow of cars and ushered youngsters across the street. To check police brutality, Panthers tracked squad cars and, with law books and tape recorders in hand, monitored police conduct during the arrests of Black citizens. Their black berets and leather jackets became well known, as did their defiant, but legal, display of weapons. On the steps of the California State Capitol building, they declared their opposition to a bill that would deny them guns. "Black people have begged, prayed, petitioned, and demonstrated, among other things, to get the racist power structure of America to right the wrongs which have historically been perpetrated against Black people. All of these efforts have been answered by more repression, deceit, and hypocrisy," the statement asserted. "The Black Panther Party for Self Defense believes that the time has come for Black people to arm themselves against this terror before it is too late."[65]

In addition to attracting men and women who were deeply committed to social justice, the Black Panther Party also drew others who were enthralled by the gun and who, once in the party, continued to commit senseless violent or illegal acts. There also were those within the party for whom violence was more than a tactic for self-defense: It was a necessary strategy to effect the revolution or to enforce internal discipline. The threat to constitutional rights that arose during this time lay not only in the government's attack on the Panthers' political program and apparatus but also in the nature of the government's response to the party's violent tendencies. Rather than constraining those tendencies, the FBI tried to exacerbate them. In describing the FBI's actions against the Black Panthers, the inquiry conducted by the Senate Select Committee on Intelligence established "that the chief investigative branch of the Federal Government, which was charged by law with investigating crimes and preventing criminal conduct, itself engaged in lawless tactics and responded to deep-seated social problems by fomenting violence and unrest." High bureau officials, the committee continued, "desired to promote violent confrontations between BPP members and members of other groups."[66]

The FBI tried to break up marriages of Panther members, induce landlords to evict them, and prevent party members from speaking to audiences at high schools and colleges. "We have been successful in the past," bureau headquarters acknowledged, "in preventing such speeches."[67] Plans were made to intercept and then "erase and distort" taped messages between Panther chapters and their national office; to create a phony underground organization "to attack, expose, and ridicule the image of the BPP in the community"; and to use informers to promote rumors "started in several chapters across the country" so that "each rumor could lend credence to the other."[68] The "purpose of counterintelligence actions," Hoover explained, "is to disrupt BPP and it is immaterial whether facts exist to substantiate the charge."[69]

FBI duplicity was also used to subvert the party's programs. The Panther leadership had rejected a proposed children's coloring book as a distortion of their views and had ordered it to be destroyed. The FBI seized it, added captions advocating violence—"Kill Your Local Hog"—and then printed and distributed copies in the party's name to businesses that supported the Panthers' free breakfast program, "to impede their contributions."[70] The FBI sent irate letters of complaint to the Bishop of San Diego impersonating parishioners of Father Frank Curran, who had allowed Panthers to feed children in his church. Within a month, the bureau could report, "Father Curran has now been completely neutralized"—transferred to "somewhere in New Mexico"—and the free breakfast program in San Diego was terminated.[71] When the San Francisco FBI office balked at disrupting the Panthers' effort to feed children, headquarters issued an ultimatum: "Eradicate 'serve the people' programs."[72]

Of the FBI's 295 admitted COINTELPRO operations against so-called Black nationalists, 233 were directed against the Panthers.[73] The bureau's attack on the Panthers was also exceptional for what Kenneth O'Reilly calls "its total disregard for human rights and life itself."[74] J. Edgar Hoover found "appealing" a proposal from his Los Angeles office to incite violence between the Panthers and a rival group, the US organization (United Slaves). It could "result in a US and BPP vendetta," he predicted.[75] On January 17, 1969, Panther leaders Bunchy Carter and John Huggins were assassinated on the campus of UCLA by two US members, an action in which the FBI might have had a direct hand.[76] While hostilities between the two volatile groups were dangerously aroused, the San Diego FBI received permission to aggravate them further. When fragile peace negotiations seemed on the brink of making headway, the FBI acted to scuttle them. After more Panthers were wounded and murdered, the FBI, according to the Senate Select Committee, "viewed this carnage as a positive development" and boasted that "a substantial amount of unrest"—the "shootings, beatings" in southeast San Diego—"is directly attributable to this [COINTELPRO] program."[77]

The Senate Select Committee found that early in 1968 FBI headquarters had instructed its field offices to encourage "local police to raid and arrest 'Black Nationalist Hate groups.'"[78] By the end of the year, the raids were in high gear: in Indianapolis, in San Francisco, and on two occasions in Denver. During the following spring, police raided Panther headquarters in Los Angeles twice as well as Detroit, Chicago, San Diego, Sacramento, and Indianapolis again. More raids were later conducted in Chicago and Los Angeles. "Frequently," Robert Goldstein notes, "Panthers were arrested during these raids on charges such as illegal use of sound equipment, harboring fugitives, possessing stolen goods and flight to avoid prosecutions, and later released."[79] In other cases, captured Panthers were accused of murder and acts of terrorism, charges that eventually were dropped for lack of evidence or were not sustained in court.[80]

Then, just before dawn on December 4, 1969, Chicago police invaded the apartment of Fred Hampton, a leader of the Illinois Panthers, ostensibly to serve a search warrant. Spraying gunfire into the rooms where Panthers were sleeping, they killed Hampton and Mark Clark and wounded four others. The police arrested all survivors for attempted murder and then devised a cover-up for the killings that grew more transparent with each telling.

The raid on Fred Hampton's apartment is described here by persons intimately connected to the terror of that night. Ron Satchel, the Minister of Health for the Illinois Panthers, was seriously wounded by police gunfire. Akua Njeri, Fred Hampton's fiancée, narrowly escaped death. Flint Taylor, a law student at the time of the raid, later served as the attorney for the survivors in their suit against the Chicago police and the FBI.

RON SATCHEL

I was a pre-med student at the University of Illinois when I first heard about the Black Panther Party. I had read an article in *Jet* magazine about Huey Newton and the Panthers in Oakland. The impression I got was that it was another street gang. In Chicago, they had the Blackstone Rangers, the Disciples, the Conservative Vice Lords. And I thought the Panthers were just like them.

Then Fred Hampton spoke at the University of Illinois. I got a different feeling from listening to his speech and talking to him afterward. I got the impression that the party was an organization for social change. He said the media was trying to create a bad image of the Panthers be-

RON SATCHEL

cause it was a socialist organization. I saw the good things they were doing, like running a Free Breakfast for Children program and planning an
alternate health center. I tried to weigh these things. Then I started going to meetings.

From there, a friendship built up between me and Fred and some of
the other members. Fred was a pre-law student. He came from a middle-
class family, you know. He was really straight. He didn't take any drugs
or alcohol. Very honest. I just don't have anything but good to say about
him.

I was nineteen when I got involved. I tried to stay in the party and college at the same time, but it got to be too much for me. Finally I dropped out of school. My family worried about me when they found out I was in the Black Panthers. My mother came to the office a few times. She had gotten the same image that I had from the news media. So I wanted her to see what we were really about, that we were involved in propaganda, political organizing. Afterward, she was more behind me, but she still worried that I would get hurt.

Well, we worked on the circulation of the newspaper. There were a lot of people who were not members who sold newspapers, too. Some of them were just community workers, friends of the party, supporters. And we'd get picked up for disorderly conduct when we were selling them. One time, two of us were at the Jackson subway station downtown with our newspaper, and someone started harassing my partner. I went over, and the next thing I knew, he said he was a policeman. I asked him if I was arrested, and he said, "Yes." I put my hands out, and he put handcuffs on me, but I was charged with assault and resisting arrest. I had to pay court costs and was put on probation for a year and a half—just for selling newspapers.

The Free Breakfast for Children program was held at different sites. Our first site opened in April 1969, at the Better Boys Foundation. We served an average of one hundred fifty children per day. Then we served breakfast to about one hundred seventy-five children at St. Dominic's Church near the Cabrini Green homes. A hundred children were served at a church near the Henry Horner homes. Another hundred at the Baptist church on Jackson Boulevard near Western, and another ninety at a restaurant called the Soul Cafeteria. At the peak, we had somewhere between eight to ten different sites where we served children food before they went to school. We felt that nutrition would help them learn. My primary responsibilities were organizing and operating the breakfast program and the medical clinic.

In an area where you had a high infant mortality rate, where you had lead poisoning, where you had inadequate medical service, where you had doctors who were more concerned with private wealth than public health, we saw a basic need for free medical service. And we worked hard over a long period of time to make that a reality. The clinic itself wouldn't solve all the health problems of the people. We believed that socialized medicine would. And we wanted to create an institution that would set an example, where people could see what socialized medicine could be like.

Even though we were under the umbrella of the central committee of the party in Oakland, we primarily followed Fred Hampton. Fred was a very dynamic person, very charismatic. He had what seemed like innate leadership qualities. He believed in taking the good from Elijah Muhammad, the good from Martin Luther King Jr. He studied Martin Luther King's speeches, and he reminded me of him, except, of course, Fred wasn't a Baptist preacher. Fred believed in socialism. That was our means of salvaging Black people.

The people in the party were very energetic, very sincere. Being in the Panthers was a learning experience. I learned a lot about life. But everything wasn't all peachy keen. Money was supposed to be used for these programs, and for the most part it was. But some of it was misspent. We were told that if we had anything to say, any gripes, to get it all out at meetings. I found that when I objected to some of the things the party was doing, I would be hushed up. But I think the good things outweighed the bad things.

The Panthers had a ten-point program: We want freedom; we want the power to determine the destiny of our Black community; we want full employment for our people, so on and so forth. It included education and giving Black people a sense of pride. But not only Black people, you know. We weren't a separatist group; we knew we had to work within society. We worked with all kinds of groups in Chicago: the Young Lords, a Puerto Rican group; the Young Patriots, a group of Appalachian whites. We had a coalition called the Rainbow Coalition. That's where Jesse Jackson got the name.

We were trying to work with the gangs. In fact, we had meetings with them long before this incident took place. When we wanted to open our health clinic, we had some difficulty with the Conservative Vice Lords. They didn't want us to operate it in "their territory." They thought we were another gang, and we had to check with them first. We negotiated with them on a number of occasions, and they finally accepted the fact. The Blackstone Rangers was the largest youth gang in Chicago. Their numbers were in the thousands, like three to five thousand. We tried to work with them, but it was very difficult. They were into extortion and selling of drugs. And there would be murders committed. But they respected Fred. He tried to convince them that what they were doing really offered no future for the Black community.

The Panthers were for Blacks finishing school and stuff like that. They were against drugs. When I came out of high school, and even when I went to college, I never used drugs. But I got introduced to drugs from an FBI informant, William O'Neal, inside the party. The first time I smoked marijuana, I got it from him.

O'Neal was in charge of security. He tried to get real friendly with everybody in leadership, but I didn't like him. I didn't like the methods he used to screen out "police provocateurs," so-called agents. Those people were no agents. He would accuse them of being informants, and he wanted to question them and beat them. I couldn't agree with that. And I kind of got real quiet and withdrawn for a while. Other people objected, too, but they were afraid to say anything because they would be accused of being agents themselves. There was a big mistrust among the members.

O'Neal gave a layout of Fred's apartment to the FBI. It showed where he slept. Fred and Deborah Johnson always stayed in the back bedroom. I would sleep at the apartment in the front bedroom a lot, but I also still went to my mother's house. Verlina Brewer, an eighteen-year-old community worker, wasn't even a member of the party. We met her at some school, and she started coming to meetings. I think it was too late for her to go home the night Fred was murdered. Blair Anderson was a member of the Blackstone Rangers. He used to come to our meetings to represent them. He and another guy, Louis Truelock, stayed at Fred's apartment, too. Fred met Louis in Menard Prison down in southern Illinois. He was one of the oldest persons in the party, almost forty. It was a communal-type living situation. A lot of times, when people didn't have anywhere to stay, they would come there. O'Neal was there earlier that night. I remember he came in and left a couple of times, but he was not there during the time of the shooting.

We had some guns in the apartment. We had them there to protect ourselves. Then we heard that the police might be coming there, and we didn't want Fred to be living in a hot situation. So they were removed. For some reason, O'Neal decided to bring the guns back over there just before the raid.

This was a time when we had members coming in from the different chapters in the state. We had been trying to reorganize. I remember we had a meeting that evening. When it was over, we came back to the apartment. I was real tired, so I went to sleep kind of early. The next thing I knew, I heard a knock. Very shortly afterward, I heard a lot of shooting. It seemed to first be coming from the front of the house. Then I heard shooting from the rear. I was on the bed nearest the door. Bullets started coming through the wall. Plaster was falling to the floor.

When I got fully awake, the first thing I thought of was to get on the floor. Blair and Verlina were in my room. We all got down there, in between the two beds. There was a shotgun in the room, and Blair wanted to know if we should do something with it. I told him, "No, just stay down. You're going to get shot." But that's where we were hit, because they shot down low, a barrage of shots real fast.

They got everybody in my room. I was hit with a Thompson submachine gun, forty-five caliber. I got hit once in the leg and three times in the pelvic area. I got wounded in my finger and thumb. My thumb was split wide open. So I had blood all over both hands.

After the shooting stopped, they came in with their flashlights. I saw two people in the doorway with guns pointed at me. I remember hearing a voice say, "If Panthers kill police, police will kill Panthers." They told me to turn the light on. I said I was hit and hurting and couldn't get up. They said, "If you don't get up, we're going to kill you." I tried to make my way around the foot of the bed, using the wall to support myself, and limped to the doorway.

They started calling me, "Nigger!" "Black bastard!" "Motherfucker!" I hopped once or twice more toward the back of the house—then I was kicked in the rear. I fell flat on the floor in the dining room area, on my chest and stomach. I remember seeing Deborah Johnson through the dining room in her nightgown, headed toward the front of the apartment. I was told to put both of my hands behind my neck, and handcuffs were placed on my wrists, real tight. I was in a very awkward position. My stomach was in pain. I had pain in my leg. Raising my arms over my neck caused more intense pain. The cuffs cut off circulation in my arms. Blair was put on the floor next to me. I seemed to be passing out. I thought I was going to die. I heard Blair say, "Be strong. You'll be all right."

I was kicked on one of my feet and told, "Get up, nigger." I tried. But I was dizzy and blacking out periodically. The same voice said, "Get up or I'll kick your ass." I don't know how I managed to get up—maybe it was a rush of adrenalin—but I did. I had to walk to the front door and down the stairs and all the way to the paddy wagon. It was freezing cold. I was in excruciating pain, and I kept passing out. I didn't get a wheelchair till I got to Cook County Hospital. There the policemen photographed me and took my fingerprints. They handcuffed my leg to one of the poles of my hospital bed, and they supplied a twenty-four-hour guard. That's the way it was for fourteen days.

I kept wondering what happened to Fred. When I found out Fred had died, I cried. I felt real bad, and I wished that I had died, too. I felt like it was a big loss, like he was a family member.

I was in the hospital and all shot up when I got indicted for attempted murder, armed violence, aggravated battery, armed assault, unlawful use of a weapon, illegal possession of a weapon—I had seven different charges. Later on, they had to drop them all. But the police came into the hospital room and tried to ask me questions. I didn't talk to anyone till I saw one of the attorneys. I didn't even talk to the doctors and the nurses.

I stayed in the hospital for about a month, in the trauma ward for a few weeks and then in the general medical ward. I was in a lot of pain for a long time. In fact, I walked with a limp and had to use a cane for about a year and a half after that. I think one bullet is still in me, because I set a metal detector off a few times.

Edward Hanrahan, the county prosecutor, went on television. He had his own little story about what had happened. He had an enactment of the raid, with each police officer telling his story. But it couldn't have happened that way. Everything he said was refuted and proved wrong.

I later found out that we couldn't have used the gun in the room even if we had wanted to, because it wasn't functioning. It was proven that nobody shot that shotgun. No bullets came out of my room. The only shot that could have come from a Panther member was at the front door, where Mark Clark was killed. The FBI firearms expert, Robert Zimmers, testified on the ballistics. He said that from the way the door was and from the angle of the shot, it happened after the police busted through and came in shooting.

The health clinic was opened in January or February of '70, right after Fred was murdered. We already had the site. We rehabilitated a storefront; we put walls and partitions up and moved in medical equipment that was donated to us. Then we came in contact with a lot of doctors through organizations like the Medical Committee for Human Rights, led by Quentin Young. They donated their time and money. Our clinic was open five evenings a week. It stayed open for two years. I just wish Fred could have seen it, because he was really the driving force behind that clinic, and he gave me a lot of support.

My title was Minister of Health for the Illinois chapter. My cadre's job primarily was getting the health center organized and taking care of the health of the party members. We also had a sickle-cell anemia screening program. We tested over fifty thousand children in the schools. We used a test that was fairly inexpensive; we called it wet preparation. If it was done right, you could pick up about ninety-five percent of the people who either had sickle-cell anemia or the trait. That was the first major screening program. Later I traveled all over the United States, except for the South. They were trying to set up health clinics in other cities. So I would go there to lend a hand in organizing them.

Well, I stayed in the party for four years after Fred's murder. When I left the party, I wanted to go back to school right away, but my wife had more credits. So I worked while she was going to school. Then my wife and I broke up. She went into the Black Muslims. I moved to Michigan, then back to Chicago, then to Arizona. Finally I moved to Oakland.

Meanwhile, we had decided to sue. I was one of the plaintiffs. We didn't go to trial until years later. And then it lasted over a year. We got a settlement from Cook County, the city of Chicago, and the FBI. I think it was one and a half million between seven parties. Most definitely, that said that they did something wrong. But I was disappointed in the settlement, because after what happened to me, I thought I should have gotten a lot more.

I tried to do the best I could with what I got. I gave my mother and the family some. I bought a couple of vehicles. I bought some property near Eureka. I'm not able to do it now, but you can get a house fairly cheap there. I'm going to go back up there next year or the year after. It's real quiet and nice.

AKUA NJERI (DEBORAH JOHNSON)

The Black Panther Party here was organized around basic inalienable rights: land, bread, housing, education, clothing, justice, and peace. We felt that children should be fed. We knew that many of them were going to school hungry. Rather than commission a group to do a study or try to get funding, we set up breakfast sites throughout the city. We went door to door: "Come on, bring your children. The Black Panther Party has a free breakfast program." The only prerequisite was that you come— not who lives with your mother, who sleeps in her bed, how many brothers and sisters you have, or who your daddy is—just that you come. It wasn't the interrogation by a bureaucracy that people had to go through to get government services, which was the beautiful thing about it.

When the kids came in, somebody would greet them: "How you doing, little brother?" "How you doing, little sister?" We'd try to make them very comfortable so they wouldn't feel they were in a threatening atmosphere. We talked to them: "You know, you gotta eat before you go to school, so you can study." And the kids just really enjoyed it. They would all come back and bring their little friends. Sometimes the par-

AKUA NJERI (DEBORAH JOHNSON)

ents would come, too, to see what this was all about. Who knows what they had heard about the Black Panther Party in the media? And they would sit down, and we would occasionally feed them, too. We never made anybody feel like, "We're doing you a big favor." We were there as the people's servants. And that's what the Black Panther Party was about.

We also organized around getting people decent housing, fighting against slum landlords. We had free clothing drives, free food give-aways. We had a free prison busing program, in which those who couldn't afford it were able to visit their families and friends in Illinois, Michigan, and Indiana prisons. We also had a free medical center. We were the first group to do door-to-door canvassing and testing for sickle-cell anemia, which primarily hits the Black community. That was before sickle-cell became well known. We were doing all this in a country where people were going hungry, people didn't have housing, people didn't have clothing. We tried to reveal the contradictions within the system—that this is America, the land of the free, but people are denied basic needs.

The Black Panther Party also believed in self-defense. We would not go out, as we were displayed in the media, looking for a policeman to shoot or anything like that. But we believed if we were attacked, we had the right to defend ourselves.

Everybody in the party had to participate in its program. We didn't have anything like a high echelon that didn't participate. You had to go work at the breakfast site, whether it was serving food, mopping floors, cleaning the table and dishes, or whatever. Everybody had to go out and try to get sites for the breakfast program. You had to participate in soliciting doctors and volunteers for the free medical center. You had to canvass the community to let them know we had a free prison busing program. Fred did all that, too. I mean, he was the leader of the party. He'd go all over the country speaking. But he also worked at the breakfast program. He worked to get volunteers for free medical service. And you could see Fred out there a lot of times selling papers.

The first time I heard about the Black Panther Party was when my brother brought this xeroxed sheet of paper home with a panther on it. You could almost see the muscles moving on the panther. It said: "The Panthers are here." So I said, "Oh, wow, this is great." Then I heard that this group was over at the Chicago Teachers College, trying to turn the curriculum around. I said, "Wow, this *is* great."

I didn't really know that much about it, but I happened to look at this talk show, the Rodney Barret show. Fred Hampton and Bobby Rush and some others were on there. I sat there, listening to Fred talk about the party's ten-point program and the things that they were doing. Whatever he said, you knew it was the truth. You knew that this man really believed in what he was doing. He wasn't in it for any power or fame or glory trip. This man was going to live and fight and die for the people. And you just knew that. I was so impressed.

Then this friend of mine said, "Let's go to a political education class." I was attending City College at the time. I had my little skirt and sweater and my little English books and everything. So I went to this class, and this guy was there, wearing dark glasses and a long leather coat. He was walking around, hitting his fist into his hand. I thought: "Oh, my God. This is not for me."

Then he came over to me and asked, "You go to school?" I said, "Yeah." I was terrified. "What school?" I told him. "What did you learn today?" Well, I hadn't learned anything. I really hadn't, but I didn't appreciate him putting me on the spot like that.

He said, "See, that education is not relevant. The people are not really learning anything in school. And not just to single this sister out, but this is typical. You have to come here to learn something." I was so embarrassed, I vowed then, "I'm never coming back. These people are crazy."

But, of course, I went back. And they had us reading to death. I mean, seriously, you had to read! And I ended up not going to school and not going to work. The party became of primary importance to me, twenty-five hours a day of studying and working.

I worked with the breakfast program, worked in the office, typed up press releases, got literature out to the community, solicited donations, worked on fund raisers, sold papers. I think we had to sell over a hundred papers a week then, each individual. It was the hardest work I ever did, if you want to call it work, but I felt good about it. You were learning so much. You were doing so much. You were doing it for yourself in particular, but also for your community. And you could see yourself being productive. It was truly an education, in terms of the things that we were doing, the community groups that we worked with, and just going out talking to people. To hear them say: "Right on, sister, I appreciate what you're doing," and to have people you'd seen at rallies come in and say, "Well, I could sell some papers this week"—it just made you feel really good.

We had wide community support. That was evident in our rallies and all of our programs. When we had our give-aways, you could hardly get into our office. And if people wanted to volunteer and work with our program, we were open to that. Some people couldn't embrace the whole party ideology, but there were certain things they would participate in: "Yeah, that's a good idea. You're feeding kids. I can work with that." Or, "This is a good idea, free medical center." Or, "I could pass some literature telling people about your program."

There were raids going on continuously on Panther offices throughout the country. And that was really to frighten us, to wear us down, to destroy us. We always said: We must be doing something right if they put that much energy into stopping us. So it kind of fired us up to work even harder, to get more donations, to get more people involved, to spread the word even more. We thought about the repression and the raids, but we didn't let it weigh us down to the point where we would have been too afraid to move. It took a lot of love for Black people, I'm telling you.

I can't remember the exact times, but I witnessed some raids on our office, which was a block north of where we lived. One time I went by there, I remember, and I saw these police cars. There were so many of them driving toward the office, I just knew it was going to be a raid. I was real pregnant then, so I kept on walking. As I passed the door, the police came out of the office and were beating up on some of the Panthers. And then the officers set fire to our supplies for the breakfast program. It seemed like whenever we got lots of donations from community groups, a raid was guaranteed.

On the night of December 3, we had a political education class. People from all over the state were here: Mark Clark from Peoria, Harold Bell and others from Rockford. People were here from Michigan. They had all come together with the central committee of Illinois to get some guidance for reorganizing and restructuring what they were doing. They'd been here maybe a week or so. We were all going to political education classes, talking about distributing and selling the paper, getting more programs organized throughout the state.

That particular night, I didn't go to the class. Everybody else was there except me and O'Neal. We were both at the house. He stayed in the dining room area; I was mostly in the back bedroom. Me and O'Neal, we didn't talk much. Later, he dropped me off at my friend's house. It was probably about ten or eleven when I talked to Fred from my girlfriend's. Fred and I were supposed to meet and go out to his mother's house, but we changed our minds.

When I came back to the apartment, Fred was already there. They had had a good class and were still talking about some of the things they had discussed there. I went back to the bedroom. Then Fred came back. Then he went up front again and talked some more. He was always fired up to talk. Sometimes we'd be asleep, and he would shake me, "Deborah, Deborah," or "Hamp, Hamp," and he'd say, "Listen to this." And he'd have another idea for a speech. I remember once we were listening to Diana Ross and the Supremes sing "Some Day We'll Be Together." Fred got all fired up about this song, and he did a speech. He did it at some of the rallies. He started naming all the Black Panthers who had been murdered. He said, "Some day we'll all be together." It was the most beautiful speech.

Anyway, Fred finally came back. We got in bed. He said, "You better call my mom and tell her we're not going to come." So I called her, and we talked for a while. Fred fell asleep while he was talking to his mother. It was unusual, but I didn't think it was anything really strange. He had been running for days, trying to do everything. So I hung up the phone. I don't know how long we slept. But it was after twelve when we were talking to his mother, and from what I understand, the raid was around four-thirty in the morning.

The first thing I remember was Louis Truelock on the side of the bed, shaking Fred: "Chairman, chairman, wake up! The pigs are vamping!" I looked up and saw bullets coming from what looked like the front of the apartment and the kitchen area. The only movement that Fred made was to lift his head up slowly. He looked up, then laid his head back down. That was all the movement that he did. He never said a word.

A lot of times, if somebody rang the bell or came to the door, Fred would jump up. He could hear it, but I couldn't. I'm a heavy sleeper. So for him to move his head up that slowly and just lay it back down was real unusual. Especially if somebody was saying, "The pigs are vamping." If he had heard that, he would have flown up. Although Fred was big, he was very swift on his feet.

All this time, the bed was vibrating. Bullets were going into the mattress. I looked up at the doorway, and I could see sparks of light, because it was dark back in that area. I thought I was dead then and I was just seeing this as a spirit or something. I didn't feel any pain. I wasn't shot, but I just knew, with all this going on, it was all over. Then Louis Truelock yelled out: "Stop shooting! Stop shooting! We have a pregnant sister in here." At some point, they stopped shooting. Fred didn't move anymore. That was it, the one time he raised his head and laid it back down, like a slow-motion movie.

Louis Truelock said, "We're coming out with our hands up." I had on a robe that was open and a pair of Fred's long underwear and his house shoes that were on the side of the bed. I'm coming out with my hands up, and I hear a couple of shots, and I jump. And I'm thinking, "Keep your balance. Don't stumble. Don't make any sudden moves because you're not dead yet, but you will be if you trip." Louis Truelock was coming out behind me.

There were two lines of police that I had to walk through. I remember concentrating on their faces and trying to remember numbers—some of them had badges. I told myself, "You have to remember this. It's very important. Remember any details in their faces." But of course, later, I couldn't remember any of it. It's still a blur. Then one of them grabbed my robe and pulled it open. I was eight and a half to nine months pregnant then. "Well, what do you know—we have a pregnant broad." Another policeman grabbed me by the hair and slung me into the kitchen area.

The back door was open. It was winter time, and it had snowed. I was cold, and I was scared. Harold Bell was lying on the floor in the kitchen when I went in there. I stood facing the wall by the refrigerator, next to the open door. Louis Truelock was standing next to me. Then the shooting started up again. I heard a woman scream. Then it stopped. I looked around and saw Ronald Satchel on the dining room floor. He had blood all over him. They brought Verlina Brewer in from the front bedroom area and threw her against the refrigerator. She was bleeding. She started to fall. They grabbed her and threw her against the refrigerator again. Ron Satchel wasn't moving. I thought he was dead. I mean, I couldn't even see his body breathe.

There was more shooting. I heard a voice that wasn't familiar to me say, "He's barely alive. He'll barely make it." I assumed they were talking about Fred. The shooting started again, just for a brief period. It stopped. Then another unfamiliar voice said, "He's good and dead now."

I remember telling myself, "Don't think about this." And in my head I kept saying the ten-point program over and over, because I just knew I would flip out if I really got into everything that was going on there.

They took us out to the front of the apartment. I didn't look toward our bedroom because I was afraid I'd see a body I didn't want to see. I did see Mark Clark lying on the floor in the living room area when we went out. I knew he was dead, but I just kept saying: "You can't lose it now. You've got to live through this. You've got to remember everything you saw."

They took me, Harold Bell, and Louis Truelock to the police station. I think we went to Wood Street first. They locked up Harold Bell and Truelock and put me in kind of a detention room. The police were playing good cop–bad cop. One was real mean, and the other was saying: "We really want to help you, Deborah." It's a routine they do: one makes you feel threatened, the other makes you feel you have a friend you can confide in. We learned about that stuff in political education class from people who had experienced it.

There was a reporter there from the *Tribune*. I don't remember his name. He said he wanted to talk to me about what happened. I said, "No, I have nothing to say." Then when he was leaving, I said, "There is something that you can quote me on. There's only one word you need to put in your story—*fascism*. It will be clear to everybody." He got mad and left.

They took us from there to Eleventh and State. Now I was handcuffed behind my back. When they took me out of the paddy wagon, a policeman jammed a revolver to my stomach and said, "You better not try to escape." I was a million months pregnant, wearing house shoes in the snow, and handcuffed behind my back. So I don't know what escaping I was going to do. They took me to the lockup and let me make a phone call. I called Bob Rush. He said, "You know Fred is dead." I knew. I knew. He said, "Be strong, sister." I said, "Okay."

Anyway, when they took me to the police station, I was not going to let the matron examine me, because they stick their fingers everywhere to make sure you're not bringing drugs in. They knew I was with Fred Hampton. And I thought, "Are they going to try to kill our baby?" I said I wasn't going to let the matron stick any fingers anywhere. They said, "Okay, put her in the hole." I had heard about the hole. People who had gone to jail before told stories about this little room they put you in, with a hole in the floor for you to use as a bathroom. There are rats and roaches and all of that stuff. Finally I let them examine me. They charged us with aggravated assault and attempted murder.

The beautiful thing about this was that the Black Panther Party allowed the community to come through the apartment. They came from all over the country. We had double lines, triple lines all around the block. And we had our skeptics who said, "After all, they had guns there." Hanrahan, the prosecutor, had gotten on TV and called it "a vicious attack by inhabitants of the Panther apartment." But anybody who went through that apartment and saw all the bullet holes that had to come from the police was automatically sympathetic. It was just too blatant. They could see that there was no way the police were met by a "vicious attack." And people were crying: "I can't believe this would happen here."

What it did was it organized a lot of support for the Black Panther Party. The community really came together. People all over were coming into the office: "What can we do?" And they were sending in money. There was so much support, not just from the Black community but from people in all walks of life. They had little parties to raise bond money for the survivors. I was the first one they got out of jail, because I was pregnant. Then I went out with various community groups and raised money for the other people.

After I got out of jail, I came and saw the apartment. A lot of people didn't know who I was. I just took the tour with the others. The apartment was all shot up. The mattresses, the beds were all shot up. The clothes on the floor were all bloody. I lived through that whole thing again. I saw Fred before he was killed, talking on a number of occasions to different people, telling them what they needed to do. I heard his voice telling me, "When you have the baby . . ." You know, everything was just coming to me. And I cried because I saw the community there, just wrapping their loving arms around us.

The funeral was held at Rainer's funeral home. People came from all over to view the body, to sign the book. They were playing "Some Day We'll Be Together." Ralph Abernathy announced that he was starting the Fred Hampton scholarship fund for minority students going to law school. Community leaders from all over came to show support and to let people know that this was not just an isolated incident. It didn't just happen to Fred Hampton and the Black Panther Party. There were so many police brutality cases and murders of civilian people by police officers. But all of them didn't have the notoriety that Fred Hampton, chairman of the Illinois chapter of the Black Panther Party, had.

We first discovered that O'Neal was an FBI informant during the Stanley Robinson trial.* It was kind of a fluke that we found out. Somebody just happened to walk up in that courtroom, and there was O'Neal sitting up there, testifying for the state. And from then on, we started getting information. I never thought O'Neal was an FBI informant. But there had been some people in the party who suspected him because he would disappear for periods of time. Most people chalked that up as paranoia. You've got to understand that at that time the police were always watching us, our phones were tapped. And, of course, we knew they had infiltrated us. It reached the point where it could be said about anybody, "Oh, he might be a pig." So the people who did suspect O'Neal—we just marked it off as their paranoia. Fred would say things like, "O'Neal is crazy." But he would sometimes give me a look, like there's some things going on that we can't talk about. And I left it at that.

Of course, after the fact, everything falls into place. You start thinking about all the times you were with this person. I remember when my son was first born, I took him to my best friend's house. O'Neal and another Panther came over there to talk to me. When they left, my girl-

*See Flint Taylor's account of this trial, pp. 238–249.

friend said, "You shouldn't talk to these people. You don't know who's an informant. Those two guys that left could have been." She had never been in the party. So, of course, I thought she didn't know anything. She said, "I just get a bad feeling, especially about that one who did all the talking." I said, "Girl, you're really tripping." Later, when I found out who O'Neal was, that was the first thing I thought about. I got a real sick feeling, because I had this man come over to her house. He had even been to my mother's house.

Then it occurred to me: he could have drugged Fred that night. I was trying to piece it together. At what point could he have done it? There were so many times in the house when I wasn't with O'Neal. He could have walked back and forth and done anything. I wouldn't have known. You try to figure out when it happened, how it happened, but you just can't. Because when you don't suspect somebody, you don't account for their every move.

Well, it shook me. I vowed never to get in another organization, not from the fear of getting killed or arrested or anything like that, but because I just didn't trust people. I always believed that there were—and I still to this day believe there were—so many more informants we'll never know about. It just makes you really kind of leery of trusting people. It's like you've been robbed, beaten, raped.

It was tragic that Fred's life was lost. Here was a person who grew up in Blue Island. His family lived in Maywood. He could have been comfortable and denied our struggle. Of course, he was a victim of oppression, too, although he wasn't hungry or homeless. But here was a person who stood up and fought for Black people's rights in particular, and poor and oppressed people's rights in general. He made a commitment. One thing Fred believed was that he was not going to die in a car accident or by slipping on a banana peel. If you live to be forty-something and don't make a commitment for the struggle, you've died at an early age anyway. And Fred said: "I'm going to live for the people. I'm going to fight for the people. I'm going to die for the people." That was his commitment.

With Fred's death, we lost great leadership that didn't live long enough to realize even half of its potential. That's the tragedy. The leadership for the party was not there anymore. The direction was not there anymore. A lot of the support we had kind of dissipated for a while because there was nothing there to channel it, to embrace it, and utilize it. But that's not to say that everything ended. A lot of good programs survived.

Fred was buried in Louisiana, near Hainesville. Some years later, I went to visit his grave site. It's down a country road, really back in the woods behind this church. There's a lot of graves there. This particular year I went, Fred's headstone was shot up. His was the only one. And it just said to me that even in death there's a hatred or fear of what he stood for, what he did, how he worked for the community.

FLINT TAYLOR

Fred Hampton grew up in Maywood, a suburb of Chicago with a large Black population. As a high school student in the mid-sixties, he became very involved in civil rights. Even then, you could see he was going to be an unusually gifted leader. He was relied on by school officials to mediate racial tensions between Blacks and whites. At sixteen, he was instrumental in organizing a youth chapter of the NAACP at the Proviso East High School. Within a year, the chapter membership increased from seventeen to seven hundred. It was at this early stage that the FBI placed Fred on its "Agitator Index," which officially targeted him under COINTELPRO.

You have to remember what was happening in those days. When Martin Luther King Jr. came to Chicago and the freedom movement marched in Cicero, people stoned them. Then, in 1967, there were riots, an uprising in the Black community here. During this period, Fred's organizing came up against the same kinds of resistance other Black activists were facing. Because he spoke out publicly against police abuse, the Maywood police started a vendetta against him. He was arrested on petty charges and not so petty charges. All this was moving Fred to the left in terms of his politics.

In late 1968, Fred connected with Bobby Rush. They opened up a Black Panther Party office on the West Side and were very successful. They had a breakfast program for children; they were working on a medical clinic; they built alliances and coalitions with other organizations. There was a lot happening here, and the Panthers were right in the middle of it. And, of course, they were into self-defense. They guarded their offices with weapons. Police would come by and shoot into the place. Sometimes there would be an exchange of gunfire, and then some people would be arrested. On several occasions, police and Panthers were wounded.

I was a second-year law student at Northwestern then. During the summer of 1969, we were working at Legal Aid as students and lawyers and were helping the Panthers and other organizations. But the city had placed

FLINT TAYLOR

strong restrictions on what we could do. Hundreds of Panthers were arrested on whatever charges the police could drum up when the party members demonstrated or sold their newspaper or were involved in confrontations with the police. We couldn't represent them in criminal court, and we couldn't bring suits for police brutality. So in August of 1969, we started our own office—the same one we have today—the People's Law Office.

Ed Hanrahan was the state's attorney and chief prosecutor for Cook County. He was an up-and-coming political official, very aggressive, the heir apparent to Mayor Richard Daley. He had really fanned up a lot of racism during his 1968 election campaign. He talked about a war on gangs, but it translated into a war on the Black community. And he treated the Panthers as just another gang.

There were all those stereotypes being put out about the Panthers, about the violence, about these gun-toting, fear-causing Blacks. And here I was dealing with them on a day-to-day basis. I saw they were real people who had concerns about their lives, about what was happening in their community and also internationally. Some of them were students. Some had been in the penitentiary. Others were working people. All were dedicated to the principle of getting the oppression off their backs and dealing with police violence and economic injustice. They strongly believed the way to do that was through revolution. They believed in self-defense, having guns to defend themselves against the police. But that was the *only* thing the media would focus on, that the Panthers had guns.

The way the Panthers were portrayed was a conscious part of COINTELPRO. The FBI fed information to the media, which in turn stereotyped the Panthers as Black racists. In fact, that's not what they were about. They were one of the few Black militant organizations that made an effort, both in their rhetoric and practice, to form coalitions with white and Latino groups. Fred often said, "You don't fight racism with racism; you fight racism with solidarity."

For the two or three months before they killed him, Fred was on this incredible roller coaster. He was always speaking at a college or a high school or at some rally. He did a lot of organizing around Bobby Seale, who had been bound and gagged during the Chicago Eight trial.[*] The Panthers had daily demonstrations in front of the federal building.

In the fall of '69, a young Black man was killed by the police on the West Side. His brother came home from Vietnam for the funeral, and the police killed him, too. It was so outrageous, and the Panthers were doing a lot of very vocal organizing against police violence. Then, two weeks before Fred was killed, in mid-November, there was a very serious shootout. A couple of police were killed. Spurgeon Jake Winters was killed, too. Winters had been expelled from the Panthers or wasn't in good standing, but he was taken to heart after he was killed. Fred called

---

*Eight antiwar activists, who had protested at the 1968 Democratic National Convention in Chicago, were tried under the newly passed anti-riot act for conspiring to cross state lines with the intent to incite a riot. A description of the trial by Abbie Hoffman, one of the defendants, appears on pp. 326–328.

him a fallen comrade, a righteous soldier who had defended himself in a battle with the police. Tension had been very high even before that between the police and the Panthers. Now it was just off the charts.

In '67 and '68, the Federal Bureau of Investigation sent out two very significant memos to all their offices concerning the counterintelligence program. The one in 1967 called on the FBI field offices to "expose, misdirect, discredit, and otherwise neutralize" the Black movement.[81] The second memo, issued in March of 1968, the month before Dr. King was assassinated, followed up on the same theme. It specified the goals of the program. One goal was to "prevent the rise of a 'messiah'" who could "unify and electrify" the Black militant movement.[82] As an example, the memo named Malcolm X. It named Dr. King. It named Elijah Muhammad, Stokely Carmichael, and H. Rap Brown. The FBI documents we obtained later, during the trial, also showed the concern they had with Fred's leadership abilities. Other goals were to prevent coalitions between Black organizations, to discredit the movement in the eyes of whites and other Blacks, and to prevent the growth of those organizations. It was "no holds barred," with the bureau relying on violent, unconstitutional, and otherwise illegal tactics in pursuit of those goals.

Early in '69, the FBI heard that the Panthers were trying to straighten out the street gangs. Gangs were very strong in Chicago, and there was a lot of Black-on-Black violence. The Panthers tried hard to reach the leaders, to get them to have a more revolutionary view, to turn their wrath away from each other and direct it toward the oppression of Blacks. When Fred and Bobby Rush met with the leader of the Blackstone Rangers, Jeff Fort, the Chicago FBI heard about it from their informants.

To stop that kind of coalition building, the FBI sent Fort an anonymous letter: "The brothers that run the Panthers blame you for blocking their thing, and there's supposed to be a hit out for you." Then it advised, "I know what I'd do if I were you." In their explanation to Hoover, the Chicago FBI wrote that the letter "may intensify the degree of animosity between the two groups and occasion Fort to take retaliatory action which could disrupt the BPP or lead to reprisals against its leadership."[83] That was a really important piece of evidence, showing that the FBI's intent was to cause actual physical violence between the Panthers and the Blackstone Rangers. There was no question that they wanted to wipe out the leadership of the Panthers. And if they could do it with the Blackstone Rangers, they would.

Among the people who first joined the Panthers was an FBI informant named William O'Neal. He was right in on the ground level. As the

Panthers got stronger, he moved into the position of chief of security. He was the classic provocateur under COINTELPRO, always suggesting far-out violent schemes. He turned out to be the Judas who helped set up Fred Hampton's murder.

One of the FBI's programs against the Panthers was to spread false rumors. They would get a rumor going that so-and-so was an informer. In an organization where informants were not welcomed, that's a very serious charge. Here was O'Neal, the actual informant, spreading rumors about other people being informants and talking about using an electric chair to ferret them out. He actually bullwhipped someone he had branded. That is pretty high irony, I would say.

O'Neal answered to his control agent, Roy Mitchell, of the Chicago FBI. After the shootout with Jake Winters in November, O'Neal and Mitchell sprang into action. Within a week, O'Neal had given Mitchell a floor plan of Fred's apartment, which laid out all the rooms, placed the furniture, and designated the bed where Fred and Deborah slept. Mitchell, who had a close working relationship with the Chicago police department, contacted the Gang Intelligence Unit, the arm of the red squad that dealt with Black organizations. He fed them the floor plan and other important information, and in late November 1969 they set up a raid on Hampton's apartment, supposedly to seize weapons. But they called off their raid after the local FBI chief supposedly told them that the weapons had been moved from the apartment.

Roy Mitchell also had a close working relationship with Hanrahan and his assistant, Richard Jalovec. Mitchell told them the weapons had been moved back into the apartment. He gave them the same floor plan and told them who would be there and when. Hanrahan must have seen the raid on the Panthers as a real political opportunity. He jumped at it.

What was unusual about Hanrahan's situation was that he had his own private police force, officers assigned to him directly. Fourteen of them, led by Sergeant Daniel Groth, actually conducted the raid. They got a perjured search warrant for weapons; that would be their cover. The question was asked afterward: "You knew only one or two people at most would be there at eight o'clock at night because Fred conducted political education classes at a church during that time. If you really wanted to get weapons, why didn't you go then rather than four-thirty in the morning when they would all be there sleeping?" They admitted they changed the time of the raid to catch the Panthers at home and asleep.

There was always this suspicion that O'Neal drugged Fred that evening to make sure he would be out of it when the police raided. O'Neal was present in the apartment that day and had access to the food and drink that was served. An independent analysis of Fred's blood done at Cook County Hospital showed that he had a large amount of the depressant drug secobarbital in his system. And you can't find anybody, including O'Neal, who said that Fred ever used drugs. The government came out with a second test that attempted to rebut the first one. But there was always this suspicion—more than a suspicion, there was a strong circumstantial case—that O'Neal had drugged Hampton.

Preparations for the raid were highly unusual. They didn't take along bullhorns, spotlights, or tear gas, which they normally did in such situations. Groth approved the use of a Thompson submachine gun, although he had never taken one on a previous raid, not even to seize warehouses of weapons from street gangs. They also brought a semiautomatic rifle. They had numerous shotguns and hand guns.

Half of the raiders broke in the front door, and half broke in the back. You have to picture this apartment, a tiny ghetto flat. Mark Clark was sitting by the front door with a gun, as a sentry, but he was asleep. When they broke in, they opened fire and shot him dead. At the same time, they came in the back, shooting. They fired more than ninety bullets into the apartment. The Panthers may have gotten off one shot. Clark most likely fired as he fell, fatally wounded.

After they came in the front door where Clark was and killed him, they shot Brenda Harris in the hand and the leg. She lay there in terror. They took the machine gun and stitched right around her body, continuously firing through the wall. They did it, according to them, to "freeze" the people in the front bedroom. But, very conveniently, the shots all went in the general direction of the bed Hampton was on. They came to the door of the front bedroom with the machine gun and shot a couple bursts of fire in there. Doc Satchel was lying down in this room. He was hit five times. He had to have part of his colon removed. Verlina Brewer was shot in her knee and her leg. Blair Anderson was also wounded.

Deborah Johnson, Fred Hampton's fiancée, who was eight and a half months pregnant with their child, was in the bed with Fred when the police attacked. Deborah said that Fred never got up, which totally supports the idea that he was drugged. The police brought Deborah, Louis Truelock, and Harold Bell into the kitchen, but they didn't bring Fred. There was a burst of fire. Altogether, Fred was shot four times. Two bullets went into his head. The angles were such that he must have been shot from above. The evidence strongly suggested that a raider executed

Fred at point-blank range, as he lay on his bed, after Deborah had been brought out of the room.

By five or five-thirty A.M., the police left the apartment. They took the bodies out, and they seized some evidence they thought would support the story they planned to tell. But an enormous amount of evidence was still inside. Instead of sealing up the apartment, they left it wide open and went back to Hanrahan's office.

Hanrahan immediately held a press conference. He put the guns they had seized from the apartment on a table and told the press that it was a shootout, that two hundred shots had been fired, and that the "vicious" and "violent" Black Panthers had started the firing. He said that the Panthers had fired at the raiders as they came in the doors, that the initiating shots in each phase of this supposed shootout had been fired by the Panthers, and that "but for the grace of God, all of our men would have been killed." Hanrahan claimed that the Panthers had fired from Ron Satchel's bedroom and that Fred had gotten up and fired several shots at the police. He pointed to the gun Fred supposedly used. The press went right along with it—"Panther Chairman Killed in Shootout"—regurgitating Hanrahan's lies on the front pages of all four dailies.

Early that morning, we had gotten a call from Bob Rush: "Fred's been assassinated. Come to the apartment." We got there about seven A.M. The walls looked like swiss cheese. They were very thin, almost like cardboard, and many of the machine gun bullets had gone through two and even three walls. We were there until one o'clock the next morning, taking evidence. We set up makeshift lights. We would take each bullet or shell and mark where we found it. We'd take a picture of it. Then we'd film the whole thing. We did that for every piece of evidence. We didn't know what would be significant and what wouldn't. We felt we had to keep working. We were afraid the police were going to come back, arrest or shoot us, and seize anything that could implicate them. So we devised this system where we would take the evidence to a minister's house. Everything was cloak and dagger. It reminded me of the Underground Railroad.

It was a very intense situation. I remember there was a door lying right at the entrance to Fred Hampton's bedroom. One of the lawyers picked up the door and underneath was a huge pool of blood. They had dragged Fred off the bed after they shot him and left his body there. Then, at another point, we were in Fred's bedroom, taking evidence. I reached for a shoe, Deborah's high-heeled shoe, under the bed and pulled it out. It was full of blood, with a machine gun bullet in it.

If I wanted to point to one thing that had the greatest effect on my development, on my commitment to social justice, being in that apartment those eighteen hours would be it. To see the horrible violence that had been inflicted was incredible.

The Panthers did an astute political thing: They organized tours of the apartment. There were lines around the block waiting to go in. All you saw was this evidence of all these bullets headed toward Fred's bedroom and his bed. You know, people's minds were blown by this. I remember an older Black woman shaking her head, saying, "It ain't nothing but a northern lynching."

The Black community was outraged. The NAACP demanded an investigation. Members of the Afro-American Patrolmen's League examined the apartment and called the killing an "obvious political assassination" and a "deliberate police set-up."[84] Jesse Jackson, Ralph Abernathy, C. T. Vivian, everybody was speaking out. After a *Sun-Times* reporter quit over the coverage and the *Sun-Times* editor toured the apartment, some of the establishment media started to tilt our way a bit and ask some questions about the official version.

Hanrahan decided to go back on the offensive. He went to a friendly reporter on the *Chicago Tribune* and offered the paper an exclusive opportunity to talk to the police. So a week after the raid, the *Tribune* ran a front-page banner headline: "Exclusive: Hanrahan, Police Tell Panther Story." The article was accompanied by pictures. One of them showed a door with two holes circled. The caption underneath read: "Black Panthers fired thru door (bullet holes circled) at states attorney policeman on back porch." Under another picture it said: "Hail of lead tore thru bathroom door in fire from opposite bedroom according to police."[85]

Well, luckily, we still had access to the apartment. We saw that the holes that had been circled were not bullet holes but were nail heads. And we looked at what was supposedly the bathroom door and found it to be the bedroom door. It was riddled with machine gun bullets from police firing in. They had taken evidence of their own shooting and claimed that it was evidence of Panther firing. The next day, we went to the *Sun-Times* and were able to show that the *Tribune*'s exclusive was based on falsified information. Hanrahan's house of cards was beginning to publicly fall apart.

Normally after a police killing, particularly one where there are allegations of excessive force, an internal police investigation is held. In this case, they weren't even going to do one until Hanrahan decided he needed it to exonerate the raiders. What an investigation! Questions *and* answers were prepared by the Internal Inspections Division (IID) and shown to the raiders. Later, the IID official in charge testified that he knew of no other inquiry conducted like this one and admitted that the whole thing was a whitewash. The rest of the IID investigation consisted of a report by firearms examiner John Sadunas. He said that he had matched two fired shotgun shells with Brenda Harris's gun. At that point, he hadn't even been given the raiders' guns to make comparisons. The IID then came out with a finding that exonerated the police. It was announced with much fanfare at a big press conference by the superintendent of police and Hanrahan. It was the crassest of cover-ups.

A federal grand jury was impaneled in mid-December as a result of enormous public pressure. An FBI firearms expert, Robert Zimmers, who examined the raiders' guns and the Panthers' guns, testified that the two shotgun shells couldn't have been fired by Brenda Harris, as Sadunas had claimed. Instead, he matched them with a raider's gun. Zimmers said he'd never in all his many years as a firearms expert seen such a "mistake" by someone of Sadunas's experience. Zimmers examined all of the ballistics evidence and documented that all but one of the shots had been fired by the police. From all signs, it looked like there were going to be indictments.

Then the grand jury was recessed for three weeks. Jerris Leonard, who had been put in charge of the investigation, went to Washington to meet with John Mitchell and perhaps President Richard Nixon. After this hiatus, there was a radical change. A Black prosecutor involved in the grand jury investigation later said that from that point on, it became a complete cover-up. An FBI document we later uncovered revealed that Leonard had returned from Washington and informed the head of the FBI in Chicago, Marlin Johnson, that there would be no indictments against the police.[86] Instead, the grand jury would merely write a report. In exchange, Hanrahan agreed not to indict the Panthers. Of course, there was no case against them anyway, particularly after Zimmers's findings. By avoiding indictments against either group, two major avenues for exposing the FBI's complicity were blocked.

In June 1970, we initiated a civil rights suit for damages against the police, Hanrahan, and Jalovec for conspiracy to murder Fred Hampton and Mark Clark, to maim the rest of the people in the apartment, and to cover up evidence of their guilt. It sought many millions of dollars in damages. In 1976, we finally went to trial, seven years after the fact. It went on for eighteen months. Both before and during the trial, a vast amount of evidence implicating the FBI was uncovered.

The day of the raid, December 4, 1969, Bobby Rush stood in front of the apartment and publicly held J. Edgar Hoover, John Mitchell, and Richard Nixon responsible for the assassinations. We knew the government was doing that kind of thing, that the FBI had to be implicated, but we had no evidence to support it in this case. We didn't know O'Neal was an informant. We didn't know there was a COINTELPRO program. They thought they had closed all doors leading to the FBI, and they had, for several years. They probably would have kept them closed forever if the Stanley Robinson case hadn't come up in 1973.

Subsequent to his Panther involvement, O'Neal got into some other very heavy stuff. There were a couple of murders that a police officer, Stanley Robinson, supposedly committed. O'Neal was along with him at the time and was implicated in the actual murders. To save himself, he surfaced to testify against the officer. Suddenly this guy we knew as a Panther—and as a client—was publicly exposed as an FBI informant. It blew our minds. Our case hadn't gone to trial yet, so we started to drive after the evidence of what he had done. We subpoenaed FBI documents. We only got thirty-four, but among them was O'Neal's floor plan. On December 4, 1974, the fifth anniversary of Fred's murder, we added O'Neal and his FBI bosses as defendants in the suit.

We had a very reactionary judge named J. Sam Perry. When he didn't like something, he'd tell us to "shut up," and he'd run off the bench. He'd order the marshals to grab us. Both my partner, Jeff Haas, and I were cited for contempt. It was like playing the Yankees with Billy Martin as the umpire. It was just like that. If you wanted to demonstrate what a trial is not supposed to be like, what a judge is not supposed to do, what unfairness is about, our trial would be a perfect example.

Judge Perry actively thwarted our efforts to get evidence of FBI involvement. We kept subpoenaing documents. The judge would examine them in secret and then tell us, "There's nothing here that's relevant. You can't have them." We knew that wasn't true, but there was nothing we could do. Then the Senate Select Committee on Intelligence shared some of their documents with us, including the one about the phony letter the FBI sent to the Blackstone Rangers to provoke a violent attack on Fred and the Panthers. We came back to the judge, guns ablazing, so to speak: "What do you mean these documents aren't relevant? Look at this one." We finally forced them to release some of the COINTELPRO papers. They included a memorandum dated the day before the raid, which said that the local police planned "a positive course of action" based on the information about the Hampton apartment that the Chicago FBI had given them and claimed this "action" as part of COINTELPRO.[87]

Three months into the trial, we had Roy Mitchell, the FBI agent who controlled O'Neal, on the stand. He made a slip-up that showed there were still more files they hadn't admitted to or produced. It came out in public, in front of the press, so the judge felt he could no longer sit on this information. He ordered them to produce all the files. I don't think he suspected what was going to happen. Up from the FBI office came more than twenty-five thousand pages of suppressed FBI documents in shopping carts.

Among the files was the "bonus" document. After the raid, the higher-ups in the Chicago COINTELPRO program wrote to bureau headquarters, taking credit for it and asking for a bonus for O'Neal. They referred to O'Neal's floor plan that the FBI had given Hanrahan. They boasted that O'Neal's information "proved to be of tremendous value" in setting up and killing Fred Hampton and in making the raid "a success."[88] After this incredible assassination and slaughter, the Chicago FBI wrote Hoover and took credit for it internally, while for seven years they had publicly denied any involvement in it. Bureau headquarters quickly approved payment of O'Neal's thirty pieces of silver. It was one of the most damning pieces of evidence we uncovered.

We also got access to the Gang Intelligence Unit's files on the Panthers and were able to uncover several other informants. One of them, Marie Fisher, had given information to both the GIU and the FBI. During the trial, she handed out a statement to us and the press in which she said that the Chicago head of the FBI, Marlin Johnson, had asked her to drug Fred Hampton before the raid. She confirmed this in an interview with us. But this was not revealed until after Marlin Johnson testified at the trial. And the judge would not let us recall Johnson to confront him with this new information under oath.

After eighteen months, the jury went out. They deliberated for three days and were deadlocked. Rather than declare a mistrial and have it tried again, the judge dismissed the entire case. He took matters into his own hands and never let a jury decide. It was, to say the least, a highly unusual move.

We appealed to the Seventh Circuit and got a reversal. It was a terrific decision, which found that we had proved a strong prima facie case of conspiracy between the FBI and Hanrahan. The court found that the FBI and the Department of Justice had obstructed justice. It said there should be a hearing to determine what punishment should be imposed against them. It found that there should be a hearing to determine whether raid leader Daniel Groth committed perjury in order to get the search warrant. The court also ordered that whatever evidence was still being kept from us must be produced at retrial. It overturned our contempt citations and removed Judge Perry from the case. The city of Chicago and the FBI took it to the Supreme Court and lost; certiorari was denied. It came back here for a new trial, and we started to hold hearings and to develop more evidence.

When Judge Perry threw the case out, it was very discouraging. I mean, it's really hard to describe what it was like to be in court for eighteen months in front of that man. No matter how outrageous the conduct of the other side was, whatever lies were being told by them, how much evidence we were uncovering daily, he would just ignore it all. You'd go into court, and you'd know your arguments were going to go nowhere. But we continued to fight. Every day we kept battling, even though we knew what was coming. It was very discouraging. But then we just threw all our energies into writing this two-hundred-fifty-page appeal brief. To win so overwhelmingly on appeal felt as good as it felt bad to lose the trial.

Ultimately, after all the appeals and before the second trial, we worked out an agreement with Cook County, the city, and the FBI. We ended up settling for just under two million dollars, which at that time was one of the largest civil rights settlements. The appellate decision was so strong and the size of the settlement was so large that we were able to righteously claim that it was a very important victory. But it couldn't change what happened or bring Fred and Mark back to life. And their assassinations sent a powerful message to those young folks the Panthers were organizing: "This is a very serious game you're getting involved in, and you could end up dead."

But we have also gained strength from the courage, dedication, and leadership of Fred Hampton. After Fred was murdered, the Panthers coined the slogan "The Spirit of Fred Lives." All these years later, that's still true. In his short life, he moved many with his inspirational leadership, and that inspiration continues to contribute to the movement even today.

Voter Rights Revisited

UNDERCUTTING AFRICAN AMERICAN
ELECTED OFFICIALS

In 1985, Albert Turner, a veteran voting rights activist in Perry County, Alabama, was indicted by the Reagan Justice Department for voter fraud. His attorney noted, with some irony, that "he stood accused of cheating black folk of the vote he literally risked his life to gain for them."[89] Now that African Americans were becoming a majority of registered voters in many areas, agents of the FBI had become vigilant about the possibility of vote fraud. They spied on the Perry County Civic League's get-out-the-vote meeting; they hid behind post office mail slots to see who mailed absentee ballots; they swept the county, getting affidavits from elderly Black voters to try to produce evidence of fraud; and they showed up at job sites to "interview" Black workers.[90] Nevertheless, Turner, his wife, and another person indicted with them were acquitted on all counts. Earlier, a federal court had overturned the convictions of two other African American voting rights activists in Alabama, Maggie Bozeman and Julie Wilder, who had been convicted by an all-white jury on similar charges.

When the government interfered with the efforts of African American citizens to register to vote, its actions clearly had serious consequences for civil liberties. When the government attacked African American political activists or public officials for alleged criminal violations, as the

Justice Department did with Albert Turner, the implications for civil liberties were somewhat masked but no less consequential. By the 1980s, direct attacks on the African American freedom struggle had been supplemented, if not supplanted, by the criminalization of dissent: false allegations of wrongdoing that tainted activists and even forced Black officials from office.

An essential feature of the criminalization of dissent, especially as practiced by the FBI and the Internal Revenue Service (IRS), is its covert nature. Claims of politically motivated investigations and prosecutions are difficult to prove conclusively when they are made against government agencies that operate in secret. Violations of civil liberties are harder to substantiate, and enduring doubt also discredits and disables activists or elected officials once criminal allegations are lodged against them. Whether investigated but not indicted or indicted and tried but not convicted, officials thus tainted are consumed with the task of defense, often without the support that otherwise would be forthcoming.

"In the late 1960s and early 1970s, many groups and persons were selected for investigation" by the Internal Revenue Service, the Senate Select Committee on Intelligence reported, "essentially because of their political activism rather than because specific facts indicated tax violations were present."[91] The IRS inquiry into the National Council of Churches, for example, which began in the mid-1960s and continued for nearly ten years, was driven by a "continuous visceral opposition" to the council's support for civil rights, according to investigative reporter David Burnham.[92] African American activists, too, were targeted, including members of CORE and SNCC.[93] The IRS investigated fifty branches of the National Urban League "in the absence of specific evidence of tax violations," the Senate Select Committee stated, "because they exercised First Amendment rights."[94] The IRS and the Alabama tax collection agency both investigated Martin Luther King Jr., who became the first person in the history of the state to be prosecuted on felony tax charges. "Despite all the bravery he had shown before, under personal abuse and character assaults, despite the courage he was to show in the future," Coretta King said of her husband's ordeal before his final vindication, "this attack on his personal honesty hurt him the most."[95]

By 1964, the IRS had supplied the FBI with a list of contributors to the Southern Christian Leadership Conference, to be used by the bureau in a scheme to "eliminate future contributions."[96] Acting in league with the FBI, the IRS improperly selected the bureau's political targets for its investigations and shared its findings with the FBI for "uses [that] were clearly illegal."[97] In the case of antiwar critics, the bureau acknowledged that seeking disclosures of tax returns from the IRS "is consistent with our efforts to obtain prosecution of any kind against Key Activists to remove them from the movement."[98] But the lion's share of the bureau's tax harassment was directed against African American activists. The FBI received tax returns for most of the African Americans it had labeled "Key Black Extremists" to use "as weapons in its campaign to 'neutralize' all of them."[99]

Richard Arrington was listed by the FBI as a "Key Black Extremist" in 1972 after he won a seat on the Birmingham City Council and became an outspoken critic of police brutality. It was the beginning of twenty years of investigation and harassment, which were most intense while he served as the first African American mayor of Birmingham. "There is no reason to believe that a federal crime has been committed, therefore, there is insufficient probable cause to go forward with an investigation," concluded a prosecutor who reviewed the FBI's preliminary inquiry into virtually every aspect of Arrington's business dealings in 1985.[100] Unable to discover incriminating evidence, the FBI set about to provoke the mayor into breaking the law. When one entrapment scheme after another failed—twice by the FBI in 1987 and again by the FBI and the IRS in 1988—Arrington was cited by the U.S. attorney as an unindicted co-conspirator in a "kickback" scheme. The U.S. attorney publicly disclosed the allegation on the eve of Arrington's reelection bid and maintained it until 1993, when the Department of Justice finally dropped the accusation.

The federal government's tenacity in the face of repeated failures to find or provoke wrongdoing suggests the selective harassment of a prominent and outspoken African American official. The case became more persuasive when, in 1989, FBI operative Robert Moussallem personally disclosed to Mayor Arrington his involvement with the FBI, the IRS, and the U.S. attorney in their efforts to entrap him. Moussallem swore in an affidavit that, "under their direction," he was "to set the Mayor up."[101] The same year, disenchanted FBI and IRS agents informed the special counsel for the city of Birmingham, Donald Watkins, of the government campaign against Mayor Arrington. "They told me [Assistant U.S. Attorney] Barnett wanted to get Arrington whether it took one year or ten," Watkins said.[102]

The agents also revealed that federal law enforcement officials had developed a "hit list" of African American officeholders they would target on public corruption charges. Selection was based not on who was suspected of criminal activity but on who was most vocal, most visible, and most complained about by conservative groups in Alabama. Richard Arrington headed the list. In perhaps the most devastating revelation, Hirsh Friedman, an FBI operative whose credibility the government had lauded in court, described an informal bureau policy called *Fruhmenschen*—a German word meaning "primitive man." "The purpose of this policy," Friedman swore in an affidavit, "was the routine investigation without probable cause of prominent elected and appointed black officials in major metropolitan areas throughout the United States."[103]

Other cases also suggest selective targeting. Cleveland Mayor Carl Stokes was indicted on 467 charges of fraud, larceny, and forgery, which were dropped a year after he left office. Charges of violating federal campaign financing laws against former U.S. Representative Shirley Chisholm were dropped after months of a highly publicized investigation. William Hart, mayor of East Orange, New Jersey; A. Jay Cooper, mayor of Pritchard, Alabama; Curtis Miller, mayor of Alortion, Illinois; and Kenneth Gibson, mayor of Newark, New Jersey, were all found not guilty after having been charged with corruption. In 1981, FBI agents began their sixth investigation of Tennessee Congressman Harold Ford: monitoring him in his home, following him as he drove his car, and spying on him from an office they rented next to his in Memphis. In 1987, Ford was finally indicted on nineteen counts of conspiracy and fraud. Unable to secure a conviction, the government retried him in 1993, and Ford was acquitted on all charges.

Half of the 26 African Americans in Congress between 1981 and 1993 were subjects of federal investigations, a ratio equivalent to 204 white representatives being under such scrutiny, when in fact only 15 were.[104] Selective targeting is even more apparent when indictments are compared to convictions. A National Council of Churches study reported in 1990 that over the previous five years, African Americans, who were only 3 percent of the public officials in the South, were defendants in 40 percent of the corruption cases.[105] Yet in Alabama, for example, of the African American public officials brought to trial during the 1980s, fewer than 25 percent were found guilty, only a fraction of the average conviction rate.[106] That African American public officials are overrepresented among those investigated and indicted and underrepresented among those convicted of crimes lends strong support to the proposition that they have been unfairly targeted.

The attack by the IRS and the FBI and its media conduits on Mervyn Dymally, one of only two African American lieutenant governors in the nation since Reconstruction, lasted years and took its toll on his political career but produced absolutely nothing in the way of evidence of wrongdoing. "At issue," Dymally said, "are the civil rights of African Americans: Can they be represented by officials who are free to carry out their duties without intimidation?"

MERVYN DYMALLY

I was born in a small multiethnic, multireligious village in Trinidad. My father's people came from India as indentured servants to work the sugar cane and coconut estates. He was Muslim; his family built the mosque in the village. My mother was of African descent. She was Catholic; her family supported the rectory. We children were caught between these two fiercely religious families. At some point, there arose a dispute about which church or temple we should go to. The Anglican canon was brought in to mediate the dispute, and we ended up as Episcopalians. Subsequently, my brothers and sisters drifted back into the Catholic Church, and I stayed with the Anglican Church.

My father would be offended if you said we were poor. We had a kind of nonpoverty status. By that I mean we had an abundance of food, and there was a communal spirit in its distribution. The workers, after they finished working on the estate, had gardens in which they grew all kinds of vegetables, casava, rice, and so forth, which they shared. You could climb up somebody's tree and get fruit. You could cut the sugar cane and the papaya, the bananas. Nobody regarded you as a thief. And there was always a lot of wild meat and fish that the butchers and fishermen shared.

After my mother and father separated, he remarried, and I went up to the city to live with him and my stepmother. I went to secondary school there. I was not a very good student. I didn't have a sense of focus, and I was troubled by my lack of status, country boy as I was. Father Boniface at the Catholic school was very elitist. He catered to the white kids who were boarding in the school. He was Dutch, and he was probably a racist. But in the islands, we did not judge things on the basis of race but rather on the basis of class. And I identified with the workers. During our growing up, we had a great deal of admiration for T. Uriah "Buzz" Butler, who started the workers' revolution in Trinidad.

I failed the senior Cambridge exam, which meant that I would have had to go back to school for another year. But I had already attracted the attention of the oil workers union by my heckling of the opposition party. So when the union offered me a job on their newspaper, the *Van-*

MERVYN DYMALLY

guard Weekly, I took it. This was during the war years. There was a de-gree of affluence, and things were relatively inexpensive. I began chas-ing booze, women, and music.

My mother was pushing me to get out of the rut I found myself in, and we did write to a number of schools. I finally decided on Lincoln University in Missouri, because the registration fee was about fifty dol-lars a semester and there was no tuition. In 1946, I came to Lincoln, to-tally unprepared for the difference in environment and culture. After that first semester, I went to New York and lived with some friends from

Trinidad. Again I was just searching. I worked on about eleven jobs in ten months: washing dishes, pushing the garment cart, and feeling very sorry for myself. I used to go to Grand Central Station and look at the people arriving, with the hope that I'd see somebody I knew. You talk about a man who was lonely in a crowd. I finally decided I wanted to go home. My father hit the roof.

You've got to understand that the whole system in Trinidad was based on class, and the only two education degrees that provided wealth and status were medicine and law. So when you left the colonies in those days, that's what you studied. Nothing else mattered. In the fall of '47, I read about a chiropractic school in Dayton, Ohio, that offered an accelerated degree. I went there, only to discover that the school was not accredited and that chiropractic wasn't even recognized in Trinidad. I ended up working as a janitor at General Motors. I left there and went to physiotherapy school in Anderson, Indiana, still trying to find something. From there, I went to Chicago and then to California. I finally ended up at Chapman College.

But it wasn't until 1951 that I recognized that those Hollywood stories we read in Trinidad were not true, that riches didn't fall from trees, and that there was no substitute for hard work and education. My grades began changing; my whole attitude changed. I got married, began raising a family, and brought the rest of the family over here. After I graduated, I started substitute teaching and working at night—two full-time jobs. I would get off from teaching about three and race down the Pasadena freeway to work at four. I did that for several years until I got too exhausted.

One day, a friend invited me to join the Young Democrats in Pasadena. The night after the meeting, the news about the sit-ins in Greensboro, North Carolina, broke. I can remember saying to myself, "I really ought to be doing something more useful than coming all the way down here with these white folks." I decided to organize a Young Democratic club in the Black community, which was kind of a first at the time. Then I was elected treasurer for the Young Democrats of California. As treasurer, I got introductions to John Kennedy and to Bobby and Ted Kennedy. I became a coordinator in Kennedy's presidential campaign.

One day the United Auto Workers had a conference in Fresno, and Gus Hawkins was there. He was the state assemblyman for South Central Los Angeles and part of Watts. He asked me for a ride home, and in the course of the conversation, I said, "Mr. Hawkins, who's going to succeed you?" He said, "I don't know." I thought that was rather odd. Here's a guy who had been in public life for twenty-eight years, and he had no successor. One of the reasons was that the Black leadership was moving out of the ghetto into better neighborhoods. So I decided to run and moved into the district. I got elected to the assembly in 1962.

While I was there, the one-person, one-vote ruling came out. By the way, the first and only time I talked to Chief Justice Earl Warren, I asked him what he considered his most important decision. He said, "The one-person, one-vote ruling." Los Angeles County, with forty percent of the state's population, had been gerrymandered so that it had only one state senator. With the reapportionment that followed from that Warren decision, the representation increased from one to thirteen. There was one Black district, and I fell right in the center of it. So I became the first Black state senator in California in 1966, the same year that Reagan got elected governor.

Those of us who had left the assembly as a result of reapportionment were part of a group in the state senate called the Young Turks. We overthrew the old guard that was tied to the lobbyists. That started the most productive period in my political career. I became Senate Democratic Caucus chairman, chairman of the Reapportionment Committee, chairman of the Joint Committee for Legal Equality for Women, chairman of the Select Committee on Children and Youth. They were very fruitful years. I authored the Child Abuse Prevention and Treatment Act long before child abuse became an issue. I did the Early Child Education Act and the very productive Child Growth and Development Act. I authored the Dymally-Seroti Child Care Construction Act, a bill to provide state funds to construct child care centers. And the Dymally-Waxman Campaign Reform Act. I sponsored the bill giving eighteen-year-olds the right to vote. I authored legislation that funded the first Black medical school west of the Mississippi, the Charles Drew University of Medicine and Science, which enrolls young people with a commitment to go back to underserved areas.

I became the "women's legislator" in California. I introduced the Equal Rights Amendment and the Community Property for Women Law. Before, when a man died, a woman did not automatically become a trustee of the estate. It had to be probated. But when the woman died, the man did become a trustee. We equalized that. And now, when there is a divorce, the wife is automatically entitled to fifty percent of the property acquired during the marriage.

In 1967, Louis Martin, vice chairman of the Democratic National Committee, put together a group of Black elected officials at a reception for LBJ in Washington. While I was there, a reporter, David Broder, asked me what I thought about the Vietnam war. Well, I took a swipe at the war, and the story was syndicated. As I understand it, Louis Martin and the rest of the folks were very upset with the story that came out in the *Washington Post*.

Right after that, I was in my office in the state building at First and Broadway. The receptionist said, "There are two men here who want to see you." As they walked in, they flashed their badges. They were from the felony unit of the Internal Revenue Service. I called my accountant, and he said, "Do not talk to them. These are felony people." Now, what is interesting about that is that usually when you are going to be audited, they send you a series of form letters telling you to come in. Then they go through your stuff with your accountant and your lawyer. With me, they started a felony investigation right away.

The IRS audited me three years altogether. One year, they got me for about six dollars. Another year, they got me for per diem. In California, all legislators received the equivalent of what was the standardized federal allowance for travel every day. There had been a gentlemen's agreement in effect between the IRS and the legislature that we did not pay taxes on the per diem, but now they said I had to pay those taxes. When I protested, they said, "Well, go ahead and file a claim." I didn't, because if you file a claim, you get audited again. The IRS kept after me anyhow. I ended up paying about twenty-five thousand dollars in legal fees.

In the sixties and seventies, there was a lot of hostility between the Los Angeles police and the citizens. There was a shootout between the Black Muslims and the police in 1962. There was a shootout between the police and the Black Panthers in December 1969. I was not the spokesperson for those groups, but as the only Black state senator then, I had to speak out about their frustrations. The night of the Panther shootout, I was called. I went over to Central Avenue, and the police just rushed in. They had been hiding in the back of a hot dog stand. Then all of a sudden, they started swinging their clubs everywhere. They hit me. Afterward, when they realized who they had hit, they kind of sobered up.

The police had such a paramilitary hold on the city that few politicians dared speak out against them. But I had organized a group called STOP, Stop Terrorizing Our People. And I was resented for that—the chief of police, William Parker, invited me to leave the country. I think that resentment stayed with the police and the *Los Angeles Times* for years afterward.

My campaign for lieutenant governor in 1974 was very exciting. Ed

Reinecke, who held that position, resigned; and Governor Reagan appointed my opponent, State Senator John Harmer, to fill the vacancy just three weeks before the election. So Harmer was able to run as the incumbent. Jerry Brown was the Democratic candidate for governor, but we never campaigned together. He kept his distance from me, and that gave reporters a lot to write about. Nobody expected me to win. But we had a coalition that represented a lot of diverse groups: women, the elderly, Blacks, Latinos, labor, and rural Californians. We campaigned in all the rural counties, and that's what brought me over. I actually ran ahead of Jerry Brown.

I got sworn in by a friend of mine, Judge Billy Mills, and I walked across the hall from the senate chambers to my office. A reporter was there from the NBC channel. He told me he had heard that I hired my brother on the staff. In California, that's against the law. I said, "I may be many things, but I'm not that stupid." That was the first day. And it never stopped. It never stopped.

By statute, the lieutenant governor is the chair of the Commission for Economic Development. The commission had been a dead duck, but I went to the legislature and got it revived and funded. There was no greater problem facing the people of California than the economy, and I saw that as my greatest challenge. We tried to get the Japanese to open up plants in the state. We wanted to help the housing industry by providing low-interest loans, help minority business development, deal with rural employment problems and women in the economy. Well, the media and law enforcement agencies waged a campaign against me for years, and they tried their damnedest to get me indicted. They concentrated on the angle that as chair of the commission I was requesting payoffs. I don't know for what. The commission had no grants to give. It had no contracts. Of course, they could find nothing.

There had been a headline in the San Francisco papers that about a hundred state legislators were being investigated. From all of those people, the FBI singled out Al Song and myself, the only two minorities in the state senate. We had been seat mates for eight years. They leaked information about Al that caused his defeat in '76, even though he was never indicted. They went through everything I had. There were about ninety-four boxes of my materials that I had transferred to the California State University archives in Los Angeles. The FBI took it all.

I was somewhat surprised that the FBI came after me, because I didn't see myself as a threat to the establishment. But they did. The FBI went to ABC News in Los Angeles with a package of materials, trying to give them the impression that I had all these hidden treasures. The assignment editor happened to be a friend of mine. When his manager said, "We ought to do this one," he said, "I know Dymally; let me talk to him." So he called me, and I went up there.

He said, "You were in a corporation with this guy." I said, "I can't remember." He said, "Hey, man, why are you lying to me? They just left here." I said, "Who did?" "The FBI. They say you were a director of the Brussard Enterprises."

"Brussard Enterprises? Oh, shit." Then I remembered. Back in the sixties, in order to incorporate in California, you had to have three signatures. So Harry Brussard, who had a neighborhood liquor store, said to me, "Merv, my wife and I would be honored if you would come on as the director of our little family corporation." That was all the way back in '62, but the FBI had dug the stuff up and given it to this guy at ABC to make it seem as if I had a lot of money. That's the way they leak stuff. Of course, he didn't use it.

But apparently the FBI went to NBC with the same package, and they bought it. The FBI even tipped off NBC that they were going to subpoena my bank papers. NBC went to the bank and filmed the FBI doing it. Unprecedented! Needless to say, the bank didn't want to do any more business with me. In fact, one of the most prominent lawyers in Sacramento, who was counseling me, asked me to sever my relationship with him, because his partners could not stand the harassment they were getting from the FBI. My accountant of many years dropped me. He said, "Hey, Merv, I hate to do this, but I can't deal with this FBI harassment anymore."

Once the words "under investigation" are hung on you, no one returns your calls. You lose contracts and constituents. The banks call in notes. Your credit is stopped. I knew all along that I had not gotten involved in any corrupt practices, but I must confess to you that I was intimidated by these negative stories.

Talk of an indictment against me was everywhere. There was never any indictment—just talk. And it never let up, with the FBI calling in friends and so forth. You feel so humiliated. The lowest day for me was when I walked in the office and the Senate Democratic Caucus staff was talking about my "indictment." It had permeated the capital so deep that it was on everyone's lips. They even called a federal grand jury and subpoenaed my sister. She had a beauty school, and the theory was that I was laundering money through her. The poor woman damn near died. But there wasn't one witness to say I was involved in anything.

The media aids and abets this whole process. In the midst of my re-election campaign, a *Los Angeles Times* reporter went to an investigator for the state attorney general's office and said, "I understand that Dymally is going to be indicted for political corruption." The investigator said he wasn't aware of that, but he wrote up a memo to his supervisor. In the memo, he put: "P.S. This is a rumor only." A deputy attorney general, who had taken a leave of absence to work for my opposition, gave the memo to the wife of a CBS commentator in Los Angeles, Bill Stout. The "P.S." had been erased. She was also working for my opposition, and, two weeks before the election, Stout read the memo on the air and said, "You heard it. Dymally knows it. He's going to be indicted." That seemed to give substance to the rumors that had been going on all along. Everybody picked it up—a big story.

I was driving down the San Diego freeway with my son and campaign manager when I heard it on the radio. I said to both of them, "It's all over with." I knew it would just kill me. As I traveled up and down the state, no one ever asked me about the fact that I pioneered in women's rights in California, in child care. It was always about the indictment. No matter where I went, it was the indictment. I was beaten up so badly that for years I felt like people were looking around and thinking what kind of corrupt politician I was.

After the election, a friend of mine from Gary, Indiana, told me, "I want to open up an engineering office in Los Angeles, and I'd like to retain you." He was going to include me as a partner to start up the business. Well, the FBI interviewed him, and he put a stop on a check he had given me for the business. Oh, it scares you. The FBI was so good at knowing my activities. Another time, my brother-in-law, who is a real estate agent, had what he thought was a good deal for us to get into. The California Canadian Bank, a branch of the Imperial Bank of Canada, gave me a credit account of ten thousand dollars, so I proceeded to write a check against it. The bank had a little visit from the FBI and canceled out the loan, and my check bounced like a piece of rubber. Fortunately, my friends loaned me some money to make the check good. All of '79, I was under this constant harassment every place I went.

It's a federal offense to make a false statement on an application from an institution that is insured by the federal government. But you know what happens on those applications. You sometimes forget. You sometimes don't have all the accurate stuff: the dates are wrong, some of the figures may be off. Well, the FBI went to every savings and loan where I had secured a loan. They tried their damnedest to get those people to suggest that perhaps one of the forms wasn't totally accurate. That was really stretching it.

I mean, this FBI thing is very intimidating stuff. Listen, I'd gotten to the point in '79 where I was damn near broke because nobody would touch me. Here I am, a Ph.D, a former college trustee, sixteen years in the legislature, a former lieutenant governor, and I couldn't even get an offer from the state colleges to lecture. I finally got a research assignment through Kenneth Clark. He's the one who did the paper on the effect of segregation on children for the *Brown* decision on school desegregation. Ken Clark had a contract to do a study on an educational program that affected migrant children. My wife and I and another researcher got a subcontract to do part of the study. Then the FBI went to Ken. He told them to go stick it. He was incensed, because I'd been a fellow at his research center, and he'd known me very intimately. Kenneth Clark was one of the few people who didn't collapse, who didn't cave in.

A friend of mine who's a psychiatrist said: "By the way, I never did tell you, but the FBI came and talked to me about you." They'd tell people that they were just doing a routine check, but it was very intimidating. Look, when the FBI visits you, you're scared. They interviewed friends of mine, and some of them just peeled off. They called in my ex-wife, figuring all ex-wives are unhappy with their husbands. She gave them a tongue lashing. She said, "I want you to leave this man alone." They never called her back, but they went to my son. That scared me. They tried every which way.

On October 1, 1979, I went to Compton to a reception. A city councilman there said to me, "You ought to run for Congress in this district." I reasoned to myself, "Maybe I ought to think about it. If I were in business and lost, I certainly would not give up. I'd try and regroup." I came back and talked to my son and my campaign manager. Well, in January of 1980, I announced on a Tuesday in Los Angeles that I was going to run for Congress. The next day, I went to Sacramento to have a press conference. Meanwhile, the investigation the FBI started in the seventies was still continuing. When the reporters asked about it, I just said, "Well, I don't know anything about it, but I'm going to bring the investigation out in the open. Let the public make a judgment on my candidacy." I couldn't deal with this cloak-and-dagger legal system anymore.

Then this reporter from the *Sacramento Bee* came to me and asked, "Have you checked with the U.S. attorney?" I said, "No." He said, "They're about to drop your case." Here's a reporter giving me this inside information. That was Wednesday. My lawyer called the Department of Justice on Thursday. Saturday I got the letter telling me they dropped the case.

Harassment is a personal phenomenon. No other person experiences the agony of that harassment. It is only when we relate our personal pain to someone else, and in the process find that our experience has been far from unique, that we begin to see the pattern. George Brown of Colorado and I were this country's first two African American lieutenant governors since Reconstruction. We met in Atlanta at a conference of the National Association of Human Rights Workers and began sharing experiences. We realized we had each been looking at small parts of a pattern, a pattern neither of us recognized until we put our two pieces together and found that they matched. I could have been in Colorado, and he could have been in California.

Dr. Mary Sawyer, who was also at the conference, felt our experiences had been too similar to be chance events. So she traveled to every corner of this country to talk to African American elected officials about what had happened to them in office. For two years, she pieced the pattern together and wrote a report.[107] It was the first detailed account ever written of the systematic harassment of Black elected officials in the United States. And it is just not an issue of the rights and privileges of these politicians. At issue are the civil rights of African Americans: Can they be represented by officials who are free to carry out their duties without intimidation?

PART THREE

Silencing Opponents of War

Wartime is no time to quibble about constitutional rights and guarantees.

William R. Vance, Dean of the University
of Minnesota Law School, 1917

"Dear parents, I must this day, the fourth of April, 1918, die," Robert Paul Prager wrote on a scrap of paper. "Please, my dear parents, pray for me."[1] Prager, a young bakery worker of German birth, had fallen victim to the accusations of a local loyalty committee. He was searched out, stripped of his clothes, wrapped in an American flag, and dragged stumbling through the streets of Collinsville, Illinois, before being taken beyond the city limits. There, on the Old National Road, some among the mob of four hundred pulled him high into a tree, where he was hanged until he was dead.

"From the facts I have been able to gather concerning the lynching of the man in Illinois," U.S. Attorney General Thomas Gregory said, "I doubt his having been guilty of any offense." The *New York Times* noted the country's democratic war aims and worried that "we shall be denounced as a nation of odious hypocrites." The *Washington Post* allowed a positive note: "In spite of excesses such as lynching, it is a healthful and wholesome awakening in the interior of the country." Meeting the next day, President Wilson's cabinet decided to sidestep the issue. Wilson was silent, and his attorney general said that it was a matter for Illinois to handle. The eventual trial of the mob leaders, who were blazoned in red, white, and blue ribbons, was accompanied by a band that played patriotic airs in the courthouse. This was a case of "patriotic murder," the defense told the jury. After twenty-five minutes of deliberation, the acquittal was celebrated with cheering and hand-clapping. "Well, I guess no one can say we aren't loyal now," one juror shouted.[2]

Whatever Prager's opposition to the war might have been—he had in fact tried to enlist in the Navy—his "disloyalty" was predicated on unsubstantiated rumors and suspicions of socialist inclinations. In the hysterical fervor of the day, any questioning or opposition to the war was considered intolerable. As the frenzy spread, labor and the left also fell victim to the complex of superpatriotic vigilantes, the press, and the government that acted in the name of the holy cause.

The crusade to "save democracy" left its dysfunctional stamp on much of the rest of the century: The clear lesson was that war, or the threat of war, would brook no dissent. Government repression of war critics during World War I would be replayed in a lower key on the eve of and during World War II, become accentuated during the decades-long Cold War, and then reach a crescendo again during the Vietnam war, when the right to dissent was dramatically reasserted. Repression—with its attendant patriotic hoopla and its equation of dissent with disloyalty—recurred, although its emphasis sometimes changed. Trials of war opponents continued to occur in significant, if lesser, numbers; police assaults on protesters became, if anything, more violent; and covert attacks against dissenters by intelligence agencies in the Vietnam era dwarfed those that had occurred during World War I, when political surveillance was in its infancy.

WORLD WAR I: TURNING DISSENT INTO DISLOYALTY

After the declaration of war on April 6, 1917, many who had opposed the U.S. entry into the conflict abruptly changed positions. Those sections of the peace movement that did not collapse—by and large, its left wing—accused the government of going to war to advance the interests of American business and challenged the constitutionality of the newly passed conscription law. As they did this, their strength increased. The Industrial Workers of the World gained thirty thousand new members in the first six months of the war; Socialist Party candidates in the municipal elections of 1917 averaged over 20 percent of the vote; and the peace coalition, the People's Council of America, held rallies across the country that attracted thousands. In addition, over three hundred thousand men were delinquent in some way with the draft. It was all evidence of a troublesome undertow of antiwar sentiment with which a war-bound administration had to contend.

The administration's newly appointed Committee on Public Information deployed a "propaganda blitz" to compel support for the war, while the nation was portrayed as being at the mercy of enemy spies. Woodrow Wilson spoke of Germans who "filled our unsuspecting communities and even our offices of government with spies."[3] Twenty thousand spies were loose in New York, the *New York Times* headlined; spies were in the State Department, the secretary of the treasury warned in a McCarthyesque charge; and the head of the Senate Naval Affairs Committee had "no doubt spies are in our departments. I want to see the German devils ferreted out and hanged."[4] Citizens of Milwaukee urged officials to provide their city with military protection from German spies. Cecil B. DeMille volunteered studio guards armed with machine guns to protect Los Angeles.[5] "The demand that spies be found and shot became louder," Joan Jensen writes, "mingled inextricably with pressure to stamp out all criticism and opposition to the war."[6]

"You should be lined up against a brick wall and shot," a chief of police told an arrested cleric who was a critic of the war.[7] Suspected war opponents were in fact beaten, whipped, and tarred and feathered by mobs of patriots. Homes, offices, churches, and people were painted yellow. Suspect citizens were forced to kiss the flag, made to recite a "catechism of loyalty," or come before self-styled patriotic tribunals for proper atonement, not only for opposing the war but also at times for not supporting it enthusiastically enough. No one was to be above suspicion. "Look up your neighbors," the Tulsa *Daily World* warned, "be careful with whom you converse, and always let the other fellow do the talking until you are absolutely sure of his patriotism."[8]

Public schools "became seminaries of patriotism."[9] University professors were dismissed or indicted for disloyalty. Christian pacifists, Jehovah's Witnesses, and others were jailed for preaching peace from the pulpit or for distributing religious antiwar messages. The virtually uncontestable power of Postmaster General Albert Burleson to refuse second-class mailing privileges for "anything that will impugn the motives of the Government for going to war," in his words, all but doomed a critical press.[10] And when an African American newspaper wrote of the Black soldiers executed by the military after a violent confrontation with white Texans: "We would rather see you shot by the highest tribunal of the United States Army because you dared protect a Negro woman from the insult of a southern brute in the form of a policeman than to have you forced to go to Europe to fight for a liberty you cannot enjoy," the newspaper's editor was sentenced under the Espionage Act to twenty years in Leavenworth.[11]

The Espionage Act of 1917 imposed inordinate fines and prison terms to punish, among other things, "false statements with the intent to interfere with the operation or success of the military or naval forces" and attempts to "willfully obstruct the recruiting or enlistment service of the United States."[12] Although the act was presented as a measure to "safeguard and protect our national defense secrets," in fact no spy was ever prosecuted under it.[13] But more than two thousand persons were, for the crime of disagreeing with the government's war policies, despite Wilson's pledge not to permit the law "in any way to be used as a shield against criticism."[14] Under the loose interpretation of the act favored by district courts, prosecutors did not have to show that defendants' statements did in actuality "interfere" with the success of the military or "obstruct" recruiting into it but merely that their statements could possibly have done that. Culpable speech could even include words drawn from private conversations or speech that had been uttered before the country's entry into the war. The "military and naval forces" to which the act applied were not only the U.S. Army and Navy but also the Canadian Army, the Salvation Army, the YMCA, and the Red Cross.

So construed, the Espionage Act produced bizarre results. A fisherman overheard complaining about the unseasonably bad weather in the spring of 1918—"Damn such a country as this"—was arrested; the producer of a film that depicted British atrocities during the Revolutionary War was given ten years; another man was sentenced to twenty years for circulating a pamphlet that endorsed the reelection of a congressman who had opposed the conscription bill.[15] Persons who complained about the draft, cast aspersions on the administration's motives for entering the war, or criticized war bond drives were successfully prosecuted. But the act's prime targets were the Industrial Workers of the World (the Wobblies) and the Socialists. Wobblies were arrested and convicted by the hundreds in mass trials that disabled the organization. Virtually the entire Socialist press was banned from the mails, and much of its leadership was indicted, frequently in the heat of election campaigns. Nor were pacifists tolerated. The Fellowship of Reconciliation journal, *The World Tomorrow,* was banned from the mails because, as one historian described, "its message of love beyond political boundaries violated the Espionage Act."[16] In 1918, the Espionage Act was made more stringent: It became a crime to "willfully write, utter, or publish any disloyal, profane, scurrilous, or abusive language about the form of government of the United States," the flag, or—ironically—the Constitution.[17]

Although the Espionage Act was the centerpiece of the government's assault on dissent, the American Protective League, with its vast, quasi-official network of volunteer homefront spies, was a harbinger of the importance that political surveillance would come to assume in American life. The APL was a private, clandestine force sheltered within the Justice Department as an adjunct to the Bureau of Investigation at the same time that it was built and staffed within financial-industrial hierarchies, mirroring their organizational structures and their anti-labor biases. This extraordinary combination, with "a cross-section of the ruling business elite" at its top and 350,000 secret operatives below, watched for signs of disloyalty in every large city and many small towns.[18] The APL cooperated with the Selective Service and joined forces with Military Intelligence, state and local law enforcement agencies, and vigilante groups. It conducted millions of investigations for the Justice and War Departments. The APL's historian proudly noted that, to uncover information on "disloyal" persons, the APL gained access to the records of banks, the confidences of ministers, and the contents of mail and telegraphs. Its minions wiretapped telephones; planted dictaphones in homes and offices; posed as salesclerks, credit bureau representatives, and reporters; and resorted to theft "thousands of times."[19] With local red squad agents and the Bureau of Investigation, the APL infiltrated antiwar groups, broke up their meetings and church services, arrested their speakers, and raided their headquarters. "In eighteen months," Joan Jensen concludes, "the United States had fielded a corps of sleuths larger than any country has done in all history. And they called it the American way."[20]

TOWARD A NATION UNITED: WORLD WAR II AND THE COLD WAR

In 1933, students at ninety American colleges and universities campaigned on behalf of a pledge originated by Oxford University students. Bluntly put, the pledge asserted that they would not support their government in any war it might conduct. This pacifist position, had it been uttered in 1917, would surely have brought indictment under the Espionage Act.[21] In the 1930s, the rise of Nazism in Germany and militarism in Japan were creating anxieties about a new war at a time when students were becoming disillusioned with the previous one, including the harsh repression that had accompanied it. In April 1934, twenty-five thousand heeded the call for a National Strike Against War, the largest political demonstration by students the nation had seen. Spring strikes for peace became annual events that lasted through April 1941. In 1936, five hundred thousand students struck, amounting to almost half of the undergraduate population.

College administrators responded by banning antiwar meetings and speakers; expelling and suspending student antiwar activists; censoring antiwar literature, including student newspapers; proscribing radical student groups; and encouraging, even organizing, physical attacks on student war protesters. Despite the negligible participation of faculty members, student protest was attributed to the cunning of Communist professors. By 1936, twenty-one states and the District of Columbia required loyalty oaths for professors. Four years later, hearings before the Rapp-Coudert Committee of the New York state legislature resulted in what was at the time the largest purge of college professors on record. Meanwhile, presidents, deans, and other college officials secretly opened student files to the FBI and supplied it with the names of student organizers, members of antiwar groups, and their sympathizers.[22]

When the United States declared war after Pearl Harbor, the red scare that had been mounting ended, or at least was held in abeyance. The near-uniform support for the war—on the left, only the Socialist Workers Party opposed it—was in striking contrast to the opposition to World War I. After the conviction of SWP leaders under the Smith Act in 1941, criticism of the war came mainly from the right. Although Attorney General Francis Biddle vowed, once the war began, to avoid "the disgraceful series of witch-hunts, strike breakings, and minority persecutions" of World War I, almost two hundred indictments under the Espionage Act were issued before the fighting ended.[23] And some seventy newspapers were barred from the mails. An unsuccessful prosecution under the Smith Act was brought against right-wing and native fascists, which, as Robert Goldstein observes, "was notably weak in showing any conspiracy or any attempt to undermine the armed forces."[24] The most egregious violation of civil liberties, however, was based not on ideological reasons but on national origin: 120,000 Japanese Americans, most of them citizens of the United States, were summarily incarcerated in concentration camps during a war against totalitarianism, with the country experiencing barely a shudder at the contradiction.[25]

At the war's end, public opinion strongly supported Franklin Roosevelt's belief that American-Soviet wartime cooperation would continue in peacetime. With the collapse of the wartime alliance, however, Harry Truman adopted an adversarial stance toward the Soviet Union—enunciated in the Truman Doctrine—and labeled opposition to his foreign policy as Communist-inspired or subversive.[26] Amid cries of "soft on Communism" from the right and stories of espionage sensationalized in the press, the red scare was resurrected. Nine days after Truman announced his doctrine, he ordered a loyalty program instituted, which swept up millions of government employees in its net. Within the week, J. Edgar Hoover had linked foreign policy with internal security by urging a domestic crusade against Communism. To that end, the FBI forces were marshaled, HUAC launched its inquisitions, and Congress enacted sweeping repressive legislation.

When former Vice President Henry Wallace headed a third-party ticket in 1948 that advocated cooperation with the Soviet Union, it was red-baited into oblivion. Goldstein notes that "the real casualty of the election was not Wallace's Progressive Party, but freedom of debate over foreign policy in America," with the result that "the mere presentation of views contrary to the official foreign policy 'line' moved 'into the realm of treasonous or at least un-American activity.'"[27] The "American peace movement," he adds, "which had shown signs of renewed vitality in the immediate aftermath of World War II, was virtually devastated by 1950."[28]

It is not surprising that opposition to the Korean war was quiescent, rarely resulting in marches and rallies or even in milder forms of protest. But in 1954, when the United States detonated a hydrogen bomb in the South Pacific, antiwar protest revived with a new focus: halting nuclear testing. In 1957, a grassroots test ban coalition, Citizens for a Sane Nuclear Policy (which came to be known as SANE), was formed; within several years, Women Strike for Peace (WSP) came into being. Newspaper ads, rallies, and civil disobedience challenged the policy of nuclear deterrence that required commitment to an unending arms race. True to form, HUAC launched an attack on WSP to undercut its credibility, and the Senate Internal Security Subcommittee's charge of Communism against SANE split that organization, seriously damaging it, after it had experienced dramatic growth.

THE NATION ASUNDER: THE VIETNAM WAR

The Vietnam war evoked "a clash unprecedented in American affairs," Tom Wells writes, noting that "never before had so many U.S. citizens defied their leaders during wartime."[29] National protests began in April 1965 with an antiwar rally sponsored by Students for a Democratic Society. As the war intensified, outrage grew, sparking demonstrations, sit-ins and teach-ins, student strikes, draft-card burnings, electoral campaigns, fasts, lobbying, vigils, street theater, and later, for a small minority, violence. Diverse—indeed, contentious—opponents of the war joined in coalitions that often split apart, only to come together again. Throughout the Spring Mobilization, the New Mobilization, the Student Mobilization, and more, activists alternated between exhilaration at each larger, more insistent demonstration and anger and exasperation at the escalation of the war that often followed. Nevertheless, Wells contends, the movement "played a major role in constraining, de-escalating, and ending the war."[30]

In cities across the nation, refurbished and greatly enlarged local police intelligence units, the red squads, declared a covert war on peace activists. Their spies within antiwar organizations amassed dossiers on personal and political activities. They vandalized equipment and stole membership lists and other vital materials, indeed, "anything we could get our hands on." They obtained positions of leadership from which they could influence policy, tried to provoke peace groups into violence, and, by their "saturation" infiltration, created an atmosphere of suspicion.[31]

The more overt attacks on dissenters ranged from creating annoyances to inflicting brutality. Philadelphia police stopped cars with antiwar bumper stickers to harass the occupants. Los Angeles "was shaken by a police riot in which a large number of demonstrators . . . were clubbed and brutalized."[32] A rally at Grand Central Station, called by the newly formed Yippies, was broken up by New York police, who charged demonstrators, punching, choking, kicking, and bloodying them with nightsticks. "One could only conclude," said a *Life* reporter who observed it, "that the current police tactic is terrorism."[33] Police at the 1968 Democratic National Convention in Chicago attacked demonstrators indiscriminately, clubbing news reporters, bystanders, and ministers from the local community as well. A climate had been created that supported the violent suppression of demonstrators. On May 4, 1970, troops from the Ohio National Guard suddenly and without warning fired on Kent State student protesters, leaving four dead as the Guardsmen turned and marched away.

Although the federal government's covert war against peacemakers reached its height under the presidency of Richard Nixon, its foundation had been laid during the Johnson administration. Both Johnson and Hoover invoked the same tactic against the antiwar movement that had been used against the civil rights movement: taint it as Communist or foreign-dominated. But as "Communism" became less credible as an investigative rationale in the late 1960s, a different menace was seized on:

the "New Left," an amorphous category that invited abuse. The FBI agent in charge of New Left intelligence testified that it "has never been defined. . . . It's more or less an attitude, I would think."[34]

The FBI surveilled diverse individuals and groups, from "free universities," which were said to be "anti-institutional" or "subversive," to persons listed in the *Congressional Record* who supported Senator Wayne Morse's criticisms of the Vietnam policy. The antiwar Institute for Policy Studies was burglarized, wiretapped, and infiltrated by scores of FBI informants. Federal agents spied on Students for a Democratic Society, the American Friends Service Committee, Clergy and Laity Concerned, the New Mobilization to End the War, SANE, Veterans for Peace, and Vietnam Veterans Against the War. Goldstein notes that between 1960 and 1974 the FBI conducted over a half million "subversive" investigations, not one of which resulted in a prosecution for attempting to overthrow the government, the purported reason for the inquiries.[35]

Political surveillance itself contributed to an inhibiting climate of fear and suspicion, but the FBI also intruded more directly in the affairs of antiwar groups. In May 1968, a counterintelligence program, COINTELPRO, was begun against the New Left. In July, the director of the FBI sent to all field offices guidelines for disrupting student and antiwar protesters that included using "obnoxious pictures" on leaflets to discredit leaders, "instigating or taking advantage of personal conflicts or animosities" among leaders, "creating the impression certain New Left leaders are informants," exploiting the "hostility" toward the Socialist Workers Party "wherever possible," and being "alert for opportunities to confuse and disrupt New Left activities by misinformation."[36] Before this version of COINTELPRO officially ended, hundreds of disruptive actions had been taken against peace activists.

In addition to the FBI, the CIA, in apparent violation of its charter, infiltrated antiwar groups and set up what it called Project CHAOS, which amassed great amounts of data on war protesters. The IRS, with no basis for suspecting tax delinquency, illegally audited tax returns of antiwar groups and individuals; and the White House complemented efforts to punish war opponents through the judicial system with extralegal operations against them. Meanwhile, legions of Army agents—as many as twelve hundred of them—probed civilians, unfettered by criteria that could protect constitutional rights. By 1969, the Army had instituted a plan for "the identification of all personalities involved or expected to become involved, in protest activities."[37] And in fact, the Senate Select Committee on Intelligence found that "political dissent was routinely investigated and reported on in virtually every city within the United States," with the accumulation of files on one hundred thousand Americans.[38] Not only did Army agents infiltrate the National Mobilization Committee to End the War in Vietnam, antiwar groups in Chicago, antiwar demonstrations in Washington, and even an antiwar vigil in the chapel of Colorado State University, they also infiltrated a Halloween party for elementary school children in Washington where the presence of a local "dissident" was suspected. So much political intelligence was being produced that the Department of Justice set up the Interdivisional Information Unit (IDIU). In 1968, the IDIU summarized thirty-two thousand intelligence reports on Black Power and antiwar protests.

Under Richard Nixon, the IDIU was incorporated into the Internal Security Division (ISD) of the Justice Department, whose staff was enlarged from six persons to sixty. By then, criticism of the war had been established as a First Amendment principle in the courts. The ISD turned elsewhere: Between 1969 and 1972, "virtually every prominent antiwar leader" was prosecuted on dubious if not outlandish allegations of conspiracy to commit criminal acts.[39] Although the use of the conspiracy charge circumvented rules of evidence otherwise in force and gave prosecutors other advantages, the government lost case after case at the trial or appellate levels. Nevertheless, the costs incurred in time, energy, and money diverted these groups from their antiwar activities. Those disruptive effects were intensified by the ISD's aggressive and abusive use of grand juries.

"The federal grand jury has become a battleground," as Moore's *Federal Practice* put it, in the Nixon administration's war "against the press, the intellectual community, and the peace movement generally."[40] The ISD subpoenaed more than one thousand persons—including antiwar and antidraft activists—to appear before federal grand juries. Grand jury witnesses stood defenseless against federal prosecutors once they were immunized—and thereby stripped of their Fifth Amendment rights—and were compelled to testify under pain of imprisonment for civil or criminal contempt.[41] Those who chose not to be imprisoned were subjected to questions about the details of their political beliefs and associations, their personal habits, and even their intimate relationships. A judge of the Ninth Circuit Court of Appeals observed that "it would be a cruel twist of history to allow the institution of the grand jury that was designed at least partially to protect political dissent to become an instrument of political suppression."[42]

A decade later, Ronald Reagan also tried to shut down opposition to his foreign policy. This time, the targets were primarily religious activists who were moved by the economic deprivation and death squad reprisals faced by the people of Central America. When these activists refused to be silent, secret political police from the FBI and the Immigration and Naturalization Service were marshaled against them.

Tainting the Antinuclear Movement

HUAC AND THE IRREPRESSIBLE
WOMEN STRIKE FOR PEACE

Little of the American peace movement survived the Cold War consensus of the McCarthy era. But by the mid-1950s, with the test of a hydrogen bomb in the South Pacific, new voices arose to challenge the strategy of nuclear deterrence. By 1960, the influence of the most prominent of these voices, the Committee for a Sane Nuclear Policy, had grown dramatically, and the Senate Internal Security Subcommittee began an investigation of SANE. Pressed to prove that it had no red tinge, SANE—like the CIO, the NAACP, and even the American Civil Liberties Union before it—adopted an exclusionary rule: Communists were to be purged from its ranks. The result was disastrous: Many members were expelled, many chapters defected in protest against the lapse in civil liberties, and SANE's entire youth section was suspended for challenging the policy.

In contrast, Women Strike for Peace refused to exclude anyone for their political beliefs. With creative, spirited protest, this organization helped to legitimize dissent against Cold War dogmas. Born in 1961 of one woman's outrage at the cavalier acceptance of the nuclear threat, Women Strike for Peace took shape as its founder, Dagmar Wilson, invited others to join her. Even as the women were planning their first "strike"—simultaneous demonstrations in sixty cities across the country in support of a test ban—the FBI began to amass what turned out to be forty-nine volumes of records, collected in the course of its long and far-reaching but fruitless effort to characterize the group as "subversive." In order to spy on the WSP delegation at the disarmament negotiations in Geneva, the FBI sought the assistance of Swiss police and CIA agents abroad. The CIA itself had already been busy investigating the group's domestic activities, an inquiry that violated the agency's statutory limitations. And WSP chapters were monitored by police departments in such cities as Los Angeles, Washington, Chicago, and New York.

At the end of 1962, leaders of Women Strike for Peace were called to appear before HUAC. The focus of the committee's inquiry was WSP's refusal to require the same ideological test of its leaders that SANE and other groups had used. At a time when Cold War hysteria was waning, these women, through ingenuity and humor, were able to respond to HUAC largely on their own terms, a development that did not go unnoticed by the press. "Peace Gals Make Red Hunters Look Silly," one paper headlined.[43]

As WSP became an established part of the coalitions that sponsored massive antiwar demonstrations, the CIA's surveillance increased and its interest shifted. At first, the CIA labeled WSP a "Communist front," but by 1967 the peace group had been classified as potentially violent and a threat to the CIA's personnel and installations. In what columnist Mary McGrory called "the CIA's most ridiculous waste of money," it infiltrated the Washington, D.C., WSP chapter with a spy who reported on its meetings, photographed demonstrators, and stole the group's records and lists of supporters.[44] After ten years of spying, however, the CIA discovered no foreign connections, no evidence of illegal activities, and "certainly no history of violence."[45]

Here, Dagmar Wilson, a longtime resident of Virginia, describes the origins of Women Strike for Peace and her encounter with the House Un-American Activities Committee.

DAGMAR WILSON

In 1983, I placed an ad in the *Loudoun Times Mirror* on behalf of Women Strike for Peace. It said: "I refuse to be counted as one of twenty million *acceptable* dead in a nuclear war in which the U.S. would hope to prevail over the Soviets." Quite a lot of correspondence in the local paper was generated by this statement.

And then an advertisement appeared in the same paper recalling the days of the House Un-American Activities Committee. It began with the

DAGMAR WILSON

headline: "The So Called 'Nuclear Freeze Movement' Is A Deception &
Fraud. Loudoun Residents Are Being Pitifully Victimized By The Notorious 'Women Strike For Peace.'" It named people as Communists and
tried to associate Women Strike for Peace with them. Much of its detail
and many of its names were taken out of context from the committee
hearings more than twenty years before. So there it was. Those investigations were still being used against us.

I was a commercial artist and illustrator in Washington in the 1950s,
and I did a lot of freelance work for the government. Although I did my

work in my own home, I had to put my hand on the Bible and swear that I never had been a Communist each time I did an assignment. I thought it was funny. I expected a smile from the secretary who was holding the Bible and reading the loyalty oath that I was required to take. Oh, no—she was deadly serious. So I just accepted the ritual, absurd as it seemed to me. I didn't realize what a terrible thing was being done to me—and to us—in those days.

Then, in 1962, the House Un-American Activities Committee subpoenaed me, along with other members of the Women Strike for Peace movement. I had reason to be quite concerned. My husband, Christopher, was working at the British Embassy as a foreign civil servant. We talked it over very seriously beforehand. This committee had gotten people jailed, and if that happened to me, it could have meant his job. He said, "Yes, but there is nothing to do but go up there and answer the questions as you think best."

Those of us who were subpoenaed had to work out how we would confront the committee. We were advised by others to play it cool, no publicity, the less the better. But one woman from upstate New York said, "They've subpoenaed Dagmar Wilson. What we should do is all volunteer to testify." That evening, we sent telegrams to our mailing tree throughout the country. We said: "Volunteer to testify. Come if you can. Hospitality provided. Bring your babies, if necessary." And that is what happened. The committee got hundreds of telegrams from people offering to testify.

Quite a number of the women did come, and that hearing room was full. Three hundred women were there with their babies and their bottles. It was much more like an enlarged PTA than a congressional hearing. But the tall guys with the helmets were there, too, standing around the wall.

There were three days of hearings, and I was the last to be called. As I listened, I could see very clearly what a simple-minded plot or scenario the committee had thought out, about who we were and how to "trap" us. They tried to set us up as being run by a group of clever Communist women in New York. They had me down as a very innocent victim, a "duped" leader, who was being manipulated by these wicked Communist ladies. If we had fallen for the committee's line, our organization, like some before us, would have been split by dissension.

But the strength of Women Strike for Peace was that we did not allow ourselves to be intimidated by the fear of Communists in our midst. We were not about to examine each other and say, "Are you or aren't you or were you ever . . . ?" The committee's ghost was not our ghost, so we were not haunted by it. We felt, really, that we were a sisterhood of fellow spirits, and we would march with Communist women and every other woman in the world to abolish war and to work on nuclear disarmament.

Each woman spoke her own lines and took her own stand. The first witness took the Fifth Amendment. She just wasn't about to answer. That was her personal vow and her decision. One woman said: Yes, she had been a Communist in her youth. So what? Others were quizzed about having written for their college papers, which were, of course, leftish, and always are if they're worth anything.

When the first woman was called, we all stood. This was by agreement beforehand. Then came the gavel and the pronouncement: "That's a demonstration. It's not allowed." The next day, we tried applause. That, too, was against the rules. Then, with the typical ingenuity of our sex, we decided that every woman who went up for interrogation would be presented with a bunch of flowers by her sisters, which we did. And everyone who came off the stand was hugged and kissed and congratulated.

By the time my turn came, the solidarity of the women had been very well established. A charming young woman with a baby on her arm came up to me with a bouquet. I took it, kissed the woman, and went up to the stand. I was nervous as the dickens. I was afraid I might be trapped into saying something that would be harmful in some way to somebody else. But as it turned out, the questions that were asked of me were so patently absurd that the only way I could answer them was with humor, almost challenging my inquisitors not to be so silly. And there was a great deal of laughter, because everything I said was true and people in the audience had experienced it with me.

Alfred Nittle, the attorney for the committee, was himself a rather poor imitation of a high-powered lawyer. He kept taking off his glasses and thrusting them at me with a question. That made me want to laugh, you know, but I tried very hard not to. He was trying to establish what he thought was a simple fact. He asked me, "Are you the leader?" I said, "No. I'm not. We are all leaders in this movement." He said, "But you are, nonetheless, called that, are you not?"

I tried to explain that it's partly the press that does these things. Anybody who had been at any of our local meetings would have seen the way we thrashed things out until we really had agreement. We were quite Quakerly in our methods, though maybe a bit more lively. We worked over things until we achieved consensus.

Nittle tried to worm out of me how we operated. Finally, in exasperation, he said, "I don't know how you manage to operate at all." I answered, "Sometimes we wonder, too." It was quite a truthful and spontaneous answer. But obviously the way we were operating in those days
was extremely effective, although we really couldn't have described it
too well to anybody. It worked because we were unified, we were together, and we had the same kind of instincts. We were responding to
our times. Our nation's policy in the face of the advent of nuclear weapons
affected us all very much the same way.

Everyone—the Congress and the country—was beginning to feel the
committee was a bit of a drag. This was a committee that had not passed
any legislation in the twenty years of its existence. It was more and more
of an embarrassment, really, even to the House. The press had a ball.
They were all so happy to see the committee put down. And we were
given the chance to do it. It was really very gratifying. But, look, were
we ever lucky! We came along at an opportune moment. We had much
more public support than victims of this committee had had before. And
our mutual support and our determination not to be intimidated saw us
through.

Women Strike for Peace started out of my own personal anger. It began with the Berlin Wall and the cavalier way newscasters were saying
that this could mean war between the USA and the USSR. Of course, it
would be a nuclear war. The fallout shelter program brought home to
everybody the danger we were in. And radioactive fallout from nuclear
tests had already found its way into the systems of children. People were
beginning to be uptight about that.

I remember a news story about some Quaker peace walkers crossing
the USA. Their destination was Moscow. It appeared on the "women's
page" as a human interest story rather than as a political event. The tone
of the article was patronizing. I thought, "The heck with this! These are
the only people who are really making a statement against this kind of
folly. If they're nuts, then so am I." My anger was beginning to build.

Bertrand Russell had just been arrested in Trafalgar Square. He said
civil disobedience was the only way he could draw attention to the danger we were in. Now, I'm an old-time fan of Bertrand Russell. I cut my
teeth on his philosophy, and I grew up reading his books. I thought if a
man of his stature, his position in England, has to go to these lengths,
this is important.

Some friends were visiting us that evening, both medical men, both
English. They were sitting in our backyard. I read them Bertrand Rus-

sell's statement and said, "This is iniquitous that they're jailing men like this. What do you think about it?" Well, these guys were making wisecracks and treating it all lightly. This angered me very much. I mean, I was close to tears. This was typical of the put-downs that women got when they brought up questions of this kind. To me, it was vitally important and way beyond making jokes over. My husband knew me well enough to see that I was getting close to an explosion. He made a suggestion: "Women are good at getting things done when they've made up their minds to do it."

I'd never been in any way politically active before in my whole life. But the very next day, I got on the telephone and called the local chairman of the Committee for a Sane Nuclear Policy: "What are you going to do in response to Bertrand Russell's jailing?" "Well, we're having a meeting on Friday," he answered. I said, "Oh, so you're conducting business as usual. You know what I feel like doing? I feel like chartering a plane, filling it with women, and picketing the jail." But the trouble with this idea was, as I knew, that by the time we could get there, Russell would have been released.

I hung up the phone and just sat there in a numb way. I thought for a while. Then I started dialing all the women in my telephone book. Some of my friends were in Chicago, some in New York. I just called everybody, no matter how far away. I said, "What would you think of Women for Peace, a women's peace action?" Almost everybody seemed ready for it. That was Monday. By Wednesday, I had set up a meeting in my house. By the end of that evening, we had concluded that we would call ourselves Women Strike for Peace; that we would demonstrate in our hometowns, wherever we were; that we would address ourselves to our local governments; that we would send out a call; and that we would get this off the ground in Washington, D.C. We got permission to announce our plan from the pulpit of the Unitarian church on Sixteenth Street at the meeting our local SANE chapter had arranged.

We set a date for a nationwide demonstration, to be held in six weeks. Many people said we were crazy, and we were. The call that we sent out said, roughly: Do whatever you think is right, but do it on the same day and let us know. It was soon being mimeographed, crisscrossing back and forth all over the country. Some people got it several times from different sources. That's how quickly the idea caught on. And that's how ready we all were to go. It just needed one trigger, and it just happened to be me.

What helped a lot was my inexperience. I was always very shy, not one to step out in the world and borrow trouble. But here I was rushing in, a fool, where angels had long since tried and failed. My language was devoid of political clichés because I didn't know any. And never having done this sort of thing before, I was living in a state of perpetual, wound-up terror. It was ages before I came down.

The women in Washington worked like crazy. We were learning everything on the job, even how to operate the darn mimeograph machines. And then we had to approach the press, approach the police, get a sound truck together. We went all over Washington, D.C., announcing this thing. Everything was a first time for us.

We had decided that we would meet at the Sylvan Theater, which is at the foot of the Washington Monument. Our little sound system was put together with wire and string. We told the press that this great event was going to happen, but we were never sure how great it would be. The park police had arranged rows of beautiful green chairs for us, freshly painted. They looked very shiny and *very* empty on a great expanse of green grass, with the Washington Monument looming over us—just me and my fellow organizers.

At last a woman appeared on the horizon. Then another and another till they began to come and come and come. All the chairs were filled, and people had to sit on the grass on either side.

I made the first really big speech of my life. We had written identical letters to Khrushchev and to Kennedy, appealing to them to rethink the U.S.-Soviet confrontation in light of the nuclear age, to turn back before it was too late. All of the women were asked to sign. There were miles and miles of signatures. We delivered them that day to the White House and to the Soviet Embassy.

News reporter Roger Mudd, in those days a rather unknown man, had come up my front door steps that morning and said, "We'd like to tape you now, before the demonstration, and then again afterward." So there I was, sitting in my living room, reading our statement for the first time on the air. And I remember him turning to his helper there and saying, "Well, you couldn't want better than that, could you?" God was on our side, I tell you. Everything was going right.

We read in the papers afterward that sixty communities had participated, one way or another. So it was a great, great day. In the next few days, the mail in my vestibule was like a mountain. Every day. Some of those letters were addressed to "The Storybook Illustrator, Washington, D.C." or just "Dagmar Wilson, Washington, D.C." But they all came to my address. What quickly became obvious was that there were thousands of women who wanted to go on with the antinuclear movement.

As we worked together, we began to feel feminist vibes. Partly it was because of the put-downs we often got from officials. Then it was the difficulties some of us began finding at home. Some husbands' noses felt out of joint. They felt neglected and found themselves pinch-hitting with the kids and the household chores. In the beginning, housewives "striking" was no more than a novel idea, something that had a bit of humor in it and would attract the attention of the press. But as time went on, it developed into a reality.

We ran the movement much as we ran our family lives, so we began to feel that there was a woman's thing going on. Then, of course, we couldn't have cared less about the kinds of things that the State Department thought were so important, such as national prestige and who's the top nation, when the future of life on earth was at stake. We felt unified by common experiences and by our common concern. And we loved each other. It was wonderful, but there was a serpent in our Eden—the House Un-American Activities Committee.

That committee was trying to discredit the peace movement, and especially us, by questioning our loyalty. They tried to make even the smallest things we did seem sinister. They threw one woman's name at me. I don't know why. I don't know whether they found that she had contributed to her college paper or been a member of some club or other. But the committee asked me: "Has she got a key to your office?" I didn't know if she had, but my reply to that was, "You make it sound very conspiratorial."

Then Nittle asked me about the day we went international, when we decided to call ourselves Women's International Strike for Peace. He asked if this idea had come from that same woman. I said, "Heavens, no. I'd had the idea for a long time. But, frankly, when we come out of one of our meetings and we've agreed upon something, we all think it's our own idea."

There was a point when I said, "Look, I don't think I want to talk to you about anyone else. Ask me about myself." Nittle let that pass. Actually, they treated me with gloved hands. I don't know what would have happened if it had been earlier, when there was still so much fear, when this country was so hysterical about Communism. It somehow became criminal to be a Communist. In every European country, there was a Communist Party, a legitimate political party. They ran candidates. Some of those candidates got elected into their government. After my European upbringing, I was just astonished to find that in America, people jumped out of their skins if you mentioned the word "Communist."

Nittle asked me about that: "Would you permit Communist Party members to occupy leading posts in Women Strike for Peace?" One hitch in that question was the use of the idea of leaders. I had already explained that we didn't have leaders. But I let that pass because I thought it was important to make another point absolutely, categorically clear: "My dear sir, I have no way or desire to control those who wish to join our efforts for peace. Unless everyone in the whole world joins in this fight, then God help us."

This is what we all had in our hearts, so it's the way it came out. But Nittle pressed on: "Would you permit Nazis or fascists to join?"

"If only we could get them!"

There was no question that I made them look awfully silly. I remained polite throughout, though, and I never lost my cool. Once in a while, I did turn around and grin at the house behind me. It was a great day. I probably will regard it as the one great moment of my life. I had the opportunity not only to confront my accusers but also to make them look like idiots. To us, they seemed so absurd. But it can be a terrible danger when that which is absurd becomes accepted as truth.

Well, the second go-round with my ever-loving government began in 1964, when I, with two others, went to the State Department to request a visa for Professor Kaoru Yasui, who was then head of the Japanese peace movement, Kon Tikyo. He had been invited to give a series of lectures under the auspices of the *National Guardian,* which was a left-wing publication. Because his visa was being held up, people such as Dr. Benjamin Spock, Linus Pauling, and Ann Eaton were asked to send telegrams urging that the visa be granted. But for us in Washington, it was obviously more effective to go down to the State Department in person, which we did. We told them our reasons for wanting Professor Yasui to come here and speak to us. The visa was granted, by the way, and Dr. Yasui came and he spoke.

It was sometime after that, then, that a subpoena arrived, and three of us were called to tell HUAC what had transpired between us and the State Department. But this was not to be an open hearing. Suddenly it dawned on us all: No, we're not going to speak in a closed hearing.

Outside the doors of the hearing room, let me tell you, women and children were crowded together in the passages. And flowers kept coming up in the elevator. Baskets and baskets of flowers kept coming up. And we, inside, were indomitably saying: "Let them come in, and let the press in, and we will answer your questions. We will speak if you open the doors."

The committee's attorney advised us that we could be held in contempt. This, however, had to be voted on by the Congress, which was just about to break for the Christmas recess. In the absence of a quorum, House Speaker John McCormack upheld the committee's recommendation himself. It was unbelievable: McCormack, alone, held us in contempt of Congress, claiming that he had no choice. This began a two-year legal battle, which we won in the end.

One of the aims of Women Strike for Peace was to work with women in other countries, and especially in "enemy" countries. Our idea was that if women across national boundaries could work together, even while hostilities were taking place, they might be able to persuade their own governments to do the same.

I went to Vietnam when the bombings in 1967 had just begun. The bridge that one had to cross to get from the airport to Hanoi had been destroyed, and we were taken by ferry. There were bombed-out areas of Hanoi, and there was dreadful damage in the countryside: villages, Catholic churches—all decimated. It was terribly sad to see.

Convoys took us by night out to a remote area, Dienbien, where much bombing had occurred. They traveled without benefit of headlights, signaling to each other on their horns. At one point, we had to wait in a dugout along the roadside while a bridge was being repaired. It was a bright, moonlit night. And I had the funniest feeling. This was the same darn moon that I looked at in our backyard in Georgetown only two weeks ago. And I was thinking, "Tomorrow, Christopher will be looking at this moon." It just gave me an uncanny "one-planet" feeling. We live together on one earth. Can we do it in peace? I still cherish that dream.

The Vietnam Era

The War Against the Peacemakers

During the fall semester of 1964, University of California students rallied in Sproul Plaza on the Berkeley campus and occupied adjacent Sproul Hall to protest a ban on political activity on campus. Thirty years before, Robert G. Sproul, then president of the University of California, had first issued rules against political expression: no literature distributed, no petitions circulated, no funds solicited, no buttons sold, and no candidates presented to the student body.

The Sproul administration had also responded to the mounting student peace movement of the 1930s with more than rules to limit protest. It organized a fraternity-based vigilante squad to combat student "strikers" and condoned the vigilantes' violence against the activists.[46] When Berkeley police arrested student activists off campus, it was "on the request," the police blotter noted, of the "University of California."[47] The administration set up a political intelligence network that included county district attorneys, sheriffs and police chiefs, American Legion commanders, the California National Guard, and the Industrial Association of San Francisco, a labor spy outfit. Information about activists was secretly channeled to the campus police and used to intimidate students.[48] After the American entrance into World War II, student activism all but died out, and the movement remained quiescent in the early Cold War years.

In 1957, however, a progressive coalition known as SLATE, which bid for seats in the student government, was founded. Between 1958 and 1960, SLATE opposed compulsory ROTC, supported a fair housing proposition, rallied against capital punishment, and fought skirmishes with the administration over the shifting rules against political expression. The pace of protest accelerated in 1960, as demonstrators opposed the appearance of the House Un-American Activities Committee in San Francisco. One day after protesters were swept down the marble steps of city hall by fire hoses, five thousand more confronted HUAC with shouts of "Sieg Heil!" This unprecedented challenge helped to legitimize protest against the red-hunters and laid the basis for what was to come at Berkeley. Opposition to the committee, participant Bob Gill remembered, "supplied a core of veterans, training and experience that passed through the FSM, the antiwar movement and the student civil rights movement."[49]

The Berkeley Free Speech Movement (FSM) came into being in 1964, galvanized by the university administration's restrictions on student political activity and demanding the right to speak and organize freely. Undeterred by a massive police presence on campus, threatened suspensions, red-baiting, ultimatums, and attempts to divide the protesters, the Free Speech Movement triumphed in less than four months. The FSM's confrontational tactics were soon reenacted nationwide, as students broadened their focus to include the war in Vietnam. It was, as Kirkpatrick Sale observes, "a signal that a new generation had been born."[50] Jackie Goldberg is a fitting representative, coming from a traditional background and drawn first to civil rights struggles and Women Strike for Peace and then to prominence in the Free Speech Movement.

JACKIE GOLDBERG

The University of California had a rule that we couldn't do any political activity on campus. Up to that point we hadn't challenged it—when they said, "You can't," we said, "Okay." We had our own place in front of the campus, on Bancroft Way at Telegraph Avenue, where people could get up and rally and make pitches and hand out leaflets and organize. The left, the right, and the center all used the same strip. We had our little card tables. And we would collect money and hand out leaflets and harangue each other and students as they walked by.

We had all believed that we were off campus and they couldn't regu-

JACKIE GOLDBERG

late us. We'd even gotten city permits to be out there. All of a sudden, we were told that we were on university property. Just before classes began in the fall of 1964, they sent a letter out to all organizations: "University facilities may not be used to support or advocate off-campus political or social action." So now, no tables. Not only that—all political activity was banned during the middle of the Goldwater-Johnson election.

It was widely believed at the time that outside pressure was put on the university to do that. William Knowland, who ran the *Oakland Tribune*, was a right-wing Republican and the California state chairman of

Barry Goldwater's campaign for president. He was totally outraged that there were Berkeley students who picketed the convention and put up a CORE banner inside to disrupt Goldwater. And there were actions by the Ad Hoc Committee Against Discrimination to integrate his all-white newspaper. According to an insider who worked within the chancellor's office, Knowland became outraged and called Chancellor Strong: "You've got to stop these people from agitating or using the university to get recruits to demonstrate." Supposedly, the trade-off was that his paper would then come out editorially in favor of the state bond issues that benefited the University of California.

Since we all had our tables on the same strip, everyone was banned, including groups they could care less about: the Wesleyan Foundation, Hillel, the Sierra Club. The Republican clubs were just as angry as the left groups. There were the California College Republicans, kind of a liberal group. Then there were the Young Republicans, as reactionary as they come and very Goldwater. But they were upset, too, because how were they going to support their candidate? You couldn't do anything now. So everybody had a stake in it. Everybody got involved.

The first name we used for the free speech movement was the United Front. The first meeting was at my brother Art's apartment—the "death trap," I used to call it, because of the poor condition of the building. And our very first action was a press conference at Bancroft and Telegraph. Then some people set up tables at Sather Gate to break the ban and were cited by the university officials. As soon as they were cited, other people would sit down in their places. But for some reason, just five were told to come to a disciplinary hearing.

When they went to report to the dean's office in Sproul Hall, we got hundreds of people to go with them. And we brought a petition with us that said we also staffed the tables and were as guilty as the five who were cited. We realized that the only way we could beat the ban would be if we were all in it together. But they wouldn't let us in the dean's office for the disciplinary hearing, so we had a sit-in right then. Three more students were cited: Mario Savio, Sandor Fuchs, and Art. The university knew where the leadership was coming from, and they picked them advisedly. Although Art neither sat at a table nor violated any of the rules, he was chairperson of SLATE. SLATE was a student political organization that ran candidates as alternatives to the fraternities and sororities. Sandor was to be the next chair. And Mario represented Friends of SNCC and had become one of our spokespeople.

That night, they suspended Art and the others *without* a hearing. We decided, this United Front of people, that we were going to up the ante a little. Since they said that Bancroft and Telegraph was now part of the campus, then any part of the campus was just as illegal as any other part. Why stay in that obscure section? So we moved right in front of Sproul Hall, the administration building, in the main plaza. We set up about fifteen tables. Not all the organizations were willing to do that. Some of the more conservative groups had a philosophical problem with civil disobedience. They issued a press statement, though, saying that they supported our right to be there.

Then a campus police car drove right in the middle of the plaza, in front of Sproul Hall. It was lunch time, with about fifteen thousand students pouring out of the classrooms into the central area, where, horror-struck, we watched Jack Weinberg being dragged from the CORE table and plunked into the police car. When they arrested someone from CORE, the Congress of Racial Equality, they picked the one group that probably had the greatest support on campus. I mean, everyone was just shocked. Then the only spontaneous demonstration I've ever seen took place—people just sat down around the car. They were saying, "Sit down! Sit down!" More people sat down than there were activists in the whole campus.

It was an extraordinary moment. We just took over. We surrounded the police car, and we used the top of the car like a speaker's platform. In a few minutes, they had a microphone up there. Inside the car were the arrested Jack Weinberg and one policeman, a bizarre scene.

We sat there for a day and a half, from noon until the next day at five or six o'clock. People would alternate; when some would leave, others would come. And these folks, probably more than half of them, were not in any organization that the people who had been doing the planning represented. So who spoke for them? What were their demands? It wasn't really clear. It was clear that some of them were militant as hell. Having finally done something, they weren't going to leave so easily. And they stayed and stayed.

All sorts of people took turns speaking on top of the car. The campus police hadn't the slightest idea what to do. They said it was okay as long as you took your shoes off. Art was one of the first up there. Mario spoke. Charlie Powell, the president of the student body, came and told us he didn't think this was the way to do things. I mean, there was debate. But most people talked about why free speech is important and why they were there.

Now, the university was absolutely dying because it was football season and parents' weekend was coming up. Not only was it embarrassing when people just normally went by the scene, but they were going to have parents from all over the state visit the campus. And in the middle of the campus is a police car trapped by several thousand students. This was not going to be allowed to go on. We knew that we were going to be out of there one way or the other by the weekend. The question was which way.

We put together an ad hoc committee of representatives of the various groups and asked to meet with Clark Kerr, the president of the university. Just before we went to Kerr's office, the Oakland police arrived. There were more police than I had ever seen, with the riot gear, with the big helmets and long sticks, mace, and all the guns. I mean, they looked like an invading army. And they were surrounding us on three sides. There was a phalanx in the shape of a V of a hundred police on motorcycles revving their engines right at the edge of where the kids were sitting. The huge din reverberated in the plaza between the student union on one side and Sproul Hall on the other.

That's what it was like when we walked into Clark Kerr's office. Up to this point, there had been a great deal of solidarity. But in that meeting, someone from the Young Americans for Freedom denounced us to the president and urged him to have us all arrested and thrown in jail. He left the room, but everybody else, including several conservative Republican groups, stayed. Even though they were not participating in the demonstration, they believed in the right of free speech.

Then the negotiations began. We wanted immediate reinstatement of the eight suspended students. The administration did not agree. If there wasn't immediate reinstatement, we at least wanted a hearing with the right to present evidence. Kerr said, "Fine, we'll do that. We'll have the Student Conduct Committee of the Academic Senate take it up." (We found out afterward that there was no "Student Conduct Committee," although he kept referring to it.)

I had had some admiration for Clark Kerr up until this time. I mean, I was not in his fan club; don't misunderstand me. But as presidents of universities go, I thought we had a good one. I was very naive, still harboring this illusion of a great university president who was going to be reasonable about all of this. But he acted in the most disgusting, despicable manner you could possibly imagine. For me, that was one of the most horrifying things of the whole several months. Almost from the beginning of the negotiations, he would have his secretary come in and whisper audibly: "The police want to move in on the students. They won't wait much longer." And she did this repeatedly. Just the crassest crap in the world, to pressure us to accept anything they wanted.

I believed the police were just going to drive their motorcycles over the bodies to move the car out. I believed someone was going to die out there. Well, I panicked. I admit it freely. We were not a disciplined civil rights movement like the people who had gone down south, who had training in civil disobedience. We didn't even know who half of these students were, literally. So I said, "Whatever the best deal is, let's take it because it at least gets the suspended students a hearing before a faculty committee." And I said, "I can't sit here and say that instead of going to that committee, I'm willing to risk anyone's life." This is where Mario and I got into a fight. Mario was saying: "No, hold out. We'll win it right now. We'll win it all." Nobody liked Kerr's offer, but I prevailed and we agreed. And Mario went out and told the people what the deal was, and the demonstration ended.

Mario did not forgive me until December. I was accused of terrible crimes and misdemeanors. To this day, I don't think we would have won it right then, but I think we would have won more if we had held out. I think he was right and I was wrong. It was a good example of where police action affected me.

Out of that weekend came the Free Speech Movement. Now we had a lot more people. Maybe sixty or seventy were on the executive committee. Independents who weren't affiliated with anything had representation. And dorms. There was a small steering committee, from which I was purged for allegedly "ingratiating myself to the president of the university" that night of the police car sit-in. Well, that's the way it goes.

I did not come out of a flaming radical, red-diaper-baby home. I grew up in Inglewood, California, where I won the Good Citizen of the Year Award from the Daughters of the American Revolution in high school. I won the American Legion essay contest. I was Rotary Girl of the Year. This was the McCarthy era, and Inglewood was the capital of anti-Communism. We had a Christian Anti-Communist Crusade there. So I was terrified of getting duped by Communists. I was afraid of signing my name to anything or being associated with anyone. McCarthyism had done its job on me. My brother, Art, considered himself a radical, but I thought he was dreadful. The only thing we agreed on was civil rights, because being Jewish in Inglewood was to be the hated minority. So I did a little bit of civil rights stuff in high school.

In 1961, when I was a student at USC, I learned through some television show that nuclear testing in the atmosphere was polluting milk with strontium 90. I thought, "I've got to do something about this." I mean, we were killing *our* kids now. So I went down to city hall, and I met Women Strike for Peace people. I was hesitant at first, but these middle-class white women looked just like me. They didn't have horns; they didn't have tails. And they were for peace. I thought, "If that's Communism, then I'm missing something here." Well, I participated in the demonstration. And I worked with them the rest of '61 and '62 and again after my transfer to Berkeley.

So I got active first through the peace movement. When I came to Berkeley, people told me there were Communists in SLATE. Even though I agreed with almost everything SLATE stood for, I refused to join it my first year there. I did my second year. By then, who cared anymore? I mean, I had changed considerably because of the events that had unfolded. In the summer of 1964, I wanted to go down south to work with the civil rights movement, but I was not quite old enough. So I got involved with the Ad Hoc Committee to End Discrimination in San Francisco. It drew tons of students from Berkeley. We did sit-ins in the car dealerships and in the hotel industry. A few of our sit-ins, like the one at the Sheraton Palace Hotel, were very successful in getting actual contracts to hire more minorities. I got arrested my first time there. And I began worrying less and less about Communism being the threat, because I was getting an education as to what America was really like.

In the late fifties and the early sixties, an awful lot of us believed our civic textbooks. We really believed in freedom, equality, liberty, and justice for all. And we were conservative because we believed that those things were already going on. I went from being very right-wing to being very left-wing, without one moment's sleep being lost, because I didn't have to change my value system a bit. The difference was this: what I thought was real and what wasn't changed. I had believed that the justice system worked. Well, when my Black lawyer was called "boy" during the civil rights trial, when some of the judges refused to let the discussion of why we were there be brought forward, I thought I was in Mississippi, not in San Francisco.

So each experience simply gave me a better insight as to what was real and what was a lie. It was just a natural progression. I think that that's something the power and the authority at the time did not understand. They accused us of being cynical, but they were the ones who were really cynical. They're the ones who didn't believe in liberty and justice for all. We believed in it completely. We said that the university and the police department took ten thousand conservatives and made them into ten thousand liberals. And then they took ten thousand liberals and made them into ten thousand radicals. That was probably a little too strong, but not by very much.

At one point, the newspapers reported that Kerr said forty-nine percent of us were followers of the Communists or sympathizers. The next day, there were buttons all over the campus saying: "I'm one of the forty-nine percent." Whereas two years earlier I wouldn't join SLATE, I was now wearing that button. I don't think that most of us were consciously attacking McCarthyism, but we had a lot to do with diminishing it nevertheless.

One of our songs that came out of the events was sung to the tune of "Oh, What a Beautiful Morning": "There are five thousand reds in the plaza / There are five thousand reds in the plaza / The microphone's loud and it's drawing a crowd / I'm sure that the rules say that this is just not allowed / This will look bad in the papers / This will look bad in the press / Call out the troopers from Oakland / They'll get us out of this mess." People who weren't even affiliated with anything would sing this at the top of their lungs.

Then it seemed as if the university had finally come up with a formula that could win. And the formula was: You can have your tables back on campus; you can organize off-campus activities; you can collect money; you can have speakers. You'll only be regulated by two rules. One is time, place, and manner—you can't interrupt classes and so on. The other is you cannot advocate an illegal act. Ahhh. Now who was advocating civil disobedience in their programs? It was the civil rights organizations and some of the more militant groups on the left. It was a wonderful formula from the university's point of view, because the center and the right didn't care about it. So we were really about to be split apart.

We have always talked about the "atrocity theory" of the Free Speech Movement, which is that every time we were about to lose, the administration committed another atrocity that swelled our ranks with people who were really, in the best sense of the word, "naive." Mostly what made the movement was not that we were brilliant tacticians, although I'd love to say that we were. It was that whenever we would get stuck, the university would do something stupid. This time, they sent letters of citation to Mario Savio, to Art, to me, and to Brian Turner. These letters said in effect that we were to be thrown out of school for leading demonstrations at various times in the previous three months.

At that point, everybody in the executive committee decided that they were not going to let them pick off our leadership. They were just not going to let the university do it. We would have a big sit-in at Sproul Hall. Mario made his most famous speech that day, which really was nothing short of spectacular: "There is a time when the operation of the machine becomes so odious, makes you so sick at heart, that you can't take part; you can't even passively take part, and you've got to put your bodies upon the gears and upon the wheels, upon the levers, upon all the apparatus and you've got to make it stop! And you've got to indicate to the people who run it, to the people who own it, that unless you're free, the machines will be prevented from working at all."[51]

I hadn't even decided that I was going to sit in. I was already a wreck. This was my senior year. I was still going to classes when I could fit them in and trying very, very hard to graduate. I was going to be a teacher, and I already had one arrest on my record. What did I need another one for? Besides that, I had been discredited, so why should I stick my neck out? Then Mario gave that speech, and I didn't have any doubt in my mind if I was going to go in and sit in or not. "Oh, God, of course I'm going in. He's absolutely right. We've got to do this."

Joan Baez, who was becoming the sensation of the country, sang "We Shall Overcome" on the steps. Then she turned around with her guitar and walked in. Maybe fifteen hundred people went into the building, not knowing when they'd come out. There were just mobs of people inside. It grew to two or three thousand. We divided people into shifts and sent some home, so we'd always have six to eight hundred at any one time, certainly enough to hold the building. We set up an alternative university. We had classes and study halls. We had living spaces on several of the floors. I don't know where they came from, but somebody brought in all of Jean Genet's films, so we had a film series that was of really sterling quality. It was also the first night of Chanukah; we had a Chanukah celebration. We organized food, shelter, sleeping, bathrooms, everything. We were determined to stay.

That evening of December 2, we believed that the university was probably going to wait us out. They were not going to come in and do this police number, because it was their building and they didn't want it torn up by the police. So we figured that they were going to try to kill us by attrition. And if they had been smart, that's what they would have done. Finals weren't far away, and that was a very big stick over us.

Well, we miscalculated. An arrest order came down from Governor Pat Brown, who, according to the story we got, was talked into it by Ed Meese.* At about two o'clock in the morning, a local Berkeley radio station intercepted word that the police were about to begin arresting us. All over campus and in all of the surrounding areas, lights started going on as people listened to the news. I was on the third floor of Sproul Hall. When I looked out toward the hills of Berkeley, I could see students running down the streets. They were running in large numbers toward the building. You'd think people would be fleeing, but instead they were trying to get in. I mean, it was really quite a drama.

The thing that was so phenomenal was that even though they were afraid, even though they had never done anything political, they were captivated by the necessity of having the right to free speech. I mean, most of these folks were defending a right they didn't intend to use. They weren't going to join a political organization. They weren't going to be involved, you know. These people were, "I'm just here to get a good education so I can get a good career." This was U.C. Berkeley in the sixties. Everybody had been filling their heads about how wonderful they were—the cream of the cream. Yet here they were, sitting in, risking everything. It was really extraordinary.

The police had already surrounded Sproul Hall. They would not let anyone in. People started climbing up the sides of the building on ropes. They hooked up a pulley between Sproul Hall and the student union building and were coming across the quad to join us. I mean, this was just a bizarre thing. Those of us who had been in the civil rights movement were doing instant workshops on nonviolence, on going limp, nonresistance, and protecting oneself from billy clubs.

By the standards of the mid-sixties, it was a very brutal arrest. The first thing that frightened us was that the police kicked the press out of the building. They kicked out the observers from the religious communities. They kicked out the professors who had come to observe. It was just us and the Oakland police. Really, give me a break! This was the *Oakland* police. This was Meese's bunch, who had a reputation far and wide as the most brutal police in northern California. And now they were covering all the windows on the ground floor with newspapers. We were terrified.

---

*Edwin Meese, the U.S. attorney general from 1985 to 1988 under Ronald Reagan, earlier was the deputy district attorney for Alameda County, California, where Berkeley is located.

Then they came for us. They went floor by floor, starting at the fourth. They made short shrift of people who were not going to walk out. There was an anger; there was an intent to harm. They would grab you by the neck or by the hair or by the heels and just drag you. Some of us were put in elevators, but they dragged most of the people down the stairs, heads hitting the cement or the marble.

Some of us were taken to the basement. They pulled about two or three dozen people off into an interrogation room, one or two at a time, to try and terrorize us. They were quite effective. I got pulled into the interrogation room, and I was certainly plenty scared. It was literally the bright lights and the "Who are you, and what are you doing here?" They asked: "Are you a leader? Who is in charge? Who is doing this? Who said that?" I mean, it was really like a grade-B movie. Honest to God.

Frankly, nobody knew anything because we hadn't done anything except sit in. There was no conspiracy to do something else. So you had nothing to tell them when they asked: "Did you mess with the records of the university?" The furthest thing from anybody's mind was to go into any of the offices. We were real clean-cut—you should see the pictures of it—we looked very straight for "flaming radicals." But there was all this paranoia on their part. And they were sure that they had this hard-core something or other here that they had to get information out of. Or maybe it was just harassment.

The cops had removed their badges and put them in their pockets, so we could not identify them. After I was interrogated, this cop reached down to get me, and his badge fell on the ground. I said, "I know your number." Was that a mistake! He dragged me up the flight of stairs from the basement to the paddy wagon. I was injured pretty severely. I had trouble walking for weeks after that. And *I* was charged with felonious assault on an officer, not the misdemeanor of going limp like everyone else.

I was going to file for police brutality for them messing up my back. I had all kinds of pictures and X-rays of my injuries. But Stan Gold, my attorney, sat me down: "Look, who is going to believe that this officer attacked you for no reason at all?" I said, "They're going to believe that little me attacked this big guy?" He said, "Yeah, you're a leader, and you've been in the papers. They're going to believe that you're a hothead and you got angry and flew off the handle." He said, "I'll defend you whatever you decide to do, but my advice to you is to make a deal: They drop the felony; you drop the charges against them." It took me two days to agonize over that. But when Stan Gold said, "Your chances of being

convicted are about seventy-five percent," I made the deal. That's why
I'm a teacher today. With felony assault, I would never have been allowed
to teach.

Anyway, we were all carted away. Some people were taken to the
Oakland city jail. Some of us went out to Santa Rita. I was there. They
didn't have any place to put eight hundred people, so they had a
makeshift prison set up in the Oakland armory. The police were panicked and paranoid. They didn't know how long it was going to take
to raise bail for this huge number of people. They didn't know whether
we were going to refuse bail, which was getting to be the new tactic in
the South.

Meanwhile, the whole community of Berkeley had become completely
galvanized. All kinds of people who had not supported us, who had not
cared about us, were horrified: "The police covered the windows! The
police wouldn't let the press inside!" So they raised a zillion dollars in
that one night for bail. I mean, a ton of money. And since it went out on
national news, people from around the country were sending money, too.
So even though there were eight hundred of us in prison, we were all
bailable within two or three hours. Now, the police didn't process us
nearly that fast. It took twenty-four hours to get everyone finally out,
but it wasn't for lack of money.

And then the strike came. Before this, most of the faculty had not been
courageous in their support of us. There were even professors who attacked us as "brownshirted Nazi youth." Then suddenly the real Nazis
had shown up in all their regalia and had dragged us away, unarmed and
nonviolent though we were. Now professors wrote on their black-
boards, "If all my students aren't here to be taught, I'm not going to teach
the ones that are here." Messages like this: "Because eight hundred can't
be here today, my lecture has been canceled." You could walk through
the halls and see no one in the classes.

The strike was very successful. Even the people who didn't support
us wouldn't go to class, because they were very upset by the magnitude
of the police action. The arrests had gone on all night and most of the
next day. Whenever people walked onto campus, they saw the vans and
buses and cops and guns and helmets and clubs. And then to see the windows covered with newspaper, to hear the people screaming inside the
building—you can imagine the horrifying scene it created. And you're
seeing an endless stream of bodies being dragged out.

We had one mass trial in the Berkeley Community Theater. Once I
dropped my charges against the police, they dropped the felony charges

against me, and I was just one of the gang now. We were all charged with trespass on public property and resisting arrest if we had gone limp. I was the first witness for the defense. I was on the stand for three and a half days. They picked me because I was the only person in leadership who was in a social sorority—I was a pledge mother at the time—so I was the model kosher student. Through me, the story of the whole movement was told. But it wasn't enough.

Everybody was convicted. Then the long process of sentencing began. Almost all of us got probation and a fine of some small amount. The conditions of probation were no sit-ins, no lie-ins, no walk-ins, no wait-ins, no sleep-ins, no nothing for two years. The people who weren't going to do anything else, of course, didn't violate the probation. But the people who were went right off into the Vietnam Day Committee and the Stop the Draft Week and everything else at Berkeley. I managed to graduate in spite of everything and was in a sit-in the next spring at the University of Chicago.

I think the biggest thing the Free Speech Movement did was help activate a whole generation of students and seriously undermine the repressive effect of the McCarthy era. Even though the Free Speech Movement ended by December 1964, activism survived and expanded. That spring of the same school year, we had the most magnificent Vietnam Day teach-in. It was really unbelievable. It went on for four days and nights, around the clock. We had speakers from all over the world. Thousands of students participated. People from San Francisco and Oakland and Berkeley came. It was an entirely student-run operation, out of which grew the antiwar movement.

HARASSING ANTIWAR DEMONSTRATORS

After the presidential election in 1964, Lyndon Johnson intensified American involvement in Vietnam. He complemented the clandestine warfare that had been in place with open military engagement, first through the deception that produced the Gulf of Tonkin resolution and later by bombing North Vietnam in Operation Rolling Thunder.[52]

In March 1965, three thousand students at the University of Michigan broke Cold War conventions by holding a debate on war policies that electrified the nation's campuses. The newly invented "teach-ins" spread, climaxing at Berkeley with three days of debates, demonstrations, and parades that attracted thirty thousand students, many fresh from the Free Speech Movement. In the midst of the teach-ins, twenty thousand students rallied against the war in Washington, D.C., under the auspices of Students for a Democratic Society. One hundred thousand across the country joined the International Days of Protest in October 1965. In April 1967, hundreds of thousands marched to the United Nations to hear Martin Luther King Jr. denounce the war. It was a symbolic joining of the antiwar and civil rights movements.

In response, President Johnson demanded that the CIA find Communist links to critics of the war, even though previous efforts to uncover such ties had failed. J. Edgar Hoover sought more than mere tainting. "The New Left with its antiwar and antidraft entourage," he instructed his field offices, required "continuous effective attention in order that no opportunity will be missed to destroy this insidious movement."[53] An onslaught of COINTELPRO actions soon followed: Phony leaflets were distributed at a college campus, listing conflicting times and places for antiwar meetings. A "New Left youth group involved in anti-Vietnam activity" was sent anonymous, cryptic messages with the expectation that they would "cause concern and mental anguish."[54]

COINTELPRO documents show that the bureau sought to "create ill-will," to "fan discontent," to "drive a wedge," to provoke "a rift" among activists.[55] The New York FBI, for example, sent to "68 peace groups and selected individuals" a fake, unsigned letter designed to "widen the split" between the Young Socialist Alliance (YSA) and the Student Mobilization Committee.[56] The Atlanta FBI disrupted attempts at reconciliation between Students for a Democratic Society (SDS) and the Socialist Workers Party (SWP) because "it would be greatly to the Bureau's advantage not to let these two major factions in the Atlanta antiwar movement become overly friendly and cooperative." FBI forgeries were cast in provocative language with obvious intent: "Keep the jewboys in their own building," the FBI has a Black student group saying, referring to SDS members at New York University. "You're a joke man," the FBI has SDS telling the Black Panthers, with "'Huey the Homo' afraid to raise his voice for fear he'll get busted again" (referring to Huey Newton, head of the BPP).[57] By April 1971, when the New Left COINTELPRO presumably ended, the bureau acknowledged that it had carried out as many as 290 disruptive actions—a rate of one every three or four days—many of which were devised to keep opponents of the war from speaking, teaching, writing, or publishing.[58]

Opposition to the war continued to build nonetheless. Local police responded with violence to peaceful protests in Los Angeles, Philadelphia, Chicago, and New York, where undercover police agents intimidated participants and even provoked their uniformed fellow officers to attack demonstrators. From the spring of 1967 to the spring of 1968, protesters in New York were attacked: at a mobilization on April 15; at a May 30 music festival at Tompkins Square Park; at a November 14 demonstration against Secretary of State Dean Rusk, organized by the Fifth Avenue Vietnam Peace Parade Committee; at a week of antidraft demonstrations in early December; at a January 24, 1968, demonstration near the Plaza Hotel; and at a March 22 protest organized by the Yippies at Grand Central Station.

However disruptive the government response, opposition to the Vietnam war persisted. It was, Tom Wells concludes, "perhaps the most successful antiwar movement in history."[59] Norma Becker, who initiated the Fifth Avenue Vietnam Peace Parade Committee, was a tireless leader in the growing ranks of opponents to the war. She drew inspiration from her work in the civil rights movement.

NORMA BECKER

To avoid implementing the Supreme Court's 1954 school desegregation decision, Prince Edward County, Virginia, closed its public schools. All the white kids went to private academies, but the Black kids were kept out of school for five years. In 1963, our union, the New York United Federation of Teachers, organized a project whereby teacher volunteers would go down to Prince Edward County and set up Freedom Schools during the summer vacation. I had already seen the television coverage of Birmingham: the dogs let loose on children. That was a turning point for me—I had young children myself—and I felt I had to become personally involved.

Just as that feeling grabbed me, I heard about the UFT project in Virginia and volunteered. We set up schools in church basements, on lawns, in living rooms, wherever there was space to accommodate a significant number of children. We had eight schools in the outlying districts and around six or eight in the town of Farmville. We taught, we had parties, we went out to register voters. We became integrated into the life of the community, the Black community.

I made contacts with people in the civil rights movement, particularly in SNCC, people like Ivanhoe Donaldson and Leon Roland. These two young men—what were they, twenty and twenty-one—they were incredible. They were training high school kids for nonviolent civil disobedience campaigns in Farmville. After we returned to New York, Ivan-

NORMA BECKER

hoe asked me if we could try to get the UFT to sponsor a Freedom School
Project in Mississippi the following summer, Freedom Summer. We went
to a UFT executive board meeting prepared to persuade them, but in two
minutes flat they adopted the program without debate. So we were able
to involve a lot of teachers and students and raise a lot of money and
materials in schools throughout the city.

    That southern experience was the beginning of my conversion to
pacifism, to nonviolence. I'd always regarded nonviolence as some kind
of cockamamie, well-meaning, idealistic stuff that was just not rooted in

reality. You know, good people, nice people, but not from the real world. That southern experience made me reevaluate. Then I began to read the literature, the theoretical literature. It confirmed what I had seen in action. I began to realize that nonviolence has a power in terms of social struggle that can be equivalent, at least, to the power of violence.

My parents came out of that East European, Jewish, immigrant, working-class, secular, socialist milieu, strongly trade unionist. My father had been on picket lines. He would tell stories of my uncle and himself on strike, about how the bosses had them beaten up with rubber hoses so it wouldn't leave any scars. Not that they indoctrinated me, but this was the life they led. And having lived through the Second World War and the Holocaust, I had become a politically conscious person. When the war ended, I believed all that stuff about a new world, democracy, freedom, justice, prosperity—all the good things that so many people had given their lives for.

The postwar period came as a shock to me. I felt personally betrayed. I found out that the United States was not a glowing democracy of kindness and compassion and justice and truth. Manifest Destiny and global dominance were the driving forces in American foreign policy. Our government supported corrupt, brutal, oppressive dictators, oligarchies, the elite living in opulence while the overwhelming majority of the population was living in poverty. By the time the Vietnam war came, it just seemed more of the same. And those people were catching hell from our weapons. I felt I had to jump into the antiwar movement because the war was such an injustice. And it was escalating, escalating rapidly.

Newspaper ads critical of our Vietnam policy were appearing. All kinds of groups—trade unionists, academics, health professionals, social workers—sponsored them. So Sandy Adickes and I decided that we would do the same thing with teachers. I had met Sandy in Prince Edward County in 1963. The next year, she and I became the coordinators of the UFT Mississippi Freedom School Project. In May of '65, we circulated a petition throughout the schools. We got thirteen hundred signatures for an antiwar ad in the *New York Times*. We had no concept of an ongoing organization. But by the time the ad came out, the war had escalated so rapidly that we decided we weren't going to disband. We called a meeting, and around eighty teachers showed up. The Teachers Committee for Peace in Vietnam was born.

The movement was just beginning to take shape. By the end of the summer, the National Coordinating Committee to End the War in Vietnam called for "International Days of Protest" for October 15 and 16,

1965. Every antiwar group in the country was supposed to organize an action. I remember that Labor Day weekend speaking to Maris Cakars, from the Committee for Non-Violent Action, about what we should do. In the course of the conversation, I said, "Well, they march those missiles down Fifth Avenue for the Loyalty Day parade. Let's march down Fifth Avenue."

I set a date for a meeting and invited every known antiwar group in New York City that was functioning at the time. A. J. Muste, who was the dean of the pacifist movement, signed the call with me. It was his name that brought people there. Most of them were from the traditional peace groups: SANE, Women Strike for Peace, Women's International League for Peace and Freedom, War Resisters League. And the Trotskyist party and the Communist Party. We also had groups from the neighborhoods, like the Tompkins Square Committee. Two unions sent representatives: the Fur and Leather Workers and District 65. Then there was this alphabet soup of youth groups like SDS, YSA, and SPU, the Student Peace Union; some pacifist groups; and some others. Dave Dellinger co-chaired the meeting with me.

Well, that meeting was mind-boggling. Except for the neighborhood committees and the campus groups, all the others had a history of conflict, distrust, betrayal, and mutual recriminations. I couldn't believe it. The suggestion was thrown out that we march behind five slogans, which would be put on placards. But these people couldn't agree on the time of day, let alone what slogans to use. I remember feeling bewildered and dazed.

We reached a point where there was dead silence. Out of sheer naiveté, I said, "Look, if the people in this room can't agree, I'll call twenty other people, and if necessary we'll march like they did in Paris, without any placards, just black armbands." Images of Pierre Mendès-France leading Parisians in a march against the Algerian war came to me. At that juncture, Abner Grunauer from SANE proposed that we march behind *one* slogan: "Stop the War in Vietnam Now." And the group agreed! We became the Fifth Avenue Vietnam Peace Parade Committee. It got abbreviated to the Fifth Avenue Parade Committee, and later just the Parade Committee.

We had six weeks to organize the march. In all that time, the police did not grant us a permit. Some people would demonstrate even if there were no permit. I was willing to. I had seen firsthand the heroism—I mean real heroism—in the South. It was inspiring. I felt: "They could do it. Why can't I?" But the more respectable-type groups like SANE and

Women Strike and some of the professional groups, and certainly the trade unions and the church groups, were all nervous about demonstrating without permission. So we put on all our promotional literature: "Permit Pending." It wasn't until the very last minute, through the intervention of the New York Civil Liberties Union, that the police granted us a permit.

The demonstration was planned for Saturday. On Friday night, David Miller from the Catholic Worker movement burned his draft card at the Whitehall Street induction center.[*] That was the first draft card burned in the anti–Vietnam war struggle. It made the front page. We were nervous because it was not an "acceptable" kind of behavior. We felt that it would deter people from coming to the march the following day. But it didn't. And David Miller's action became one of the forms of protest others emulated. The next day, twenty-five thousand marched. It was beyond most people's fondest dreams. I was ecstatic. And that first demonstration launched the New York City antiwar coalition.

After a pause in the bombing of North Vietnam on Christmas Eve 1965, there was a threat that Lyndon Johnson would resume it in January 1966. We had a TDA—"The Day After"—contingency action planned. It was to be the first mass civil disobedience in the New York antiwar movement. An ad hoc committee organized it, because the Parade Committee couldn't endorse civil disobedience. I remember I got a call from Staughton Lynd at six or six-thirty on the morning of February 1, telling me that the bombing had resumed. I set the telephone tree in motion. Our arrangement was that everyone would march around Times Square, and then people who were willing to risk arrest would sit down and block traffic, a tactic we'd learned from the civil rights movement.

Well, I'll tell you, I had to do some real soul searching. By that time, I was divorced and supporting the family myself, or mostly myself. I had to decide whether I was going to risk losing my job. I'm not a brave person, but the war had already become such a bloodbath, and there were no signs that there was going to be any deviation from that path. Roger LaPorte, a young father from the Catholic Worker movement, had immolated himself outside the United Nations. He was following the

---

[*]The Catholic Worker movement, founded by Dorothy Day and Peter Maurin in 1933, is composed of communities that are committed to nonviolence, voluntary poverty, prayer, and hospitality. The movement has protested injustice, war, and all other forms of violence and racism.

model of the Buddhist monks in Vietnam who poured gasoline over themselves and set themselves on fire in protest against the war. This young man we knew immolated himself. When things like that happened, I just felt I had to take the risk. That was the first antiwar action where arrests were made. And the front-page article in the *Times* listed the names and addresses of all of us who were arrested.

There were so many antiwar actions. There were forums and student demonstrations. In March of '66, a rally of fifty thousand was held at the Bandshell in Central Park. That same year, three uniformed soldiers refused to serve in Vietnam—the "Fort Hood Three." When they came to us for support, we held a press conference and organized a mass meeting. The three were abducted by the Army on the way to that meeting and put in the stockade. That was so outrageous that we had a spontaneous march to Times Square.

But it was the university teach-ins that did the most to raise the awareness and consciousness of the Vietnam war. They took place on campuses throughout the country: huge meetings with all kinds of speakers, open mikes, questions and debate from the audience. I watched them on TV or listened to them on the radio. It was electrifying. It broke through the wall of silence that had prevailed in the media.

All these actions and events had a cumulative effect on people. They inspired, they encouraged, and, especially with the Fort Hood Three, they made you feel, "Jesus, they're sacrificing their lives." It just kept you going. I mean, it would get so discouraging. Each demonstration we had was bigger than the one before, but it was followed by a major military escalation. Inevitably. We didn't know what to do.

I was at a terrible loss to understand the mentality of our government leaders. It just seemed to me that the brutality in Vietnam was so horrendous, the loss of life was so immense, the destruction of the land was so widespread. There didn't seem to be any possibility of military victory. Why did they keep going? And I didn't understand people who supported them, the Al Shankers of this world, the leaders of my own union, which I had broken with. I had worked with them in the civil rights movement, but then they followed the government line on Vietnam. I didn't understand why liberal, progressive, humanistic-type people continued to support the war. I still don't. I guess it's the herd instinct, nationalism, "my country right or wrong," "anything's better than Communism." I don't know.

Late in 1966, the Spring Mobilization Committee to End the War was organized. This was a coming together of the civil rights and antiwar movements. In January 1967, at Riverside Church, Martin Luther King had come out against the war. James Bevel and Bernard Lafayette and a lot of the former SNCC organizers had come up north to work in the antiwar movement. Bevel became national director of the Spring Mobilization Committee, and we planned a mass rally and march at the United Nations for April.

That was a monstrous demonstration. Central Park was filled with throngs of people, four hundred thousand of them. It began to rain as we marched down to the U.N. to hear Martin Luther King speak.

Out of Cornell University, Bruce Dancis and a couple of other guys had been mobilizing students from various campuses for a massive draft-card burning at the demonstration. I'll never forget that night. Some of those parents begged their sons to reconsider at the last minute: It would ruin their college education; it would ruin their careers. Well, those guys burned their cards anyway. And they had enormous support. Lots of actors and actresses from Broadway shows came. The entire cast of the musical "Hair." That was the first national draft-card burning. And nineteen-year-old Bruce Dancis, whom I had worked with closely, was later sentenced to a year and a half in Leavenworth.

We had the Pentagon demonstration in October of '67. After the rally, thousands of college kids surrounded the Pentagon. They were going to occupy it, and Abbie Hoffman was going to "levitate" it. Most of the people were not taking part in the civil disobedience. They had come back to the parking lot, where they were to board their buses. But the authorities had moved the buses, and thousands of people were stranded. The parking lot was chaos.

Suddenly they started bringing down the wounded from the Pentagon. Bloody heads were coming down, one after the other. They had been hit with rifle butts or clubs. Within minutes, it was clear that there was a pattern: Almost everyone who came down with a bloody head was a female, a young college girl.

Two or three weeks after the Pentagon demonstration, the Parade Committee called for a rally at the Hilton Hotel, where Secretary of State Dean Rusk was to speak. It was a very silk-stocking, hoi-poloi kind of crowd, women in furs and gowns and chauffeured limousines. We were penned in behind the police barricades, hundreds and hundreds on each block around the Hilton and on the side streets. There was no room to move. When I got there, I was very uneasy, because I picked up the tension in the air immediately. And sure enough, at one point the cops charged into the crowds of demonstrators.

I saw a New York City police officer—badge number 23337—without provocation jump out of line, grab a young man by his hair, yank him backwards to the ground and crack his head on the concrete.

N.W.

About 6:20 the police on the wall descended into the crowd swinging their clubs and hitting people, without any provocation so far as I could see. Almost simultaneously, the police on the outer edge waded into the crowd, also swinging their nightsticks and clubbing people. We were thus caught between two lines of attacking police. People were falling to the ground and crying out. . . . I was bleeding profusely from the head wound, blood was running down my cheeks. . . . As I lay on the ground I was kicked in the back repeatedly.

T.M.S.

I was smashed over the head with a billy club by a policeman on the street. I fell to the ground and was promptly encircled by policemen, I would say 5 or 6 of them, who all beat me repeatedly with their clubs until I could manage to break through the circle. I ran down 53rd Street toward 5th Avenue, dripping blood from the original head wound, and as I passed the numerous police along the street a number of them also beat me with their nightsticks.

I would like to add that I am the holder of an award medal for bravery given to me by the Police Commissioner in the fall of 1966 when I chased two purse snatchers into Riverside Park and retrieved the purse containing $130 which had been snatched from an old lady on Broadway.

T.W.[60]

The police were usually hostile and uncompromising. Earlier, at a women's demonstration at the Whitehall induction center, police had charged into a line of guys standing across the street chanting antiwar slogans in support of the young women. The police slammed people into the wall of the building, pushing the barricades and sending the whole sidewalk of onlookers into a wild scramble. They took one guy, Matt Weinstein, a college student, a big, husky football-player type, beat him mercilessly, and pushed his face down to the ground. Then about six or eight of them circled around, kicking him while his hands were manacled behind his back.

And the police were never, ever held accountable for any of the violence that they perpetrated against the demonstrators. I sent letter after letter of complaint, but I was never called to answer questions about anything that I had been an eyewitness to. Never. Not once.

A month after the Rusk demonstration, we had a nonviolent sit-in at the Whitehall induction center. It was the first day of Stop-the-Draft

Week. I was with a group led by Grace Paley.* We were sitting down behind the police barricades, when suddenly the mounted police started
charging. My twelve-year-old daughter and her friend were with me, and
we were terrified. It's a terrifying thing to have horses charging at you.
And I'll never forget this: Grace jumped up, grabbed the commanding
officer by the lapels of his jacket, and shook him: "I'm holding you responsible for this. I'm holding you . . ." And he's saying, "Lady, please,
lady, please," and he pulled his men back. In retrospect, it was funny,
but at the time it wasn't. There had been no provocation. We were a nonviolent group. In fact, our civil disobedience action had all been worked
out in advance with the police authorities. The following day of Stop-
the-Draft Week, when students demonstrated, the police were violent.

Sometimes when there was violence, we didn't know whether it was
provoked by a paid agent, a kid who had lost his head and panicked, or
some person who believed in revolutionary violence. But I had come to
learn that the NYPD Bureau of Special Services provoked violence in order to clamp down on us. The threat of agent-provocateurs was always
there. You could put in hours and hours and days and weeks of preparation and nonviolence training—and then a government agent would
screw the whole thing up.

I know the FBI was involved. The Amalgamated Bank of New York,
where we did our banking, turned over every check we deposited to the
FBI. We had deposited tens of thousands of them because we were selling train and bus tickets for demonstrations in Washington. The ACLU
filed suit on our behalf. They pointed out that this kind of surveillance
had a "chilling effect" on people. But we lost. The FBI would also contact bus drivers and either persuade them or harass them into not taking us. Hundreds and sometimes thousands of people—like in 1969—
were stranded around the city.

Sid Peck, who had been instrumental in organizing the local teach-in
at Case Western Reserve, became one of the stalwarts of the national
movement. His group, the Cleveland Area Peace Action Council, had
called together a national convention to plan an action for the fall. It
voted to endorse a Moratorium to begin on October 15, 1969, and to
hold a Mobilization in Washington one month later. The Moratorium
was to take place all across the country, where each locality would do
its own thing. I thought that was a brilliant strategy. It enabled people

*Grace Paley is an award-winning author and poet.

to organize whatever kinds of actions they chose, from prayer services in churches to teach-ins on campuses to rallies, demonstrations, and candlelight vigils. The Quakers began to read the names of the war dead on the steps of the Capitol and were arrested. Then some antiwar members of Congress took up where they left off. It was picked up by local groups everywhere. They'd set up a booth in the town square or center and read the names of the war dead. In some places, muffled drums accompanied them. In others, there was the blowing of taps. The Moratorium turned out to be a stunning success. Two million people took part in it.

In New York, we had rallies in different parts of the city. I remember I spoke at a huge rally at Columbia University. And Mayor John Lindsay spoke. By this time, establishment figures were trying to jump on the bandwagon. Apparently, public opinion, as they or their staffs perceived it, had begun to swing against the war. We got a call from Jacob Javitz's office: Why wasn't the senator invited?

Meanwhile, the New Mobilization Committee to End the War in Vietnam was planning its demonstration for November in Washington, D.C. That's when the demand by the D.C. Black United Front for a "head tax" came up: The "New Mobe" would have to pay them so much for each person who came to Washington. Some groups wanted to pay it. Some didn't. It was a very divisive issue.

It turned out that the whole thing was set up by the FBI. There were government agents within the Black United Front, who had been instructed to push for that "head tax." Then the FBI put out a forged flyer in Sid Peck's name that attacked the Black United Front in the most racist terms for demanding the "head tax." It called the BUF leader a "Zulu king" and ended with: "Suck on your bananas, brothers and some day you will learn how to make fire or build a wheel. Affectionately, Sid." They had forged his signature. They distributed the flyer throughout the movement. It exacerbated existing tensions, which is just what they wanted to do. J. Edgar Hoover said: "We have been trying to create a split between these two groups based upon this demand. This leaflet may serve such a purpose."[61]

But the Mobilization could not be stopped. It started the night of November 13. Stewart Meachum, of the American Friends Service Committee, conceived the idea of the "March Against Death." For forty hours, people walked single file across the Arlington Memorial Bridge to the White House. Everyone carried a candle and a placard with the name of an American killed in action or a Vietnamese village that had been destroyed. They marched all night, in the rain, forty-five thousand of them. I think it was one of the most dramatic demonstrations. The next day, three-quarters of a million people came. There was a very moving moment in which people lit candles and held hands and sang "Give Peace a Chance," led by John Lennon and Yoko Ono.

When Nixon ordered the invasion of Cambodia at the end of April 1970, the Mobilization immediately called for a demonstration at the White House for May 9. During that period, the whole thing escalated. The killing of the students at Kent State electrified campuses.* There was a nationwide student strike, and over five hundred schools closed down. The country was in upheaval.

In New York, five hundred students from Pratt Institute, many of whom were demonstrating for the first time, rented half a train. They expected to commit nonviolent civil disobedience. They brought vaseline, canteens of water, first aid equipment, and kerchiefs to wet in case of tear gas. I was very impressed with them. I was already a seasoned demonstrator, but I wasn't ready to get maced. I mean, after the Pentagon, forget it. Seeing masked, uniformed men shooting tear gas canisters—you have to see these guys with their khaki uniforms, their big gas masks with the snouts. You know, you have feelings of unreality.

Anyway, the students were supposed to march to the White House behind caskets they were going to deliver to Nixon. But the government parked all these buses bumper to bumper around the White House. And our marshals, who were controlled by the SWP, steered the demonstrators away because they were against civil disobedience. Those who favored civil disobedience were in disarray and unable to provide any leadership. The students felt betrayed. Many people returned from that demonstration very depressed, very bitter. And there was a profound anti-leadership sentiment.

By this time, the SWP had broken with the Mobilization and organized its own group, NPAC, the National Peace Action Coalition. So you now had two national peace coalitions competing for funds and for support. That's when VVAW, the Vietnam Veterans Against the War, made such a tremendous impact. They revived us when we were demoralized, after Kent State and Cambodia, when the movement was at an ebb. The VVAW "Dewey Canyon" actions had us mesmerized. These scruffy-looking Vietnam combat veterans, some in wheelchairs and on crutches,

---

*The events at Kent State University in Ohio are described by Roseann Canfora and Alan Canfora on pp. 349–367.

tossed their medals away at the Capitol. Unbelievably poignant. It made the movements' internal conflicts seem so ridiculous.[62]

Right after Dewey Canyon, in April of 1971, there was a demonstration sponsored by NPAC and the People's Coalition for Peace and Justice. Around four or five hundred thousand people came. But before that, the FBI sent out a leaflet to many campuses. It spoke of those who would come as "every white fag group in the country . . . , every Jew leader . . . , white female lib group, every lesbian collection of coo coos, every ranting pervert, every liberal maniac." And it concluded, "Dellinger and company are a cancer in the movement's bloodstream. They must be removed, and now. . . . Write Vietnam Peace Parade Committee." *That was a total forgery.*

As part of COINTELPRO, the FBI issued other leaflets under our name and sponsorship. I have a flyer that was ostensibly put out by the National Black Anti War Anti Draft Union, NBAWADU. It was anti-Semitic in content. At the bottom of the leaflet was our name, the "Vietnam Peace Parade Committee." The Anti-Defamation League got hold of it and sent me a copy. I had never seen it before. I wrote to the ADL, telling them that this was a blatant fraud. NBAWADU no longer existed. It was definite provocation, a deliberate, conscious attempt to discredit our efforts to stop the war.

Recently, I was watching some of the coverage of the fiftieth anniversary of Hiroshima. In one of the documentaries, the narrator made a comment: "And so the people of Hiroshima were treated like matter." That grabbed me because that's what war does. It reduces human beings to the level of matter—inorganic matter. That's how our government was treating the people of Indochina.

"Do you understand what napalm does to people?" a U.S. volunteer in South Vietnam, with the Agency for International Development, wrote in a letter to the Episcopal Peace Fellowship:

> It explodes and spreads a jelly all over everything in the vicinity. This jelly is on fire. It burns through clothing and destroys the skin with burns. It leaves the people not already dead to die a horrible death by burns. It burns trees, houses, everything. Do you understand what a phosphorus bomb does? It gets on the body and burns and it does not stop burning until it reaches bone. What does it feel like, I wondered, to have phosphorus on your face and feel it eating away right down to the skull. Do you like that picture? Well, that is what your government and mine is doing. . . . Can you even begin to imagine the utter horror of being in a village where the planes come in, dropping fragmentation bombs to drive people into the open, and then following with napalm and phosphorus bombs to get an effective kill? . . .

If you've been able to grasp even a tiny fraction of the anguish and desperation of this letter, and I have been able to record a fraction of what I feel,
and I feel only a fraction of what my people in the countryside feel, then
you will do everything in your power and in the power that God offers you
to stop this war.[63]

It did drag out from 1972 until 1975, for the final peace treaty to take
place. There was vast relief that the bombing was over, that the carpet
bombing of Vietnam was stopped. When the final treaty was signed, we
organized the War Is Over rally. Cora Weiss from Women Strike for Peace
got Joan Baez and Phil Ochs and a number of entertainers, and we had
this big celebration in Central Park. But there was no overwhelming joy.
I think that on an intellectual level I felt some satisfaction—you know,
recognizing that our movement had some historical impact. But I wasn't
happy. The carnage had been so vast. The death toll of Vietnamese was
staggering. The loss of our men for nothing. Fodder. Fifty-eight thousand dead, thousands crippled. It was not the kind of situation that gave
one joy.

HUAC, THE POLICE, THE FBI, THE COURTS:
CONTAINING AN EXTRAORDINARY GENERATION

In the aftermath of the October 1967 Pentagon demonstration, the Justice Department under Lyndon Johnson indicted Dr. Benjamin Spock and
other antiwar leaders for conspiring to violate the Selective Service Act,
"as a warning," Robert Goldstein writes, "to all antiwar demonstrators
and spokesmen that they might very well face similar charges."[64] In fact,
the government's position was that all twenty-eight thousand persons
who signed an antidraft statement and even those who had applauded
the defendants' speeches could be indicted. Under Richard Nixon, the
Justice Department brought conspiracy charges against outspoken critics of the president's Vietnam policies, including the Chicago Eight, Daniel
Ellsberg, Philip Berrigan and his co-defendants, and the Gainesville
Eight.*

That the government lost case after case, either at trial or in appeals

---

*Daniel Ellsberg describes the Pentagon Papers case on pp. 330–339 of this book. Philip
Berrigan and his co-defendants were accused of conspiring to raid draft boards, bomb heat-
ing tunnels in the Capitol, and kidnap Henry Kissinger. The Gainesville Eight, members
of Vietnam Veterans Against the War, were accused of conspiring to disrupt the 1972 Republican National Convention in Miami.

court, is particularly revealing in light of the advantages that conspiracy charges confer on the government's side. The ordinary rules of evidence are relaxed, and all "conspirators" are held liable for the acts of each individual. A conspiracy charge can be sustained even if the "conspirators" acted completely openly, even if they never met, even if they agreed with each other only implicitly, and even if they never acted illegally. First Amendment scholar Thomas Emerson warns that when conspiracy charges are applied to political activity, it "becomes dangerous for any individual to participate in a campaign or demonstration that in the course of its unfolding may give rise to some violation of the law. It is hard to conceive of a more chilling effect upon the system of free expression."[65]

In the months after the Pentagon demonstration, Abbie Hoffman, Jerry Rubin, and Paul Krassner founded Yippie!, a group that, they believed, would bring the disenchanted children of the middle class, who had turned down rat-race America for a kinder, communal vision, to protest the 1968 Democratic National Convention in Chicago. A play on the word "hippie," Yippie! fashioned satire and symbol into a political weapon intended to shock, confront, and capture media attention. After dumping dollars down on Wall Street brokers and plastering the Times Square Army recruiting booth with "See Canada Now" stickers, the Yippies scheduled a "Yip-In" at Grand Central Station to observe the spring equinox. The six thousand people who poured into the train terminal at midnight were met by what a New York Civil Liberties Union lawyer called "the most extraordinary display of unprovoked police brutality I've seen outside Mississippi."[66] One squad went for Abbie Hoffman, clubbing him unconscious. It was a harbinger of what would happen at the Yippie! "Festival of Life," which was slated to be celebrated in Chicago alongside the more staid protests organized by the National Mobilization.

By the time the demonstrators arrived in Chicago for the Democratic Convention protests, five thousand National Guardsmen had been mobilized; a thousand FBI agents were deployed; six thousand troops with flame-throwers, bazookas, and bayonets were stationed at the ready; all twelve thousand city police had been put on twelve-hour shifts; and barbed wire sealed off the convention site. What followed was a rampage by the Chicago police, characterized by the indiscriminate beatings and teargassings that a presidential commission later termed a "police riot."[67] But it was Rennie Davis, David Dellinger, John Froines, Tom Hayden, Abbie Hoffman, Jerry Rubin, Bobby Seale, and Lee Weiner—the

Chicago Eight—who were charged with conspiracy to cross state lines with the intent to carry on a riot.*

The stage was set for an extraordinary trial, dominated by the spectacle of Bobby Seale gagged and chained to his chair in the courtroom. The judge's hostility to the defense was undisguised and frequently expressed: the bench warrants issued for the arrest of pretrial defense lawyers, the unprecedented number and severity of contempt citations, the refusal to permit critical defense witnesses to testify before the jury, and the belittling comments about the defendants and their lawyers. The defendants responded by directly challenging both judge and prosecutors, sometimes puncturing courtroom decorum with Yippie! chutzpah and lampoon.[68]

ABBIE HOFFMAN

MR. WEINGLASS [DEFENSE ATTORNEY]:   Will you please identify yourself for the record?
THE WITNESS: My name is Abbie. I am an orphan of America.

MR. WEINGLASS: Where do you reside?
THE WITNESS: I live in Woodstock Nation.

MR. WEINGLASS: Will you tell the Court and jury where it is?
THE WITNESS: Yes. It is a nation of alienated young people. We carry it around with us as a state of mind in the same way as the Sioux Indians carried the Sioux nation around with them. It is a nation dedicated to cooperation versus competition, to the idea that people should have better means of exchange than property or money, that there should be some other basis for human interaction. It is a nation dedicated to—

THE COURT [JUDGE JULIUS HOFFMAN]:   Just where it is, that is all.
THE WITNESS: It is in my mind and the minds of my brothers and sisters. It does not consist of property or material but, rather, of ideas and certain values. We believe in a society—

THE COURT: No, we want the place of residence, if he has one, place of doing business, if you have a business. Nothing about philosophy

---

*The defendants were later referred to as the Chicago Seven, after Bobby Seale's case was severed from those of the others.

ABBIE HOFFMAN

or India, sir. Just where you live, if you have a place to live. Now you
said Woodstock. In what state is Woodstock?

THE WITNESS: It is in the state of mind, in the mind of myself and
my brothers and sisters. It is a conspiracy. Presently, the nation is held
captive, in the penitentiaries of the institutions of a decaying system.[69]

In a series of demonstrations up through 1968, we had established a
kind of momentum in the antiwar movement. Our focal points for symbolic targets were the decision makers: the Pentagon, the Capitol, draft
boards. The Democrats were gathering to plan the next four years of ac-

tivity at their convention in Chicago. Vietnam was the war of liberal Democrats, and it was up to them to do something about it. So it would have
been impossible to overlook their convention as a target. Various factions of the antiwar movement, in their own style and in their own language, began preparing in December of 1967 to bring large numbers of
people to Chicago.

We felt we could have brought from one to two hundred thousand
people there. But events over the next four months or so led us to believe that we were going to be greeted with hostility by the authorities
and that our numbers would be much smaller. There had been a peaceful demonstration in Chicago that spring that was attacked by the police. The Yippies had been beaten by police at Grand Central Station.
There had been violent confrontations—clubbing of students—at Columbia University. Also, there was an attitude on the part of Mayor
Richard Daley and the police authorities that they were simply not going to allow a large presence.

A large presence requires an immense amount of staging, of logistical
work. We would have had to secure permits well in advance to assure
the demonstrators and the performers that the city authorities were not
going to be hostile. We had to know where the bands could set up their
equipment, where two hundred thousand people were going to sleep. I
must have gone to Chicago a half dozen times between New Year's and
August to make arrangements. Now, we were not the easiest people to
negotiate with, but anyone who checked the Yippies' relationship with,
say, authorities in New York City would have known that when we go
into negotiations, we stick to agreements. We were not interested in having a bloodbath because it would be our own blood.

By now, all the groups involved had gone through permit negotiations
many, many times with city officials in Washington, in New York City.
But Chicago was a little more difficult. We negotiated with the deputy
mayor. He was courteous and polite, but we did not get a permit. It
seemed to us that the authorities were saying: "As long as we can, hold
off." Still, we thought they were going to stall and then give us our permits a week before, just as a public relations ploy. But as events subsequently proved, they weren't that interested in public relations.

There was real tension in the air. But people from around the country were determined to come and make a statement against the war in
Vietnam. They were not going to be deterred by Mayor Daley going on
television and saying: "Nobody's going to mess with my city." They were
not going to be intimidated by parades of police whacking their batons

against the palms of their hands, or pictures showing the National Guard setting up an encampment on the outskirts of Chicago, or the stories in the press claiming that suspected "terrorists" were headed there. Daley was doing his symbolic warfare, but we were doing ours, too.

When you're up against forces of superior financial and military power, superior numbers, you play a game of destroying the symbols of authority, of making authority overreact to look foolish. Well, Yippies excelled in symbolic warfare. And, of course, when we baited them, they went for it. We said we were going to put LSD in the drinking water; they called out six thousand National Guard troops to protect the reservoir. We said we were going to strip naked and have orgies on the beach; they had thousands of police patrolling all the beaches in Chicago. Whatever we said we were going to do, no matter how outrageous it sounded, they would marshal their troops. They didn't understand our language.

We burlesqued the whole process of electoral politics. We said, "We're going to run a pig for president, Pigasus the Pig." We built a campaign around it. We got real pigs and let them loose in the streets. So then they arrested the pigs. It was a clash. What can I say? It was a cultural clash that was played out in the media. And negotiations at the center of it weren't making any progress.

The Yippies were not the only ones who didn't get permits. The other groups didn't get them either. But for all of us to have backed down, for us to have said, "There's not going to be any demonstrations," would have been unthinkable. Of course, within the context of what we were doing, we kept backing down. We made a symbolic stand that we would stay in the park, that we had a right to be there. But we didn't want people to get wiped out in the night. We knew the cops were coming in with tear gas and clubs. So every night we asked people to leave the park after the eleven o'clock curfew.

But the police acted like enraged, crazed animals. They chased people in the park, in the streets. They chased them right into houses, into restaurants, into hotels, clubbing the shit out of anybody they got. Everyone was fair game. There's a woman, a suburbanite, with two kids in a car, and the police are surrounding her. They've got their bayonets sticking in the window and poised at the tires, and tear gas is going off all around. I mean, there were a lot of very poignant scenes that just couldn't be hidden from the photographers. News reporters and photographers got assaulted in the streets, as did just passersby. It even happened inside the convention hall! Daley had a praetorian guard of plainclothes detectives. Dan Rather was hit with a blackjack, clubbed to the floor by them.

I was what you would call a hardened veteran by the time Chicago happened. I had seen police behave like that a number of times, you know, in Mississippi, in San Francisco, in Washington, in New York. What shocked me here was the duration. Those other events would happen for half an hour, an hour. Sometimes city officials would apologize: Something didn't go right, you know, something got out of control. But here, the city officials were justifying it. And it kept going on night after night. It went on for four days. It gave you the sense that there was a complete breakdown of law and order.

Chicago police were on me twenty-four hours a day. They followed me visibly and surreptitiously. Everywhere I went, there was a car with two plainclothes policemen behind me. They would come up and introduce themselves. I even managed to con a couple of meals out of them. They let it be known that I was going to be arrested on Wednesday. That morning, police came into the restaurant where I was eating and said, "You're under arrest." I asked, "Did you call Commander Brash about this?" I just picked out a name. I said, "If I'm to be arrested, you're supposed to check with him right away." They went out, and I kept eating breakfast.

The next thing I know, there are police cars surrounding the restaurant. They dragged me across the table and threw me out the door. I was kept for about fourteen hours without food or sleep. They beat me up a few times and moved me from station to station, while my lawyers were running around trying to find me.

Up until the demonstrations in Chicago, the antiwar movement was spontaneous, decentralized. There were hundreds of groups. The government has difficulty dealing with that kind of an amorphous mass. So they proceeded to go after the leaders, whether we called ourselves leaders or not. To build a national movement, you have to be able to develop a strategy, develop a language that's America, that's going to appeal to large numbers of Americans. We were the ones who had a national strategy. And we were the ones the government singled out a little bit more than others—Jerry Rubin, Dave Dellinger, Tom Hayden, Rennie Davis, and me—first through HUAC and then through the Justice Department.

HUAC originally got me pissed off at the system of oppression in this country back in 1960, when I saw what was going on in San Francisco. Actually, I didn't see—that was the point. The public was not allowed to go into their hearings. HUAC let their cronies in, DAR members and the American Legion. Those of us who had waited since dawn began chanting, "Down with HUAC." The police clubbed students to the ground, turned water hoses full force on them, and threw people down the marble steps.

HUAC was impaneled to disgrace you, to dishonor you in the community. And in the 1950s, many witnesses accepted the legitimacy of the committee. There were very few moments, like Zero Mostel's, of what you would call outbursts. I'm not passing any judgment. The times were different; they had economic leverage on the people they called; there wasn't a movement in the streets.

By the time our moment came, HUAC had lost its bite. They didn't have economic leverage on the Yippies. They couldn't ruin our careers—we didn't want to work anyway. Because of what happened in Chicago, because of what was happening in Vietnam every single day, because the country was going to split apart, we didn't give a fuck what they called us. What's this committee going to do—put us in jail? We'd all been in jail. Our attitude was "Throw your best punch, you asshole. You can't hurt us." By 1968, when HUAC came after us, we were determined to use our strategy of mockery and satire and take the offensive.

HUAC? Oh, fucking hey, I loved it. While the lawyers were playing this rational game, making various legal points and raising their hands politely, we had witches going up and down the aisle with brooms. And of course, we were dressed as freaks. Rubin is naked to the waist, with a bandolier and a plastic machine gun and painted face and barefooted. I remember at one point I raised my hand and said, "May I have permission to swear?" And the answer was, "There's no swearing in this room."

I said, "Well, I'll go outside." So I walked out the door and yelled, "Bullshit!" really loud. I mean, you could hear it a mile away. Guards came running up the aisle. Then I opened up the door and said, "Oh, I feel much better now. Thank you."

We'd just walk up to them and cuss them out: "Fascists! You're the illegitimate ones, not us. You jerks, you're un-American." And it's interesting, they never held any of us in contempt. There were people in the audience from the Hollywood Ten and others who had been pilloried by HUAC. They had tears in their eyes watching us stand up there and scream at them. Those were just about the last hearings HUAC ever had.

The strategy was to put yourself in a situation where the opposition, no matter what it did, lost. But this is a dangerous game. You're going to have to pay some. You might have to go to jail. You might get beat up—I had my nose broken in seven places by cops. In the midst of the hearings, I walked up the Capitol steps in a shirt that looked like a flag. Here come all these guards, yanking at me and ripping it off. They started jumping all over me, beating me up. The cameras were filming the whole thing. On the one hand, they looked totally stupid, arresting me for wearing a shirt I had just bought at a store. Lots of people in the country were wearing that shirt. On the other hand, the story in the media was that I had desecrated the flag. It made people think that I had spit on the flag or wiped my boots with it.

The guards at the D.C. jail heard that and said, "You sonofabitch commie, we're going to get you." When they came to take a blood sample, I said, "I don't want to do that. I'm only going to be here a few more hours." They said, "You've got to." I'm screaming, "Lawyer! Lawyer!" and it isn't working. They got me down on the ground, spread-eagled, and injected me. Eight weeks to the day, the exact incubation period, I got serum hepatitis. By the time it was my turn to testify before HUAC, I was in the hospital. I'm sorry I didn't get the chance, because I was going to say, "I have nothing to hide," and take my clothes off.

In Chicago, I was under investigation from at least half a dozen agencies that I know of. I had been under surveillance for a long time before that. But after the Pentagon demonstrations in October of 1967, when it became pretty clear that the next national action would be at the Democratic Convention, we started to come under pretty heavy surveillance. And then, with the passage of the Interstate Anti-Riot Act in April of 1968—the Rap Brown Law, as it was euphemistically called—we were under almost daily FBI surveillance.

The FBI committed burglaries, stealing lists and papers from me. Hundreds of illegal wiretaps. God, we had one lawsuit in Washington alone where they revealed a hundred and forty-four illegal wiretaps on me. I mean, they would wiretap everyone I was connected with. And then if I went to give a speech at a university, the FBI would show up there a couple of weeks ahead and try to get them to cancel it. They followed my parents, photographing them. They'd walk up on the beach, Miami Beach, and take their picture while they were sitting there. They went to my father's customers and got them to cancel their business, even though he didn't agree with me. Just totally harassing things. Character assassination stories about me in lots of magazines and newspapers—the FBI would use their contacts to have them printed. Set-ups. People were constantly coming up and offering me weapons. I was offered bazookas. I was offered machine guns. You wouldn't believe it—I was offered a tank! Frame-ups. A guy showed up at the office, left the room, and twenty minutes later in come the police and arrest everybody. He had brought guns in a bag and left it there.

All these things done to us were completely illegal. And no one listened to what we were saying. No newspaper, no reporter in this town was interested. And I did not act like a paranoid person in that period. But when your apartment is broken into and lists and papers are gone through and nothing else is taken—something suspicious is going on. And I always, to this day, maintain an element of naiveté about that kind of stuff. It pretty well shocks me and offends me as an American.

The FBI could not understand what motivated us. We were brought up in the 1950s, believing in the American empire and all the values of shopping mall suburbia. And we were well educated and white. We had it all, yet we were saying, "No." I'm talking about people like Tom Hayden, Rennie Davis, Jerry Rubin, and myself, and, in a sense, the white radicals of our generation. I'm not talking about Dave Dellinger, who was a career pacifist for thirty years, and he'll be doing it for another thirty. And I'm not talking about the Blacks in SNCC. I'm talking about, why us? The FBI could not understand.

Reading my files, there were immense moments of high comedy when the FBI was trying to fathom something like the gibberish of the Yippie language. If you say, "I'm going to tear this country down," the FBI sees tanks and jets. They can't see that as a poetic expression. There's no poetry in the FBI. You're talking about accountants. You're talking about accountants trying to interpret poets, and mad poets at that.

At one point, they hired someone to psychoanalyze me and Jerry. I met that person three years ago. Their main conclusion seemed to be that I was an exhibitionist. You know, if you run naked through a church or throw out money at the stock exchange, it's safe to assume that. They just did not understand our motivations or our strategy or the world around them. They thought the country was on the absolute brink of catastrophe, falling apart at any minute. And here was a handful of people—me, myself included—who had enormous power. I didn't even have a secretary. At some points, I didn't even have a telephone. But we had figured out ways of communicating ideas that were somehow threatening to them. So that's power.

You read these FBI files, and it's like here's a general of a vast army. One time I was arrested, and they needed a hundred police to take me in. A hundred! Another time I was arrested on Thirteenth Street, and they had both ends of the block barricaded. They had squad cars all up and down. When the police approached me, they had their guns drawn.

I just thought they were going to make some stupid mistake and shoot me. I mean, it was just incredible.

The so-called Rap Brown Law was passed in April of 1968 to prevent national demonstrations. It's so broad that they can use it to stop any national movement in this country. It's a state-of-mind law, because it deals with your intentions. We were charged under that law with conspiracy to cross state lines with the intention to incite a riot. Eight of us were selected and packed off to what the ACLU said was the "Trial of the Century." We couldn't very well dispute the fact that we had traveled from New York to Chicago. So there's the crossing of the state lines. But if a riot is defined as an act or a threat of violence, what does it mean? Obviously there was violence. Anyone who looks at the footage of those demonstrations can see that there was a riot. But it was outrageous that we were put on trial for what happened in Chicago. The government's own study called it a police riot.

They would have police or police agents testify, "I heard him give a speech telling people to get sticks and stones and go downtown." Total lies, you know. Those of us who were on trial, at every speech we'd give there were fifty or sixty tape recorders. But they never had any tape recordings as evidence. And they never had any legitimate reporters, civilian eyewitnesses. It was all their police agents. So now it's my word—a long-haired, disreputable radical—against the word of a government agent. The evidence was us. Look at us: long hair, unshaven, freaky, disrespectful of the court. That's what the trial was about.

We didn't try to hide things. We didn't try to get our school teachers from the fifth grade to testify about what terrific, nice people we were. We would bring in revolutionaries. Black Panthers would say what they thought was wrong about America. We tried to conduct a political trial. But the court system doesn't have a mechanism for that, so you've got to try to do it within the context of a criminal trial. We would testify, "Oh, yes, we had a conversation." "What did you say?" And then we'd give some long indictment of the war in Vietnam or something on racism.

We all, in our various ways, had the attitude "Fuck them," the same as with HUAC. We were not going to legitimize the courts. This is just another institution that's corrupt. Now that attitude itself was a bit original, because liberals think the courts are where you'll get your just due. That's where truth will come out. Our attitude was we might as well yell out, because what's the difference? They invented the rules. They got the hanging judge. They're building the gallows downstairs. I mean, we might as well rip it down.

At the same time that we were romantic utopians, there was some fatalism involved because we just felt we were going to get it. We were going to prison forever. We were going to get shot. I remember before the trial began just searching the whole scene, trying to figure out where the snipers were going to shoot at us, where they were going to assassinate us. But once the trial began, I threw every ounce of my being into it. Prison? Assassination threats? None of it mattered.

We used instant analysis to try to highlight what we thought was outrageous. Of course, we were being victimized, but we were not taking it lying down. So we waited for the judge to do something outrageous, for him to shoot off his mouth or make some stupid ruling, and then we'd respond by calling attention to it. And the way in which we responded was to go outside the accepted form of courtroom behavior. No one did that before. No defendant stood up and said, "Why did you say that, judge?" Not only that, but at some point, I was calling him Julie: "Julie, cut that shit out." Anything. Anything, like when we showed up with judge's robes on.

Of course, it was outrageous what Hoffman did. First, he wouldn't let Bobby Seale have the lawyer of his choice. Then he wouldn't let him defend himself. Then, when Bobby kept interrupting the proceedings, they bound and gagged him. What astounded me was that they couldn't shut Bobby Seale up. They must have tried five or six different contraptions to gag him. Nothing worked. Within three or four minutes, he was loose and screaming at the judge again. I thought that part of it was pretty great. It was a testament to the human spirit and will. It was powerful and it was symbolic.

Our response to the chaining and gagging of Seale? When they said, "Hear ye, hear ye, all rise for His Honor Julius Hoffman"—we didn't rise. And in comes his honor, the judge. He's just totally shocked: There's people *sitting!* He orders us to rise or be in contempt. Our stand was that free speech was a lot more complicated than just words, and this was free speech. We eventually won that in the appeals court.

Ramsey Clark was not allowed to testify because he might have swayed the jury a little too close to our side—the attorney general of the United States! As the attorney general at that time, he had access to all these FBI reports and everything. He was going to say that we were no threat, that the mayor was way out of line, that you could negotiate with us, that the Justice Department had urged the city of Chicago to negotiate permits. But that would have made the police and the city of Chicago look pretty bad. So when he showed up in court that day, the judge said: I don't want the jury to hear it. He claimed that Ramsey Clark's testimony wouldn't be relevant. It was one of the more outrageous aspects of this judge's outrageous behavior.

When our case came up to the appeals court, they said that of course Ramsey Clark had valuable information and had a right to testify. I believe the appeals court agreed with something like a hundred and twenty-eight out of a hundred and twenty-nine reasons we stated as grounds for reversal. The only one they didn't want to make a ruling on was the constitutionality of the law.

So there's the law. It's still on the books. Now, we did not go to Chicago with the intention to incite a riot. But if you asked me a year later, "Did you go to San Francisco, did you go to Washington to incite a riot?" I probably would have been cocky enough to say, "You bet your fucking ass. How are we supposed to change this country? What are we supposed to do? Get some permits? They won't give us permits. We're supposed to have a nice la-de-da? We've already got the shit kicked out of us. You want to talk about law, go up and look at my apartment. The FBI's just gone through it."

You know, we were angry. All the legal ways to change the country had been closed down. And the police, the FBI, the Justice Department were all using illegal means against us. We felt it was just a matter of time before they started picking us all off. After the trial in Chicago, I had a suitcase with phony identification and disguises all ready to go. I figured I'd be underground any minute.

RETRIBUTION FOR ACTS OF CONSCIENCE

Richard Nixon's Vietnam policy was two-sided: a public position of "Vietnamization," to completely disengage American troops and turn the war over to the South Vietnamese; and a secret position of U.S. escalation, to win the war at all costs. Nixon announced the first withdrawal of twenty-five thousand troops in June 1969, followed by more withdrawals in September and December, in no small part to defuse domestic opposition. Secretly, however, he ordered the bombing of a neutral nation, Cambodia, and plans were made to bomb North Vietnam's cities, mine its harbors, and invade the country.[70]

A former Defense Department official and State Department representative in South Vietnam and, in 1967, a strategic analyst at the Rand Corporation, Daniel Ellsberg was seeking ways, within the administration, to forestall military escalation. But he was meeting with no success.

Told of the secret bombing of Cambodia and convinced that Nixon was in fact on a course that would escalate the war, Ellsberg began to photocopy the documents that came to be known as the "Pentagon Papers," part of which he had authored. The classified Defense Department history revealed that U.S. involvement in Vietnam had been "either deliberately distorted or withheld altogether from the public."[71] In November 1969, Ellsberg gave portions of the Pentagon Papers to William Fulbright, chairman of the Senate Foreign Relations Committee. But it would be more than a year, on June 13, 1971, before Ellsberg succeeded in having them made public, on the front pages of the *New York Times*.

The administration claimed that the publication of the documents jeopardized the nation's defense. Henry Kissinger, especially, railed against Ellsberg—"the most dangerous man in America today," who "must be stopped at all costs."[72] But whatever danger Ellsberg's release of the Pentagon Papers posed, it was not, apparently, to national security.[73] The secretary of defense estimated that 98 percent of the documents could have been declassified, and the Defense Department itself soon published virtually the same material.[74] Solicitor General Erwin N. Griswold, who argued before the Supreme Court that the publication of the Pentagon Papers constituted a "grave and immediate danger to the security of the United States," later admitted that he had "never seen any trace of a threat to national security from the publication."[75]

Richard Nixon sought and won a temporary injunction prohibiting the further publication of the papers. "Never before," David Wise notes, "had the federal government gone into court to try to censor a newspaper."[76] Two weeks later, the Supreme Court struck down the injunction. Then, after Nixon's Justice Department had secured an indictment against Ellsberg for releasing the papers, it continued to interrogate witnesses using grand jury proceedings that had less to do with the grand jury's function—securing indictments for criminal acts—than with the aim of fishing for information.[77] Subpoenaed were Southeast Asia scholars, journalists, congressional aides, and the records of the Unitarian Church and Beacon Press, which had published the Pentagon Papers. Harvard professor and Vietnam expert Samuel Popkin testified before the grand jury that he knew nothing of the Pentagon Papers release, but he was pressed to reveal the sources of his own scholarly research, which he refused to do. Popkin went to prison for his principles, "a long step toward legitimizing the misuse of grand juries as instruments of political intimidation," the *New York Times* editorialized.[78]

The president also created a clandestine White House unit, known as "the Plumbers," ostensibly to plug information leaks to the press. In fact, this group operated outside the law to exact retribution by seeking and leaking derogatory information about Ellsberg to the press or by engaging in direct acts to humiliate or harm him. "Get it out, leak it out," the Nixon tapes revealed the president ordering his top aides. "I want to destroy him in the press; is that clear?"[79] Then, late on the night of September 3, 1971, Plumbers E. Howard Hunt and G. Gordon Liddy stood guard outside the office of Ellsberg's psychiatrist, Dr. Louis Fielding, as their three Cuban accomplices broke in. According to Special Watergate Prosecutor Leon Jaworski, they were in search of information to "smear and defame [Ellsberg] before he came to trial" and to "discredit him as a Vietnam War critic."[80] The president's chief domestic affairs adviser, John Ehrlichman, had approved the Plumbers' robbery attempt; and Richard Nixon, according to his chief of staff, "had ordered it himself."[81]

The legal case against Ellsberg, based heavily on the Espionage Act, did not go to trial until 1973. Ellsberg was charged with conspiring with others to steal classified materials and deliver them to persons not entitled to receive them. When the judge in his case learned of the Fielding burglary and other instances of government misconduct, he declared a mistrial and dismissed the charges. The Plumbers' illegal activities against Ellsberg were among the abuses of power cited by the House of Representatives in considering Nixon's impeachment. "By leaking the Pentagon Papers, Daniel Ellsberg had promoted the downfall of the Nixon administration, a downfall that," Tom Wells believes, "played a pivotal role in ending the war."[82]

DANIEL ELLSBERG

The fact is that in Vietnam we were forcing a war on a nation that overwhelmingly would have preferred peace under either competing regime. We were choosing war for the people of Vietnam. And I believe that most officials who knew the situation at all, including my colleagues, were well aware that it was without the consent of the Vietnamese. There's really nothing worse you can do to a people than to fight a war in their country to which they do not assent.

And being in Vietnam was enough to teach me, as it did nearly everyone who went there, that we had been massively lied to. The truth was that we were involved in a hopeless stalemate, which was in fact getting larger and larger in scale. That perception was very widely shared in the Pentagon and in the armed services—among infantrymen. Most every-

DANIEL ELLSBERG

thing they had heard before they went had been a lie. And everything that was being said to the public while they were there was a lie. But they didn't have the proof, the documentary proof, that the president, Lyndon Johnson, was consciously lying. In fact, most people in the system were under the misapprehension that it was only their own colleagues and their immediate superiors who were doing the lying and perhaps were fooling the president. What the Pentagon Papers revealed was that the president himself was directing this deception to the public and, in fact, was getting quite adequate information about the realities in Vietnam.

Even though the papers were history and didn't apply to Richard Nixon directly, I hoped that releasing them to the public would be worthwhile. But if I had not been aware through friends of mine who were still in the administration that new escalations were very likely, I do not think that I would have put out the Pentagon Papers simply for the satisfaction of educating the public. The reason for my being willing to tell the American people what I knew with documentary evidence—and to go to prison for it, even for the rest of my life, if necessary—was above all an urgent feeling that they had to be alerted to this secret past in order to recognize it in what was going on at the moment and act to avert further escalations in that same war.

My immediate concern in the fall of '69, when I copied the papers, was that Nixon would publicly commit himself to the war and that it would then prove almost impossible for him to withdraw. My further concern was that in the course of attempting to achieve an outcome that was acceptable to him, he would be escalating the war. Very specifically, I was afraid that 1969 and 1970 would be a replay of 1964 and 1965, when secret plans had finally led to a major escalation of the war while I was in the Pentagon. Indeed, the Pentagon Papers did not come out until over a year and a half later; during that time, there were two invasions in Indochina—the invasions of Cambodia and Laos—and a renewal of heavy bombing over North Vietnam. So my fears were justified.

But some of the worst of the escalations were averted: We never used nuclear weapons, and we never invaded North Vietnam. And contrary to what most scholars, as well as the public, normally believe, those two possibilities were not remote at all. They were very possible, indeed probable, if the public had not acted vigorously. We now know that it was only the massive mobilization against the war, known as the Moratorium in October and November of '69, that deterred Nixon from carrying out heavier escalations than anything undertaken before. And the Pentagon Papers, of course, helped to encourage the public to act in the later stages of the war.

Before I made the Pentagon Papers public, I had spent over a year intermittently reading work by Martin Luther King Jr., Gandhi, and others. Just in March of 1968—by coincidence, the week Martin Luther King Jr. was killed—I became aware of this approach. King was very self-consciously a scholar of Gandhi. However, he said in his book *Stride Toward Freedom* that it wasn't until he encountered the actual situation brought about by the decision of Rosa Parks that he was challenged to put Gandhian thought into action. It does take the example of someone like that, I think, face to face, to make you aware that you have the capability of doing such a thing and that it's a meaningful kind of action for someone like yourself.

Having read the theory, I met people, younger people, who shared these ideas, and they were going to prison. That suggested to me: What should I be doing if I were willing to take the risk of jail? And that question immediately, of course, suggested to me the Pentagon Papers, because they were in my safe.

I first gave the information to Senator William Fulbright at the end of November 1969, but he didn't actually put it out. In the meantime, the FBI became aware of what I'd done. My former wife had told her stepmother, who was very conservative and who immediately informed the FBI. Then the FBI investigated me. When they came to my former wife, she refused to talk to them. They then went to my employer, the Rand Corporation, and told them that it was the bureau's impression that I had given the Pentagon Papers to the senator. Rand didn't do much because they assumed the FBI was taking care of it. The FBI, in fact, more or less dropped it, on the assumption that I'd only given it to Fulbright. It could have gotten them into trouble, taking on the Senate, so they didn't pursue it.

After all, it wasn't illegal, as they knew. What I had done was clear grounds for firing and clear grounds for depriving me of my security clearance, which, in a way, is worse than firing. It means you can't get a similar job elsewhere. It's like a blacklist. But firing and revoking clearance are both administrative steps. I had not, in fact, broken a law.

What I'd done was copy information, and whether information can be stolen turns out to be a very murky area of the law. In fact, by virtually every precedent, the answer is no. When you are copying information, you're not really stealing. If the person still has the information, you're just sharing it, in effect. You can steal paper, and you can steal a form of words. But copyright, for instance, is almost entirely a civil matter, for civil damages and civil suits. Criminal copyright is a very restricted kind of thing. In any event, the government can't copyright anything. So I hadn't violated that, as most people imagined I had. By any previous interpretation of the law, I simply hadn't broken the law.

What challenged the government about what I did was that it was an open act. If they didn't prosecute me, they would admit that there was no law against it. Well, I was prosecuted, but that doesn't mean they expected to win. That's why, in large part, they had to go after me with the

White House Plumbers. They didn't have a case that they really were confident of winning in court.

Of course, when they're coming heavily at you, they have a chance of winning, whatever the law, whatever the strength of their case. As my lawyer, Leonard Boudin, said, "When they say, 'U.S. versus Daniel Ellsberg' and claim you've broken these laws, and the jury hears all this, you're not sure you'll walk out of there free."

I asked him, "What are my odds?" He said, "Fifty-fifty. Face it, Dan. Copying seven thousand pages of 'top secret' documents and giving them to the *New York Times* has a bad ring to it." So we went through two years of proceedings, five months in court.

The FBI early on took the position, which was correct, that I had had no real confederates. Except for a few people who helped me from time to time actually copy the papers, like Tony Russo and my wife, they felt that there was no grand conspiracy. However, the Defense Department and the White House were convinced that there was a big conspiracy, with which they would be able to get the Rand Corporation. They actually didn't care much about the Rand Corporation, but through them they really wanted to get Paul Warnke and Mort Halperin and, perhaps they dreamed, Robert McNamara, Clark Clifford—and Ted Kennedy; he's the one they really wanted to get.[*]

Actually, they had a good prima facie case. It was a plausible assumption on their part, because I had had associations with these people. The FBI had studied it closely, and they concluded that, plausible or not, there was no conspiracy. And that was another reason why the White House didn't trust the FBI entirely. So they assigned their own people to smear these others, if possible, without relying on doing it in court with legal evidence.

Why did the White House Plumbers go into my psychoanalyst's office? The explanation they preferred to give was that they wanted to see who I'd given the papers to. But the real reason for the break-in was to get information that they could blackmail me with. Someone who interviewed the Cubans involved in the break-in told me that they had been

---

[*]Founded in 1948, the Rand Corporation conducts research on national security and domestic policy matters, often for government agencies. Robert McNamara and Clark Clifford were both former secretaries of defense. Paul Warnke and Morton Halperin had been high-ranking Defense Department officials, and Halperin had been a senior staff member of the National Security Council. Edward M. Kennedy, first elected to the U.S. Senate from Massachusetts in 1962, was number one on Richard Nixon's "enemies list." All had questioned or opposed some aspect of the government's conduct of the war in Vietnam.

led to be as interested in my family's personal life as in mine. William Merrill, who prosecuted the Plumbers for the break-in, told me he thought they wanted to scare me off so I wouldn't take the stand in my own trial. If I hadn't testified, my case would have disappeared. The jury had to see what my motives were, to see who I was.

Another thing Merrill suggested was that if they couldn't scare me off the stand, they would get me to leave the country. Escaping from prosecution, of course, would have totally given up the case. They didn't even exclude the idea of causing me to commit suicide. This was a most ambitious thought. This is what they tried to do with Martin Luther King Jr. J. Edgar Hoover sent tapes to Coretta of King's supposed lovemaking, with the inference that it was a good time for him to commit suicide.

The White House didn't get what they wanted with the break-in, so they tried other things. They investigated all my former girlfriends from when I was a bachelor. It was quite a list. They got a lot of sexual promiscuity during that period when I wasn't married, but what could they do with that? It wouldn't hurt my reputation in this society. It just wasn't what they were looking for. So they really didn't get much out of that.

G. Gordon Liddy, one of the Plumbers, made a very interesting revelation. He had proposed, and it eventually had been agreed, that someone should put LSD in my soup at a reception at which I was speaking. I think, by the way, it must have been a reception in my honor by the Federal Employees for Peace in Washington. Liddy said the okay came from on high, which could only mean either the special counsel to the president, Charles Colson, or the president himself. However, it was too late to recruit the waiters for this purpose, and they weren't able to carry this through.

My wife was very worried in that period about crowds and the possibility of somebody getting me. I thought that the government didn't do that sort of thing to Americans. But I was simply wrong. They were trying to do it to me. There was discussion of killing me among the Plumbers and their people, who were CIA people, of course, and were used to this. On May 3, 1972, just before my case was about to come to trial, I was speaking on the steps of the Capitol. Mexican-laundered money, which was later used for Watergate, was first used to bring up eleven Cubans from Miami to Washington. Their orders were to totally incapacitate Ellsberg at this rally.

Of course, that didn't come out until much later, when I learned it from the prosecutor. The story that first appeared in *Time* was that they were just to punch me in the nose. Well, I couldn't think of any reason for doing that. They were already calling me a traitor and stigmatizing me and having a trial. I couldn't think what punching me in the nose would do. But when I heard that the order was to incapacitate me, I immediately felt sure I knew who ordered it and why. It came from the president, probably with advice from Henry Kissinger and Alexander Haig. It wasn't a matter of punching me in the nose to discredit me. It was a matter of shutting my mouth seriously or forever.

They had given the Cubans the cover story that I was, of all things, going to desecrate the coffin of J. Edgar Hoover, which happened to be lying in state at that moment in another part of the Capitol. Needless to say, our rally had nothing to do with the mourners for that. But the Cubans were told that we were infiltrating the Hoover mourning procession and that they were to protect Hoover's body.

When the Cubans got there, being ex-CIA men or current CIA men, they got very suspicious that they were being set up for something when they realized that the crowd wasn't friendly to their calling me "traitor." They suspected that they had been lied to, as they had been, and were smart enough to choose not to be fall guys. So they threw it. They deliberately punched at people on the side of the crowd and got themselves led away by the police. They were released after two men, one showing FBI credentials and one showing CIA credentials, told the police, "These are good Americans. We vouch for them." Undoubtedly the two were E. Howard Hunt and Liddy, using expired credentials and thus impersonating officers.

I didn't know about the incident at the time, although I recall the people shouting at me and the fighting. I actually saw Frank Sturgis in this fistfighting. I recognized him later in photos taken when he was arrested at the Watergate. He was the potential assassin, the guy who'd been involved in attempted assaults against Fidel Castro and Omar Torrijos of Panama.

In the meanwhile, the president's special counsel, Charles Colson, pled guilty to an operation to defame me in the press by putting out materials that would attack my lawyer, Leonard Boudin. He admitted providing a newsman, who later became President Ford's press secretary, with material for an article on Boudin that would have attacked him as pro-Communist. Colson pled guilty to this mainly, it seems, to avoid being prosecuted for his part in the chain of command that planned to have me incapacitated, which would have been a much more serious charge.

The break-ins at Dr. Fielding's office and at Watergate were not peculiar to Nixon. Nixon did have an innovation, which was to apply tactics that had been used on the Communists and the Socialist Workers Party and other left-wing groups to people who were moderates and liberals, centrists of various kinds. The latter category actually applied to me. It also applied to most people on Nixon's "enemies list." And that's what got a lot of people very excited, that Nixon was using tactics on others that were to be reserved for left-wingers. He was using them profusely against the Democrats and the liberals.

But as far as techniques were concerned, they had all been used. Nothing that Nixon did was worse than what Lyndon Johnson and, for that matter, Bobby Kennedy had done to Martin Luther King Jr. in the way of wire-tapping and blackmail and everything else. Nothing. It's part of the way the country is run. It doesn't mean it has to be that way forever or that it can't be changed. But it's part of the reality. How do you maintain a society that on the one hand consistently conducts an imperial policy, which is no worse or better than any other major imperial country, and on the other hand sees itself as an anti-imperial country that favors self-determination, opposes torture, and is in favor of freedom throughout the world? While it is a country that is democratic in many ways, more than almost any other country, its actions abroad oppose its own institutions.

In actual fact, it took me a long time to learn this. It was long after the Pentagon Papers that I learned that our policy in Vietnam was not an exceptional case. We were supporting, quite consciously, a highly unpopular dictatorship against, let us say, the alternative either of democracy or of a more popular dictatorship, popular in the sense of enjoying wide support and legitimacy. The very widely held idea that the United States favors and supports free institutions abroad is, in respect to the underdeveloped world, very simply a big lie, in the Hitlerian sense of the "big lie." And I don't refer to Hitler just to stigmatize it, but to refer to a matter of authorship here and a technical term. Hitler's point was that large, overarching, comprehensive lies are actually more easily believed and more effective than small lies, which are more subject to incredulity and disproof.

In any case, the notion that the United States backs free institutions in the third world is very simply a lie—and a big lie. We don't favor, we don't support, but we oppose free institutions in the third world when they interfere with our corporate and strategic interests. We are mostly in the position of either overthrowing free institutions, in the rare cases where they exist—as in Chile under Allende, as in Guatemala under Arbenz, as in Iran under Mossadegh—or preventing them from emerging. We simply stamp them out where they threaten our interests.

Now the question is, how do you behave in that way—which is not a way we invented but is a classical imperialist mode—and at the same time preserve the impression in our people's minds that they and their government are on the side of liberty throughout the world, including the poor, underdeveloped parts of the world? And the answer is by lying to them, by protecting those lies with an effective secrecy system, and by knocking down people who would attempt to give a more truthful picture.

And so you've got to stigmatize those people. I was a particular threat, I suspect, not only because of my actual expert background but because the special form of stigmatization chosen for me backfired. The articles that came out in *Life* magazine and elsewhere chose to emphasize my "instability," since there was nothing on which to base an accusation of left-wing or Communist sympathy. Well, the way of doing that was to stress how radically I had changed psychologically. So they emphasized the fact that here I was, being very actively antiwar although I had earlier been very actively pro-war. They showed lots of pictures of me as a marine or firing weapons in Vietnam, with a helmet on and actually armed to the teeth. Of course, in our society, they could hardly have given me a more favorable image. What the hell—that gave an impression of me in the public eye as a thoroughly reliable patriot. After that, it was very hard for them to knock me down, even though the headline in *Life* actually said: "From Hawk to Violent Dove." I'm sure they very much regretted printing such pictures.

From the very beginning, the White House Plumbers wanted to get a "psychological profile" on me and to use the psychological smear as much as possible, an interesting analogy to the Russian technique of putting dissenters into psychiatric hospitals. I once did a vigil for General Petro Grigorenko outside some Russian agency in New York, I remember, and I was thinking about that analogy at the time. He was assigned to a psychiatric hospital because he was a dissenter. It struck me how similar that was to the techniques they had used on me, trying to smear me as a psychiatric case. Hunt told the CIA that he wanted to show me as a broken man. They wanted to be able to refer to my oedipus complex knowingly. It was actually a fairly outrageous approach.

They were afraid that the reality of what they were doing and planning would get out to the public if more and more people imitated my own act of conscience and responsibility, if other officials began to act like responsible citizens and human beings instead of automatons and began to uphold their oath to the Constitution above their loyalty to a particular boss. So they hoped to deter that basic human loyalty by scaring them with the threat of major prosecutions like mine, or with other acts they had in mind. They failed to put me in prison, but the spectacle of having to conduct two years of legal proceedings did act as a very considerable deterrent. I know that there were people who were prepared to put out information. But when they saw the possibility of the hundred-and-fifteen-year sentence facing me, they held back to see, till the dust settled, and never did get around to it.

For any citizen to put himself or herself in direct opposition to government policy takes some risk. And jail is in fact not the most important consideration in most cases—rather, it's the risk to their reputation, with their spouses, and above all risks to their jobs, whether they work for the government or not. I don't think that we can avert such wrongful wars in the future, or other grave dangers to our environment elsewhere, without people taking risks. And that requires courage. So since courage is contagious, I think that examples of that in the form of major exposures and nonviolent peaceful disobedience or civil resistance are essential to the process.

I think it's going to be a very great challenge, but it's not without some compensation. I think that in the course of it, there will be a mobilization against imperialism that will be broader than anything we've ever seen before. If I'm wrong, then the public can be sold anything. The implications of that would be very sinister. But I'm not convinced that that's really true. In the end, they didn't sell Vietnam. It took a long time, but the public did finally see through it.

SAMUEL POPKIN

I knew Dan Ellsberg very well. He and I were two of the few Vietnam nuts in Cambridge who could talk about Vietnam for hours at a time, day and night. We had been there at the bottom, living in the villages. And both of us were writing about it. Although I knew an enormous amount about Dan's work, I did not have any idea whatsoever that the Pentagon Papers were going to be released. I knew zero about that. So I didn't have to worry about: Do I want to protect my friend or not?

The FBI visited me right after the papers were released. I had just returned from Hong Kong, and the next day they came to my office. The agents said, "Classified documents are out." They were polite, not evil

SAMUEL POPKIN

and not scary. But it was, of course, very scary being interviewed, because an awful lot of classified material floated around in Vietnam. And
I'd talked to many people about things that were not public. I didn't know
what the FBI was trying to do. I was a little upset by the tone of their
very strange questions. I made it clear to them that I had never seen the
Pentagon Papers, that I didn't know Ellsberg had them, and that I had
no idea this was going to happen.

They asked me a thousand questions of the "Does Daniel Ellsberg
still beat his wife?" kind. They were really questions you couldn't pos-

sibly answer, like "Would you say he's excessively demented?" I couldn't figure out where they came from until I read Seymour Hersh's book about Henry Kissinger. The things Kissinger was saying about Ellsberg were literally what the FBI was asking me to confirm: "Would you say Ellsberg was a madman?" "Would you say he hates his country?" And I said, "No. He may be single-minded. He may be intense. But he is very patriotic, and he is anything but a madman." I answered all the sane questions. For questions like "Is he still obsessed with sex?" I made it clear that I just didn't know how to answer one way or the other.

Certainly one of the things they wanted was Ellsberg dirt. Not criminal dirt, but smear dirt. I thought at the time that the reason they were trying to destroy Ellsberg was partly because he was so credible. He's very effective, one of the smartest people I've ever known, and not a person you'd easily want to debate. They were also afraid of what else he knew. He did know more than any civilian at that time about American nuclear planning, strategy, and targeting. Yet he never released a single word about any of that. Ever. Nor did he release the diplomatic volumes of the Pentagon Papers that could have been extremely damaging. But I think Nixon—he was so leak-crazy—was worried about the other shoe dropping with Daniel Ellsberg. So if you make the guy look demented enough, nothing he says will be taken as credible or serious by the press. They were out to discredit him, to make him out to be a kook and a weirdo.

David Nissen, the man in charge of prosecuting Ellsberg, pulled in a big team of prosecutors to go after everybody. They set up a grand jury in Los Angeles and another one in Boston, where I was subpoenaed. I just felt like I was a marked man. Once it's in the paper that you're being subpoenaed, it looks like you're guilty. There's no way to prove otherwise. When that happened, I talked with a career CIA official I knew. "I know you think something went on that didn't," I told him. "You're wrong, and I want to tell you why." Later, that person went out of his way to say to me, "Your quarrels are with people on the other side of the river." He meant: Your problems are at the White House.

In fact, now we know from the document that put John Ehrlichman in jail that he was the one who authorized the break-in at Dr. Fielding's office. It was part of an effort that was initiated by the White House after the release of the Pentagon Papers. But the break-in at Dr. Fielding's was only one part of the document. Another part said: We're going to set up a grand jury, and we're going to subpoena the following people. And I was one of them.

I was very scared at first because the conspiracy laws are so vague. When conspiracy to commit a crime is a crime, any link in the chain can be a crime, even if the act, by itself, is perfectly legal. That's what makes conspiracy laws really dangerous. Maybe when I was talking with Dan about Vietnam and said, "Dan, this is great. You ought to write it up," that could have been a "conspiratorial" act. Discussing other documents, discussing other studies that were done in Vietnam that I knew about when I was there and that he knew about—any of that could have been considered part of a conspiracy.

Because we didn't know if they were after me or not, the first thing I did was claim the Fifth Amendment. The government right away said, "Well, aha. He must be hiding something." Most of the prosecutors in the Pentagon Papers case, with one or two exceptions, were "good soldiers." They didn't think about the possibility that the government could be wrong or that the conspiracy rules could be misused. It never crossed the minds of those upright little prosecutors that the purpose of the case was not to protect government security or to stop Communism but was just to prevent bad publicity for Henry Kissinger and Richard Nixon.

So I'm thinking: They could be out to cast a wide net, to set up a conspiracy. And they're thinking: We're upright. Why should he be nervous? If he's nervous around upright prosecutors, obviously he's hiding something. It was hard for them to understand what I was saying because they just assumed there were two kinds of people in the world: the people who wanted to nail Daniel Ellsberg and the people who wanted to protect him. I was trying to protect a principle—the right not to reveal confidential sources for my scholarly research—and they just weren't willing to see that.

We tried every which way to answer questions to make it clear that I knew nothing about Ellsberg and that, as long as they didn't ask about other names, I would answer them.

PROSECUTOR: Has Daniel Ellsberg ever discussed with you the possibility of releasing a copy of the Pentagon Papers to Neil Sheehan?*
POPKIN: No.

---

*Neil Sheehan was the *New York Times* reporter to whom Daniel Ellsberg gave the Pentagon Papers.

PROSECUTOR: Has anyone else ever discussed with you the possibility of releasing a copy of the Pentagon Papers to Neil Sheehan?
POPKIN: No.

PROSECUTOR: Has anyone discussed with you the possibility of releasing the Pentagon Papers to anyone else?
POPKIN: To the absolute best of my knowledge and memory, no.[83]

The connections that my knowledge had with what Dan Ellsberg had done were as tenuous as tenuous can be. But the connections between my knowledge and a lot of people's careers were very strong. I'd gotten interviews from people in Vietnam who wanted to remain anonymous. Ironically, some of them were military officers who were probably not the least bit sympathetic to Dan Ellsberg. But their promotions were being blocked and their files were, in effect, being put in limbo at the Department of the Army, waiting to see whether their names came out in the Pentagon Papers case. I have reason to believe, and I did at the time have reason to believe, that grand jury minutes were being secretly leaked by people in the Justice Department to people at the Defense Intelligence Agency, which is illegal. And that's what was dangerous.

The people who had written the Pentagon Papers were military men coming in and out of Cambridge. Of course I knew them and talked with them. But I didn't realize until afterward that they were working on such a big deal. And then I remembered, "Oh, yes. When I talked with Colonel X, he said he was doing a study of such and such. And General Y—Oh, that's what he must have been doing." I realized after the fact that I knew there may have been such a study. Big deal. That's all I knew. I never saw a page of it.

But the prosecutors weren't satisfied. They wanted my opinions about who might have worked on the papers or who might have had them. They asked, "Who were the persons you interviewed to acquire this knowledge of who participated in the study?" And later, "Please name them, those persons who furnished you with the information which caused you to form an opinion as to who possessed the Pentagon Papers in Massachusetts prior to June 13, 1971." And they also asked, "Mr. Popkin, you've told us you have opinions based upon your conversations with others. With whom were these conversations held?"

There were more questions. I answered them all by stating that they violated my rights under the First Amendment to freedom of press, speech, and assembly. You can't, as a scholar, have people suffer damage because they were interviewed. And I'd given them my word. The government's questions, in effect, required me to break my oath, to trample for no justifiable reason the constitutional rights I care about. But the government just figured, "If he won't answer and then calls on the First Amendment, he must really have something."

I have to tell you that being in the grand jury room was the most extraordinarily grueling thing I ever did. You can't imagine what it's like to have your honor threatened and your whole identity called into question. It was a lot more scary than walking around unarmed in the middle of a revolution in a Vietnamese village. You're in this room. And you feel like you want to stop and look at the grand jury and say, "I don't know a goddamn thing about the papers—I told you that under oath—but the prosecutors are trying to stop my research. These men are asking questions that will hurt innocent people."

You have the feeling that every time you don't answer a question, the prosecutors are telling the jury, "See? See what he's up to?" For all I knew, those sleazy prosecutors were saying, "Watch it. We're going to ask him an innocent question, and he'll probably assert the Constitution. Why do you think he's doing that?" You don't know what they're doing, how they're manipulating. You're only there when you're being asked questions.

You do not have a right to have a lawyer in the room. Every time they asked me a question I thought was important, I demanded to see my lawyer, who was waiting outside. You can do that if you know you have that right and if you're tough enough not to crack when you're in there. But it's hard not to feel the pressure against you. It's hard not to crack.

PROSECUTOR: Mr. Popkin, do you recall an immediate reaction that was formed in your mind upon hearing about the original stories in the *New York Times* about who might have been the source?
POPKIN: I request permission to see my counsel.

PROSECUTOR: Mr. Popkin, how can your counsel be of use in this case? We are asking you about your immediate reaction.
POPKIN: I request permission to see my counsel.

PROSECUTOR: Mr. Popkin, you are being asked about your immediate opinion, how can counsel be relevant?
POPKIN: I request permission to see my counsel.

PROSECUTOR: Mr. Popkin, you are stretching things for this grand jury. Your exits from the grand jury have been ranging about five minutes. This is being an inconsiderable inconvenience to the grand jury.

The fact was that at that point they were fishing, because I'd already made it a hundred percent clear that I didn't know about this damn release. And it was chilling to be asked about your opinions, to be asked about everybody you interviewed. I had to put my work aside. I couldn't conceivably interview people on Vietnam when they might think I could be coerced into divulging their names. I mean it really was: "Here comes the chill." Many people in the scholarly community were scared by that.

At Harvard, there was a lot of support because we did not cast the issue narrowly, as an absolute First Amendment privilege—that there are never times when you should talk. We instead took the position that whenever a grand jury asks a scholar questions, it may be doing harm to the First Amendment, to the free flow of ideas and information. Therefore, it should only be done when the government can demonstrate a strong need for the information. That position was supported unanimously by a vote of the Harvard faculty. But the prosecutor wouldn't even say why the government needed the answers to the questions he asked me.

POPKIN: What is the pertinence of my opinion on this subject to the subject under inquiry?
PROSECUTOR: The grand jury does not answer questions.

Scholars should not be forced to answer questions without restriction just at the whim of any prosecutor. Whenever there is possible damage to the Constitution, it should go in front of a judge, question by question. And that's what we were saying—that you shouldn't put the Constitution in the hands of the prosecutors.

That position got me an extraordinary amount of faculty support from Republicans, Democrats, conservatives, liberals—people who felt very strongly because of the McCarthy days, like John Kenneth Galbraith and John K. Fairbank; people who were very close to the Nixon administration as well, like James Q. Wilson; and others with national stature, like Harrison Salisbury and Edwin O. Reischauer, the former ambassador to Japan.

Every single faculty member I approached wrote thorough and thoughtful affidavits for the court about the necessity of protections to do their research, making clear why my case was important to their work. They couldn't study decision making, the Cuban missile crisis, Lyndon Johnson, or any aspect of public policy without some ability to protect people. It would be a disaster. I, one hundred percent, unequivocally, think that scholars must be able to talk to people about how decisions are made at any time and for any decision.

In the past, prosecutors had not gone after professors in this way, pushing so hard to use the grand jury as a political weapon. It shook a lot of people at Harvard. After all, I was a middle-of-the-roader. I was far too ambivalent, full of real existential angst about the war, to be a vocal activist. I was neither willing to stand with the government and say the war is wonderful nor willing to take it seriously when people were ga-ga over the brave new world being developed by the National Liberation Front. I'd had lunch at the White House with Henry Kissinger to discuss my research in the villages, and I talked about abuses of CIA programs. And he'd sent memos to the head of the CIA in Vietnam. I talked with all the ambassadors in Vietnam. I gave seminars about my work in the villages to all the people in Saigon. I was considered the honest, fair critic, neither a tame house scholar nor a flaming antiwar radical.

So a lot of people were very shaken when the government started going after me, because it was a real attempt to shut down the middle. Maybe the people who disagreed with my criticisms were trying to get me. I mean, that's very plausible. There were a fair number of people who thought that one faction of the government was trying to purge dissenting moderation from within the policy process.

The faculty was behind me, but for a long time Derek Bok, the president of Harvard, simply didn't understand what was going on. He was such an honorable man that he assumed that when the government dealt with Harvard, they'd be honorable. And I suppose he assumed that I had to be a little bit paranoid. Once he saw my grand jury transcripts and understood what we were doing, he tried to help us finesse the whole thing. He went to people in the Justice Department and told them I now would agree to answer all questions of any kind that weren't about confidential sources. In turn, the government wouldn't ask me questions about confidential sources. That way, the government wouldn't look as if they had backed down. Popkin wouldn't have to play hero. And Harvard would be safe.

So we went into court. Derek Bok came before the federal district court as my lawyer to make the point that this was a serious Harvard case. He got up and said, "I've talked to people at the Justice Department in Washington, and they authorized me to tell the court that they are not going to ask Samuel Popkin any questions about confidential sources. And my client is willing to answer all other questions." At that point, the Justice Department prosecutor got up and said, "There's a misunderstanding. We *do* want to ask questions about confidential sources."

Then the judge asked me, "Will you answer?" I said, "No." They put me in chains and took me to prison. When Derek Bok left the courtroom, he was so furious I thought he was going to go through the wall instead of the door. He even forgot to say good-by to me on my way to jail, he was so upset. My reaction was: "I told you. I told you." Nobody wanted to believe how devious this whole thing had gotten.

From beginning to end, it dragged on for about a year and a half. You make your appearance before the grand jury, plead the Fifth Amendment, and go home. A month later, they call you back and hold a hearing to give you personal immunity. Now you can't use the Fifth Amendment. Then they ask you more questions, and you plead the First Amendment. You're cited for contempt, and you appeal. Then you go to the Supreme Court, but they refuse to grant certiorari. That's when Derek Bok worked out the compromise with the Justice Department. It took a year and a half from the first time I was questioned by the FBI in July of 1971 to when I went to jail, right before Thanksgiving in 1972.

As I was being taken off to jail, my wife, Susan, read my statement before television cameras: "If scholars are to be questioned without restriction about their sources, grand juries will become the government's instrument to limit the free flow of information about government to the public. This is intolerable in a democracy, and I could not justify any part I might take in setting that precedent."

I went to Dedham County Prison, Sacco and Vanzetti's old jail, for a week. I got out after that because the solicitor general was embarrassed about lying to the Supreme Court on my petition for certiorari. He had probably lied inadvertently because he had also believed the Justice Department. He had told the Court, "There is no First Amendment issue here at all because we are not asking scholarly opinions. We're not asking confidential sources." If it had become known that the solicitor general had lied to the Supreme Court, the potential scandal could have destroyed his entire reputation.

When I was released, I said, "Beyond all else, I hope my case has brought concern to bear on the need to look at grand juries more carefully—at the coercive powers vested in grand juries. . . . The grand jury was originally designed to stand between the people and the government, and it's time it was brought back to that role."

THE SHOOTINGS AT KENT STATE

On April 28, 1970, without the consent or knowledge of Congress, President Richard Nixon ordered American troops to join the South Viet-

namese army in the invasion of Cambodia, a country the United States
had been secretly bombing for over a year. Two days later, the president
announced the "incursion" with an appeal for support that, as Seymour
Hersh describes it, "included a number of major lies—notably Nixon's
statement that the United States had previously done nothing to violate
Cambodian neutrality."[84] That night, antiwar demonstrations erupted
at Princeton, Rutgers, Oberlin, and Stanford. Within days, student
strikes, reminiscent of the peace strikes of the 1930s, broke out on a hundred campuses.

Then, shortly after noon on Monday, May 4, Ohio National Guardsmen occupying Kent State University fired down from their vantage point
at the crest of Blanket Hill into unarmed students, some of whom were
the length of a football field away, killing four and wounding nine. Dead
were Allison Beth Krause, Jeffrey Glenn Miller, Sandra Lee Scheuer, and
William K. Schroeder.

More than four million students, 60 percent of the nation's student
body, walked out of classes. One-third of the country's colleges and universities shut down. More than ten thousand young men pledged to turn
in their draft cards. Amid the widening protest, thirty-seven college and
university presidents told Nixon that they shared their students' "ap-
prehensions" and urged a prompt end to the war.[85] Although dissent was
overwhelmingly peaceful, serious violence nevertheless erupted in some
places. At more than two dozen schools, police wielding clubs and firing
tear gas clashed with students as windows were broken and fires were
set. Between May 1 and May 15, eighteen hundred were arrested. The
National Guard was activated at twenty-one campuses in sixteen states.
"The month witnessed," Tom Wells writes, "the greatest display of campus dissent in American history."[86]

In June, Richard Nixon appointed a presidential commission to study
the campus unrest, with the admonition not to "let higher education off
with a pat on the ass."[87] But while the commission held that some Kent
State students had been reckless and even criminal, it clearly indicted the
Ohio National Guard: "The indiscriminate firing of rifles into a crowd
of students and the deaths that followed were unnecessary, unwarranted,
and inexcusable."[88]

The facts do not bear out either the Guardsmen's claims that their
lives were imperiled by onrushing students or the claims of the highest-
ranking Guard officers, made within hours of the shooting, that their
troops were responding to attack from sniper fire. Although "the FBI's
sympathies were with the Guardsmen," the bureau stated flatly: "There

was no sniper."[89] Nor does the evidence indicate that Guardsmen were otherwise threatened. Pictures of the scene show that what little rock throwing there was had all but ended before the Guard fired their weapons. Moreover, the closest students were sixty feet away, not within a few feet or even inches of the Guardsmen, as some had said. The students who were killed were as far away as 375 feet and were not, the FBI determined, "in a position to pose even a remote danger to the National Guard."[90] The FBI concluded: "We have reason to believe that the claim made by the National Guard that their lives were endangered by the students was fabricated subsequent to the event."[91]

Alan Canfora and Roseann Canfora, brother and sister, who were students at Kent State, barely escaped with their lives from the rifle fire. Less than a month earlier, California Governor Ronald Reagan had spoken menacingly of campus unrest: "If it takes a bloodbath, let's get it over with."[92] In fact, it had already begun. The death toll included Samuel Hammond, Delano Middleton, and Henry Smith, three African American students killed two years earlier by a volley of state trooper gunfire on the South Carolina State College campus in Orangeburg after civil rights protests. "They committed murder," then Attorney General Ramsey Clark said of the troopers.[93] Ten days after the shootings at Kent State, Mississippi Highway Patrol officers and Jackson city police fired shotguns, carbines, and submachine guns "indiscriminately," according to the presidential commission, into and around a dormitory at Jackson State College, a Black school, wounding women in the building and killing Phillip Gibbs and James Earl Green, who were outside.[94] As it had concluded about Kent State, the commission found that the "barrage of lethal gunfire" had been "completely unwarranted and unjustified."[95]

ROSEANN (CHIC) CANFORA AND ALAN CANFORA

ROSEANN CANFORA: To this day, in the city of Kent they talk about those "outside agitators" Governor Rhodes alluded to in the speech he gave before the shootings. Who are those outsiders? When Guardsmen opened fire, the only targets their bullets hit were students, not outsiders. Those the Ohio grand jury chose to indict, those they felt were the most active, were twenty-four students and one faculty member. This whole idea of surreptitious outside agitators negates the fact that we went through a metamorphosis of awareness, that we made a conscious decision to oppose the war and a conscious decision to do what we could to stop it.

ROSEANN (CHIC) CANFORA

ALAN CANFORA: For my first year of college, in 1967, I went to a
branch campus of Kent State. It was about five miles from my home in
Barberton, which is just outside Akron, one of the most industrialized
areas in the country. I was in a political science class where everybody
was opposed to the Vietnam war except me. It was not so much that I
was in favor of the war. I just thought America was such a great country that I would never question decisions of any significance that the government made. After a while, I began to listen to what the others were

ALAN CANFORA

saying, and for the first time I started to consider whether or not it was a proper war. Within a short time, I had some serious doubts.

In the spring of 1968, the assassination of Martin Luther King was followed by the assassination of Robert Kennedy. Both of those events, but especially the killing of Robert Kennedy, had a profound impact on me. I had been wearing an RFK badge for months. I didn't have time to be active in his campaign—going to school, working full time, hardly getting any sleep—but I felt he was going to be the savior of America. I remember my father screaming and yelling the morning after he was shot, "Jesus Christ, they just killed Bobby Kennedy!" I was devastated.

By summer, I was opposed to the war, but it was more like an intellectual question with me. Then, on television, I saw all those students at the Democratic Convention in Chicago being beaten so severely in the streets. I immediately felt a great deal of sympathy for them. I had to seriously consider the motivations of the police and, of course, of the political leaders who were promoting a war and then repressing opponents so severely.

In the fall of 1968, I came to the campus at Kent State. By coincidence, that's right when the Students for a Democratic Society was forming here. I didn't join SDS then. In fact, I joined the Young Democrats, and I went to their meetings with my roommate, Tom Grace. Even though I became antiwar, I still supported Hubert Humphrey. I was strongly Democrat.

In October, we went over to Akron University with the Young Democrats to hear Richard Nixon give a speech. SDS was up in the bleachers. About two hundred of them were screaming and yelling and chanting slogans. They shouted Nixon down repeatedly. And here were Tom Grace and I, down on the floor with about fifteen members of the Young Dems, meekly chanting, "Debate Humphrey," which seemed so inconsequential. We looked up at those SDSers, and I just said, "Let's go sit with them." That was a big turning point.

ROSEANN: I'm a year younger than Alan, but we came here together. He moved into Johnson Hall as a sophomore, and I moved into Lake Hall as a freshman. I was one of those students who was very unconcerned about the war. I was here to complete my education. But I was aware of SDS's presence. It was a constant, very visible presence. You couldn't go into the student union without being approached by them. I can remember throwing away their antiwar leaflets as I walked by.

It wasn't until my sophomore year, when the government instituted the draft lottery, that the war touched me personally. Realizing the possibility that my brothers, my own brothers, could be put in a kill-or-be-killed situation, I took the time to read the leaflets. I wanted to understand what they would be fighting for or against. It was at that point that I started to attend some of the SDS gatherings.

ALAN: Only a few weeks after the Nixon speech in Akron, recruiters came from the Oakland police department—Oakland, California! They had been going after the Black Panthers and had shot some of them. The Black students and SDS had a sit-in to protest racist police recruiting on our campus. I was going to my dorm, and the sit-in was in the building adjacent to it. I looked in and thought, "This is a legitimate cause." I stood around at first, but within five or ten minutes, I was sitting on the floor with them chanting slogans. That was my first militant action with SDS.

As fate would have it, our evolution, Tom Grace's and mine, continued during a time when SDS itself was going through a lot of changes. We'd go to their meetings and consider the different points of view that were advocated by the moderates and the radicals. There were always these big debates about what tactics to use and what strategies to follow. We were torn by which faction to support. As it turned out, when SDS split in the spring of 1969, Tom and I both gravitated toward the more moderate faction. But most of the leadership of SDS at Kent went with the Weather Underground.

SDS was unbelievable. They started out with about six people in the fall of '68. By the time spring rolled around, two and three hundred were coming to their rallies. They had their first "spring offensive" rally on April 8, 1969, to abolish ROTC on campus. Students were opposed to ROTC because it was training officers to lead an unjust and immoral war in Southeast Asia. About a hundred and fifty, two hundred people marched around, chanting slogans—and I was into it.

When we got to the administration building, we wanted to present our demands, but campus cops were guarding the back door, so we went around to the front doors. A fight broke out between the cops and some SDSers, with elbows and fists flying. I was holding the one door open, while people were trying to get into the building. But the police held their own. So a few people made militant speeches, and we left the area. That evening, they arrested some of the SDS leaders. The university was going to hold a hearing on April 16 to decide whether to expel them.

ROSEANN: There were four leaders of SDS up for expulsion. I was rather intrigued by their leadership and persistence and dedication to their cause. So, out of curiosity, I went to the administration building to attend the hearing. When we got there, a couple of students on the front steps were saying, "They tricked us. They moved the hearings over to the Music and Speech building." Years later, it was learned through the Freedom of Information Act that those students were police informants.

ALAN: The university said it was to be a closed hearing. Our slogan was "Open it up or shut it down." When we got to the front doors of Music and Speech, the Greeks, approximately sixty fraternity boys, were chanting: "SDS go home! SDS go home!" We started to shout back. It was a volatile situation, people confronting each other face to face, with no police there. Inevitably, somebody's going to throw a punch. Well, a wild fight broke out. There was still fighting when somebody said, "Hey, the Main Street door is open."

ROSEANN: We followed the crowd and walked in the door and started up the stairs, heading toward the expulsion hearing. The next thing we knew—I mean, within seconds—there were helmeted patrolmen locking the door behind us.

ALAN: By the time we got up to the third floor, some of the big SDS guys pried open the steel doors to the hearing room. Everybody just flooded in, and that was the end of the hearing. As soon as we did that, both ends of the corridor were sealed off. Immediately! They had us trapped.

ROSEANN: Actually, I thought I was just going to be an observer. Then someone turned on the television, and there on the newscast was: "Three hundred students have seized a building at Kent State." I thought, "Holy shit! My mother's going to be watching this." It was the first indication I had that the news doesn't always report what's happening. They said we took over the building, and here we were locked inside it.

At times it was very jovial, and at other times very frightening. After we were there a few hours, we looked out the windows, and there were thousands of students below. They had raided the cafeteria and were sending up bread, milk, and orange juice. I'm thinking, "How long will we be up here?" It was my first demonstration, and I was like trapped for life. There was a rumor they were bringing in the paddy wagons, and we were all going to be arrested. And there was no escape. I mean, patrolmen were at either end of the corridors.

But the building was angled in such a way that the freight elevator couldn't be seen from where they were. At one point, Alan and I walked out of the room, and the elevator door opened. There was Carl Moore, one of our professors. When we saw him, we just rushed for the elevator. This was our great escape. Carl Moore said, "When you leave, go out the back door of the loading dock and run. Don't tell anybody we're doing this."

ALAN: He must have taken down six or eight elevator loads full of people. It was really kind of funny. If he had only been able to get out a few more loads, the police would have been guarding an empty corridor. I'll never forget the feeling when we got off the elevator, because I was really worried up there. I was thinking what the political repercussions would be for my father—he was on the Barberton city council. When we hit that cool, fresh air of a spring evening, it was such a great feeling.

ROSEANN: I remember being so excited, falling on the ground, saying, "Freedom, at last!" as if it had been some horrible experience. Alan
and I ran right back to our dorms. But as fate would have it, some kids
were so excited that they went around to the front saying, "I just came
down the elevator!" The cops took the elevator key from Carl Moore,
and the last sixty or so students were caught. I think his key is still state's
evidence somewhere.

ALAN: That was the end of SDS. The leaders were thrown in jail for
six months. The group was kicked off campus. But in just one year, SDS
had raised the awareness on the campus so significantly that three thousand students marched in April of 1969, in the rain, to defend their right
to exist as an organization.

ROSEANN: You can imagine what an educational experience that was
for me. I felt that I'd been baptized. I'd become a part of it. And, of course,
the continuation of the war, and the always-present possibility that my
brothers would have to serve, was a very personal motivating factor in
my involvement in the antiwar protest. I would much rather have just
gone to classes. I wanted to be a cheerleader, a sorority sister, a good
student. But my life was changing.

The first thing I would read in the newspaper every day was the obit-
uary column. If there were flags next to the names, I'd look to see if the
person who died at war was somebody I'd met at a park dance or some
school event. When so many lives were being lost and so many people
were coming home in bags and boxes, protesting the war suddenly became far more important than anything else. I went everywhere there
was to go. If there was a moratorium, if there was an action in Cleveland or down in Washington, I'd skip classes and go. Ending the war became a priority.

ALAN: Going into the spring of 1970, there was no organized antiwar group here. With SDS gone and the leaders in jail, the rest of us were
kind of dissipated and demoralized and unorganized. But when Nixon
invaded Cambodia on April 30, I think the consciousness of the students
was so great, because of the work of SDS, and the invasion of Cambodia was seen as such a serious provocation that there was a spontaneous
uprising here at Kent State.

ROSEANN: We were absolutely fed up. I mean, you go to so many
moratoriums; you go to so many peace rallies; you march so many miles;
you raise your fists or you raise the peace sign so many times; you write
so many letters; you do so many things to stop the bloodshed. And then
after Nixon promises to wind the war down, they announce that there's

going to be more. It wasn't surprising to me that students took to the streets.

ALAN: We knew when Nixon invaded Cambodia that we were going to be getting involved in some serious protests. As it turned out, the next morning, Friday, May 1, I hitchhiked home with my girlfriend. We'd fallen deeply in love that winter, and for those three or four months we were practically inseparable. I wanted to introduce her to my parents. While we were there, we got a phone call from one of our roommates. He said, "Hey, the rumor is there's going to be a street action tonight. Get some material; we'll make protest flags." I stopped at the fabric store a block from my house and bought this black material before we hitchhiked back to Kent.

That evening, we got another call: "People are getting pretty riled up. Hurry on over." So a bunch of us went down to the section of town called North Water Street. That's where the bars were and where everybody used to hang out.

ROSEANN: People were congregating, saying, "We've got to stop the bloodshed." But there was a feeling like, "What should we do?" First it was just chanting: "One, two, three, four! We don't want your fucking war!" And then spraypainting on the walls: "U.S. out of Vietnam, U.S. out of Cambodia now." If it would speak louder than marching another mile, I saw nothing wrong with it. I didn't care that somebody would have to wash that paint off or blast it off with a sandblaster. I figured, Let them think about our generation being sent off to the slaughter every minute they're doing it.

ALAN: The street was jammed with about three hundred people. Some trash was dragged into the middle of it and set on fire. Then a few students went through the crowd: "On a signal, we'll move down the street toward the main intersection. Okay, let's go!" Nobody went. There was a second attempt. This time, the whole crowd moved down North Water Street shouting antiwar slogans. An SDS veteran street fighter tossed the first rock through a window. Others followed.

There was just chaos on the streets of Kent for the next half hour. A total of forty-three windows were broken, twenty-eight of them in one bank. Mostly it was the banks, the loan companies, and the utility companies— kind of symbolic targets that linked the economy to the war.

ROSEANN: When the windows started smashing, there was a feeling of elation. The feeling was just, "This is righteous anger." These kids were saying, "There's nothing left to do to make people listen." And they weren't committing violence against human beings. They weren't hurting people. They were inflicting damage against property in an effort to wake human beings up and stop the bloodshed. I know there are those who have a problem justifying damage against property. But there are ways to prosecute people for that. And the politically motivated students who took that chance were willing to make that sacrifice. But I'll tell you something—I don't think there was a kid who smashed a window or spraypainted a wall who ever thought that those incidents would be used time and again for years to justify the shootings that took place three days later.

ALAN: On Saturday evening, May 2, we went to the anti-ROTC protest. Many colleges had already kicked ROTC off campus. In fact, that was one of the main goals of SDS the year before. There were about three hundred of us at the beginning of the rally around the old ROTC building. Only a few plainclothes campus police were standing around, smoking cigarettes and laughing. We yelled at them. It was like a family thing, back and forth. Then we left the area. When we returned to the Commons a half hour later, the crowd had grown to about two thousand. We came charging back down the hill toward the ROTC building, whooping it up, yelling antiwar slogans, anti-ROTC slogans.

The police were gone when we returned. It was very mysterious why, in the darkness for the next one-and-a-half hours, this ROTC building was absolutely unprotected, even though the police headquarters was just up over the hill, about two hundred yards away. Did they want the building burned? They allowed the students to have every opportunity to set it on fire. But the attempts were feeble. The firemen finally came an hour later. The building was burning in one small corner, and they started to put it out. Then some students pulled the hoses away and squirted them. The firemen jumped back on the truck and took off. Someone reignited the building, just slightly again, in one corner. The firemen came back a short while later, this time with tremendous protection. The police and the sheriffs had finally come. They started shooting tear gas and taking flash photographs. The crowd moved away. As we left, we could see that the fire was out. They had put the fire out.

We marched almost a mile around the front campus. The ROTC building was out of our sight then. When we walked back toward the Commons, very mysteriously the building had been reignited. Pretty soon the whole thing flared up. The building burned to the ground, with flames shooting two hundred feet into the air. Thousands of students stood on the hillside, chanting: "Burn, ROTC, burn!" But the question of who reignited that building while it was under police protection has not been answered to this day. In fact, that portion of the FBI investigation, about the fire, is still sealed.

ROSEANN: The ROTC building was an Army barracks that was deteriorating. It was a temporary structure, already scheduled for demolition, and was only being used for storage. And it went up in smoke while it was under heavy police protection. I believe it was started by a police provocateur to justify the military takeover of the campus. At the precise moment that the building burned, the National Guard arrived at the outskirts of the city of Kent.

ALAN: During that time, the FBI and the intelligence community of the United States government hired police agents and provocateurs, as part of the COINTELPRO program, to commit acts of violence in an attempt to discredit the antiwar movement and also the civil rights movement. It was done in the same way that Hitler and his agents burned the Reichstag in Germany to discredit the opposition and create a climate to smash it.

The burning of the ROTC building created the pretext for Governor Rhodes to come to the campus the next day and deliver a hostile and inflammatory speech. "These students are the worst type of people we harbor in America," he said. "They're worse than the Communists, the brownshirts, the night riders, and the vigilantes." He concluded by saying, "We're going to eradicate the problem." And the National Guard—eight hundred of them on the campus, four hundred in the city—had the speech beamed into their barracks. That set the stage for what happened later on Sunday, May 3.

ROSEANN: Sunday was an awful day. We woke up and came downstairs, and at the entrances to every dorm were armed Guardsmen with military rifles and bayonets. I used to look out my fourth-floor window and see football games on the field below. But the view that Sunday morning was like Nazi Germany. There were a hundred and fifty pup tents, jeeps, and tanks on that field. And armed soldiers. I mean, it was like a complete military takeover of our campus. The Guards were belligerent and anti-student, taunting long-haired kids who walked by. Those who guarded Lake Hall, I'll tell you right now, were sexist beyond belief. When we walked out, they'd say things like, "I got one like you last night."

When Governor Rhodes said, "We're going to eradicate the problem" using "every weapon," I was, honest to God, too naive, too young to realize the kind of danger he had put us in. Students were bayoneted Sunday night. I mean, here we were, peacefully sitting in outside the campus. We were told that President White was going to meet with us. We had wanted to talk to him about the fact that he had allowed a total military takeover of our campus. But he never showed up. Instead, the National Guard showed up and chased us with tear gas. Several students who were climbing into the library windows to get away were stabbed in the backs and legs by Guardsmen's bayonets.

ALAN: I wasn't there. I had stayed home to study. But that night, we heard a radio broadcast about the helicopters with searchlights. We could see them, even though we were in the city, helicopters everywhere, patrolling with spotlights. It was like something out of a police state. When we woke up Monday morning, May 4, we heard on the radio about the bayoneting.

That morning, I finally made the flags. I had the material all weekend, but it had been so hectic that I didn't have time to do it. I sawed an old broom handle in two and taped the black material to each half. My girlfriend had been with me the whole weekend: Friday night downtown, Saturday night during the ROTC confrontation, Sunday night when we stayed in. At the last minute, when we were getting ready to go to the noon rally, she worried about a possible confrontation with the Guard and began to feel very upset in the stomach. It got so severe that she just said, "Alan, I'm not going."

It was getting close to noon, so I left and walked up Summit Street, heading toward campus. Guardsmen were on every street corner. As I got to the Commons, there was a long line of them. The end Guardsman said to me, "Hey, boy, what are you carrying there?" I said, "Just a couple of flags." He said, "Well, today we're going to make you eat those flags."

I'd always been kind of a wise guy, raised up in the pool halls of Barberton. I responded, "Don't get too close, motherfucker, or I'll stick them down your throat." It was just a crass wisecrack. I had no intention of allowing him to get close to me, because I knew that they had stabbed people with bayonets the night before. I've always been very quick on my feet, and I figured that as long as I kept my distance, there would probably be no problem.

I walked away and went to the gathering of students. I recall talking to my friend, Jeff Miller, just briefly at the Victory Bell area. Within the hour, of course, he would be shot through the head and killed. But now we talked about the invasion of Cambodia and the need to stop the war. Jeff was always pleasant but quiet, relatively shy, a very gentle person. I remember there was a very somber air about him that day. Then I saw Tom Grace and talked with him for a while and a couple of other people.

ROSEANN: There were a number of reasons why students attended the rally. Originally, it was planned to protest the U.S. invasion of Cambodia. We wanted to go on strike until U.S. troops were withdrawn. Some students were there specifically for that reason. Others came to protest the military takeover of our campus and the oppressive tactics of the Guards. Some students had been gone all weekend and wanted to find out what the heck was going on. There were possibly some who were there to protest the protest. Who knows? Someone rang the Victory Bell to call people together.

No one told me that meetings were prohibited. But if someone had, I would have gone anyway, because in my heart I would have believed it to be a violation of my constitutional rights. A huge contingent of Guardsmen with rifles stood some distance away. Ken Hammond, who later was indicted as one of the Kent Twenty-Five, gave a speech about how we were there to participate in a national student strike.

It was at that point that the National Guard jeep drove up, and someone read the riot act to an absolutely peaceful gathering. A riot act is to be read to a mob that's out of control and showing evidence that there's a threat to life or property. When we were told that we "must disperse immediately," the gathering became more spirited. The students made it apparent they weren't leaving. They raised their fists in the air and chanted: "Pigs off campus!" and "One, two, three, four! We don't want your fucking war!"

ALAN: The National Guard began to fire a tremendous barrage of tear gas. Then they came marching toward us at a fast pace. Some of us threw the tear gas back at the Guards. Of course, they had the helmets on and gas masks. And they kept charging toward us.

ROSEANN: The Guardsmen advanced on the crowd, bayonets in hand. You could just see them kind of going in V formation, chasing us up the hill. The air was filled with tear gas. Some students started to run into Taylor Hall. I remember people yelling: "No, don't go in there! You'll get trapped in the building." We'd been through that before. So the majority of students ran around either side of Taylor Hall. It was at that point, too, that a National Guardsman was photographed clubbing a student.

ALAN: When the Guard came charging at us, we ran up over the top of Blanket Hill. They followed in pursuit at a quick pace, up over the hill, and down into the practice football field, adjacent to the parking lot.

ROSEANN: The majority of student activists assembled in the parking lot. Some went beyond the paved lot into the gravel parking area, next to Prentice Hall. That's where a few students picked up some stones. I remember seeing it. As the Guard assembled in the football field two hundred feet away, there was one very brief stone-throwing incident. I didn't see one stone ever hit a Guardsman. And the evidence shows that no Guardsman was ever treated, even for a minor injury. Some stones were picked up by Guardsmen and thrown at the students. And that was it. That ended it. I'm not condoning the throwing of stones, but it was brief. And no Guardsman shot at that point. If the shooting was in response to stone throwing, as they have claimed all these years, it would have happened then. It didn't.

People were wiping their eyes from tear gas and looking for the friends they'd lost on the way. It was utter chaos. Everyone was just kind of milling around saying, "What are they doing? What's going to happen now?" The Guard was still assembled, the majority of them, on the football field.

ALAN: That's when that picture was taken of me, which was later reproduced in *Life, Time, Newsweek*, and many publications. I was waving a black flag of protest in the foreground of the photograph with my back to the cameraman, staring straight ahead at the line of Guardsmen, two hundred feet away from me. About a dozen Guardsmen were down on their knees, aiming their rifles toward us in the parking lot area.

ROSEANN: I was standing with Alan when they knelt down and aimed their guns at us. I actually saw a man looking through his scope right at me. God, that was the turning point. It hit me that there might be somebody crazy enough to kill college kids just for what they stood for or the way they looked. I said to Alan, "Let's get out of here." He said, "Wait a minute. I want to see where they're going." That was the last thing he said to me before he was shot.

ALAN: It was Troop G that had their fingers on the triggers. A few minutes later, they would do the killing. If they had fired the moment they were aiming at us, there's no doubt I would have been killed. I think it can be said that, among all the protesters, I was probably the most visible and the most vocal. I waved the flag and shouted—mostly antiwar slogans, but a few obscenities as well, I have to admit.

I was directly motivated by the death of my friend Bill Caldwell. He had been killed in Vietnam on April 13, 1970. We found out about it the next morning. I remember I started to cry and smash my fist into the pillow. Bill was one of the nicest people, very kind-hearted, a very gentle person, very peace-loving. He was absolutely opposed to the war, but he had been drafted. I spoke to him a day or two before he went to Viet-

nam and tried to talk him out of it. He thought about going to Canada.
In fact, his father wanted to pay for him to go there. But Bill said, "I
think I'm going to take my chances." He mentioned how several of our
friends from Barberton had gone to Vietnam and come back. "They made
it," he said. "Just like those guys, I'll take my chances." That's the last
thing he ever told me.

We had gone to his funeral on April 24. It was a very traumatic experience seeing his closed coffin—he had been run over by an American
tank in the middle of the night as he slept. It was a "friendly fire" type
of thing. I remember seeing the coffin and the flag draped over it. I'll never
forget how angry I was. It wasn't just a war far away from home. This
war killed one of my best friends.

While I was waving the black flag at the Guards, I was thinking about
Bill's death, about the deaths of many other soldiers I didn't know. Even
though I was very concerned about the deaths of the Asian people, that
was relatively abstract to me. But the death of my friend and the experience of his funeral caused me to want to make as powerful a statement
as I could to stop the killing of other young men. I think my participation at that moment can be described as a sublime act of patriotism.

Within a few minutes, the Guard was ordered to get up from their
firing position. It seemed as if they were in retreat, because they marched
back in the exact route from where they had come a few minutes earlier.
So we thought the confrontation was over. The stone throwing had
stopped. They stopped shooting the tear gas. They had stopped aiming
their guns. They were marching away.

ROSEANN: Before they went back up Blanket Hill, the same Troop
G that had aimed at us huddled briefly. It's my honest belief—having
heard all the trial testimony, having seen all the evidence, and having witnessed the actual shootings—that the conspiracy and the decision of when
to shoot and from where to shoot occurred in that huddle. I believe the
triggermen saw that Pagoda on the hill. They knew the hill was strategically the best point from which to shoot, and I believe they said: "We'll
go up; we'll let the others continue on; we'll stop there at the Pagoda,
and we'll turn around and shoot."

I started walking back in the opposite direction of the Guard. I watched
them leave the practice field. I clearly remember Troop G lagging back
as they neared the crest of the hill. It was kind of weird. I was looking
over my shoulder at them, and they were looking over their shoulders at
us the whole time. The other Guardsmen continued over the hill.

But as soon as Troop G reached the Pagoda, they turned in unison and, without warning, leveled their guns and started firing. I was still looking at them at that time. I saw the smoke and I heard the shots before I ever had the thought to turn and run, because it was such an incredible sight: American soldiers turning their guns on American people.

ALAN: It was so shocking! Students were walking to their classes; they were going back to their dorms, when Troop G stopped, turned, and suddenly began to fire down the hillside. They shot mostly at the distant parking lot where the most visible, the most vocal, and the most radical students were located. From the top of the hill down, Joe Lewis, the closest student to the Guard, was sixty feet away. He was shot twice and wounded. He survived by some miracle. On down the hillside, John Cleary was wounded, about ninety feet away.

I was near the bottom of the hill when I saw them begin to raise their guns to shoot. Then I heard the guns fire. I thought to myself at that moment, "They must be shooting blanks." It was unbelievable to think that in broad daylight, on a college campus while classes were in session, they would fire a barrage of bullets down into students.

As I turned to take my first step away, I could see people at the bottom of the hill lying flat on the ground to make smaller targets of themselves. And I thought about doing that. But I was fortunate enough to be about six feet away from the only tree on the hillside in the line of fire. I took a couple of very quick steps, and as I began to kneel behind the oak tree, I felt a bullet pass through my right wrist.

I stayed tucked in behind the tree during the thirteen seconds of gunfire. As I knelt there wounded, I could hear bullets hit the tree. I could hear many other bullets zipping through the air on both sides of the tree, into the parking lot behind me, where all four students were killed. And I could hear many bullets ripping through the grass next to me. I'm absolutely convinced that they were aiming at me intentionally and that that oak tree saved my life.

ROSEANN: I think they picked specific targets to make examples of us at Kent. There's no doubt in my mind that Alan was a prime target. He was probably one of those who unnerved them most, because he was bold and he had the flag and he was in the forefront. Look at the tree that shielded him—the bark in front of it was shot off. I think even as they saw him get behind that tree, they were determined to shoot right through it into his body.

ALAN: I looked off to my right during the shootings. I could see my roommate, Tom Grace, about ten feet away. The bottom of his foot was blown open. He started to sit up to grab his ankle. I yelled out to him,

"Keep your head down!" He says to this day that he thinks I saved his life by preventing him from sitting up while the bullets were still flying. It was very ironic that two roommates who had gone through this metamorphosis from the Young Democrats to SDS to the spring of 1970 were both wounded.

ROSEANN: It wasn't until Jimmie Riggs pulled me behind a parked car that it hit me that they were firing live ammunition. The car that shielded us was riddled with bullets. Bullets were ricocheting off the cars around us, and glass from the windows of the car we crouched behind shattered all over us. You could hear bullets zipping through the grass beside us. There was all this scuffling and commotion—then there was this hideous silence of shock and disbelief as it sunk in that they had done this.

When I came from behind the car, I saw Bill Schroeder lying on his back, three feet behind me. He had crystal blue eyes. His eyes were open, and he was looking up at a very blue sky. He had blood all over his shoulder. And I knew he was dead. I looked over and saw a girl lying prone on the lawn of Prentice Hall, four hundred feet away from the Guard. I walked over, and it was Sandy Scheuer, whom I'd grown to know that year. She rode home most weekends with my roommate to Youngstown. When I saw Sandy dead, I remembered that Alan had been standing much closer to the Guard than Sandy or Bill. At that moment, my friend Jeff Hartzler came up to me and said, "Alan and Tom both got hit."

ALAN: I started to get up to help Tom Grace, but I saw there were other people who rushed to his aid. So I thought I'd try to get to the hospital myself. I ran through the parking lot. There was a scene of outrage and terror in those seconds after the shooting. People were screaming in pain and crying for ambulances. Some people were in shock. It was just an unbelievable nightmare.

I ran over to the home economics building to get a bandage or cloth or something. A student got me a towel, and I went to a drinking fountain to rinse my wound off. The bullet had gone in the front of my wrist and come out the other side. Outside the building, I ran right in front of the first car that came to the stop sign. I told the driver, "Look, I've been shot. Would you give me a ride to the hospital?" He said, "Yes," so I jumped in the back seat. I was suffering a great deal of pain. I had lost a lot of blood and almost fainted. But I didn't shed one tear, and I kept my cool.

I got to the hospital, and as I started to go into the emergency room, I looked in the back of an ambulance and saw Jeff Miller lying on a stretcher. I thought to myself, "It's Jeff!" I thought again about what a nice guy he was. He had a bloody wound on his cheek as big as a silver dollar. I thought about his smile, because he was always smiling. I thought, "They'll have to do some kind of plastic surgery to fix this wound in his cheek." Of course, he was dead, but I didn't know that.

In the hospital, I saw Tom Grace on a table in the hallway. He was just lying there, not being treated by anyone. He was in extreme agony. The bones were protruding out of the bottom of his foot. He was crying and screaming and asking for something to kill the pain. I tried to calm him. Then I was grabbed by a policeman and forced to go into a treatment room. I had to wait about forty-five minutes. They were treating the others who were dying and who were wounded more severely.

Finally an intern came in, a young Asian doctor. He looked me over for a minute or two. I asked, "How many people were shot?" He said, "Three dead. Two girls." I knew my sister had been in the parking lot. I showed him my plastic hospital bracelet and said, "Could you please check to see if one of them is named Canfora?" I'll never forget those five minutes I waited for him. Then he came back and smiled: "No, it wasn't her."

ROSEANN: When I got to the hospital, a policeman was at the door. I said, "My brother and his roommate have been shot, and I'm the only one who can identify them." He wouldn't even let me in the lobby. I kept trying to get through the door, so the policeman picked me up and threw me on the pavement. There was a photographer who snapped his picture doing that. He turned with his billy club and started beating the photographer, smashing his camera and exposing his film. I went around the side of the building, crawled in through a window of the laundry room, and found a doctor: "My brother's been shot, and I want you to find him for me if you would." I told him my name. Within minutes, Alan came walking down the hall. I can't tell you the feeling.

ALAN: It was a difficult time to be a young person. Only ten days earlier, I had attended the funeral of my friend. Now, it turned out that my other friend, Jeff, was killed, too. And I'm wounded and my roommate is wounded. Each day, I waited for the National Guard to be charged with murder. I thought for sure it would happen. I still had enough faith in the system to think that these murderers would be brought to justice soon.

ROSEANN: In October of 1970, the Ohio grand jury convened. Of course, we thought there would be criminal indictments against the Guard. I mean, were we idiots or what? I got a phone call from my mother the day the grand jury returned their indictments. I had moved to Boston because I wanted to forget politics for a while. Fortunately, that feeling didn't last. I asked her, "How many got indicted? Did they get them all?"

She goes, "Well, they've indicted twenty-five people, but none of them are Guardsmen." I said, "You're kidding." And she started going down the list of all my friends: "Jeff Hartzler was indicted, Jimmie Riggs was indicted, Alan was indicted . . ." It was like, "Oh, my God, all these people." And then she said, "There's one more—you've been indicted."

I'd witnessed probably the most shocking incident that I'll ever witness in my entire life. Yet the victims were made out to be the criminals, and the National Guardsmen were hailed for their bravery. Seabury Ford, the special prosecutor who led the grand jury, had a birthday cake that year that said "Shoot the bastards." And he said publicly, "They should have shot more of them."

The Ohio grand jury report itself was so biased that the federal court ordered it burned. They actually had to go outside the county courthouse with the news media there and burn the report in a trash can. But the court allowed our indictments to stand. The majority of the Kent Twenty-Five were indicted for Monday, the day of the shooting. My charge was second-degree riot. They said I acted in concert with five or more persons in order to create a tumultuous disturbance.

ALAN: The grand jury was appointed by Governor Rhodes, who had ordered the Guard in. The indictments were the first step in the cover-up—the victims were blamed. Joe Lewis, who was standing sixty feet away from the Guard, was giving them the finger when he was shot. He was indicted. So two of the wounded students, Joe and I, were charged with participating in a riot. I suppose we were guilty of assaulting the bullets with our bodies.

ROSEANN: It was so hard for middle America to accept the fact that American soldiers did something like this without provocation, without warning, without reason. They had to latch on to something. And the idea that the Guard shot in self-defense was the most convincing. "Well, of course there was a sniper. Why else would they shoot?" I remember my own aunt, whom I love dearly, came in the house in tears, saying, "You know there was a sniper." I mean, here's Alan bandaged with a wound, and my aunt is shaking a finger in his face, saying, "You know there was a sniper." And we're saying, "No, there wasn't." When the sniper theory was disproved, relatively early, then they fabricated the story that rocks, bricks, and bottles were thrown at the Guardsmen.

The FBI investigators believed that the self-defense theory was fabricated by the Guard. The President's Commission on Campus Unrest concluded that the shootings were "unnecessary, unwarranted, and inexcusable." Some Guardsmen admitted it. James Farris testified that from the time he left the practice field to the time they shot, not a single rock was thrown. Lloyd Thomas said he fired only because he was told to but personally saw no necessity to shoot. John Martin said his first thought when the shooting began was, "What idiot is firing with a weapon in this situation?" And then there was a Guardsman, Captain James Snyder, who admitted he had lied to the grand jury when he said he took a gun from the body of Jeff Miller and brass knuckles from a student he clubbed earlier.[96]

There had simply been no riot, so there was no evidence to prove second-degree riot. In December of 1971, our indictments were thrown out. But the killers walk free to this day.

ALAN: The country was in an uproar. Five million students shut down about five hundred universities in May 1970. The national student strike was the pinnacle of student activism in America. And President Nixon in his memoirs said that the days after Kent State were the darkest days of his presidency. It was just an unbelievable crisis in our country.

ROSEANN: It was Kent State and the student movement that hastened the end of the Vietnam war. Within six months, Nixon was forced to bring more troops home. When the war finally ended, an Army lieutenant named Richard Shandline wrote a letter home: "One thing worries me. Will people want to hear about it, or will they want to forget the whole thing happened?" His concerns are much the same as the concerns of those of us who survived the shootings here at Kent State. I worry, too, that people will not want to hear about it, that people will want to forget the whole thing happened.

The Heresy of a Modern-Day Social Gospel

THE FBI AND THE COMMITTEE IN SOLIDARITY WITH THE PEOPLE OF EL SALVADOR

In the wake of revelations of "Orwellian excesses" by the nation's established intelligence agencies, Gerald Ford's attorney general, Edward Levi, issued new FBI guidelines in 1976.[97] These guidelines sought to contain the bureau's fishing expeditions, to restrict its work more closely to criminal investigations, and to provide oversight by the attorney general. Domestic security investigations dropped sharply.[98] Imposed by one administration, however, the guidelines were subject to change by another. In December 1981, President Ronald Reagan issued Executive Order 12333. Two sets of new FBI guidelines followed early in 1983, one concerning domestic security and terrorism and another, largely secret, governing foreign counterintelligence and terrorism. Together, they provided the FBI with vaguer and lower standards for beginning an investigation and even less of a reason for ending one.[99]

Meanwhile, the administration shifted its foreign policy priorities. "Central America is the most important place in the world for the United States today," Ronald Reagan's ambassador to the United Nations said in 1981.[100] The president himself drew a more cataclysmic conclusion from developments in the region's small nations: "If we cannot defend ourselves there . . . the safety of our homeland would be put in jeopardy."[101] In numerous Central American countries, with their extremes of poverty and wealth, revolutionary movements were on the rise. Portraying the insurgents as "terrorists," the Reagan administration supported the repressive regimes in El Salvador and Guatemala and sought the overthrow of the newly established Sandinista government in Nicaragua.[102] "The idea is to slowly demonize the Sandinista government," an administration official bluntly asserted, "in order to turn it into a real enemy and threat in the minds of the American people, thereby eroding their resistance to U.S. support for the contras* and, perhaps, to a future U.S. military intervention in the region."[103]

President Reagan's policies never won widespread public support, despite his enormous popularity. In fact, they inspired passionate opposition, especially among church people. His denial of asylum to thousands of refugees fleeing those repressive regimes intensified the opposition. The result was the Central America peace movement, composed of some fifteen hundred groups in fifty states, which organized predominantly local actions: holding candlelight vigils to mourn the Salvadoran dead; adopting Nicaraguan cities; shipping clothes and tools to the Guatemalan poor; and carrying out hunger strikes. The national organizations that participated in this movement included Witness for Peace, Sanctuary, Pledge of Resistance, and the Committee in Solidarity with the People of El Salvador (CISPES).

CISPES, which opposed U.S. aid to the Salvadoran regime and provided humanitarian support for the rebels, became a prime target of the administration's repressive response. After the group was founded in 1980, the FBI began an investigation to determine whether it was controlled by the rebel Farabundo Martí National Liberation Front (FMLN) and would therefore stand in violation of the Foreign Agents Registration Act. In Dallas, Frank Varelli, whose father had been head of El Salvador's national police, posed as Gilberto Antonio Ayala Mendoza, a poor refugee whose family had been murdered by the death squads—and was welcomed into the local chapter of CISPES. In fact, Varelli was turning in the names, addresses, and license plate numbers of persons who attended the CISPES gatherings to his FBI handlers, reporting on them "almost on a daily basis."[104] The FBI officially closed its investi-

---

*The contras, an anti-Sandinista exile army funded, trained, and directed by the U.S. government, committed atrocities against civilian populations that "were not isolated incidents, but reflected a common pattern of behavior," a former contra leader acknowledged (Edgar Chamorro, quoted in Christian Smith, *Resisting Reagan: The U.S. Central America Peace Movement* [Chicago: University of Chicago Press, 1996], p. 48).

gation in February 1982, concluding that "there was no evidence indicating CISPES was acting on behalf of, or at the direction of a foreign power or group."[105]

Yet, thirteen months later, the bureau began a second investigation of CISPES under secret provisions of the Foreign Counterintelligence and Terrorism guidelines. This investigation lasted more than two years. Despite instructions from bureau headquarters that agents were not to interfere with First Amendment rights, FBI records obtained by the Center for Constitutional Rights show that political activity, not terrorism, was the bureau's concern. Legal political activities were monitored in Pittsburgh, Mobile, Norfolk, Chicago, Phoenix, San Juan, San Francisco, Los Angeles, and elsewhere. Shortly after the San Diego field office proposed closing down the investigation because it had found "information to indicate that the organization is involved with information campaigns, fund raising functions, and peaceful demonstrations," FBI headquarters extended its probe to all fifty-nine field offices.[106] The Center for Constitutional Rights noted that bureau headquarters instructed local offices "to invade campuses, insert undercover agents, stake out residences, monitor radio programs and broaden the investigation to include any group that opposed the Administration's foreign policy in Central America."[107] And, indeed, the investigation expanded to include more than one hundred organizations, among them the National Council of Churches, the Maryknoll Sisters, Oxfam-America, the United Auto Workers, and the National Education Association.[108]

In mid-1985, the House Subcommittee on Civil and Constitutional Rights, headed by Representative Don Edwards, questioned FBI officials about the nature of the CISPES investigation. One week later, the Justice Department's Office of Intelligence Policy and Review ordered the case closed, advising the bureau that CISPES was engaged only in legal political activities.[109] Edwards concluded: "Not one criminal act was expressly charged to CISPES, yet through innuendo and guilt by association, CISPES was prosecuted, tried, and found guilty of subversion."[110] It was, FBI Director William Sessions later told Congress, "an investigation of which the FBI is not proud."[111]

In 1987, Frank Varelli, disillusioned with the FBI, revealed a darker side to the investigation. Under FBI instructions, he had supplied the Salvadoran National Guard, whose officers were in the death squads, with the arrival dates of persons being deported back to El Salvador from the United States as well as the names of Americans traveling there who opposed the administration's policies.[112] He had prepared a file, under FBI instructions, of persons with "terrorist tendencies," which included such administration critics as Senators Christopher Dodd and Claiborne Pell and former Ambassador to El Salvador Robert White. He was told by FBI agents that they had broken into the office of the Dallas chapter of CISPES and into an apartment of one of its members.[113] In response, the FBI discredited Varelli, its prized informant, and placed responsibility for its probe of CISPES on him. Before a congressional committee, Director Sessions testified that the investigation was "an aberration."[114]

The CISPES case was hardly an aberration, however. Bureau records that came to light in 1995 show that the FBI had also conducted a nationwide "international terrorism" investigation of the General Union of Palestinian Students from 1979 to 1989, even though the agency knew that the group's purpose was educational and political and that it had committed no illegal acts.[115] Indeed, the government's General Accounting Office found at least two thousand separate FBI investigations that monitored First Amendment activities between 1982 and 1988.[116] Also, administration critics returning from Nicaragua reported that the FBI had interrogated them; that FBI agents, with Customs officials, had confiscated their personal belongings; and that agents had investigated them at their homes and jobs, questioning their friends, neighbors, and landlords.[117] Belonging to a Central America peace group, contributing to it, or attending its meetings could qualify one for a visit from the FBI. Simply opposing administration policy over the radio could result in an FBI file being opened on the dissenting individual.[118]

While phantom terrorists were relentlessly sought from among the president's critics, actual terrorism directed against administration opponents was carried out unimpeded. Yanira Corea, a Salvadoran CISPES volunteer, was abducted in Los Angeles and tortured while she was questioned about CISPES organizers and her family in El Salvador. The letters "EM," the initials of the Salvadoran death squad, were carved into the palms of her hands; her tongue and neck were cut; her face and fingers were burned.[119] Two hundred Central America activists reported death threats or death squad activity in the United States between 1984 and 1987.[120] In these cases, as in the more than one hundred documented break-ins at activists' homes, offices, and churches, the persons responsible had accurate information about their victims' schedules, relationships, and commitments.[121] The break-ins appear to have been politically motivated acts intended to intimidate, obstruct, and get information: Money and items of value were ignored, while membership lists, files on legal cases, correspondence, and photographs were taken, and threatening messages were left behind.[122] The FBI was resolute in its refusal to investigate what Congressman Edwards believed to be the work of Central American operatives or domestic right-wing groups.[123]

At the very time FBI Director William Sessions called the bureau's antiterrorism probe of the nonviolent CISPES "an aberration," veteran FBI agent Jack Ryan was fired for his refusal to investigate other nonviolent protesters under antiterrorism guidelines. He and his wife, Peggy Ryan, describe their experience in the story that follows. This section also includes an account by two of the bureau's targets in CISPES: Linda Hajek, at the time a Catholic nun, and Jose Rinaldi-Jovet, both leaders of the Dallas chapter, where the FBI probe centered.

JACK RYAN AND PEGGY RYAN

JACK RYAN: I was an FBI agent for twenty-one-and-a-half years. During the Vietnam war era, I had a hard time with all those people who protested. I knew they had to be unpatriotic, part of a big conspiracy. I felt very threatened by their outcry, because I realized some of it was aimed at me. That's not a comfortable position, especially when you feel you're right. I never examined my point of view critically. It was more or less a given. The way I was brought up and the institutions I was part of affirmed it: my own family, my schools, my government, my church.

I grew up the oldest of eleven children, in a totally Catholic setting not too far from here, in Peoria. My wife, Peggy, is the oldest of twelve, all Catholic. I went to Catholic schools and then to a seminary, studying to be a priest. After I got my B.A. degree, I dropped out. I got on at the police department, but I remained a very active Catholic. I was a lector at church, involved in the men's club. We made sure our kids all went to Catholic schools. This was seen as part of our obligation. I'm a practicing Roman Catholic right now. I consider myself devout. But I also look at being Catholic very differently than I used to. And a lot of it has to do with the blind obedience sort of thing.

I was fired from the FBI in September 1987 for insubordination or failing to live up to my oath of office. It stemmed from an event in 1983. At the time, I was caught up with the U.S. Bishops' Peace Pastoral; their statement moved me very much. I found it so different from anything I had read by bishops or the church in general. It put the focus on me as an individual and my own conscience. It said that you cannot look the other way on issues like our country's overall military or nuclear posture. These were matters you had to face if you wanted to continue call-

JACK RYAN

ing yourself a Christian. "Peacemaking is not an optional commitment," the bishops wrote. "It is a requirement of our faith. We are called to be peacemakers, not by some movement but by our Lord Jesus." I agreed. I began to feel that I couldn't justify nuclear weapons under any circumstances. So I saw that a conflict could arise at work.

Every ninety days, I would go to our Springfield headquarters for a file review of my cases, a rather routine matter. At the end, I would normally meet with the boss. In the conversation, he'd usually throw in: "Anything else going on, any problems, personal problems?" This time

I said, "Yes, something is bothering me a great deal." I told him about the Bishops' Peace Pastoral and said, "I could have problems of conscience in some work I might be asked to do."

He really didn't know how to field that. He went into a problem he once had. A doctor who performed abortions had been kidnapped by a group of anti-abortionists. He said, "You know, I'm Catholic, too, and that brought up some questions, but I didn't see any conflict." I believe he was really groping for something to say. Finally he asked, "Is it an issue right now?" And I said, "No." So he kind of left it: "Well, if it becomes one, you drop me a memo, and we'll take it from there." The next couple times I met with him, he asked, "That other matter—has anything come up?" I knew what he was talking about and said, "No." And that was it.

Gradually I began to feel very strongly that what we were doing in Central America was wrong. I thought it was horrible that we were supplying weapons, training, and surveillance photos that were being used mainly on the innocent populations of almost all of Latin America. It was just inexcusable, and I didn't personally want to be any part of this.

But while I felt those government policies were wrong, I didn't know of anything I'd been asked to do that was in line with them. Then one day I got a memo and a teletype containing a lead to investigate an incident up in Chicago. The memo was very innocuous, but the teletype that it referred to talked about somebody in the Chicago area who had put a sticky substance on the front door locks of eleven military recruiting offices. Stuck to the doors were some statements that protested U.S. actions in Central America and described the Veterans Fast for Life. A license plate registered to Joe and Jean Gump had been picked up. After checking bureau indices, they were identified as having previously broken into a missile base under the name "Silo Plowshares."

This was all on the teletype that the Chicago office sent out nationwide, as a Domestic Security/Terrorism matter. I didn't know the Gumps, but it listed some other people who were associates of theirs. One of the names, Larry Morlan, was a shock. He was somebody I met previously. He was from Rock Island, Illinois, and had been in Peoria a few years ago at a sit-in demonstration at the cathedral. That group was trying to get our bishop off his rear end about the nuclear issue. They were there about four or five days, fasting. I knew a couple of the people who were there, so I went down to give them some support. I was introduced to Larry Morlan then. I remembered being very impressed by his sincerity. So to see his name on the teletype under terrorism kind of threw me.

The name Plowshares comes from a biblical edict: "They shall beat their swords into plowshares." My belief was—and I know that I'm right—that this Plowshares group wasn't a conspiracy. It started during the Vietnam era, as a nonviolent movement protesting the war. If there was violence of any sort, it couldn't by its very nature be a Plowshares act.

The other group to be investigated was Veterans Fast for Life—four veterans who were in the middle of a fifty-day hunger strike on the steps of the U.S. Capitol, trying to call attention to our policies in Central America. I'd read about it in the Catholic press. I didn't know any of them at the time, but I did know what they were doing, and it was very difficult to call their peaceful protest an act of violence. I just felt it was absurd.

So I drew up a memo, like I had been told to do if something came up that bothered my conscience. I said that if this case had been an investigation of destruction of government property, I would have no problem. I feel everybody is responsible for their actions. And I think the people who did this went into it realizing they were responsible for theirs. But this investigation was carried out under the Domestic Security/Terrorism guidelines. It was, in effect, calling these people terrorists. Well, who controls the definition of terrorism? I thought it was obvious that they were not terrorists but were speaking out in a nonviolent way against terrorism on the part of our government.

I also said I felt that the FBI was ill advised to be involved in this sort of investigation after what happened in the past. When the FBI was burned, we should have learned our lesson. Now it looked like we hadn't. I was surprised to see, in fact, that we were involved in a blatant political-type investigation. That's what it was.

PEGGY RYAN: I had been away at the University of Illinois for a year, working on my master's on campus, while Jack was taking care of Paul, our youngest. Jack was coming to a realization that he might have to make an important decision. When I came home for Thanksgiving, he showed me the memo. I didn't know he could write like that. I told him, "Wow, that's the greatest thing." It was really excellent.

I had always been active in peace groups and women's groups here in Peoria. But Jack was not able to participate because of his job. He fully believed in what they were doing, but he couldn't say anything himself. So he kind of stood on the sidelines. I think he was beginning to feel like a hypocrite. I could see how he wanted to be this open, honest person. So I didn't care that he took the risk.

PEGGY RYAN

JACK: I guess I had painted myself into a corner, morally. Now, I'm wondering along the way what's going to happen. I'm looking at June 19, 1988, my fiftieth birthday, as the day I can retire. As that gets closer, I'm wondering, am I going to make it or will I lose my pension? All of a sudden, here it is. I've got to make the decision now.

There were other things I could have done. The particular lead was kind of innocuous: "All agents contact logical sources"—we got that kind of lead a lot—"see if anything like this occurred in your area." That's all it asked. I didn't, in fact, know of anything, so I could have said, "No, nothing like this occurred." Or I could have ignored it.

But I felt I had to address this now. I felt I was being ordered to participate directly in a case that involved opposition to a violent, immoral, and illegal foreign policy on the part of our government toward Central America. It appeared evident that the FBI was again being used to quell dissent.

And I knew that when the FBI investigated somebody, it could be very intimidating. This used to be our number one technique. We worked a lot of cases that we never intended to prosecute because we just weren't able to. But we could investigate the devil out of them. And it hurt the groups. It dried up their sources of funding; people backed off. Just think what an awesome power it is, to be able to pick and choose who you want to investigate or who you want to demolish.

I guess the moment of truth had occurred. In November 1986, I submitted the memo. A couple of weeks later, the boss called back. We had a short talk. He said, "If you would like me to tear this memo up, I'll forget the whole thing happened." I said, "No, I am serious." He said, "But refusing to handle this investigation borders on insubordination. Why don't you sleep on it and get back to me?"

About a week later, I received a memorandum from him, ordering me to investigate and report the results of any outstanding leads. If I still refused, I should indicate this in writing, and he would have no choice but to initiate insubordination proceedings against me. My answer was due Christmas Eve.

PEGGY: When I came home for semester break in December, Jack showed me the memo and asked what I thought he should do. He said it could cost him his job. I said, "Whoa, we don't need to do this. Our plan was that you were going to retire in June, I'd get a job, and you'd be home to watch the kid. Let's just do that plan." Jack had lost touch with the older kids because of his work, and I had been virtually a single parent through all those years. Now he was coming back to the family through our new little boy. It had been working out pretty good.

But here he was, telling me that this plan could be wrecked. How was I going to pay for my education? I didn't know. I said, "Do what you have to do, but I vote to just take their money and get out."

JACK: I was called in in January, put under oath, and told to sign a statement that I had been reordered to conduct this lead on the Silo Plowshares and the Veterans Fast for Life and that I would not do it. I said again that they were not terrorists; that I knew one of the individuals mentioned in the teletype personally and was totally convinced of his nonviolent posture; and that I thought the FBI was wrong and would best distance itself from this sort of thing again. I termed our government's posture in Central America as violent, bordering on illegal. And I said, "I also believe that for me as an FBI agent to cooperate with such an effort places me directly and firmly in complicity with the activity targeted by the dissent. This is the position I refuse to take."

I still had mixed emotions. I was very popular among the other agents, and I had a lot of good friends. We talked sports, families, FBI, crime. But the social conscience side of me was not well known. I knew that in taking this stand, I was going to be painted as weird.

PEGGY: They could twist everything he wrote and make him look like a religious nut.

JACK: That bothered me a great deal. But it would bother me more to be called a disloyal, unpatriotic American, because my loyalty, patriotism, and love of this country so strongly affected my actions. When I did show the others my statement, there were no comments, no questions. And I knew the way the FBI worked, that this was a big issue. There would be buzzing; everybody would be talking. But to me, nothing, no curiosity at all.

After I submitted the sworn statement, I was taken off Foreign Counterintelligence/Terrorism assignments. I'd been the agent who handled that in Peoria. Some of the work would be legitimate, like when we'd get visitors from Iron Curtain countries. The presumption quite often was that the KGB would have somebody within a group of, say, Russians who were looking at Caterpillar tractor factories.

But counterintelligence is not popular work in the FBI. In a lot of ways, it's Mickey-Mouse: wheel-spinning, going back to the old ways of doing things. Our program of interviewing people from the Middle East to see if they had any information about terrorism in this country was also a way of letting them know that we're here and we know where they are. A lot of it was done for harassment. You just had to knock on one door in a particular area, and the whole Palestinian community or the whole Iranian community was alerted. It was also done with South Koreans. We weren't necessarily always watching them, but they didn't know that.

When I came into the FBI back in 1966, all we did was chase car thieves. I saw a figure once that sixty-five percent of federal prisoners were car thieves, usually kids between eighteen and twenty-two years old. The police departments did all the work: They'd arrest the person, find out they'd crossed state lines, and then call us. And boy, we were right there. We were going after statistics. We'd pick up their reports and play editor: claim the recovery of the car at the high book value, write our own report—and there's your statistic. Eventually the courts got sick of that. Then, just when we were losing our "bread and butter" there, the Vietnam war kicked off, and we had Selective Service violators. It was the greatest thing that could have happened. Statistically, we made a killing.

The FBI is a bureaucracy, and Hoover was a genius at running it. A big part of running a bureaucracy is to spend money and say the right things to Congress. J. Edgar Hoover would go to Congress every year. It's funny, when you read the testimony—Hoover and Representative John Rooney went back and forth like Edgar Bergen and Charlie McCarthy. And every year the FBI outdid itself with statistics of its accomplishments: convictions, fines, savings, and recoveries. It was a farce.

We never really expected to prosecute a major mob figure. The FBI usually went after the street-level bookies or runners. When you hear the chronology of a good case, a big case, the hardest part was getting over the initial hurdle of people in management who were trying to stop it. The bureau viewed a big case as a problem: the toes you'd be stepping on, the irregularities you were going to have, the press scrutiny. Hoover didn't even want us to work organized crime till we were forced into it.

Our big emphasis had been on political investigations. And it might have seemed great when the FBI had secret files on "them," our mutual enemy. But when persons outside the bureau saw the kind of people involved, they realized, "Hey, Hoover might have something on me." And he probably did. He had things on a lot of people. I think this was the main reason for the congressional outcry. It involved their own vested interests.

As a result of the outcry, "strict" guidelines were slapped on the FBI. You almost laugh when you hear what they said: The FBI will no longer investigate any person or group unless it's believed that a federal crime has been committed or that these people are violating a federal law. "Well," you say, "what's wrong with that? It makes good sense." But we viewed these guidelines as handcuffs.

Before that, we investigated someone hoping to get them on some violation and realizing that the mere fact that they were being investigated hampered their activities. This was the way the FBI handled countless groups that protested government policies, even when they did it legally and peacefully. Since normal, lawful investigative procedures rarely produced the results we desired, we went by the guideline "Do what you have to do, but don't get caught."

When we were pulled out of that, we thought it was the end of the world. Just the opposite happened. The FBI became very effective in legitimate law enforcement investigations. That was pretty much the kickoff, I would say, of the real impact that the bureau had on crime in the recent past. You take organized crime, government corruption, municipal corruption, police corruption, union corruption—these were areas that had really never been addressed from a criminal standpoint. Work was being done against drug activity, and legitimate work against terrorists. And it was neat. There's a lot of pride in being part of an organization that can come through some real trying times. To admit its mistakes, I think, was part of being able to move on and become better. I saw the FBI doing this. Then all of a sudden I saw the FBI going back the other way. And I felt bad about that. I felt deceived.

After I took my stand under oath and was reassigned to other matters, my boss talked to me. He had just been on the circuit, on what we called the "goon squad," going around the country handling discipline cases. So he was up to date on what could happen. He told me I wouldn't get out of this: "You've taken on the bureau. They're going to have to respond. My guess is they're going to give you a two-week suspension."

But he warned, "You're coming into a collision course with your retirement. You're messing with your job, your pension, everything." I told him I realized it, but I also wanted it to be realized that that's how seriously I felt about this, about what we were doing in Central America.

I saw a movie once about a German conscientious objector. He was a Catholic farmer, with a wife and a couple of small children. He said he wouldn't serve in the Nazi army, and he wouldn't let anybody serve in his place, either. He just refused to do what he felt was wrong. His parish priest tried to talk him into going along with it. His bishop said he'd be following church practice, church law, if he served in the Nazi army. They told him, "This is a separate issue. It's not a matter of conscience." At the end, the camera lit on an old lady—one of the actual persons alive at the time—and her comment was, "Well, that was silly, what he did. What if everybody had done that?"

In June 1987, I got a letter from an assistant director. His recommendation was not for a two-week suspension—it was that I be fired for insubordination, violation of the oath of office. It shocked me. I didn't really think they would go this far.

I answered with a long memo. I asked that I not be fired. I pointed out that I had tried to conduct this whole thing in-house; I had talked to no one outside except a few confidants and my family. I had made no issue of this, and that wasn't my intention. The only reason I brought it up to my boss was that I didn't want any ambiguity to exist. I didn't want people who had to work with me not to know where I stood. I said I think it's best to work this out in a moot situation in my boss's office. That was my hope.

This was an interim period when William Webster, the FBI director, had resigned to go to the CIA, and the new director hadn't been sworn in yet. So there was kind of a hiatus. Webster had apparently been procrastinating on several other disciplinary actions. When the new acting director came in, they cleared off all these cases. Mine was one of them.

In September, I was officially fired. Two bosses came up, number one and two. When I saw both of them, I knew this was it—the axe. They were very sympathetic, like they normally are when they do this to somebody.

PEGGY: You know, every day I waited for them to say, "You're fired." I dreaded it. And then once he was fired, I was relieved it was over.

JACK: That was on Friday. Over the weekend, I saw a cousin of mine in church. I didn't know how to tell him, because absolutely nobody had any idea anything was going on. We went to a parish picnic, and I saw a state trooper I worked with very closely. I just couldn't tell him; to tell somebody would require a long explanation. I did tell my mom, a couple of my sisters, and my wife's sisters.

On Monday, I decided to call a newspaper. I could never have predicted what happened. Two days later, my picture was on the front page with a big headline: "FBI Agent Says Peace Views Cost Him Job." The article was very favorable, very positive. Friends all over town called. The phone rang the instant I hung up. And they were all calls of support. It was very edifying. The wire service picked up on it. The *Boston Globe* had a story—it got that far. I don't know what's been said inside the bureau, but I don't think I've been written off as a nut by the public, by the media.

I made an appointment with a lawyer. Right away, he said, "Let's stop the press releases. We don't know that the door is shut. Let's not get them mad." So I stopped. I didn't talk anymore.

When the FBI fires somebody, it's final. The bureau is exempt from civil service; they hire and fire on their own. However, as an Army veteran, I was able to appeal through the Merit System Protection Board. There's an informal letter of appeal to the FBI—"please reconsider"—

which we sent out. The answer came back three weeks later: We've reviewed it, and there's no chance.

After that, my lawyer said, "You can talk to anybody you want." *Newsweek* had persisted all along, so I was interviewed by them. In Chicago, I spoke to religious groups like Pax Christi. A reporter from San Francisco, Angus Mackenzie, interviewed me, and his story appeared in the *National Catholic Reporter*. A big part of it made the connection with Brian Willson, one of the four veterans involved in the Fast for Life. He had both his legs cut off by a train that refused to stop for him when he was protesting at the Concord Naval Weapons Station. That was September 1; I was fired September 11. Here an FBI agent is fired for refusing to investigate Willson as a terrorist. Mackenzie made the link.

We were all set for a hearing date before the Merit System Protection Board, when out of the blue the FBI called my lawyer and said, "We would like to open negotiations." We were floored. This was very close to the time when William Sessions started as director, so it would be my guess that he had looked at it. Somebody must have said, "We've got problems here."

Of course, the hearing in St. Louis was postponed while the lawyers were trying to make a deal. They finally hammered one out. I didn't like it, but it was nothing I couldn't live with: a two-week suspension, which is what my boss had initially recommended. I was to work out of the Springfield office. In effect, I'd have to commute ninety miles without compensation, which is very unusual in the FBI. I didn't like that either, but, again, I could live with it. And I would have to agree to retire on the date I was eligible. Well, that was easy.

But there was another problem. My normal performance evaluation came up. Through my whole career of over twenty years, I was always given the top adjective without exception—excellent, excellent. All of a sudden, while this other matter is brewing, I get a low mark. So I wouldn't sign the thing. I wrote a memo back saying, "This is a cheap shot." It was that old Hoover-think.

Afterward, I wished I had been quiet, because when I didn't go along with it, the next person in charge, the number two guy in Springfield, reviewed it. He replied that my evaluation was much too high, that I should have gotten the rock-bottom mark. So they worked it out that I would get a pay-grade reduction. These were the munchkins at the home office playing their little games. It really irked me. But again, I could live with it if I had to.

Finally it was all worked out; they would send the document, and I would sign it and air-express it back. Well, when I got the document, there was a new demand: that I never talk to the media about the incident or what led up to the incident—which you might say covers my whole life. It was now clear that the whole reason for their agreement was to silence me. This floored me, but my lawyer talked me into going along with it. So I signed it and sent it out on Friday, figuring they'd get it Monday.

In the meantime, Angus Mackenzie had lined up ABC Nightly News to do something on Brian Willson and myself. ABC wanted to interview me, but when they came out, I was right in the middle of these negotiations and wouldn't talk to them. So they found a film clip of me speaking to a high school group in Springfield. They got other pictures of me and put it all together. Then they were going to go to the FBI.

The timing was horrible. I had mailed the agreement to Washington for them to sign on Monday, but they had a big snow storm that day, so nobody showed up. Tuesday, ABC went to the FBI: "We've got a little segment with Brian Willson and Jack Ryan; we'd like your side of the story." The FBI wanted to know what was going on: "Here we're negotiating with him, and now he's talking to ABC."

We had a three-way conversation: the FBI, my lawyer, and me. That was funny, too. Just as I was waiting for this big call, my sister-in-law's son swallowed some medicine, and she needed somebody to watch the baby. So I was over at their house, watching her baby and trying to conduct this three-way conversation. The FBI was coming on very strong to somebody who no longer worked for them, trying to pin down what I had done with ABC. I told them everything. They were satisfied at last that ABC had done it on their own. It looked like things were finally set.

But suddenly the negotiations were stopped, by somebody else above and outside the FBI. I have no idea who it was. I would guess it came from the White House or the Justice Department. They just said: "No deal."

Now the hearing was coming up in St. Louis. The date had previously been set, but during the negotiations we didn't think there would be a hearing. When they broke down, we had about a day and a half to prepare. We challenged the bureau's action on First Amendment grounds, arguing that mine was a religiously motivated decision. We said that the FBI was bound by the Constitution to respect my religious beliefs.

Their reply was, "What religious beliefs? There's nothing here that is in any way religious." I referred to the Bishops' Peace Pastoral, in which the purpose of religion seemed to shift from just getting people into heaven to a focus right here in the real world. I could no longer put my religion into a separate compartment: This is something I do on Sunday morning, and that is what I do the rest of the week. Or, this concerns me and my afterlife, and that concerns me and the real world. I couldn't make those separations any more.

After I testified, they had to agree that I had acted based on my religious beliefs. There were two priests who were going to testify on my behalf, and I think the government and the FBI didn't want them heard. So they put on record that it was a religiously motivated action. Then they changed their argument: It would put an undue hardship on the FBI to have to accommodate to my religious beliefs. "That would set a precedent," they said. "Everybody could do this." They brought out that my refusal in this one area would make me unacceptable to go back.

They also leaned heavily on a statement I made during their questioning. They had asked me whether I could carry a gun if I came back as an agent. I said that I had carried a gun up to the day I was fired. And I had never worn a gun I didn't intend to use if I had to. But an evolutionary process had taken place since I was fired, and I came to feel that I never wanted to take another person's life, even in defense of my own. I would like to say I'd behave nonviolently, but I had been trained to behave in another way, and I'd been trained very well. The government said the FBI expected instinctive obedience. My lawyer asked, "Is that the same as blind obedience?" They didn't answer.

PEGGY: I had a delusion for quite a while that we'd win. Then I realized that we would never win, because they owned the courts.

JACK: The verdict was totally in favor of the FBI. It was ironic. The same day that the decision came out against me for refusing to investigate Plowshares and Veterans Fast for Life as terrorists, Sessions came out with the startling admission about their snooping into CISPES under the terrorist guidelines.

LINDA HAJEK AND JOSE RINALDI-JOVET

LINDA HAJEK: CISPES held its founding meeting in California in the fall of 1980. We started our community-based chapter here in Dallas at that time. Up to then, there had been a small group of church people exchanging information on Central American events.

JOSE RINALDI-JOVET: We got to know more about El Salvador. We learned about the oligarchy there, how fourteen families controlled

LINDA HAJEK

the country. Because of the way things are there, when you don't have a future, your children and your grandchildren don't have a future. After you die, your little bit of land is divided up. Each generation has less and less. With no land, you can't grow food, and you can only eat what you grow. With no jobs, you don't have money for medicine, clothing, shelter, or food—the basics.

Every time the Salvadoran people petitioned the government by peaceful measures—strikes, demonstrations, or even elections, every way they tried to bring a change to the system—the answer from the au-

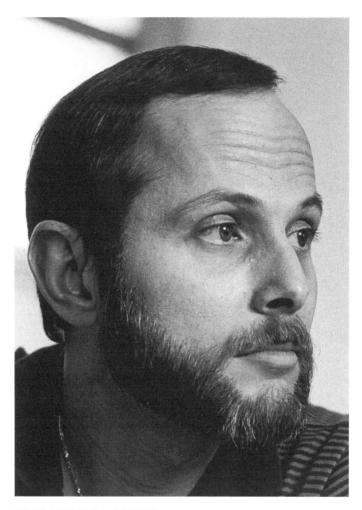

JOSE RINALDI-JOVET

thorities was a violent one. They would annul the elections, break the strikes, or open fire on public demonstrations.

The assassination of four American religious workers in 1980 in El Salvador was something that forced a lot of people here in Dallas to open their eyes to what was going on in that country. After the coup in October 1979, there was a pretense that a more humane government was going to be established. But the real power stayed in the hands of the military. Nothing had changed. Murders by the thousands were still being committed. People were dragged from their homes and killed in the streets, and no one was allowed to move them or touch them. Their bodies just lay out there to terrorize the people into silence. We saw that, and the increase of it, and we supported the people who opposed it.

LINDA: Priests were threatened. Rutilio Grande and another priest had been killed. When Archbishop Romero was assassinated,* you couldn't even go to the funeral without snipers up in the buildings shooting at you. It became very clear then that those of us sitting in our comfortable living rooms up here could no longer demand: "They should be nonviolent in their struggle." They were there on the spot, and they needed to be making the decisions. So my basic stance was at that time, and continues to be, that the people of El Salvador have a right to figure out what they want to do in their country without big brother up here calling the shots for them.

CISPES, from the very beginning, supported the guerrilla groups in El Salvador in their attempt to overthrow the dictatorship and hopefully establish some kind of democratic government. "Support," for us, meant publicly saying we believed in their right to do that. We did not have stashes of arms that we were sending down there. We did not send guns, and we did not send money for guns. We sent money for humanitarian aid. And we made sure it was channeled through organizations we felt were reliable.

We tried to speak to as many groups as we could about El Salvador. We did lobbying. Our first demonstration was in collaboration with others all over the country during Central America Week in the spring of 1981. In Dallas, about a hundred and fifty people marched down one main street and back up another. Our activities were well covered by the media—and appeared in my FBI files later. I had asked for my file through the Freedom of Information Act, and there was the article that had appeared in the *Dallas Morning News*, just after the march. So their surveillance of me had started very early on.

CISPES broadened its activities to include Guatemala and Nicaragua. Once contra aid became an issue, we did a lot of work on that. The administration had also been bringing soldiers from El Salvador to North Carolina to train them. So in January of 1982, we began a special series

---

*On March 24, 1980, Archbishop Oscar Arnolfo Romero of El Salvador was assassinated while conducting mass. The day before, he had called upon men in the army and the national guard to refuse to obey orders to kill their fellow citizens. His assassination signaled an all-out war on those who had challenged the control of the traditional elite in the country.

of vigils. We stood out in front of the federal building from four-thirty to six-thirty every Thursday afternoon, for about twelve weeks straight.

In the early eighties, we had a Maryknoll sister living in our community. Sister Celine was sixty-eight or so, teaching at an African American college here. She had been to China and the Philippines. Someone of that age, so involved and so clear about the issues, had a great impact on us. After the murder of Archbishop Romero, a group of us tried to get a memorial service together. But it kind of got diffused, and we never did do anything. Well, when Sisters Maura Clarke, Ita Ford, Dorothy Kazel, and lay worker Jean Donovan were killed, it brought it home. Celine knew those women, who were murdered in El Salvador. She had taught them at the Maryknoll College up in New York. It was like someone in our family had been touched.

Our convent here evolved into a community of seven or eight people. We worked at different places, but we lived together, and we had a focus on peace and justice issues. In 1983, our church declared Sanctuary.* A three-generation Salvadoran family moved in with us: grandparents, parents, and two children. What an impact they had on this conservative Dallas–Fort Worth community, where it had been hard to get the issues across! They were talking to the same people about the same things we had talked about, but all of a sudden it became humanized.

Here was this eighty-four-year-old man saying, "I had a Bible and a picture of Archbishop Romero in my house. My daughter was a catechist in the local parish. The National Guard came to my house and found the Bible and the picture of Romero, and they said, 'You're a Communist!'" I mean, this man is smaller than I am, and they beat him up in front of his wife. They held a gun between her body and her clothes and shot it off, just to terrorize her. Then they hauled them off to the jailhouse and held them there for about a week. Some people intervened, and the family managed to escape. They lived in hiding in El Salvador for a while, went to Guatemala, and then to Chiapas, Mexico. They finally ended up here with us.

The old grandfather had been an overseer at the plantation, so he was better off than some of the other folks we saw coming up. He talked to

---

*Sanctuary, a movement composed mainly of clerics and lay church workers, helped Central American refugees enter the United States at a time when most such refugees were being denied asylum under the Reagan administration's ideological criteria for admission. By 1987, more than four hundred church congregations had offered sanctuary to those fleeing repression and political upheaval in Central America.

a lot of church and community groups and to schools. To hear that story from him made it so clear and so real. He destroyed those images floating around in people's minds, of the guerrilla guy with this machine gun who's going to mow everybody down, the image that they all wear red berets and are Soviet Communists. It totally destroyed all that junk we were being told by the administration. Then it became clear to me: This is why the government is so opposed to these refugees being up here.

JOSE: The refugees spoke of thousands of people being killed, and President Reagan would certify that human rights were being protected. We found out that the death squads came from the same military that was running the country, and yet Reagan would say it had nothing to do with the government. We would hear what was happening in El Salvador; then we would hear and read what Reagan would say. It was totally different. I think the lies the administration came up with radicalized a lot of people. I believe in my case it made me persevere, stay and keep on. And I haven't lost my enthusiasm.

LINDA: I have a background in theology and had taught scripture in Zaire for a number of years. Having lived in a third world country for a long time, I kind of had the experiential part of it. Then I studied liberation theology. It helped me see that one cannot be neutral.

Western theology claims it is neutral; you take a step back and say, "This is the objective approach." You tell people, "Well, folks, this is the way life is, and we're sorry. Would you please pray a little harder? And the next time we bury one of your children because she didn't get adequate medical care, we'll weep with you for a while. But please don't cause trouble up there on the hill with the master of the plantation. He's a good man, and he goes to church every Sunday." I think that was the traditional stance. My theology teachers might have told me, "Don't take sides. Try to reconcile. Try to keep all these people loving each other." Well, that's already taking a stand—to keep things as they are—even if they don't want to admit it.

Liberation theology says no matter where you're standing, you have a perspective and a bias. It certainly helped me to see more clearly that as a religious person, in one way or another, I'd be taking sides. I realized that, as Christians, we had to be true to this gospel that's presented to us about sharing with the poor, about empowering the poor. And I knew that if we helped people learn they have a basic dignity, that they can respect each other as poor people and don't have to be the man on the hill, it would be threatening to the status quo. That was liberation theology, not the FBI's version of it. And there was no question about where I wanted to place myself in that. The timing was right in my own life, I guess.

So our basic stance in CISPES was: We're not doing anything wrong. Then, in April 1986, a *Dallas Morning News* reporter came and said, "I'd like to confirm some facts with you all." She'd been doing an investigative story on Frank Varelli. She sat down and told us all this stuff. And we were just reeling from it.

We had suspected there might be government plants in CISPES, because we knew they had been placed in other organizations. But I have to say that every time I took the idea seriously, I felt I was being arrogant. We were a small group, and what we were doing certainly didn't seem to merit that kind of attention. Besides, I never suspected a Salvadoran would be used to infiltrate us. So the fact that the reporter verified: "Yes, there is a plant, and he's Salvadoran," surprised me.

She said Varelli had piles of xeroxed papers all over his apartment. When he had first come to CISPES, Varelli wrote to me: "I want to read what the solidarity movement is doing in this country." So I sent a stack of everything we had to his post office box. The reporter was going through some of these papers with me and asked, "Do you recognize this?" It was a copy of a postcard that I had handwritten. We were doing a spaghetti fund-raiser here, cooking it ourselves and charging five dollars for all-you-can-eat spaghetti. We didn't have enough money for the printer, so I wrote the invitations by hand. That's what Varelli sent to the FBI office, a xeroxed copy of my handwritten postcard.

I mean, that kind of stupidity was being considered secret information. I can't get into that mindset where you secretly go around trying to find out what's public. They're paying a man to come to meetings that we announced all over the place. To me, it just reveals the sort of paranoia that they're working out of.

Varelli had gone to the *Dallas Morning News*, mad because the FBI didn't give him his back pay. He wanted the paper to do a story, and they picked up on it. This reporter did a lot of research; she talked to the FBI and tried to talk to his former boss. Then the story came out, a long front-page, Sunday morning type of thing. And there was my name in the middle of it! I thought, "Oh, my Lord, what are people going to think?" It read like a soap opera, like "Dallas": a guy was supposed to get me in a motel room and seduce me and have the sex scene recorded on film.

When Varelli couldn't come up with the kind of stuff the FBI wanted, I think it threw their whole operation. His supervisor, Flanagan, said, "Well, you better go back and find something." They figured, "If we can't break them by finding something illegal, maybe we can do it by ruining reputations, making them lose their personal credibility in the community."

The FBI must have been watching too many movies. I mean, it was so ridiculous—at that time, I was a Catholic sister. I thought: What scum of the earth, that this is the kind of thing they're trying to do in the name of national security.

JOSE: Varelli claims his superiors in the FBI told him to seduce Linda. These were the instructions he received. But he said, himself, that he never was going to do it, because by then he respected her as a nun.

LINDA: He was a Catholic as he was growing up. And even though he became a fundamentalist preacher, I think his basic cultural reaction to that sort of suggestion from his supervisors was, "Are you crazy?"

Varelli came and spoke at our CISPES meeting. That was almost a year after his story first broke. It was very dramatic. He and his attorney and our attorney and I were at the head table. We had a lot of media and a packed room. And he told why he did what he did, and why he had flipped sides.

JOSE: We found out that Varelli came from a family that had been in power. His father had been ambassador to Egypt and Guatemala, a military man who served as director general of the national police of El Salvador.

But we had known Varelli by the name of Gilberto Mendoza. He had told us he was a Salvadoran who was active against the government there. And he claimed he was so thankful for the work we were doing here because of the situation in his country. This is what he had said to us. And people had almost cried, listening to him. I was very impressed myself, and I said, "This is why we're struggling."

LINDA: He had told us, "I had members of my family hurt by the right wing." Varelli always had a flair for the dramatic.

When he flipped, he was equally dramatic. Suddenly he was confessing his sins. I went into this meeting with him very, very cautious and mad as hell at the man. I still don't appreciate anything that he did. But by the end of the meeting, I thought, "Well, maybe, I don't know." His flair for speaking did that to me.

JOSE: Varelli apologized for what he had done. He said he had been under the impression that he was going to inform on a terrorist organization. He admitted he had killed people in El Salvador during shootouts, and he feared anyone who was sympathetic to their struggle. He believed we were terrorists. But after coming to the meetings, he started changing his mind. He met Sister Patricia and Linda and thought that these people were not really bad, as he had been told.

LINDA: From the story in the *Dallas Morning News,* we knew most of what Frank Varelli was going to say. But to hear it from the mouth of the man himself certainly had an impact different from seeing it in the newspaper. I think it was clear in the minds of all of us that we had no reason to throw tomatoes at him politically on that particular night.

In a sense, Frank Varelli was not the real problem. He was recruited by the FBI. He was being paid by our government. The real problem was that the government believed it had a right to spy on its own citizens when they publicly dissented from its policies. That's the dangerous part of this: If people dissent from the government's policy, that automatically gives the FBI the right to break into their homes, put taps on their telephones, and send people to meetings to spy on them.

Varelli told us they had a device that could record conversations. He said they used it mostly to keep track of the numbers we phoned. And Varelli said they tampered with our mail. At the meeting, he pointed to me and said, "The FBI is still holding a big envelope sent to you from the city of Dallas." It did make sense. At that time, we were working really hard to see if we couldn't convert these low-income apartments into some kind of cooperative housing. And we had correspondence coming in from the city of Dallas. He said, "There's still an envelope down in the office that we confiscated from your mail."

They watched where we lived, the Bethany House of the Holy Cross Catholic Church. Varelli said they sat out there in the parking lot and copied down the license plates of all the people who came here. He claimed they had broken into the CISPES office here twice. First he said that two agents had broken in. Later on, he changed that; he said he had broken in twice. We weren't aware of a break-in. They didn't do what they did in some of the Sanctuary churches, where they left things torn up. CBS showed us some of our papers and asked, "Can you verify that these were stolen?" I couldn't. We had no secret papers, so there was no way for me to know if anything was missing.

I was coordinator of the CISPES chapter. I had a high profile in the media. I think that was one of the reasons I was targeted. I also lived and worked here. This is where all the CISPES mail was sent, where all the phone calls came to coordinate events that were going on. Jose also seemed to be especially targeted.

JOSE: I asked myself, "Why me?" I think, personally, it's because I'm for the independence of Puerto Rico. I've been an activist since I was fifteen years old, against the wishes of all my family members. On one occasion, the internal security people of Puerto Rico stopped me on the street to ask me how come I was going to certain meetings around the independence movement. With Puerto Rico being a colony, these people do answer to the FBI in one way or another.

William Webster himself, the FBI director, said that Puerto Rico was the Achilles' heel of the United States. And the FBI is very much aware of the Puerto Rican struggle. When my brother, who's in the military, transferred to Panama, the FBI talked to him about me. He said they knew where I lived, where I worked, where I traveled, where I'd spoken in public, who my friends were, the organizations I belonged to. I had been under surveillance a long time.

According to Varelli, the FBI had asked the manager for permission to go into my apartment. She refused. Then they went through the window. Varelli said he wasn't there, but he could describe what my apartment looked like from information that the agents—Flanagan and the other one—had given him. He talked about the posters and books and flags I had. What he described was correct. And the window was broken. It was down in the alley. I thought it was strange, because it was like someone took the pane out and couldn't put it back, and it had been knocked over from the ledge.

LINDA: Some things Varelli admitted doing were ridiculous. We had put out stationery and stamps for people to use to write letters to Congress. Varelli told me he stole those stamps. I asked, "Why did you do that?" He said, "You know, just to harass you." I said, "We put the stamps out there to be used. So if they were gone, I just thought that a few more letters got to Congress."

JOSE: One of the worst things Varelli did for the FBI was to communicate with the National Guard in El Salvador and tell them who from here was going down there. We believed that when people were deported by U.S. Immigration, they ran the risk of being killed in El Salvador. Varelli himself said that he thought some of those people he reported were killed.

LINDA: The FBI also infiltrated other CISPES chapters. Varelli said that he traveled all around the country, training other Salvadorans to do the same thing he had done. Finally the FBI dropped Varelli. The way they put it was: "The former asset of the Dallas Division primarily furnishing information re captioned organization (CISPES) is no longer in operation." Then they said: "Will increase efforts to penetrate the Dallas chapter of CISPES through the development of assets."[124]

More FBI informers! Instead of them having enough sense to say, "There's nothing here; let's leave," they kept pushing it. They kept talking about "We're going to break this CISPES chapter. We want to break this chapter." Varelli said that was the vocabulary the FBI used.

JOSE: It's what Varelli repeated all along, that they would break us, that they would break the opposition to Reagan's policy in Central America.

PART FOUR

Preserving the Right to Dissent

The Bureau of Investigation is not concerned with the political or other opinions of individuals. It is only concerned with their conduct and then only when such conduct is forbidden by the laws of the United States. When a police system passes beyond these limits, it is dangerous to the proper administration of justice and to human liberty, which it should be our first concern to cherish.

> *U.S. Attorney General Harlan Fiske Stone,*
> *on appointing J. Edgar Hoover acting director*
> *of the Bureau of Investigation, 1924*

No, we never gave it a thought.

> *Senate testimony of the former head*
> *of the FBI's Racial Intelligence Section,*
> *when asked whether, in the fifteen years*
> *of COINTELPRO's operation, anyone*
> *had ever discussed its constitutionality*
> *or legal authority, 1975*

On the night of March 8, 1971, when much of the nation was watching the Muhammad Ali–Joe Frazier fight, some unknown persons broke into a second-floor office in the Delaware County Building in Media, Pennsylvania. Inside, they rummaged through office files and left with more than a thousand pages of documents.

It was an audacious turning of the tables. The office burglarized was that of the FBI. The burglars, who were never found despite an intensive investigation, called themselves the Citizens Commission to Investigate the FBI. Throughout April and May, the Citizens Commission released batches of documents to the press and to others. To an African American congressman went J. Edgar Hoover's order to investigate all Black student unions; to the president of Swarthmore College went documents identifying the campus police chief, the secretary to the registrar, and a switchboard operator as FBI informants; to another congressman went information showing that his daughter had been the subject of FBI inquiries because of her "dovish" stand on Vietnam. One memorandum instructed agents to increase the number of interviews with New Left activists because "it will enhance the paranoia endemic in these circles and will further serve to get across the point that there is an FBI agent behind every mailbox."[1]

And, of great significance, one single-page memorandum was headed with a cryptic caption never before revealed publicly: "COINTELPRO." It was the first of thousands upon thousands of documents from this secret FBI counterintelligence program that would eventually be produced in the course of congressional investigations and court cases. The Senate Select Committee on Intelligence (the Church Committee) found in 1976 that, under COINTELPRO, the FBI had "conducted a sophisticated vigilante operation aimed squarely at preventing the exercise of First Amendment rights of free speech and associations."[2] COINTELPRO methods ranged from the disruptive to the illegal: misdirecting and defaming political activists, turning them against one another, inciting violence against them, and burglarizing their homes and offices.

Although the FBI officially discontinued COINTELPRO immediately after the Pennsylvania disclosures "for security reasons," when pressed by the Senate committee, the bureau acknowledged two new instances of "Cointelpro-type" operations.[3] The committee was left to discover a third, apparently illegal, operation on its own. Were there others? The senators could only conclude: "The Committee has not been able to determine with any greater precision the extent to which COINTELPRO may be continuing."[4]

Twelve years later, in 1988, the House Subcommittee on Civil and Constitutional Rights asked the General Accounting Office to review the bureau's international terrorism program for possible violations of civil liberties. The GAO discovered that the FBI did indeed monitor First Amendment–type activities; then it added, "Because of the limitations placed on access to its files, however, GAO cannot determine if the FBI abused individuals' First Amendment rights when it monitored these activities."[5] Indeed, from 1947 to 1989, the executive branch was successful in "severely restricting or even at times entirely withholding information from intelligence overseers."[6]

The problems epitomized by J. Edgar Hoover's "Do Not File" file, in which records of the FBI's own illegal activities were hidden until after his death, remain. Enforceable limits on the FBI and oversight to ensure the enforcement of these limits do not exist. Limits and guidelines set by attorneys general to control the bureau—virtually the only restraints under which it has operated—are neither permanent nor effective. At the same time Hoover assured senators that he endorsed Harlan Stone's 1924 admonition limiting the bureau to violations of federal law, he was secretly circumventing it. Earlier, in 1919, Attorney General A. Mitchell Palmer had disregarded his predecessor's promise to Congress to confine the bureau to investigating violations of federal laws and had directed Hoover to amass files on hundreds of thousands of persons, including radicals, social activists, and government officials. Later, in 1943, Hoover evaded Attorney General Francis Biddle's order to stop compiling a list of persons to be held in "custodial detention" in the event of a national "emergency." He simply renamed the list and secretly continued to place political activists on it.[7]

The problem persists after Hoover. As described in Part Three, FBI guidelines issued by Attorney General Edward Levi in 1976 in the wake of COINTELPRO revelations accorded civil liberties greater respect. But these guidelines were effectively undercut by Ronald Reagan, with an executive order and new "counterterrorism" guidelines, large parts of which are classified "secret." The result was hardly surprising: "The record before this court," Federal Magistrate Joan Lefkow stated in 1992, "shows that despite regulations, orders and consent decrees prohibiting such activities, the FBI had continued to collect information concerning only the exercise of free speech."[8]

It is true that legislative and judicial oversight as well as the Freedom of Information Act, which provides citizens with some access to FBI records, have resulted in significant benefits, revealing abuses and, in some cases, allowing redress. But oversight is variable, conditioned by the prevailing political climate and the disposition of the persons responsible and provides no assurance of access to FBI operations and records.[9] Some committee chairs and judges, for reasons of political affinity or political expediency, will not confront a recalcitrant bureau.[10] Those who do often find themselves hamstrung.[11]

For example, as Magistrate Lefkow noted, looking into the bureau's probe of CISPES, "ten individuals were investigated for reasons the FBI refuses to disclose."[12] The FBI's argument for refusing to provide the court with information about its other targets was ironic, the judge observed: The bureau claimed that it didn't want to violate the privacy of those it had spied on by revealing what had been learned. Judge Ann Claire Williams castigated the bureau for its "obstreperous conduct of spoon-feeding objections" that were "typical of the FBI" and for its "continued lack of candor to the court."[13] But even when oversight is at its best, how do the overseers gain access to incriminating files of which they have no prior knowledge? How, for example, could they have learned about COINTELPRO before the burglary in Media, Pennsylvania, uncovered it? Short of random leaks or inadvertent disclosures, no mechanism currently exists that can pierce the bureau's veil of secrecy.

A congressional charter for the FBI, proposed by the National Committee Against Repressive Legislation, was endorsed by 590 professors of law. Among other points, it limited "FBI investigations to situations where there are specific and articulable facts giving reason to believe that the person has committed, is committing, or is about to commit a specific act that violates federal law"; prohibited "investigations of groups because of their members' exercise of First Amendment rights"; prohibited "preventive or covert action by the FBI designed to disrupt or discredit organizations engaged in lawful political activity"; required "a warrant before the FBI may engage in the most intrusive investigative techniques"; and called for the "creation of an independent office with responsibility for auditing FBI investigations and, if necessary, prosecuting those who violate the law in connection with such investigations."[14] Essential elements of the proposal were introduced as an FBI charter bill, HR 50, by House Representatives Don Edwards and John Conyers Jr. four times between 1988 and 1994, without success. Legislation prohibiting the FBI from investigating activities protected by the First Amendment was eventually enacted as an amendment to a 1994 crime bill. A partial measure, it was nevertheless the first such congressional limitation in the FBI's history. Only two years later, however, at the insistence of the Clinton administration, that provision was eliminated in the Antiterrorism and Effective Death Penalty Act.

Holding repressive agents within the constraints of the Constitution has never come easily. It is true that some mechanisms that posed serious threats to constitutional rights are now, after years of use, by and large dormant: The use of sedition, espionage, or criminal syndicalism laws to prosecute persons exercising their First Amendment rights is no longer common; loyalty programs of state and federal governments have been abandoned or struck down by the courts; and congressional investigations of citizens' beliefs and associations, defied by opponents and discredited by their own inquisitorial methods, have fallen into disuse. But other repressive measures have persisted. Ideologically driven immigration laws, first inspired by a fear of anarchism in 1903 and then by a fear of Communism in 1952, are, in their latest manifestation in 1996, represented as a defense against terrorism. Under the Clinton administration's Antiterrorism and Effective Death Penalty Act, immigrants can be imprisoned and held for deportation based on secret evidence from anonymous accusers. Citizens can be imprisoned for supporting the humanitarian activities of foreign groups designated by the secretary of state as "terrorist." And the FBI, released from its short-lived prohibition against intruding on First Amendment rights, enjoys expanded investigatory power that, as James Dempsey and David Cole argue, "effectively authorizes FBI surveillance and infiltration of political, religious and ethnic groups engaged in peaceful humanitarian and political work."[15]

For much of the century, local secret police intelligence units, known as "red squads," have also been promiscuous with respect to targets and casual with respect to constitutional rights. The Maryland state senate committee that investigated the Baltimore police in 1975 said of the department's Inspectional Service Division: "The feeling seemed to prevail in the ISD that persons who deviated from the norm, who were outspoken or criticized the status quo, members of organized labor, picketers, and protesters, these people were 'potential threats' and society must be protected against them."[16] In response to the African American freedom struggle and the antiwar movement, especially, police in Philadelphia, Detroit, Chicago, New York, and Baltimore, to name only a few cities, kept files on hundreds of organizations. Los Angeles police could boast of a similar, ecumenical collection of dossiers, thousands of pages of which they shared with an ultraright-wing group.[17] In those cities and in New Haven, Seattle, Memphis, Washington, D.C., and elsewhere, red squads were refurbished for the 1960s with new, more euphemistic titles, more hostile tactics, and more sophisticated technologies. More than collectors of gargantuan secret files, these units employed aggressive methods that were intended to intimidate, provoke, and disrupt.

Accounts of abuses by the Chicago red squad are particularly instructive beyond demonstrating the multiplicity and durability of repressive agents and the broad-gauged targeting of hundreds of legal organizations and thousands of persons who committed no crime. Because the Chicago police were severely set back in their ability to spy on and disrupt constitutionally protected activities, these accounts make the point that victories over formidable repressive forces are possible. Indeed, restrictions on police surveillance of legal political activities were also won in New York, Washington, D.C., Detroit, Los Angeles, and Seattle.

A Notable Reversal

HOLDING THE CHICAGO RED SQUAD ACCOUNTABLE

On March 20, 1975, the *Chicago Daily News* reported in a front-page story that police spies had infiltrated civic groups. That information was given to the *Daily News* by the Alliance to End Repression, a civil liberties group in Chicago. The investigative work of the Alliance, itself a police target, laid bare the expansive reach of Chicago police into the political life of the city so clearly that it led directly to the dismantling of the red squad in 1975. This represented a reversal of the surge in local police political intelligence operations of the 1960s—indeed, a historic reversal of a century of covert operations.

In addition, in 1982 the work of the Alliance won protections in court against future repressive activity by Chicago police, the FBI, the CIA, and Military Intelligence. Chicago police were prohibited not only from disrupting but also from spying on the political activities of the city's citizens. The police were required to make information in their files available, fully and without restrictions, to an independent auditing firm that would periodically monitor their adherence to the court's requirements and report publicly on its findings. Violations, if found, carried the sanction of contempt of court. By compelling the Chicago police to abide by the terms of this consent decree, the federal district court attempted to provide significant protections for Chicago's citizens, the very protections that are not available at the national level.

Telling the story of the Chicago effort to keep police surveillance within constitutional bounds are Richard (Rick) Gutman, attorney for the Alliance to End Repression; John Hill, the executive coordinator of the Alliance; Jack Spiegel, co-chair of the Chicago Peace Council; Janet Nolan, a witness in a lawsuit against the Chicago red squad; and Father Donald Headley, a witness to police provocation.

CHICAGO RED SQUAD TARGETS:
RICHARD (RICK) GUTMAN, JOHN HILL, JACK SPIEGEL,
JANET NOLAN, AND FATHER DONALD HEADLEY

RICK GUTMAN: The Alliance to End Repression was a coalition of several scores of religious and community groups that dealt with violations of civil liberties in Chicago. What sparked its formation was the assassination of Mark Clark and Fred Hampton in late 1969.[*] That pushed things to the point where people said, "We've got to do something." And it did seem like more political repression was occurring then, locally and in the rest of the country. The executive coordinator of the Alliance was John Hill, a priest who had organized the first union of priests in Chicago.

JOHN HILL: The slaying of the two Panther leaders was like the ultimate in repression. This really got a lot of people off the fence. Even the Chicago Bar Association, which was as much a part of the establishment as you can find, called for an investigation. And we did. We went out and got about seventy groups, block clubs and all kinds of organizations, to write a petition. That's when the Alliance to End Repression got started.

We moved into our office on April 1, 1970. We decided we were going to attack repression wherever it was. There were so many wrongs that needed to be righted. We had a lot of people with a religious background. There were Catholics. There were Protestant housewives who had been visiting inmates in prisons for fifteen years. There were tiny organizations that had popped up all over, either having to do with prisons or with bail reform or with the rights of welfare mothers. And we became the place they could gravitate toward.

What had motivated me in this direction was that a few years earlier I had been the organizer and founding chairman of the Association of

---

[*]These police killings are described in "The Assault on the Black Panther Party: The Murder of Fred Hampton," pages 221–249.

RICHARD (RICK) GUTMAN

Chicago Priests. We wanted to have something to say about bread-and-butter issues and our careers: how we were assigned to parishes, how we operated, and our retirement. We wanted to have an elected personnel board. But we had an adamant archbishop, John Cody, who told me that under no circumstances would there be one.

Well, we got thirteen hundred priests together at Mahomick Place for a constitutional convention. That was of historic importance, the first independent association of priests within the Roman Catholic Church. We went into a meeting with Cody—by then a cardinal—a few days later.

JOHN HILL

This time, he asked me, "Can you give me two weeks to set up the machinery for the election of a personnel board?" At that point, I could be gracious. I said, "Take three."

I walked away from that meeting and thought, "My God!" I felt the blood coursing through me in ways it never did before. It was very heady. We had been a handful of priests who got together two or three times a week and used our common sense. Then I began to realize that all you needed was a handful of people with normal intelligence and experience. If you were steadfast and continued to meet; if you were flexible, able to say, "That one will never work"; and if you were sufficiently courageous—but more than anything else, if you were persistent—you would be able to answer most of the social problems confronting the community. So I had this feeling right in my gut that it was possible to make a change.

I had been a priest for twenty years, and I was marinated in ideology. What the sixties meant to me was a time to leave that aside and to be pragmatic. I think all of us in the Alliance had that kind of pragmatic sense. We were a group of liberals with a radical name and a conservative style. From the very beginning, we realized we would not be a street organization.

RICK: The Alliance worked within the system quietly to get results. It was: "We have repression in the city. What can we do to decrease it?" They tried to reform the criminal justice system.

JOHN: The bail project was just one of several. There were a hundred people at our first organizational meeting, the most colorful I had ever been at. We had Black Panther Party members. Black street gangs were represented. We had gay and lesbian people. Then there were nuns and priests and the religious laypeople. It was a really disparate group, but they all wanted to do something about the right to bail, which the Bill of Rights assures us we have.

Illinois law encouraged judges to depend on recognizance bonds. It said that what you rely on to get somebody to trial is not a threat of forfeiture of bail money but a threat that you would prosecute that person for not showing up in court. Judges weren't following that.

So we went to see Chief Judge Boyle. A great big American flag that had flown over the Capitol building in Washington covered his entire wall. He stood at the dais, about six foot four, a very imperious presence. He said, "What right do you people have to meddle with my courts?" Four years earlier, Cardinal Cody had asked me, when we talked about an elected personnel board, "What right have you to meddle with my church?" Anyway, Boyle said there were no circumstances under which he would agree to our plan for bail reform.

Most arrests took place on Friday and Saturday nights. The police made sweep arrests, ending up with several hundred prisoners. We decided to go to the bail hearings and time them. Some lasted only four seconds. Once, before the prisoner even got to the bench, the judge said, "Two hundred dollars." We wrote everything down and summed it up in a four- or five-page report. We called a press conference and said that it was like a debtor's prison, that the place was built for twelve hundred and there were nineteen hundred in there. Of those inmates, eighteen hundred and fifty hadn't been found guilty of anything; they were awaiting trial. This made the papers—not the front page, but people wrote articles on our report.

When we called to see Judge Boyle again, his secretary said he was going on a long lunch. We were getting this answer every day. Finally we decided to go where he lunched. Forty-three of us paraded right into the lobby of the Sherman Hotel. The judge sent word out that we could meet with a deputy of his. That afternoon about four o'clock, the deputy called back and said, "Judge Boyle said okay to the bail plan." He caved in the way Cody had caved in.

So we went into court with our three hundred volunteers, about thirty at a time, to interview prisoners. You had to work fast because they had three courts with hundreds of defendants going through there in about two hours. Somebody got the information about residence, employment prospects, and community ties from the detainee. Another person would be on the phone to verify the information. It had to be run back in time to feed it to a volunteer lawyer, who could then say, "Your honor, this prisoner is likely to return for his trial. We have verified that he belongs to this church, that he has worked part time at such and such a place a number of years, and that he's got his family here." A lot of reasonable judges were just looking for information like that. Recognizance bonds went way up, and the population of the jail went way down.

We formed a prison visitation group. We got twenty organizations to support the idea of having citizens conduct unmonitored inspections of state prisons. We met with Peter Benziger, head of the Department of Corrections in Illinois. Our first attempt to see people was always successful because it was just to gather information. Then once you get there, you're for real. It's like the little puppy you thought you could handle; now he's biting your ankle.

Benziger said there was no way he would meet with us again. He vented his spleen in a sarcastic and condescending letter: "These are my prisons, and I'll take care of them." So we wrote to the governor: "Is this the kind of director of the Department of Corrections we have? He refuses to meet with us. He impugns our credibility. We pay taxes, and we are not going to have this." You know, just hard-nosed. Well, Benziger finally caved in: "I'm not saying it's going to work very well, but I'll go along with you." Illinois became the only place in the United States where citizens could go into the prisons, and the guards would have to take them where they wanted to go.

There was a pattern to this process of change. If you could apply it to other things, you could replicate your successes. And we did, to a considerable extent. It kept increasing the size of our organization. After several years, we had about a hundred and fifty board members at our meetings. The bail board alone had twenty-two directors. The steering committee had between sixteen and eighteen. There were people representing the prisons group, a citizens committee on the media, and Citizens Alert, which dealt with police matters.

Citizens Alert had two main focuses. One was discrimination in police hiring. In 1972, only seven percent of those entering the police training academy were Black, while thirty-eight percent of the people in Chicago were Black. The result was that these heavily congested Black areas were patrolled by white police officers. It was like the apartheid system in South Africa. We filed a lawsuit that eventually changed the gender and racial composition of the Chicago police department. Our other focus dealt with the red squad.

RICK: "Red squad" is the colloquial name for the Subversive Activities Unit of the Chicago Police Intelligence Division. The police had an intelligence unit that gathered information on criminal activity: vice, organized crime. But the Subversive Activities Unit was separate. It gathered intelligence exclusively on lawful political activity, on people who weren't breaking the law.

There was a red squad cop in the Chicago police department in the 1890s. They were targeting anarchists then. In the 1920s, the major targets were labor unions. Later it was Communists. They expanded as time went on. In the 1960s, they included civil rights and antiwar groups. The red squad acted like any other secret police. They'd find out who was dissenting. If a group was considered a threat to the status quo, they'd try to destroy it, directly or indirectly. Because it was such a blatant violation of the First Amendment to have a unit that did nothing but harass citizens and spy on their political activities, the Alliance decided that the best thing to do was to file a lawsuit.

JOHN: We filed suit against the city in November of '74. We had a press conference in the lobby of the federal building. It was treated with benign neglect; tiny news notices appeared. I guess people didn't think it was destined to go anyplace. The history of lawsuits like this had been very poor because the judicial branch was not about to interfere with the judgment of the executive branch when they claimed "national security" was at stake.

RICK: One of the reasons I got involved in the suit was that few other lawyers wanted to. It was considered a high-risk case because in 1972 there had been a Supreme Court ruling in *Laird v. Tatum,* which said that mere spying doesn't create grounds for a lawsuit. My first job out of law school at the end of 1973 was with the Illinois American Civil Liberties Union on a one-year project. While I was there, Alliance lawyer Val Klink came to the ACLU for assistance in preparing the complaint for filing. Later, at a board meeting, the legal director reported that he hadn't been able to find any lawyer to supervise the lawsuit. There was a long silence. Finally, one board member, Lance Haddix, agreed to work on the case, but he also had a private practice. Nobody else wanted to get involved. So I picked up the ball and ran with it.

I'd rather have this than any other kind of case I can think of. I didn't become a lawyer to practice law as an end in itself. I became a lawyer because that was the way I saw myself participating politically. I had always been interested in politics. I was active in the antiwar movement. I thought about myself and what my capabilities were. I had organized in the Peace Corps and concluded that I was not an organizer. And I am not a leader-type individual. I decided that I could best contribute as a lawyer. When I learned of this case, I knew how important it was. A unit of government whose purpose is political repression, that does nothing but target lawful political dissent—to me, that's an extremely important type of litigation. It's something that affects all political groups, everyone.

So I went to John Hill and said, "I'd like to work on this case full time for the Alliance to End Repression." He said, "Well, we can't pay you anything, but we can give you a table over there." They had this really big room, and I worked at a table in the corner. I didn't get a telephone till three or four months later.

Anyway, I rewrote the complaint and filed it with the assistance of Klink and Haddix. We included a general allegation like "The red squad engages in harassment." Then we'd give specific dates, times, and places. At antiwar rallies, the red squad would openly harass people. They would take pictures. They would banter with the demonstrators on a first-name basis, using information they had about their personal lives: "Hi, Fred, how's your daughter? Heard she couldn't get a job she wanted." It was very intimidating, an attempt to discourage people from demonstrating.

The red squad would also funnel derogatory information to the media. Articles would appear smearing people and organizations by emphasizing "Communist associations." There was a conference on nonviolent civil disobedience that several groups sponsored, including the American Friends Service Committee and the Chicago Peace Council. They used a retreat administered by the Catholic Church. The red squad brought a team of photographers to film the people coming in and out, which was by itself intimidating. They also brought along a reporter from the *Tribune*, Ron Koziol, and fed him material. Then he wrote an article about "radicals" and "Communists" using church property for a "secret revolutionary planning session."[18]

We had a number of other allegations in the complaint. The red squad had broken into the offices and stolen all the files of the Chicago Peace Council, the Women for Peace, and the Fellowship of Reconciliation. John Valkenburg, a red squad cop, later explained at his deposition why they did it. I asked, "What was taken from the offices at 1608 West Madison?" He said, "Mimeograph, typewriters, stamps, money, membership files." "Why did you take office equipment?" "Well," he answered, "the best way to destroy the left would be to destroy their press or their publications."[19]

JOHN: One of the complaints was about my wedding. I was married in Evansville, Indiana, on March 3, 1973. The Episcopal priest who performed the ceremony later told me, "I received a call from the county clerk down here. She wanted the names of everyone at the wedding." When he asked her why she needed that information, she said, "I got a call from an Evansville detective saying they would like to know." The priest called to find out what this was about, and the detective said, "We're simply honoring a request from the Chicago police department." Chicago police were spying on my wedding!

RICK: At first, there wasn't too much to do in court because the city had made a motion to dismiss the suit, and the judge had frozen all discovery. So I was trying to figure out other ways to expose the red squad. It was crucial to get access to more information to show how broad their targeting was. The first major breakthrough came as a result of my being an attorney in an employment discrimination lawsuit against the Chicago police department. I had intervened on behalf of females. As part of discovery, the city had to produce a list of all the police in order to determine whether there was discrimination. It was a payroll list that had the officers by name, race, sex, disciplinary actions, unit, and assignment. There was a classification "Assignment Unknown." I thought that was a little strange. Why would the police department not know their own officers' assignments?

Eight names were in that category. I knew two of them immediately. One was Howard Pointer, a leader in Operation PUSH. He had come forward voluntarily a couple of weeks after we filed suit and confessed to Jesse Jackson that he was a red squad cop. There was very little publicity at the time, probably because he was spying on Blacks. I recognized another name, Geno Addams. He was active in the Alliance to End Repression. People all along had suspected he was a police spy, but they couldn't prove it. And there was his name on the police payroll.

JOHN: Geno Addams had been involved with us from day one. All along, we thought he was a police officer. I mean, he wasn't for real. Most people went to meetings out of a sense of moral obligation. There was a kind of irritability we all had. We didn't want anybody making long speeches. You'd look around the table, and there would be one person who wasn't irritable. If we needed volunteers for a subcommittee to get a job done, there'd be a chorus of nos. We'd only do it out of commitment. Then you'd hear that person eagerly say, "I'll do it." And no matter what was said, he thought it was a good idea. I mean, he had to be a police spy.

RICK: I thought there had to be something relevant to the other names in the "Assignment Unknown" category. So I went around with the list. First I went to left-wing groups, but nobody recognized the names. I started going to nonleft groups. I went to Citizens Action Program. CAP was a mainly white, lower-middle-class group trying to get people involved in issues like housing and Social Security. Somebody from their staff looked at the names and recognized Melvin Barna as head of the Garfield Ridge chapter of CAP. Then I showed the list to a guy named Milt Cohen. He said, "That can't be the same Marcus Salone I know. The Marc Salone I know is president of Organization for a Better Austin." Salone was its first Black president. He was also very involved in the Metropolitan Area Housing Association.

That made four red squad police who had infiltrated community groups: Marcus Salone in OBA and MAHA, Melvin Barna in CAP, Geno Addams in the Alliance, and Howard Pointer in Operation PUSH. I met with John Hill, and we decided to expose them by giving an exclusive to one newspaper. On March 20, 1975, the *Chicago Daily News* had a banner headline: "Bare Police Spying on Five Civic Groups." It went on for a week, banner headlines in all the Chicago papers.

A group from CAP immediately went down to police headquarters to confront them. They were really angry: "You'd be well advised to take police out of community groups that are working to better life for Chicagoans and put those police on the street to fight crime." The Republican state's attorney, Bernard Carey, recognized Marc Salone's picture in the *Daily News*. Salone had led a demonstration at Carey's house. Carey was furious when he found out Salone was really a full-time police officer. He thought Mayor Daley was using this cop to direct the group against him. That very day, he convened the Cook County grand jury to investigate the whole red squad thing. But I don't think Carey would have done it if he didn't think he had personally been a target.

The real significance of this exposure, the reason this got banner headlines and the filing of our suit didn't, was that the mass media—and, I think, the courts and the state's attorney—were much more responsive to information about spying on so-called mainstream individuals and organizations. The Socialist Workers Party was frequently burglarized by the federal government, but it wasn't until the Democratic Party was burglarized that President Nixon got in trouble. It was the same way here. There is always a double standard. When radical or Black groups are being spied on, the media really doesn't care too much. They think: "It's probably good that the government watches them." But when it's mainly white mainstream-type groups, all hell breaks loose.

Just a few days after our exposure of police spying, it was revealed that a right-wing terrorist group, the Legion of Justice, had worked closely with the red squad. The Legion of Justice was a paramilitary organization led by a guy named Thomas Sutton, who had previously worked against Blacks moving into white neighborhoods. The group had been formed in the late sixties to fight "Communist infiltration" in the Chicago area. Their tactics were violence and threats of violence.

Then a couple of members of the Legion confessed to a whole range of terrorist activities. They had tried to talk to the newspapers even before our suit was filed, but nobody would listen. After our exposures came out, the *Daily News* printed it. They told of such things as the Legion sending death threats to people, breaking into the offices of left-wing groups to steal their files, and physically attacking people at demonstrations. They threw tear gas grenades during performances of the Soviet Moiseyev Dance Company and a Chinese acrobatic troupe.

Instead of arresting Legion people, the Chicago police department worked closely with them. They had the same goals and the same targets. If the red squad wanted the files of some group, they sometimes would arrange it so the Legion of Justice would do the break-in and steal the files for them. The red squad would be parked out front during those burglaries, to cover and protect them. If the regular police came, they were told: "This is a police operation. You can leave."

After the exposures, the red squad was abolished voluntarily. It had been completely discredited. All these things kept the headlines going through April and May. The judge in our case still hadn't ruled on the city's motion to dismiss our lawsuit. We were concerned because he had been close to Mayor Richard Daley since childhood. They had grown up in the same neighborhood; they had been partners in the same law firm; Daley had helped get him his job as a federal judge. But with the headlines revealing red squad illegal activities and the grand jury investigation, it would have looked like a cover-up if our suit had been dismissed. We got an incredibly good ruling, totally affirming our entire complaint.

On July 11, 1975, the Senate Internal Security Subcommittee held hearings in Washington, D.C. They were closed executive sessions on the so-called nationwide drive against law enforcement intelligence operations. The Chicago superintendent of police, his deputy, and informers who had infiltrated the Alliance testified. Then in November of 1975, the Cook County grand jury came out with a very damning report. It said, "The evidence has clearly shown that the Security Section of the Chicago Police Department assaulted the fundamental freedoms of speech, association, press and religion, as well as the constitutional right to privacy of hundreds of individuals."[20]

JOHN: The police came to realize that their effort to defend themselves had to be more than just legal. They had to try to discredit everything we said, even though it had been documented.

RICK: Two months later, the Senate Internal Security Subcommittee released a press statement summarizing its hearings. They tried to change the issue: "Let's not talk about how the red squad broke the law or violated the Constitution; let's talk about Communism." It was just bullshit—half-truths, distortions, and some whole fabrications. They said they had proved two theses: first, that our lawsuit had virtually destroyed the police department's entire intelligence capability. Well, it may have affected their *political* intelligence capability, but it had no effect on their *criminal* intelligence capability.

JOHN: They made it look as though we were against the common good, because we somehow or other had deviously kept the police from using the intelligence they needed in order to save people from being bombed to smithereens by terrorists.

RICK: Their second thesis was that the Alliance was a Communist-front group.

JOHN: I guess the best answer to that is, "So what?" But we simply were not. And, politically, we had to answer that we were not. But that is the thing that made the papers when the Senate committee finally came out with their report.

RICK: Normally, when a newspaper reported on something like a Senate press statement, it would just give the government's version, period. This time, they called us up and asked, "What's your side?" And they printed it. The *Sun-Times* had an article on Senator Charles Percy's response: "The dangerous subversive threat to our way of life is not the Alliance to End Repression, but widespread illegal police surveillance," Percy said. "The guilt-by-association and 'Communist-front' allusions contained in the release accompanying the document hearken back to the smear tactics of the 1950s."[21]

The hearings were an effort to destroy the lawsuit. I'm sure they did some damage to us, but not nearly as much as they would have liked. If this had happened in 1966, I think it would have destroyed the suit and the Alliance. But this was 1976, shortly after Watergate and after the exposure of COINTELPRO by the Church Committee. And we had already discredited the red squad.

When we got the police payroll list with "Assignment Unknown" on it, that was our first big break. The next one was when we won access to all the files of the red squad in entirely undeleted form. We had made a motion to get the files for all the named plaintiffs. They produced the files but deleted the hell out of them. We said there were no grounds for these deletions, but the magistrate upheld every one. When we appealed to the district court judge, he ruled in our favor. They had to produce them uncensored. There were thirty-three named plaintiffs, but since we were certified as a class action suit, we got the files on everybody.

Some files had already been destroyed. When we first exposed the red squad infiltrators, the media called the police department to get their response. Superintendent James Rochford said: "That's just a bunch of old stuff. We're actively purging all irrelevant materials from the files." We immediately went into court and got an order forbidding them to destroy anything else. When we did discovery, we asked, "What did you purge?" They gave us the list of the material destroyed. It looked like they had purged all the files from the 1920s, '30s, '40s, and '50s. The red squad had deleted their files on thirteen hundred organizations and more than a hundred thousand individuals!

But the amazing thing is all the reports they kept. They must have thought they would win the suit, and then they could continue doing what they had been doing. Their lawyers probably told them that there was a Supreme Court case that said there's nothing illegal about keeping files. And before the mid-1970s there had never been a period where the contents of red squad records were exposed.

On March 26, 1976, we won the right to go into the red squad file room and copy anything on anyone. When we went through their file cabinets, the thing that especially struck us was how promiscuous they were. I mean, files on the PTA, the League of Women Voters, the Catholic Interracial Council, any kind of liberal or moderate group like the Chicago Council on Foreign Relations. Hundreds of thousands of pages were there. It was just incredible.

And when you read their stuff, you see how ultraright-wing they are. I'm not saying they're all members of the John Birch Society, but they basically have that mentality. They don't believe in democracy. They don't believe in the First Amendment; they think it's a threat to national security. They think racial integration, modern art, extending the franchise—all of these are part of the "international Communist conspiracy." That's how they train their people.

There was a red squad memo about the Black Strategy Center. The Black Strategy Center was set up by the big corporations after the rioting following the assassination of Martin Luther King. It was established by corporate executives like Gaylord Freeman of the First National Bank and Arthur Wood of Sears, Roebuck and Company. The red squad thought this was a Communist plot, that they were planning a "political and/or social revolution in the United States."[22]

After we obtained access to the files, we wanted the right to show all these reports to the people who were spied on. The Chicago police fought it tooth and nail, but they lost. Then we won the right to let people give the police reports about themselves to the media. We then generated numerous newspaper articles exposing the specifics of the police spying.

One red squad spy who had infiltrated the Alliance to End Repression was David Cushing. A document we uncovered was a report on the Alliance, prepared for the police by Cushing. He talked about all the strengths of the Alliance. And with unintended flattery, he compared the red squad to King George and the British, while likening the Alliance to George Washington and the colonials. Cushing was active on the board of the Alliance's Cook County special bail project and on the steering committee of the Alliance. At one of the meetings, Val Klink said that he was about ready to file the lawsuit. Dave Cushing reported that to the red squad. Cushing warned: "The people in authority better do what they have to do, because pretty soon it's going to be too late." Shortly after that was when they started purging their files.

JOHN: Dave Cushing was the preeminent police spy in our organization. It was probably the safest police assignment you could have. He was working with people who didn't have guns, who didn't believe in violence. And he even felt socially useful in the bail project. It kind of salved his conscience for the undercover work that he was doing. After Rick uncovered him, I found out that he had a job in security at the University of Illinois, so I called and asked to talk with him. I was told, "He's not here. He's graduating from the police academy today."

You find yourself asking questions you never had to ask before like, "How do you confront a police spy?" I decided to go to his graduation with an Alliance volunteer from the North Shore, Mary Powers. It was like something out of the '50s. She wore white gloves. We looked just like parents at a graduation. And we chuckled when some bigwig spoke: "People think there's a lot of glamour in being a police officer. Let me tell you, this is not Hawaii Five-O." As far as Mary and I were concerned, it was. Here we were, about to confront a police spy at his graduation.

Cushing finally came down the aisle, and we went up to him. We said, "Hi." He said, "Oh, hi." I said, "I see you're a police officer." But he didn't admit a thing. It was just like a general denial and "I'm in a hurry now."

RICK: In the red squad files on the Alliance, we saw many reports on our legal preparations. When the Alliance first thought of suing, Val Klink asked for volunteers to help prepare the case. He made up a questionnaire to be used in interviewing people to see if they would be plaintiffs. Adele Noren volunteered to help find potential plaintiffs. She was on the executive committee of the Alliance as a paid informer of the red squad. Every time she questioned someone, she'd give a copy of it to the police. When we got access to their files, there were the reports of the people she had interviewed.

JOHN: Here a police spy was asking people about their experiences of being spied on. That's unconscionable. It's as close to infiltration of a legal team as you can get, other than to have a police spy be our lawyer.

I had known Adele Noren very well. She was the representative to the Alliance from the United Methodist Church. Adele was active in Citizens Alert. When we found out about her, I got a staff person to come with me to one of the meetings as a witness, and we went up to her. I said, "Adele, I've got thirty-seven reports in this bulging pocket that seem to imply you are a police spy." She denied it. I said, "Why don't you come down to the office, and I'll spread them out for you to see if anything rings a bell, because if you're not the spy, we'd like to know who is." That was the last time I ever saw Adele.

RICK: We had considerable evidence that Adele Noren had infiltrated our legal team and that Dave Cushing had gathered information on our lawsuit. There had been very few injunctions against police spying up to then. We saw this as an opportunity to get our foot in the door, because, to a judge, spying on legal preparations is the most egregious kind of spying. We were able to get a ruling against it. The Chicago police then appealed to the Seventh Circuit Court of Appeals and lost. Unfortunately, the judge's ruling was very narrow. He just said, "Under the rules of procedure, if you want some information in a lawsuit, you have to file a request. You can't just send somebody into the organization to spy on them." He didn't even deal with the First Amendment.

But the city appealed to the Supreme Court, where certiorari was denied. Their absolutist position totally discredited them. They could have said, "We are not going to do it again." Their position wasn't even "We can spy on criminal activity," or "We can spy on people planning to overthrow the government." Instead they insisted: "We can spy on anybody we want for any reason we want, including the other side in a lawsuit."

The public thought this was crazy. The *Sun-Times* said: "Barefaced and shamelessly, the city has taken the whole dishonorable project to heights of absurdity few would have imagined possible. . . . The Red Squad's disgraceful history already involves burglarizing the homes and offices of law-abiding citizens, illegal eavesdropping and the use of agents-provocateurs to incite violence."[23]

People usually assume that those being spied on deserve it. "Why would the police be involved with them?" You know, "Where there's smoke, there's fire." "They must be subversives or something." But when people find that they themselves are spied on, they're outraged. They feel their privacy has been violated. You see that again and again. When we showed there was spying on state legislators, all of a sudden they got hysterical. And they were sincere. When you are the target, you feel a personal reaction you don't get otherwise. I remember when I first saw a report with my name on it, there was an anger I never felt before.

If the spy is someone you know, a friend, then it's even worse. That's what happened to someone in the Chicago Peace Council, one of the chief targets of the red squad. The Peace Council coordinated and organized the major demonstrations against the Vietnam war.

JACK SPIEGEL: We had had marches against nuclear testing and military spending, but it wasn't until 1965, with the escalation of the Vietnam war, that the Chicago Peace Council was officially organized. Sid Lens and a number of other peace activists were involved. It was formed

JACK SPIEGEL

as an umbrella organization. Within a year, we had as many as thirty affiliates: antiwar activists, pacifists, radicals, trade unionists, women's groups, and some church organizations.

We had a very successful operation because we were able to compromise and negotiate differences. We did lobbying work, saw members of congress and state legislators. We were able to organize a number of labor conferences. And we involved intellectuals like Erich Fromm and trade union leaders Emil Mazey of the UAW and Frank Rosenbaum of the Amalgamated Clothing Workers.

There were two co-chairs. One was Carl Meyer, the son of a congressman in Vermont. The other was me. I was director of the Shoe Workers Union in the Midwest then and had come out of a radical background. Even though I had a major responsibility to my full-time union job, I gave many evenings and weekends to help build the Peace Council.

The council became the coordinating body of all the peace groups in the city. When we first had marches and rallies against the war, none of them were bigger than a thousand, fifteen hundred. But then in March 1967, Martin Luther King Jr. agreed to come to Chicago. We had a big rally, and eight thousand people marched down State Street. That was a major event. It gave the antiwar movement a new dimension because it linked up the civil rights and peace movements. It was the spark that really got us going here. Then we affiliated with the Mobilization Against the War in Vietnam

In April of '68, we organized a demonstration against the war. While leaders of the movement made assurances to the city administration that it was going to be a peaceful march, the police let go with their clubs, and a lot of innocent people had their heads smashed. It was really a small-scale massacre.

Then Mayor Daley went bananas when he heard that people were coming here to demonstrate during the Democratic Convention in August. The Chicago Peace Council became the coordinating body for many of the participating groups. We had assured the Daley administration that we were not out to disrupt the convention. But Daley was intent on showing his power. We never anticipated all that violence. Over six hundred people were arrested. Day and night we were engaged in raising money for bail. Some of us didn't have more than two, three hours' sleep during that period.

As the Peace Council developed, the red squad sent in a number of police agents. At that time, we weren't too suspicious. We felt that people who came in were sincerely dedicated against the war, just like we were. And we were a little bit naive. Besides, you just can't distrust people and still be able to do what you want to do. I mean, you can get immobilized. We were too busy running the leaflets and passing out handbills and picketing and going to jail and getting bail for people who got in jail. But things started unraveling, and we began getting one piece of information after another.

Some agents were sent in to instigate violence. Others were much more low-key, just there to listen and report to the police. Michael Randy said he was a veteran and was disenchanted with the war. He volunteered to work in the Peace Council. He knew carpentry and actually redid the floor of our office, a very good job. Later on, we found out that he was really a policeman and had planted some electronics in there.

Another instance shows how disruptive some of these agents were. There was an organization, the Chicago Area Draft Resisters, CADRE. They would counsel young people about the draft and tell them their rights. CADRE was an affiliate of the Chicago Peace Council, so whenever they had meetings, officers of the council would attend. Police infiltrated CADRE. At one of the meetings, Morton Frankin, a red squad spy, proposed that all the adults sign a statement saying that we would do everything possible to aid and abet draft resistance. On the face of it, it was illegal.

So there I was with Max Primack, co-chair of the Peace Council at that time. And there was Frankin, challenging us and being supported by half a dozen young draft resisters. They attacked us as being cowards. And it was quite an effort to get across that this was going to play into the hands of the government and could involve us in legal matters, which would not be helpful. So the role of the infiltrators was to mislead people, especially young people, and try to create a division within the peace movement.

John Valkenburg, another policeman, operated on the South Side, in Hyde Park. He was chairman of the Citizens for a Democratic Society. He was very presentable: tall, blond, Germanic-looking, handsome, and persuasive. He advocated that some of the people in the peace movement get up on the roof, to actually fire at the police! Frankin also advocated that when police attack us, we should fight back. And for young people who were new in the movement, this was not such an unnatural thing. They knew the police in many instances were brutal at demonstrations. In Chicago, they were particularly brutal. They felt, "Well, if they're going to beat us up, what's wrong with getting back at them?" without realizing that this could destroy the movement. But people were there who knew this would play into the hands of the police. So while Valkenburg and Frankin kept advocating violence, it never became the position of the organization to engage in it.

In June or July of 1967, the office of the Chicago Peace Council was burglarized and vandalized. We came in one day and found things broken up and everything gone: our files, typewriters. They took our mailing lists. They took everything they were able to get hold of. And they tried to mislead us. They wrote something on the wall to make it appear like it was a Black radical group that actually invaded. This was a real provocation.

A couple of weeks later, Sid Lens got a call in the middle of the night from a man who told him where he could find the stuff. We found the typewriter and the xerox machine, but not the money or the records. Later on, we got some inside information. Two people from the police department, who were very dissatisfied on the force, got in touch with Sid Lens. They told him who broke in. Michael Randy had the key, and he let Valkenburg and the others inside.

One of the police spies, Irwin Bock, sat on the executive board of the Chicago Peace Council as a representative of the Vietnam veterans. He was not provocative like Valkenburg or Frankin. We became suspicious of him because he always had a pad and pencil and marked down everything that was taking place. But mainly it was that we weren't able to nail down where he came from, how he made a living. At the Chicago conspiracy trial, he came out and told a bunch of lies, that we were going to attack the Democratic Convention. This police agent claimed that at meetings where we discussed demonstrations, we also proposed violent action against the police. Well, there were people who made speeches like that, but they were made by police provocateurs like Valkenburg and Frankin.

RICK: One of the paid informers we exposed was Sheli Lulkin. She infiltrated the Chicago Peace Council. The executive secretary of the Peace Council was Sylvia Kushner. Sheli Lulkin became Sylvia's best friend. She'd go everywhere with Sylvia. And all the while Sheli was sending in reports.

JACK: She was the spy that hurt me the most because I was closest to her. Sheli Lulkin was a hard worker, a very capable person. She always volunteered to do the typing, mimeographing, filing of lists, compiling names of personalities and trade union and church people. Later on, we found out that all these lists went to the red squad. And she made personal friends with Sylvia Kushner, our executive secretary. Sylvia was not in a good position financially; we couldn't pay her very much. And Sheli was easy with money. She treated Sylvia to concerts and operas. They would go out together, stay in each other's homes. They became bosom friends.

RICK: When I told Sylvia that Sheli Lulkin was really a red squad informant, she could not accept it. She argued with us: "No, you don't know what you're talking about. She's not a police spy." But we had reports with extensive personal information about Sylvia. There was information in there that you couldn't have gotten even if you had tailed Sylvia, things like "On June 4, Sylvia Kushner went into her house and found three pieces of mail. Two of the letters concerned so-and-so." It was very clear that it was coming from somebody who was walking around with her. But Sylvia couldn't believe it because Sheli was her best friend. It's like finding out your spouse is spying on you.

Sheli Lulkin was a big wheel. She was co-chairperson of the American Federation of Teachers' committee on women's rights for the whole country. She had joined all kinds of groups. When we finally took Sheli's deposition, she listed eighty-six organizations she had gathered intelligence on. In June of 1968, a blue ribbon committee was appointed to investigate a police attack on a peaceful, lawful demonstration. Sheli, the police spy, became the recording secretary. The red squad had copies of the drafts of all the reports by this blue ribbon commission.

JACK: It was a rough period. Some of these agents became leaders of the movement. Joyce Stover was secretary-treasurer of the Peace Council. She was a plant. Irwin Bock was on the Peace Council. Michael Randy was part of the Peace Council. Sheli Lulkin attached herself to Sylvia. There were the provocateurs like Frankin and Valkenburg who tried to instigate violence. And there were others like William Frapolly who proposed sabotaging police cars and public facilities.

Everybody who honestly came to the meetings and heard our position knew we were merely advocating peace in Vietnam. Yet the government attempted to detour our program and to direct it in a way that was contrary to our basic policy. It tried to make the Peace Council out to be a violent organization. It presented a wrong perception of our aims and of our individual integrity. There's no question that this was a planned decision by the government.

And there's no question there was a lot of demoralization. There was a lot of fear. Many people fell away. Some of them felt that by being there they could get hurt. Their names, maybe, would appear in the paper. Some of them lost their jobs or were in other ways penalized by the lies of these provocateurs.

RICK: It took us years just to look through the red squad files. We had a number of people reading the reports. One of them found something about a Spanish Action Committee of Chicago. The red squad had infiltrated SACC back in 1966. A police agent, Tom Braham, told SACC members that he was concerned about the community, but his real concern was revealed in a red squad report: "The objective of this undertaking was to destroy the SUBJECT [Spanish Action Committee of Chicago], its leaders and community influence."[24]

Juan Díaz was the leader of SACC. He had been a former military police officer during the Korean war. He was very active in the Knights of St. John, a group of Catholic laymen. And the Spanish Action Committee was just a community group. It came into being right after the riot in the Puerto Rican community. The most radical thing they did was to have a peaceful, lawful march from Humboldt Park to city hall, where they hoped to express their concerns to the mayor on housing and police harassment. That was the organization that was smeared for being associated with Communists. The whole thing was incredible.

When we found the red squad reports, I immediately contacted the Spanish Action Committee. There were different people in leadership then, but they agreed to become plaintiffs. I gave the story to a reporter from the *Sun-Times*. When Janet Nolan saw the article, she called and told me she had contemporaneous records. I thought she'd be a very effective witness. She had been an observer doing an academic study, so she could set the scene. And she was not going to gain financially from the lawsuit.

JANET NOLAN: In 1952, I became a Maryknoll sister. My first assignment was in the South Bronx, teaching in a school that was mostly Black. Two years after that, I was assigned by my community to go to Mexico. I became very involved in early childhood education, as well as in developing a Mayan inner-city community to meet their own needs through social action. I was able to get some funds to build a social center run completely by the people. And a day-care center. I was absolutely committed to my work.

On April Fool's Day 1966, I got a telegram telling me that I must leave Mexico and report to Chicago. That was a tremendous blow for me—I was a basket case for a while—because I truly wanted to stay there. My new assignment was to work as an area director on a research project conducted by the University of Notre Dame to study how Puerto Rican people cope with city life.

I arrived here after having been away from Chicago about fourteen years. Just coming from the Yucatán to a big city was a culture shock in itself. But they told me there was someone who would assist me in setting up an office. He worked for the University of Notre Dame also. They felt that he was the person who represented and understood this community and could best interpret it to me. So when I arrived out of the clear blue, I was introduced to Juan Díaz.

Juan was the director of the Latin American Boys Club, and we had our first briefing there. He drove me around, trying to locate a place where we could set up our community information referral center. And he in-

JANET NOLAN

troduced me to all kinds of members of the community. He was really a great help.

During the week leading up to the riot on June 12, we had been working very hard. There had just been a celebration of Puerto Rican Day. They also had a carnival in Humboldt Park, and I had participated in Juan Díaz's booth. I took off Sunday and stayed in my little apartment the entire day. About four-thirty, I decided to go out and get some air. It was very hot. I walked down to Division Street and found myself in this huge crowd.

I heard someone say, "A boy was shot in the leg three times by the police!" Then I found out that, earlier, two people had gotten into an argument outside a bar. The police came to quiet it. Their dogs attacked one of the bystanders, who was just watching. I heard someone say, "What do they think we are, animals, that they have to put dogs on us?" More and more people came to see what was going on. Everyone was out: women with babies in carriages, old people, young girls, and, of course, the teenage boys, some of whom thought this was the perfect opportunity for mischief.

At one point, I saw this phalanx of I don't know how many policemen marching toward Division Street, wearing their riot gear. The Jewel parking lot at the corner of Damen and Division was filled with police cars. It looked like a war about to happen. In the midst of all this, I saw my friend Juan Díaz. He was running back and forth, telling people to be calm, not to fight, to cool down.

There were two apparently abandoned police cars near the corner of Division and Hoyne. A local priest, Father Headley, was standing on one of the cars, talking to the people. I remember seeing a thin Black man reach into the police car, take out a notebook, and throw it into the air. Papers came flying down. They gathered some of the papers and built a bonfire. Then they set the car on fire. I was standing right there while the tires were popping. That was the real beginning of the riot.

A fire truck arrived, and there was a tug of war between the boys and the firemen for the hose. A second fire truck came, but it was full of policemen. They got off and started to head into the crowd. The phalanx of police that had been out of sight up to then entered the Division Street intersection. The young boys saw what was happening and ran into the crowd. All of a sudden, there was a mad stampede.

I was knocked down. So were other people all around me, people who were just there trying to see what was happening. Someone ran across my back. My blouse was ripped; my skirt was torn. I ran into a doorway and tried to get inside. There were people behind the door, but they wouldn't open it.

The boys were already way down the street. And we, who had been knocked down, were standing there when the police came. They had nightsticks. I watched while an officer hit a man on the head until he knocked him down to the ground. Right next to me! I looked across the street and saw other men bleeding. I saw Carlos Castro, a young man who had become very interested in our work. He was trying to help people get up. He got hit a couple of times, too. At that point, I was trying to get out of the area, as many people were. We were right between the police and the boys during the barrage of rocks and bricks. They were flying both ways. I finally moved back off Division Street and just stayed close by, listening. When I heard gun shots, I went home and turned on my radio.

The riot continued for the next week. There was looting. Buildings were burned. During that time, I started interviewing people in the neighborhood. Juan would help me get them into the office to get their various viewpoints. Many of them felt that there was a lack of respect for Puerto Ricans as a worthy group of people. There was the whole thing of being poor, feeling discrimination, the frustrations—and the heat. Also, at that time, there were no city services. But the big issue was police brutality.

When Juan interviewed some of the Junior Latin Kings, he started preaching to them. I was a little concerned because I wanted him to pull out ideas from the young people. But he would tell them they shouldn't take advantage of the situation and make it worse: "This isn't the way we do things." In no way did he think that the rioting was right.

RICK: Yet in his reports red squad officer Tom Braham made it seem as if Juan Díaz had advocated violence: "He [Díaz] made every effort to convince the Puerto Rican people that they had been victimized by the Chicago 'Power Structure' which left them no other recourse than to engage in violent, riotous conduct."[25]

JANET: Juan never condoned rioting. But he could see why it happened. He said he himself was walking down the street once and the police threw him up against the wall and said, "Somebody was just robbed. Did you do it?" He remembers other people standing around while he was spread-eagled and feeling very humiliated. He told me, "You can just take so much of that, and then it all bursts out."

But there may have been more to the riot than that. Recently at a gathering, I met Father Headley again. I told him, "The last time I saw you, you were standing on top of a car telling people not to get involved and not to burn the police car." And he said, "Yes. Do you know why I was telling them that? Because the two men who started the fire were police officers in plainclothes." I said, "You're kidding." He said, "No. I knew those two." I was just astounded.

FATHER DONALD HEADLEY: There were two young men who happened to be Black standing next to the police car. They were trying to talk Spanish. They were telling the young people: "Burn the car! Down with the city!" I watched this for about two minutes. Then I realized I

FATHER DONALD HEADLEY

knew them. They were policemen, the two who were telling the kids that they should burn the car. I knew them from the Monroe Street District. It was a set-up!

So I got up on top of the police car. I tried to tell the kids, "Something strange is going on here. Be careful of these people—they're telling you to burn the police car, and they're policemen!" I said, "Don't burn the car—let's get out of here." But the car was set on fire.

JANET: What the Puerto Rican people wanted after the riot was to achieve political power in Chicago. The only way many of them thought they could do that was to align themselves with the Daley machine. But Juan scoffed at that, saying: "Mayor Daley tries to pit one against the other, so we will all fail." He told me that the man who owned the newspaper *El Puertorriqueño* was on Mayor Daley's Council of Puerto Rican Rights, but he did not speak for the people. According to Juan and others, he was strictly a "Tío Tomas"—an Uncle Tom. Juan kept saying to me, "I have to do something for my people. I don't want to be a leader, but if nobody else is there except the Tío Tomases, then I will." That's when the Spanish Action Committee was started.

Juan would always check in with me to report what he was doing. He said that the demonstrations he organized were a way of uniting the people to get something of value for their community: more case workers who speak Spanish, less brutality by the police, more employment, and better housing. In August, Juan was still officially working for Notre Dame, but he was up to his ears in SACC activity. I told him, "I think you're going to have to make a decision. Are you going to work for the Spanish Action Committee or for Notre Dame?" Then he left our research project and recommended Victor Guitard Rodríguez to take his place. Victor was one of the five who later turned against Juan.

On Saturday, September 3, 1966, an article came out in the *Chicago Tribune*. It said that Juan Díaz was linked to the Communists. I thought it was completely ridiculous. Juan Díaz!? He wanted no part of Communism. And he was always telling everybody not to do things to disturb the police and not to give the community a bad name. The paper said that he had been arrested on a drug charge. Some of his own people from the Spanish Action Committee, including Ted and Mirta Ramírez and Victor, attacked him in the article, calling him a dictator. A week later, an article appeared in *El Puertorriqueño*: "SACC Is a Nest of Communists."[26] It talked about what was in the *Tribune,* and it made Juan a target of ridicule. After that, Juan Díaz was completely discredited in his community.

The people in the Spanish Action Committee who attacked Juan formed a new organization. If you look at who they were, Mirta and Ted Ramírez were never leaders of the people. And Victor Rodríguez was not a leader of the community either. Then I found out they really turned against Juan because there had been an instigator there. One day, Victor came in to give me some information for my report to Notre Dame. He didn't realize—nor did I—what he was telling me at that time.

He said, "You know, we really didn't want to do that to Juan. I didn't, especially." I asked him, "Do you think anybody is behind the Ramírezes?"

"Oh, yes," he said. "There's a Dr. Baron.* They say he's a doctor in advertising. He said he's going to project this new organization to the world. He talked about putting it on TV and the radio and in the papers." I asked Victor if Dr. Baron had been a friend of the Ramírezes before. He said, "No, he was introduced to them by Tom Braham."

RICK: The red squad had engineered everything. There had been some friction in SACC, based mainly on personalities, especially between Juan Díaz and Ted and Mirta Ramírez. Braham manipulated this, using allegations of Communism. He reported that he "spoke with Mr. and Mrs. Ramírez for 2 1/2 hours," during which time he "led the conversation into a discussion relative to communists who have been trying to gain influence within SACC."[27] Braham said that he launched an "all out . . . anti–Juan Díaz campaign." He said, "It brought about the resignation of the entire original committee" that had founded SACC, except for Juan Díaz and one other person.[28]

And it was Braham who set up a rival group called the American Spanish Speaking People's Association. He reported that it "was secretly organized by members of the Intelligence Division and composed of former members of the Spanish Action Committee of Chicago. Although the members knew nothing of the part played by the Intelligence Division, they have been directed to a point where they will publicly denounce SACC and it's [sic] leader, Juan Díaz."[29]

When Juan Díaz testified in court about this, he said:

> I was confused, depressed and disappointed . . . and also ashamed. . . . And I was really hurt because I never expected Mirta or anybody to accuse me of communism and to resign from the organization. I'm still suffering from that. . . . Membership dispersed. Many of them left the town. And others went and made their own organizations. . . . Nobody wanted anything to do with us.[30]

JANET: In 1975, I read the article in the *Sun-Times* about Rick Gutman's discovery that it was really the red squad, and I was shocked. I couldn't believe that the police department would infiltrate the Spanish Action Committee and try to discredit Juan Díaz! My first impulse was to call Rick Gutman and tell him that I had a transcript of my interview with Victor from years before.

---

*"DR. BARON is in actuality Officer James Zarnow of the Chicago Police Intelligence Division" (memorandum from Patrolman Tom Braham, #12116, to Director Wm. J. Duffy, Subject: Spanish Action Committee of Chicago, Intelligence Division, Chicago Police Department, August 19, 1966, p. 3).

Then I became a little fearful, too. If I did this, if I took this step, would there be any repercussions? At the school where I'm teaching? Would my house be watched? Would I be harassed? I was aware of police brutality and that there were different treatments for different people. I mean, those thoughts did cross my mind. But I called the Alliance to End Repression that night. It just had to be done.

In a way, I was a perfect witness because I had no bones to pick. And the lawyer for the city, Peter Fitzpatrick, seemed so inept. He asked me to read from my documents, something I wouldn't have been able to do otherwise. So I read my interview with Victor, in which he admitted that they knew that Juan had been set up. I quoted Victor: "I feel bad that we did this to him, and I know that he's not a Communist." I read that to the jury.

RICK: In 1984, we obtained a ruling for the Spanish Action Committee that the police disruption of their organization was unconstitutional. The jury also awarded sixty thousand dollars for damages and forty-eight thousand dollars in attorneys' fees against the defendant, the city of Chicago.

Before that, we had won another important victory. On April 24, 1981, we got a court order outlawing political spying and disruption in the future. It's one of the strictest in the country. The police can't gather intelligence on political groups unless they first have concrete evidence that would lead a reasonable person to suspect that the group is engaging in or about to engage in something criminal. *That would eliminate just about everything the red squad ever did.*

We also have a provision stating that they can't gather intelligence on irrelevant matters. For example, if they suspect that you're conspiring to break into a draft board office, they can't start gathering intelligence on the meetings you go to about the civil rights movement. And they have to document everything. Every time there's an investigation, they have to have prior written permission. The superintendent of police or a member of his staff has to authorize it. There has to be a paper trail. And a leading national accounting firm regularly audits all the files to make sure the police are not violating these rules. The police agreed to it. It was an out-of-court settlement to avoid a trial. The judge approved it, and the court now has continuing jurisdiction to enforce the settlement order.

The city wanted to end the whole case at that point and offered us a monetary settlement for our damage claims. But we wanted to litigate our damage claims in order to obtain a ruling on the constitutionality of police spying. Police disruption of lawful political activity, like in the case of SACC, had long been held to be a violation of the First Amendment. But there had been no judicial decision that "mere" spying was unconstitutional. Even today, there are few places in the country where it's illegal for a government agency to spy on you for political reasons.

The city didn't want a jury trial. So we agreed to a ruling by a judge based on a statement of facts that both we and the city accepted. They signed the statement admitting much of their spying and disruption, including the fact that they "targeted for neutralization peaceful civic organizations," but they argued that the spying was not illegal.

In her ruling, the judge said that the red squad had violated the First Amendment rights of the Alliance to End Repression when they falsely testified before the Senate Internal Security Subcommittee that it was a Communist-front organization and when they infiltrated the Alliance's board. She also ruled that infiltration of the Chicago Peace Council was a violation of their First Amendment rights. And, most important, we obtained a ruling that the police must have a reasonable suspicion of criminal activity before they can gather intelligence. In addition, we won about four hundred thousand dollars in damages as well as attorneys' fees.

I think our lawsuit had a tremendous effect. It resulted in the red squad being abolished in the city of Chicago. And there's been very little activity by the Chicago police department of this nature ever since. Not that I think it's permanent, but it had an effect. They definitely retreated.

What the police did against the Spanish Action Committee, the Chicago Peace Council, and the Alliance—against lots of groups—wasn't something done only in Chicago. Every state police agency had a subversive unit. Every major metropolitan police department had a subversive unit. They were all doing the same thing. We discovered that the Chicago police department was exchanging information about lawful political activity with over one hundred fifty-seven other red squads throughout the country.

When you take a civics class or a political science class in high school, they don't teach that the police department has a subversive unit or that the FBI has a unit that spies on and disrupts lawful political activity. They just don't talk about it. It's invisible. And why? Because it contradicts our democratic ideology. It contradicts the Constitution.

Our professed political philosophy is that not only are people free to speak out on public issues, but they have a civic duty to do so. People who don't speak out aren't good citizens. But that's not the reality. The government doesn't like to be criticized. And there are units of government— not a few bad apples of overly aggressive individuals, but entire units of government—whose purpose is to monitor and suppress dissent, no matter how lawful it is, if it challenges the status quo.

I think the police are always going to do this to some extent, in every government. In every country in the world, whether it be the former Soviet Union, the United States or Switzerland or Sweden or Monaco, the police are going to target people who criticize the government. It's a problem that's never going to go away, never going to be completely eliminated. But it's very important that people fight it in order to keep it within bounds.

POSTSCRIPT

In 1997, the city of Chicago filed a motion in federal court to weaken the 1982 consent decree that prohibited police spying on First Amendment activities. The city claimed that the decree created "an undue burden on law enforcement" because, among other things, it inhibited investigations of gangs, organized crime, and terrorism.[31] When we learned of this development, we spoke again with Rick Gutman, who has continued to serve as the lead attorney for the Alliance to End Repression.

"The city has misrepresented the consent decree," Rick Gutman argued. "It does not prohibit surveillance of criminal activity. If it did, the city would not have co-authored it, the city would not have signed it, and the city would not have waited all these years to complain about it. The nonpolitical and nonreligious associations of street gang members or organized crime figures are not First Amendment activities, so the consent decree has no effect on police surveillance of them. It's as simple as that."

Magistrate Judge Edward A. Bobrick agreed. "Under the decree," he said, "'investigations as a law enforcement technique, including collection, analysis and dissemination of information about systemic criminal conduct' are allowed."[32] Nor is the investigation of terrorism impeded by the decree. "By its very definition," Gutman noted, "a terrorist group has either committed a crime or is planning a crime or both. Either situation would give the police justification under the consent decree to investigate." And, according to the Chicago police in charge of those investigations, the decree in fact has had no detrimental effect on them. Judge Bobrick stated that "the head of the Chicago Police Department's Gang Crimes Investigation Sections has testified . . . that he knows of no gang crime investigation that has been thwarted by the decree."[33] Rick

Gutman deposed the police sergeant who had been assigned full time to antiterrorism investigations for fourteen years. "I asked him," Gutman said, "whether the consent decree had ever stopped him from doing what he wanted to do—and he said, 'No.'"

Judge Bobrick concluded, "When looking to the consent decree as a whole, we perceive nothing in it that would hobble or place 'blinders' on legitimate police activities or trifle with public safety; nor should it."[34]

"In addition to falsely claiming that the consent decree prohibits most intelligence gathering on criminals," Gutman said, "the city inadvertently revealed its real intent: It wants the police to be able, in its own words, 'to gather and maintain information about individuals or groups that hold extreme political views,' even though they have no record of crime.[35] They want to have total discretion to spy on 'extremists,' with the police defining what an 'extremist' is. Before it was disbanded, the red squad had subversive files on everybody. In their opinion, those people all had extremist ideas. The red squad had defined the Jewish War Veterans, the Catholic Interracial Council, the League of Women Voters, and eight hundred other lawful civic, political, religious, and community groups as extremist. By changing the consent decree, the police could once again engage in indiscriminate snooping with no fear of being sued."

The consent decree prohibited investigating First Amendment conduct unless there is "reasonable suspicion based on specific and articulable facts that the subject has committed, is committing, or is about to commit a crime."[36] The city wanted to replace that prohibition with language stating that the Chicago police cannot investigate "any person for the purpose of punishing or retaliating against that person for engaging in conduct protected by the First Amendment."[37]

The new language may seem benign. But Gutman explained: "What that change does is eliminate any enforceable restrictions on spying and gathering intelligence." "They could spy on anybody they wanted for any reason they wanted, unless that person could prove that the intent of the police was to disrupt. Instead of the police having to prove that they have a reasonable suspicion of criminal activity, the person who is being spied on would have to prove that the police had improper motivation, which would be practically impossible to do. Besides, if you could prove that they were disrupting, it would be against the First Amendment even without a consent decree."

On March 9, 1999, Magistrate Judge Bobrick recommended that the city of Chicago's motion to change the consent decree be denied, thereby upholding the decree's firm protection of First Amendment rights. His recommendation was accepted by U.S. District Judge Ann Claire Williams, who denied the city's motion. On January 11, 2001, however, the Seventh Circuit Court of Appeals reversed Judge Williams's decision, effectively ending a twenty-year experiment in which repressive forces were tightly restrained.

Can we reach a point where the fundamental rights to free expression and association are permanently assured? If anything is to be learned from the stories in this book, which span the better part of a century, it is that keeping repression from intruding upon constitutional right is, indeed, a constant struggle.

Notes

INTRODUCTION

Epigraph excerpted from "Stipulated Statement of Material Facts as to Which There Is No Genuine Issue," signed by Richard M. Gutman, attorney for plaintiffs, and Peter Fitzpatrick, special assistant corporation counsel, attorney for defendant [City of Chicago], *Alliance to End Repression et al. v. City of Chicago et al.*, case no. 74 C 3268, U.S. District Court for the Northern District of Illinois, Eastern Division, November 14, 1985, pp. 2–3.

PART ONE

Epigraph quoted from Robert M. La Follette Jr., Senate Committee on Education and Labor, *Violations of Free Speech and Rights of Labor: Preliminary Report,* 76th Cong., 1st sess., report no. 6, pt. 2, February 13 (Washington, D.C.: Government Printing Office, 1939), p. 3.

1. Richard O. Boyer and Herbert M. Morais, *Labor's Untold Story* (New York: United Electrical, Radio and Machine Workers of America, 1955), p. 314.

2. Dee Garrison, *Rebel Pen: The Writings of Mary Heaton Vorse* (New York: Monthly Review Press, 1985), p. 29.

3. Senate Commission on Industrial Relations, *Final Report of the Commission on Industrial Relations,* 64th Cong., 1st sess. (Washington, D.C.: Government Printing Office, 1916), vol. 1, p. 94.

4. Ibid., pp. 54, 41, 11, 43, 53.

5. Irving Bernstein, *The Lean Years: A History of the American Worker, 1920–1933* (Boston: Houghton Mifflin, 1960), p. 130. Also see Robert Justin Goldstein, *Political Repression in Modern America: From 1870 to the Present* (Cambridge, Mass.: Schenkman, 1978), p. 190.

6. Senate Committee on Education and Labor, *Violations of Free Speech and Rights of Labor,* pp. 4, 6, 11. For a firsthand account of repression by company-town police systems, see Pete Muselin's story in Bud Schultz and Ruth Schultz, *It Did Happen Here: Recollections of Political Repression in America* (Berkeley: University of California Press, 1989), pp. 65–74.

7. Thomas R. Brooks, *Toil and Trouble: A History of American Labor* (New York: Delacorte, 1964), p. 180.

8. David Montgomery, *Workers' Control in America: Studies in the History of Work, Technology, and Labor Struggles* (Cambridge: Cambridge University Press, 1979), p. 165.

9. See Kim Moody, *An Injury to All: The Decline of American Unionism* (New York: Verso, 1988), pp. 19–20, 26–35; Montgomery, *Workers' Control in America,* pp. 161–169; and Brooks, *Toil and Trouble,* pp. 201–208.

10. Goldstein, *Political Repression in Modern America,* p. 33.

11. Robert L. Friedheim, *The Seattle General Strike* (Seattle: University of Washington Press, 1964), p. 132.

12. Murray B. Levin, *Political Hysteria in America: The Democratic Capacity for Repression* (New York: Basic Books, 1971), p. 41.

13. For an account of the Palmer raids by Sonia Kaross, one of the victims, see Schultz and Schultz, *It Did Happen Here,* pp. 159–164.

14. Saul Alinsky, *John L. Lewis: An Unauthorized Biography* (New York: Putnam, 1949), p. 337.

15. Lee Pressman, Eugene Cotton, and Frank Donner, *Analysis of the Taft-Hartley Act* (Washington, D.C.: Congress of Industrial Organizations, 1947), p. 49.

16. The HUAC investigation into the film industry began with the case of the Hollywood Ten. Ring Lardner Jr. and Frances Chaney Lardner describe those hearings and the subsequent blacklisting in Schultz and Schultz, *It Did Happen Here,* pp. 101–116. See also pp. 75–90 in the same volume for an account of the Smith Act trial of leading Communists by one of the defendants, Gil Green.

17. Ibid., p. 397.

18. Jack Miller recounts his experience in the 1916 Everett Massacre, in which sheriff's deputies opened fire on a ferryboat loaded with IWW workers as it docked in Everett, Washington; see ibid., pp. 237–248.

19. Melvyn Dubofsky, *We Shall Be All: A History of the Industrial Workers of the World* (Chicago: Quadrangle Books, 1969), p. 432.

20. The 1969 Supreme Court ruling in *Brandenburg* is quoted in Thomas Emerson, *The System of Freedom of Expression* (New York: Vintage, 1970), p. 156. The Court struck down Ohio's criminal syndicalism law, which was "similar in text," Emerson says, to the California law.

21. Richard C. Cortner, *A Mob Intent on Death: The NAACP and the Arkansas Riot Cases* (Middletown, Conn.: Wesleyan University Press, 1988), pp. 30, 31.

22. See Howard Kester, *Revolt Among the Sharecroppers* (New York: Covici, Friede, 1936), p. 37.

23. Daniel Tobin is quoted in Walter Galenson, *The CIO Challenge to the AFL: A History of the American Labor Movement, 1935–1941* (Cambridge: Harvard University Press, 1960), p. 484.

24. Goldstein, *Political Repression in Modern America*, p. 245.

25. Galenson, *The CIO Challenge to the AFL*, p. 485.

26. The investigating committee is quoted in Jeremy Brecher, *Strike!* (San Francisco: Straight Arrow Books, 1972), pp. 165–166.

27. Louise Pettibone Smith, *The Torch of Liberty: Twenty-Five Years in the Life of the Foreign Born in the U.S.A.* (New York: Dwight-King, 1959), p. 400.

28. William Preston Jr., *Aliens and Dissenters: Federal Suppression of Radicals* (New York: Harper and Row, 1963), p. 32.

29. David Caute, *The Great Fear: The Anti-Communist Purge Under Truman and Eisenhower* (New York: Simon and Schuster, 1978), p. 589, n. 21.

30. Goldstein, *Political Repression in Modern America*, p. 351.

31. See Caute, *The Great Fear*, p. 432, for membership figures in 1963. Caute lists the Teachers Union membership at 4,000 in 1953 (p. 437).

32. Boyer and Morais, *Labor's Untold Story*, p. 356.

33. F. S. O'Brien, "The 'Communist-Dominated' Unions in the United States Since 1950," *Labor History* 9, no. 2 (Spring 1968): 187.

34. Bert Cochran, *Labor and Communism: The Conflict that Shaped American Unions* (Princeton: Princeton University Press, 1977), p. 292.

35. Ibid., p. 293.

36. Frank Donner, *The Un-Americans* (New York: Ballantine, 1961), p. 65.

37. Cochran, *Labor and Communism*, p. 293.

38. Caute, *The Great Fear*, p. 216.

39. Ibid., p. 217.

40. Ronald W. Schatz, *The Electrical Workers: A History of Labor at General Electric and Westinghouse, 1923–1960* (Urbana: University of Illinois Press, 1983), p. 188.

41. UE activist and union officer Tom Quinn provides an account of the government's role in the factional struggles at Westinghouse's East Pittsburgh plant in Schultz and Schultz, *It Did Happen Here*, pp. 117–126.

42. William Peeler, the UE opponent, is quoted in Schatz, *The Electrical Workers*, p. 194.

43. Ibid., p. 200.

44. Ibid., pp. 91–92.

45. Michael Yates, *Power on the Job: The Legal Rights of Working People* (Boston: South End Press, 1994), p. 113.

46. Hardy Green, *On Strike at Hormel: The Struggle for a Democratic Labor Movement* (Philadelphia: Temple University Press, 1990), p. 157.

47. Ibid., p. 274.

48. Walter Galenson, "The Historical Role of American Trade Unionism," in Seymour Martin Lipset, ed., *Unions in Transition: Entering the Second Century* (San Francisco: Institute for Contemporary Studies Press, 1986), p. 64.

PART TWO

Epigraph quoted in Herbert Shapiro, *White Violence and Black Response: From Reconstruction to Montgomery* (Amherst: University of Massachusetts Press, 1988), p. 34.

1. Ibid., p. 85.

2. Ibid., p. 50.

3. Colonel Alfred Waddell is quoted in H. Leon Prather Sr., *We Have Taken a City: Wilmington Racial Massacre and Coup of 1898* (Cranbury, N.J.: Associated Universities Press, 1984), p. 102.

4. Jane Murphy Cronly is quoted in ibid., p. 128.

5. Robin D. G. Kelley, *Hammer and Hoe: Alabama Communists During the Great Depression* (Chapel Hill: University of North Carolina Press, 1990), p. 99.

6. Roy Talbert Jr., *Negative Intelligence: The Army and the American Left, 1917–1941* (Jackson: University Press of Mississippi, 1991), pp. 118–119.

7. Kenneth O'Reilly, *"Racial Matters": The FBI's Secret File on Black America, 1960–1972* (New York: Free Press, 1989), pp. 39–40.

8. Talbert, *Negative Intelligence,* p. 113.

9. *The Crisis* is quoted in Patrick S. Washburn, *A Question of Sedition: The Federal Government's Investigation of the Black Press During World War II* (New York: Oxford University Press, 1986), p. 18.

10. Talbert, *Negative Intelligence,* p. 119.

11. Ibid., p. 117.

12. Washburn, *A Question of Sedition,* pp. 17–18.

13. Report by Harry D. Gulley, February 24, 1923, in *Marcus Garvey: FBI Investigation File* (Wilmington, Del.: Scholarly Resources, 1978), microfilm, reel 1.

14. O'Reilly, *"Racial Matters,"* p. 19. For an account of National Negro Congress activities, see Raymond Wolters, *Negroes and the Great Depression: The Problem of Economic Recovery* (Westport, Conn.: Greenwood, 1970), p. 361; and Shapiro, *White Violence and Black Response,* p. 261.

15. Washburn, *A Question of Sedition,* p. 180.

16. The special agent in charge is quoted in ibid., p. 170.

17. Michael K. Honey, *Southern Labor and Black Civil Rights: Organizing Memphis Workers* (Urbana: University of Illinois Press, 1993), p. 151.

18. David Caute, *The Great Fear: The Anti-Communist Purge Under Truman and Eisenhower* (New York: Simon and Schuster, 1978), p. 166.

19. James W. Silver, *Mississippi: The Closed Society* (New York: Harcourt, Brace and World, 1966), p. 8.

20. David J. Garrow, *The FBI and Martin Luther King, Jr.* (New York: Penguin, 1983), p. 95. Also see O'Reilly, *"Racial Matters,"* pp. 132–133. The bureau's case for a Communist connection rested almost exclusively on the presence of two advisers to Dr. King who it claimed were hidden Communists seeking to fashion the civil rights movement in some unspecified way to the Communist Party's advantage. (See Senate Select Committee to Study Government Operations with Respect to Intelligence Activities, *Supplementary Staff Reports on Intelligence Activities and the Rights of Americans,* 94th Cong., 2d sess., Final Report, no. 94–755 [Washington, D.C.: Government Printing Office, 1976] [hereafter referred to as Senate Select Committee on Intelligence], bk. 3, pp. 85, 89. See also Garrow, *The FBI and Martin Luther King, Jr.,* p. 43.) But the Senate Select Committee on Intelligence concluded: "We have seen no evi-

dence establishing that either of those Advisors attempted to exploit the civil rights movement to carry out the plans of the Communist Party." Further, it stated that the allegation of Communist influence "was certainly not justification for continuing the investigation of Dr. King for over six years, or for carrying out attempts to destroy him" (bk. 3, p. 85).

The FBI's surveillance and disruption of the activities of Dr. King and SCLC suggest that in fact the bureau was interested not as much in Communist connections as in the movement for racial equality itself. According to FBI reports, SCLC was formed "to organize a register-to-vote campaign among Negroes in the South." Hoover, then dismissing the possibility of Communist infiltration, called for opening an investigation "in view of the stated purpose of the organization" (Morton H. Halperin, Jerry J. Breman, Robert L. Borosage, and Christine M. Marwick, *The Lawless State: The Crimes of U.S. Intelligence Agencies* [New York: Penguin, 1976], p. 63). Years later, William C. Sullivan, who was in charge of the FBI's campaign against Dr. King, testified regarding Hoover: "I think behind it all was the racial bias, the dislike of Negroes, the dislike of the civil rights movement. . . . I do not think he could rise above that" (Senate Select Committee on Intelligence, bk. 3, p. 91).

21. Senate Select Committee on Intelligence, bk. 3, p. 481. Also see Halperin et al., *The Lawless State*, pp. 79, 80.

22. Senate Select Committee on Intelligence, bk. 3, pp. 81–82, 120, 123, 129, 131–146, 158–163, 172–184.

23. Ibid., bk. 3, p. 81.

24. Paul Bermanzohn, a demonstrator who was wounded in the attack, describes the Greensboro Massacre in Bud Schultz and Ruth Schultz, *It Did Happen Here: Recollections of Political Repression in America* (Berkeley: University of California Press, 1989), pp. 333–346.

25. Memorandum from Director, FBI, to SAC [Special Agent in Charge], Albany et al., August 25, 1967.

26. Senate Select Committee on Intelligence, bk. 3, p. 20.

27. J. Edgar Hoover is quoted in ibid., bk. 3, p. 187.

28. Ward Churchill and Jim Vander Wall, *The Cointelpro Papers: Documents from the FBI's Secret War Against Dissent in the United States* (Boston: South End Press, 1990), pp. 124–125. Also see memorandum from Director, FBI, to San Francisco, September 30, 1968, for Hoover's instructions to field offices concerning ways to "create suspicion" within the Black Panther Party.

29. Letter from Donald V. Watkins, Special Counsel to Richard Arrington Jr., Mayor, Birmingham, Alabama, to Joseph Biden Jr., Chairman, Senate Judiciary Committee, and Frederick Goldberg, Commissioner, Internal Revenue Service, October 23, 1990, p. 5.

30. L. A. Nikoloric, "The Government Loyalty Program," in John C. Wahlke, ed., *Loyalty in a Democratic State* (Boston: D. C. Heath, 1952), p. 55.

31. W. E. B. Du Bois, *The Autobiography of W. E. B. Du Bois: A Soliloquy on Viewing My Life from the Last Decade of Its First Century* (New York: International Publishers, 1968), pp. 394, 395.

32. Paul Robeson is quoted in Martin Bauml Duberman, *Paul Robeson* (New York: Knopf, 1988), p. 305.

33. The North Carolina newspaper is quoted in ibid., p. 345. Also see Shapiro, *White Violence and Black Response*, pp. 46, 108, 311–312; and James Forman, *The Making of Black Revolutionaries* (Washington, D.C.: Open Hand Publishing, 1985), p. 446.

34. Memorandum from Director, FBI, to SAC, New York, October 28, 1958 (100–12304–545), quoted in Duberman, *Paul Robeson*, p. 725, n. 21.

35. The quotation from Hoover appears in Paul Robeson Jr., "The FBI vs. Paul Robeson: The Case for F.O.I.A.," in *Rights*, periodic report of the National Emergency Civil Liberties Committee, March–April 1982, p. 5.

36. Duberman, *Paul Robeson*, p. 676, n. 36.

37. Pete Seeger, who also sang that day, provides additional details about the Peekskill riot in Schultz and Schultz, *It Did Happen Here*, pp. 15–16.

38. Memorandum from American Consul, Accra, 179, to Department of State, Re: Request for Special Story on Paul Robeson; facsimile and quotations printed in the *Daily World*, October 13, 1977.

39. Paul Robeson, "Speech at the Peace Bridge Arch," August 16, 1953, in Philip S. Foner, ed., *Paul Robeson Speaks: Writings, Speeches, Interviews, 1918–1974* (New York: Brunner/Mazel, 1978), p. 366.

40. The State Department is quoted in Duberman, *Paul Robeson*, p. 434.

41. The HUAC testimony cited here and in following passages is quoted in Eric Bentley, *Thirty Years of Treason: Excerpts from Hearings Before the House Committee on Un-American Activities, 1938–1968* (New York: Viking, 1971), pp. 778–779, 784, 789.

42. Paul Robeson, *Here I Stand* (Boston: Beacon Press, 1971), pp. 38–39.

43. Paul Robeson, "Thank God Almighty, We're Moving," in Foner, ed., *Paul Robeson Speaks*, p. 473.

44. Schultz and Schultz, *It Did Happen Here*, p. 254.

45. For a discussion of the case against the Albany Movement activists, see Taylor Branch, *Parting the Waters: America in the King Years, 1954–1963* (New York: Simon and Schuster, 1988), pp. 866–868; and Halperin et al., *The Lawless State*, p. 69.

46. O'Reilly, *"Racial Matters,"* pp. 89, 86.

47. Ibid., pp. 179–180, 337.

48. Others also observed: "The FBI watched as the second bus, the Trailways, pulled into Anniston within an hour" (O'Reilly, *"Racial Matters,"* p. 84).

49. See Susan Blank, "FBI Ruled Responsible for Klan Violence It Could Have Stopped," *Civil Liberties* (Fall 1983): 6, for an excerpt from the FBI memorandum.

50. See O'Reilly, *"Racial Matters,"* pp. 216–217; and Branch, *Parting the Waters*, p. 421.

51. O'Reilly, *"Racial Matters,"* p. 43.

52. John Salmond, *A Southern Rebel: The Life and Times of Aubrey Willis Williams, 1890–1965* (Chapel Hill: University of North Carolina Press, 1983), p. 223.

53. Kim Lacy Rogers, *Righteous Lives: Narratives of the New Orleans Civil Rights Movement* (New York: New York University Press, 1993), p. 33.

54. Frank Wilkinson describes these hearings in Schultz and Schultz, *It Did Happen Here*, pp. 263–278.

55. Rogers, *Righteous Lives*, p. 104.

56. For Myles Horton's account of Highlander Folk School and the government's attacks against it, see Schultz and Schultz, *It Did Happen Here*, pp. 23–33.

57. Margaret Herring McSurely recounts this experience in ibid., pp. 365–376.

58. O'Reilly, *"Racial Matters,"* pp. 265, 286–287, 301, 300.

59. Memorandum to Director, FBI (100–448006), from SAC, New York (100–161140)(P), Re: Counterintelligence Program, Black Nationalist–Hate Groups, Racial Intelligence, September 9, 1968.

60. Airtel from Director, FBI, to SAC, Albany, Re: Counterintelligence Program, Black Nationalist Hate-Type Groups, Racial Intelligence, March 4, 1968.

61. Cleveland Sellers provides an account of his resistance to the draft in Schultz and Schultz, *It Did Happen Here*, pp. 255–257.

62. Memorandum to Director, FBI (100–448006), from SAC, New York (100–161140)(P), July 10, 1968.

63. National Advisory Commission on Civil Disorders (Otto Kerner, Chairman), *Report of the National Advisory Commission on Civil Disorders* (New York: Bantam Books, 1968), p. 204.

64. The National Commission on the Causes and Prevention of Violence is quoted in Philip S. Foner, ed., *The Black Panthers Speak* (Philadelphia: Lippincott, 1970), p. xvii.

65. David Hilliard and Lewis Cole, *This Side of Glory: The Autobiography of David Hilliard and the Story of the Black Panther Party* (Boston: Little, Brown, 1993), p. 122.

66. Senate Select Committee on Intelligence, bk. 3, p. 189.

67. Robert Justin Goldstein describes the FBI's plans to disrupt marriages and instigate evictions; see *Political Repression in Modern America: From 1870 to the Present* (Cambridge, Mass.: Schenkman, 1978), p. 525. For the FBI's admission of its interference with free speech, see Senate Select Committee, bk. 3, p. 218.

68. The plan to tamper with Panther tapes is described in an FBI document; see memorandum from [deleted] to SAC, Springfield (157–802), November 13, 1969. The planned underground organization is discussed in a memorandum from San Francisco (157–601) to Director, FBI (105–174254), June 17, 1970. For information about the plan to promote rumors, see memorandum from SAC, Los Angeles (157–4054) to Director, FBI (100–448006), July 1, 1969; and memorandum from Director, FBI (100–448006), to SAC, Los Angeles (157–4054), July 14, 1969.

69. Airtel from Director, FBI (100–448006), to SACs, Baltimore (157–2520), Detroit (157–3214), and Los Angeles (157–4045), September 16, 1970.

70. Senate Select Committee on Intelligence, bk. 3, p. 210; O'Reilly, *"Racial Matters,"* p. 316; Frank Donner, *The Age of Surveillance: The Aims and Methods of America's Political Intelligence System* (New York: Knopf, 1980), p. 225; Roger Rapoport, "Meet America's Meanest Dirty Trickster: The Man the FBI Used to Destroy the Black Movement in Los Angeles," *Mother Jones*, April 1977, p. 21.

71. Senate Select Committee on Intelligence, bk. 3, p. 211; Donner, *The Age of Surveillance*, p. 225.

72. Airtel from Director, FBI (100–448006), to SAC, San Francisco (157–601), May 27, 1969; O'Reilly, *"Racial Matters,"* p. 302.

73. Donner, *The Age of Surveillance,* p. 221. Consider, for example, the following FBI efforts to disable and divide the Panther leadership. In 1968, the bureau attempted to arouse suspicions in Huey Newton about other Panther leaders while he was still in prison; see memorandum from SAC, San Francisco (157–601)(P), to Director, FBI (100–448006), October 10, 1968. The Los Angeles bureau office proposed sending a death threat to Newton in 1970; see airtel from SAC, Los Angeles (157–4054)(P), to Director, FBI (100–448006), August 10, 1970. The Detroit office proposed to tell Newton that David Hilliard was stealing party funds and depositing them in a foreign bank; see airtel from Director, FBI (100–448006), to SACs, Baltimore (157–2520), Detroit (157–3214), Los Angeles (157–4054), New Haven (157–785), San Francisco (157–601), and Washington Field (157–1292), September 16, 1970. An airtel from SAC, New York (100–161140)(P), to Director, FBI (100–448006), August 11, 1970, contained a proposal to send New York Panthers an anonymous letter accusing Newton of being a police spy and an "outsider and a leech"; for Hoover's approval of this proposal, see memorandum from Director, FBI (100–448006), to SAC, New York (161140), August 24, 1970. For FBI letters sent to *Ebony* and the *Village Voice* charging Newton with being the "finger man" responsible for the arrest of Angela Davis, see airtel from Director, FBI (100–448006), to SACs, New York (100–161140), Chicago, and San Francisco, November 3, 1970.

In 1971, Hoover took credit for Newton's "paranoid-like reactions" and then instructed the FBI field offices: "It appears Newton may be on the brink of a mental collapse and we must intensify our counterintelligence"; see airtel from Director, FBI, to SACs, Boston, Los Angeles, New York, San Francisco, January 28, 1971. For an FBI death threat to Newton written as if it had come from Eldridge Cleaver, see teletype from Director, FBI (100–448006), to SAC, San Francisco (157–601), February 10, 1971. On the FBI's campaign to split Newton and Cleaver, see Ward Churchill and Jim Vander Wall, *Agents of Repression: The FBI's Secret Wars Against the Black Panther Party and the American Indian Movement* (Boston: South End Press, 1988), p. 40; and Senate Select Committee on Intelligence, bk. 3, pp. 203–206. The FBI attempted to keep Cleaver from sending his wife, Kathleen, to the United States to try to settle the dispute; see teletype from San Francisco (157–601) to Director (100–448006), FBI, February 2, 1971, cited in Churchill and Vander Wall, *The Cointelpro Papers,* pp. 151–152. In a 1970 memo, Hoover stressed that it was important to "demythicize Newton, to hold him up to public ridicule, to tarnish his image among BPP members"; see memorandum from Director, FBI (100–448006), to SAC, New York (161140), August 24, 1970. Also see Senate Select Committee on Intelligence, bk. 3, p. 205, where the committee termed the FBI's campaign "the Bureau's fictitious chorus of critics of Newton." After the Cleaver-Newton split, Hoover commented that "now new targets must be established"; see Senate Select Committee on Intelligence, bk. 3, p. 207.

For information about FBI proposals to harass the BPP with tax audits, make phony threats from other radical groups, and spray the party's printing press with a foul-smelling chemical, see Senate Select Committee on Intelligence, bk. 3, pp. 214–215. The FBI also pressed an airline to charge higher, prohibitive shipping rates for the Panthers' newspaper; schemed to create friction between the BPP paper and that of the Nation of Islam; and harassed the paper's distributors (Donner, *The Age of Surveillance*, p. 224; Senate Select Committee on Intelligence, bk. 3, pp. 213–220). For information about the FBI's extraordinary effort to effect the cancelation of a handful of subscriptions to the Panthers' newspaper at a high school in Rochester, New York, see memorandum from SAC, Buffalo (157–746)(P), to Director, FBI (100–448006), February 5, 1970; memorandum from Director, FBI (100–448006), to SAC, Buffalo (157–746), granting authority, February 17, 1970; memorandum from SAC, Buffalo (157–503), to Director, FBI (100–448006), June 4, 1970; and O'Reilly, *"Racial Matters,"* p. 316.

74. O'Reilly, *"Racial Matters,"* p. 294.

75. Memorandum from Director, FBI (100–448006), to SAC, Los Angeles (157–1751), October 31, 1968. The Los Angeles special agent in charge, too, "hoped" for a "vendetta"; see memorandum from SAC, Los Angeles (157–1751)(P), to Director, FBI (100–448006), November 29, 1968.

76. The two US members convicted of the murders later escaped from San Quentin prison, a difficult feat indeed. A sworn affidavit by a former FBI informant charged that when the murders were committed, the men had been controlled by FBI agents who also engineered their prison escape, a charge denied by the government. The informant asserted that the actual murderer was a third man, also an FBI undercover informant (sworn affidavit by Darthard Perry, February 10, 1978; Donner, *The Age of Surveillance*, p. 222). Retired FBI agent M. Wesley Swearingen confirms Perry's account—"I know Darthard Perry was an FBI informant and that he is telling the truth about the FBI"—and then he adds: "I then discovered the unthinkable, that FBI informants had actually been instructed by FBI agents to assassinate several other Black Panther members" (M. Wesley Swearingen, *FBI Secrets: An Agent's Expose* [Boston: South End Press, 1995], p. 83).

77. See Senate Select Committee on Intelligence, bk. 3, pp. 191, 192.

78. Ibid., bk. 3, p. 220, n. 156.

79. Goldstein, *Political Repression in Modern America*, p. 526.

80. See Frank Donner, *Protectors of Privilege: Red Squads and Police Repression* (Berkeley: University of California Press, 1990), pp. 181, 191, 216, and 265; and Goldstein, *Political Repression in Modern America*, p. 529.

81. Memorandum from Director, FBI, to SAC, Albany and twenty-three other cities, FBI, August 25, 1967.

82. Airtel from Director, FBI, to SAC, Albany and forty-one other cities, Re: Counterintelligence Program, Black Nationalist Hate-Type Groups, Racial Intelligence, March 4, 1968.

83. Memorandum from SAC, Chicago, to Director, FBI, January 13, 1969.

84. Roy Wilkins and Ramsey Clark, *Search and Destroy: A Report of the Commission of Inquiry into the Black Panthers and the Police* (New York: Metropolitan Applied Research Center, Inc., 1973), p. 7.

85. "Exclusive: Hanrahan, Police Tell Panther Story," *Chicago Tribune*, December 11, 1969.

86. Airtel from SAC, Chicago, to Director, FBI, April 8, 1970.

87. Memorandum from SAC, Chicago, to Director, FBI, December 3, 1969.

88. Airtel from SAC, Chicago, to Director, FBI, Re: Bureau Airtel 12/8/69 and Chicago Letter 11/24/69.

89. J. L. Chestnut Jr. and Julia Cass, *Black in Selma: The Uncommon Life of J. L. Chestnut, Jr.* (New York: Farrar, Straus and Giroux, 1990), p. 374.

90. Ibid., pp. 378, 379.

91. Senate Select Committee on Intelligence, bk. 3, p. 837.

92. David Burnham, *A Law Unto Itself: Power Politics and the IRS* (New York: Random House, 1989), pp. 264–266.

93. Donner, *The Age of Surveillance*, p. 337.

94. Senate Select Committee on Intelligence, bk. 3, p. 842.

95. Mary R. Warner, *The Dilemma of Black Politics: A Report on the Harassment of Black Elected Officials* (Washington, D.C.: Voter Education and Registration Action, 1987), p. 16. For an account of the IRS's collaboration with the FBI's 1964 attempt to use tax returns from Dr. King and from SCLC for disruptive action, see Senate Select Committee on Intelligence, bk. 3, pp. 855–856, 861.

96. FBI memorandum from Atlanta Field Office to FBI Headquarters, April 14, 1964, quoted in Senate Select Committee on Intelligence, bk. 3, p. 856; also see p. 861.

97. Senate Select Committee on Intelligence, bk. 3, p. 839.

98. Memorandum from C. D. Brennen to W. C. Sullivan, February 3, 1969, quoted in ibid., bk. 3, p. 851.

99. Ibid., bk. 3, p. 855.

100. Donald V. Watkins, *A Report from the City of Birmingham, Alabama, to the United States Senate Judiciary Committee on the Harassment of African American Birmingham City Officials by Offices of the United States Attorney, the Federal Bureau of Investigation, and the Internal Revenue Service (Criminal Division)*, February 21, 1990, p. 11.

101. Affidavit of Robert Moussallem, June 5, 1989, reprinted in the *Congressional Record*, 101st Cong., 2d sess., March 9, 1990, vol. 136, pt. 26, p. 52544.

102. Mary A. Fischer, "The Witch-Hunt," *Gentleman's Quarterly,* December 1993, p. 248.

103. Affidavit of Hirsh Friedman, December 1, 1987, reprinted in the *Congressional Record*, 100th Cong., 2d sess., January 27, 1988, vol. 134, pt. 24, p. H31. In addition to the admissions by Robert Moussallem and Hirsh Friedman, Darthard Perry, an FBI operative in Los Angeles, disclosed that Congressman Mervyn Dymally was the real target of an FBI-inspired tax case against one of Dymally's political allies (Rapoport, "Meet America's Meanest Dirty Trickster," pp. 60–61).

104. Fischer, "The Witch-Hunt," p. 244, cites the Justice Department as the source of these statistics.

105. Mark Curriden, "Selective Prosecution: Are Black Officials Investigative Targets?" *American Bar Association Journal* 78 (February 1992): 55.

106. Ibid.; also see Watkins, *A Report from the City of Birmingham,* pp. 36–38, for a table itemizing the cases.

107. Warner, *The Dilemma of Black Politics*. (Author Mary R. Warner is also known as Dr. Mary Sawyer.)

PART THREE

Epigraph quoted in H. C. Peterson and Gilbert Fite, *Opponents of War, 1917–1918* (Madison: University of Wisconsin Press, 1957), p. 73.

1. Ibid., p. 203.

2. All quotations concerning the Prager lynching are drawn from ibid., pp. 203, 204.

3. Woodrow Wilson is quoted in Joan Jensen, *The Price of Vigilance* (New York: Rand McNally, 1968), p. 31.

4. The *New York Times* is quoted in Patrick S. Washburn, *A Question of Sedition: The Federal Government's Investigation of the Black Press During World War II* (New York: Oxford University Press, 1987), p. 46. Other quotations are drawn from Jensen, *The Price of Vigilance*, pp. 54, 55; also see pp. 26–27, 293.

5. Jensen, *The Price of Vigilance*, pp. 27, 28. A Justice Department proposal to arrest "dangerous leaders and plotters in New York and elsewhere of whom we have absolutely no evidence" received tacit approval from the president's cabinet (p. 29).

6. Ibid., p. 110.

7. Peterson and Fite, *Opponents of War*, p. 117.

8. Ibid., p. 175. Also see Jensen, *The Price of Vigilance*, pp. 142, 171; and Roy Talbert Jr., *Negative Intelligence: The Army and the American Left, 1917–1941* (Jackson: University Press of Mississippi, 1991), p. 81.

9. Peterson and Fite, *Opponents of War*, p. 102.

10. Ibid., p. 95.

11. Ibid., p. 90.

12. Thomas Emerson, *The System of Freedom of Expression* (New York: Vintage, 1970), p. 62.

13. Peterson and Fite, *Opponents of War*, p. 15.

14. For information about the number of prosecutions, see Zachariah Chafee, *Free Speech in the United States* (Cambridge: Harvard University Press, 1941), p. 51; Wilson is quoted on p. 38 of Chafee's book. For a firsthand account of a prosecution under the Espionage Act, see Scott Nearing's story in Bud Schultz and Ruth Schultz, *It Did Happen Here: Recollections of Political Repression in America* (Berkeley: University of California Press, 1989), pp. 5–12.

15. See Peterson and Fite, *Opponents of War*, pp. 182–183, for the arrest of the fisherman. See Robert Justin Goldstein, *Political Repression in Modern America: From 1870 to the Present* (Cambridge, Mass.: Schenkman, 1978), p. 114, for information about the two cases in which prison sentences were imposed.

16. Charles Chatfield, *The American Peace Movement: Ideals and Activism* (New York: Twayne, 1992), p. 45.

17. Ibid., p. 215; Chafee, *Free Speech in the United States*, pp. 40–41.

18. Jensen, *The Price of Vigilance*, pp. 140, 234.

19. Ibid., pp. 142, 148–152.

20. Ibid., p. 234.

21. Robert Cohen, *When the Old Left Was Young: Student Radicals and America's First Mass Student Movement, 1929–1941* (New York: Oxford University Press, 1993), p. 73.

22. Ibid., pp. 323–336.

23. Goldstein, *Political Repression in Modern America*, p. 264.

24. Ibid., p. 269.

25. Minoru Yasui describes his experience during the internment of Japanese Americans in Schultz and Schultz, *It Did Happen Here*, pp. 347–359.

26. Richard Barnet argues that Truman's polices "set a direction for the United States that eventually led to the jungles of Vietnam in the 1960s and 1970s and to American participation in the 'low intensity wars' of El Salvador and Nicaragua in the 1980s" (*The Rockets' Red Glare: When America Goes to War: The Presidents and the People* [New York: Simon and Schuster, 1990], p. 267). Also see pp. 254 and 256 of Barnet's book as well as Fred J. Cook, *The Warfare State* (New York: Macmillan, 1962), pp. 149–150; and Goldstein, *Political Repression in Modern America*, pp. 289, 299.

27. Goldstein, *Political Repression in Modern America*, p. 314. (Goldstein quotes Karl M. Schmidt in this passage.)

28. Ibid., p. 371.

29. Tom Wells, *The War Within: America's Battle Over Vietnam* (Berkeley: University of California Press, 1994), p. 1.

30. Ibid., pp. 3–4.

31. Frank Donner, *Protectors of Privilege: Red Squads and Police Repression* (Berkeley: University of California Press, 1990), discusses all these activities: the theft of membership lists (p. 258); the informers' attempts to insert themselves into positions of leadership (pp. 115, 336); attempts to provoke violence (pp. 164, 169, 257); vandalizing of equipment (p. 337); and the tactic of saturation infiltration (p. 302). The quotation from the informer appears on p. 337.

32. Ibid., p. 253.

33. Robert Vaughan is quoted in Alan H. Levine, "Yip-In Massacre," *Civil Liberties in New York* 16, no. 6 (June 1968): 12.

34. Senate Select Committee to Study Government Operations with Respect to Intelligence Activities, *Supplementary Staff Reports on Intelligence Activities and the Rights of Americans*, 94th Cong., 2d sess., Final Report, no. 94–755 (Washington, D.C.: Government Printing Office, 1976) [hereafter referred to as Senate Select Committee on Intelligence], bk. 2, p. 72.

35. Goldstein, *Political Repression in Modern America*, p. 465.

36. Memorandum from Director, FBI, to All Field Offices, July 6, 1968; cited in Ward Churchill and Jim Vander Wall, *The Cointelpro Papers: Documents from the FBI's Secret War Against Dissent in the United States* (Boston: South End Press, 1990), pp. 181–182. See also Senate Select Committee on Intelligence, bk. 3, p. 26.

37. Senate Select Committee on Intelligence, bk. 3, p. 789, n. 16.

38. Ibid., bk. 3, p. 789

39. Goldstein, *Political Repression in Modern America*, p. 487.

40. Quoted in Frank Donner, *The Age of Surveillance: The Aims and Methods of America's Political Intelligence System* (New York: Knopf, 1980), p. 356.

41. Jill Raymond provides details of a case of grand jury abuse in Schultz and Schultz, *It Did Happen Here*, pp. 289–302.

42. The judge is quoted in Donner, *The Age of Surveillance*, p. 356.

43. Amy Swerdlow, *Women Strike for Peace: Traditional Motherhood and Radical Politics in the 1960s* (Chicago: University of Chicago Press, 1993), p. 117.

44. Mary McGrory is quoted in ibid., p. 123.

45. Morton H. Halperin, Jerry J. Breman, Robert L. Borosage, and Christine M. Marwick, *The Lawless State: The Crimes of U.S. Intelligence Agencies* (New York: Penguin, 1976), p. 147.

46. On the organization of vigilante squads, see Cohen, *When the Old Left Was Young*, pp. 106–107.

47. James Wechsler, *Revolt on Campus* (New York: Convici, Friede, 1935), p. 283.

48. Cohen, *When the Old Left Was Young*, pp. 100–101.

49. Bob Gill is quoted in David Lance Goines, *The Free Speech Movement: Coming of Age in the 1960s* (Berkeley: Ten Speed Press, 1993), p. 74.

50. Kirkpatrick Sale, *SDS* (New York: Random House, 1973), p. 167.

51. W. J. Rorabaugh, *Berkeley at War: The 1960s* (New York: Oxford University Press, 1989), p. 31.

52. See Wells, *The War Within*, pp. 10–11.

53. Senate Select Committee on Intelligence, bk. 3, p. 25.

54. Churchill and Vander Wall, *The Cointelpro Papers*, p. 207.

55. Ibid., pp. 143–144; Opinion of U.S. District Court Judge Thomas P. Griesa, *Socialist Workers Party et al. v. Attorney General of the United States et al.*, U.S. District Court for the Southern District of New York, 73 Civ. 3160, August 25, 1986 (published as *Decision: Government Spying and Disruption Is Unconstitutional and Illegal*, by the Political Rights Defense Fund, n.d.), pp. 79–80; Memorandum from SAC, New York (160303), to Director, FBI (100–449698), Re: Cointelpro–New Left, August 28, 1969, p. 2; Churchill and Vander Wall, *The Cointelpro Papers*, pp. 209, 211.

56. Churchill and Vander Wall, *The Cointelpro Papers*, p. 138; Griesa, *Socialist Workers Party et al. v. Attorney General of the United States et al.*, pp. 78–79.

57. These FBI documents are quoted in Churchill and Vander Wall, *The Cointelpro Papers*, pp. 145–146, 203, 213.

58. Goldstein, *Political Repression in Modern America*, p. 452.

59. Wells, *The War Within*, p. 579. Also see Seymour M. Hersh, *The Price of Power: Kissinger in the Nixon White House* (New York: Summit Books, 1983), pp. 127–132.

60. These quotations are taken from personal statements that are in the possession of Norma Becker. Initials are given here to replace full names.

61. Memorandum from Director, FBI (100–449698), to SAC, New York (100–163303), October 15, 1969, in which Hoover grants authority "to prepare and anonymously distribute" the Give Them Bananas leaflet.

62. For a firsthand account of Vietnam Veterans Against the War and the repression directed at this organization, see Scott Camil's story in Schultz and Schultz, *It Did Happen Here,* pp. 319–333.

63. The letter from a U.S. AID volunteer in South Vietnam, addressed to the Episcopal Peace Fellowship, is in the possession of Norma Becker.

64. Goldstein, *Political Repression in Modern America,* p. 440. For Dr. Benjamin Spock's account of the trial, see Schultz and Schultz, *It Did Happen Here,* pp. 91–100.

65. Emerson, *The System of Freedom of Expression,* p. 411.

66. The New York Civil Liberties Union lawyer is quoted in Todd Gitlin, *The Sixties: Years of Hope, Days of Rage* (New York: Bantam Books, 1987), p. 238.

67. Daniel Walker, *Rights in Conflict: The Violent Confrontation of Demonstrators and Police in the Parks and Streets of Chicago During the Week of the Democratic National Convention of 1968* (New York: Signet Books, 1968), p. xxii.

68. The seven defendants were acquitted of the conspiracy charges, but five of them were found guilty of the lesser charge of inciting to riot. In November 1972, a federal appeals court overturned those convictions. Bobby Seale's case was severed from the others in the middle of the trial, and he was never retried.

69. The courtroom transcript is quoted in Judy Clavir and John Spitzer, eds., *The Conspiracy Trial* (New York: Bobbs-Merrill, 1970), p. 344.

70. Hersh, *The Price of Power,* p. 53; also see pp. 54, 120, 126, 175–177; and Wells, *The War Within,* pp. 290–291, 356, 357.

71. *New York Times* editorial, June 21, 1971, quoted in Neil Sheehan, Hedrick Smith, E. W. Kenworthy, and Fox Butterworth, *The Pentagon Papers: The Secret History of the Vietnam War* (New York: Bantam Books, 1971), p. 646.

72. Hersh, *The Price of Power,* p. 385.

73. The designations "classified," "secret," and "top secret" were loosely applied and referred more often than not to political secrets, not state secrets. See Peter Schrag, *Test of Loyalty: Daniel Ellsberg and the Rituals of Secret Government* (New York: Simon and Schuster, 1974), pp. 184–186. Also see David Wise, *The Politics of Lying: Government Deception, Secrecy, and Power* (New York: Vintage, 1973), p. 210.

74. Donner, *The Age of Surveillance,* pp. 376–377.

75. Wise, *The Politics of Lying,* p. 214. Also see Michael Linfield, *Freedom Under Fire: U.S. Civil Liberties in Times of War* (Boston: South End Press, 1990), p. 144.

76. Wise, *The Politics of Lying,* pp. 214, 207–224. Also see Sanford J. Ungar, *The Papers and the Papers: An Account of the Legal and Political Battle Over the Pentagon Papers* (New York: Dutton, 1975), pp. 112, 124.

77. Donner states that the Ellsberg grand jury proceedings in both Los Angeles and Boston were leaked to the White House "Plumbers unit" for use in Project Ellsberg (*The Age of Surveillance,* p. 381).

78. "Deepening Shadow," *New York Times,* November 23, 1972, p. 34.

79. Evan Thomas and Lucy Shackelford, "Nixon Off the Record," *Newsweek,* November 3, 1997, p. 53.

80. Leon Jaworski, *The Right and the Power: The Prosecution of Watergate* (New York: Pocket Books, 1977), p. 28.

81. David Wise, *The American Police State: The Government Against the People* (New York: Random House, 1976), pp. 159, 403; Wells, *The War Within*, p. 520; H. R. Haldeman and Joseph DiMone, *The Ends of Power* (New York: Dell, 1978), pp. 159–160.

82. Wells, *The War Within*, p. 520.

83. All quotations from the grand jury proceedings are taken from an unofficial transcript published in the *Harvard Crimson*, March 29, 1972, pp. 1–8.

84. Hersh, *The Price of Power*, p. 191.

85. See Wells, *The War Within*, pp. 425–426; Sale, *SDS*, p. 636; and Hersh, *The Price of Power*, p. 194. The university presidents' message to Nixon was reported in "4 Kent State Students Killed by Troops," *New York Times*, May 5, 1970, p. 1.

86. Wells, *The War Within*, p. 426.

87. Nixon is quoted in ibid., p. 448.

88. William Scranton, *The Report of the President's Commission on Campus Unrest* (New York: Avon Books, 1971), p. 287.

89. Peter Davies, *The Truth About Kent State: A Challenge to the American Conscience* (New York: Farrar, Straus and Giroux, 1993), p. 221. Also see William A. Gordon, *The Fourth of May: Killings and Cover-Ups and Kent State* (Buffalo: Prometheus, 1990), pp. 31, 61, 62, for the nature and conclusions of the FBI's investigation; for example, the bureau studied not only what Kent State professors taught in their classrooms but even the credit ratings of the dead victims. Gordon states that "it is clear that the FBI's sympathies were with the Guardsmen and not with the students" (p. 61).

90. Davies, *The Truth About Kent State*, p. 222.

91. The FBI report is quoted in ibid., p. 223.

92. Gitlin, *The Sixties*, pp. 414–415.

93. Ramsey Clark is quoted in Frank Beacham, "A Forgotten Tragedy in the Long History of Civil Rights Crimes," *Hartford Courant*, February 10, 1993, p. D13. Cleveland Sellers, an activist who survived the Orangeburg Massacre, describes this experience in Schultz and Schultz, *It Did Happen Here*, pp. 249–262.

94. Scranton, *President's Commission on Campus Unrest*, pp. 453, 434.

95. Ibid., p. 462.

96. See Joseph Kelner and James Munves, *The Kent State Coverup* (New York: Harper and Row, 1980), pp. 97, 123, 128; and Gordon, *The Fourth of May*, pp. 141–142, for the testimony of the National Guardsmen.

97. Loch K. Johnson, *Secret Agencies: U.S. Intelligence in a Hostile World* (New York: Oxford, 1996), p. x.

98. Geoffrey R. Stone, "The Reagan Administration, the First Amendment, and Domestic Security Investigations," in Richard O. Curry, ed., *Freedom at Risk: Secrecy, Censorship, and Repression in the 1980s* (Philadelphia: Temple University Press, 1988), p. 277.

99. The Domestic Security/Terrorism guidelines (also known as the Smith guidelines) are quoted in Gary Stern, "The FBI's Misguided Probe of CISPES," Center for National Security Studies, CNSS Report no. 111, June 1988, p. 26, n. 56. See also Stone, "The Reagan Administration," pp. 278–279, 282.

100. Jeane Kirkpatrick is quoted in Christian Smith, *Resisting Reagan: The U.S. Central America Peace Movement* (Chicago: University of Chicago Press, 1996), p. 18.

101. Ronald Reagan is quoted in ibid., p. 18.

102. Smith, *Resisting Reagan*, pp. 22–23. Smith quotes John Kelly, deputy assistant secretary of the Air Force and a specialist in low-intensity warfare as saying: "The most critical special operations mission we have today is to persuade the American public that the communists are out to get us" (p. 28).

103. Ibid., p. 28.

104. Statement of Frank Varelli, House Judiciary Committee, Subcommittee on Civil and Constitutional Rights, *Hearings on Break-Ins at Sanctuary Churches and Organizations Opposed to Administration Policy in Central America*, 100th Cong., 1st sess., serial 42, February 19 and 20 (Washington, D.C.: Government Printing Office, 1987), pp. 439, 440.

105. Stern, "The FBI's Misguided Probe of CISPES," p. 5.

106. James X. Dempsey and David Cole, *Terrorism and the Constitution: Sacrificing Civil Liberties in the Name of National Security* (Los Angeles: First Amendment Foundation, 1999), p. 21.

107. Center for Constitutional Rights, "News Release: Statement of the Center for Constitutional Rights in Response to FBI Director William S. Sessions' Defense of the CISPES Investigation," New York, February 2, 1988, p. 2.

108. Tamar Jacoby, "Going After Dissidents: Do Hoover's Tactics Live on at the 'Reformed' FBI?" *Newsweek*, February 8, 1988, p. 29. Also see FBI memorandum from Dallas (199–795), to Director (199–8488) and field offices, April 2, 1984.

109. Press Release, FBI Director William S. Sessions, February 2, 1988, p. 3. Also see testimony of William S. Sessions, House Judiciary Committee, Subcommittee on Civil and Constitutional Rights, *Hearings on FBI Investigation of El Salvador Support Committee (CISPES)*, 100th Cong., 2d sess., September 16 (Washington, D.C.: Government Printing Office, 1988), p. 2; Ross Gelbspan, *Break-Ins, Death Threats, and the FBI: The Covert War Against the Central America Movement* (Boston: South End Press, 1991), p. 136; Smith, *Resisting Reagan*, p. 287; and Dempsey and Cole, *Terrorism and the Constitution*, p. 30.

110. Remarks by Representative Don Edwards, which are also part of the *Congressional Record* (March 3, 1988), are quoted in Stern, "The FBI's Misguided Probe of CISPES," p. 9.

111. William Sessions is quoted in Gelbspan, *Break-Ins, Death Threats, and the FBI*, p. 210.

112. At a congressional hearing in 1988, Congressman Don Edwards stated: "Another FBI official strongly denied in February 1987 that the FBI was passing information to the National Guard of El Salvador through Varelli. It now appears pretty clear that he did" (Dempsey and Cole, *Terrorism and the Constitution*, p. 30).

113. Varelli statement, House Subcommittee on Civil and Constitutional Rights, *Hearings on Break-Ins at Sanctuary Churches*, p. 518.

114. Sessions testimony, House Subcommittee on Civil and Constitutional Rights, *Hearings on FBI Investigation of El Salvador Support Committee,* pp. 3, 10. Also see Smith, *Resisting Reagan,* pp. 312–319.

115. Dempsey and Cole, *Terrorism and the Constitution,* pp. 44–46.

116. Ibid., p. 29.

117. Smith, *Resisting Reagan,* pp. 281–284, 284–285; Gelbspan, *Break-Ins, Death Threats, and the FBI,* pp. 2, 15, 27–28; Athan Theoharis, "The FBI and Domestic Surveillance," in Curry, ed., *Freedom at Risk,* p. 270.

118. Smith, *Resisting Reagan,* pp. 282–283; Theoharis, "The FBI and Domestic Surveillance," p. 270; Matthew Purdy and Alphonso Chardy, "Expansive Probe by FBI Spurred by Fabrication," *Hartford Courant,* October 9, 1988, pp. AA1-AA2.

119. Gelbspan, *Break-Ins, Death Threats, and the FBI,* p. 33; Smith, *Resisting Reagan,* p. 309.

120. Smith, *Resisting Reagan,* p. 309.

121. Christian Smith reported 140 break-ins from the Movement Support Network in 1989 (*Resisting Reagan,* p. 301); Ross Gelbspan in 1991 reported 200 (*Break-Ins, Death Threats, and the FBI,* p. 23). See Smith (*Resisting Reagan,* pp. 301, 307) regarding the accuracy of the information the terrorists and the intruders had.

122. Smith, *Resisting Reagan,* pp. 301–302; Gelbspan, *Break-Ins, Death Threats, and the FBI,* pp. 32, 200; testimony of Margaret Ratner, House Subcommittee on Civil and Constitutional Rights, *Hearings on Break-Ins at Sanctuary Churches,* p. 177.

123. Representative Don Edwards is quoted in Gelbspan, *Break-Ins, Death Threats, and the FBI,* pp. 220–221.

124. Memorandum from Dallas (199–795)(P) to Director (199–8848), FBI, March 3, 1985.

PART FOUR

First epigraph quoted in Athan G. Theoharis and John Stuart Cox, *The Boss: J. Edgar Hoover and the Great American Inquisition* (Philadelphia: Temple University Press, 1988), p. 86. Harlan Fiske Stone later became a Justice of the U.S. Supreme Court.

Second epigraph quoted from the testimony of FBI section chief George C. Moore on November 11, 1975; see Senate Select Committee to Study Government Operations with Respect to Intelligence Activities, *Supplementary Staff Reports on Intelligence Activities and the Rights of Americans,* 94th Cong., 2d sess., Final Report, no. 94–755 (Washington, D.C.: Government Printing Office, 1976) [hereafter referred to as Senate Select Committee on Intelligence], bk. 2, p. 140.

1. Theoharis and Cox, *The Boss,* p. 426.

2. Senate Select Committee on Intelligence, bk. 3, p. 3.

3. Ibid., bk. 3, p. 13.

4. Ibid.

5. U.S. General Accounting Office, *International Terrorism: FBI Investigates Domestic Activities to Identify Terrorists,* September 1990 (Washington, D.C.: Government Printing Office), p. 3.

6. Frank J. Smist Jr., *Congress Oversees the United States Intelligence Community, 1947–1989* (Knoxville: University of Tennessee Press, 1990), p. 276.

7. See Theoharis and Cox, *The Boss,* pp. 42–43, 56–57, 86, 92, 93–94, 172–174; and Frank Donner, *The Age of Surveillance: The Aims and Methods of America's Political Intelligence System* (New York: Knopf, 1980), pp. 162–164.

8. Joan Humphrey Lefkow, "Report and Recommendations," to the Honorable Ann Claire Williams, U.S. District Judge in the case of *Alliance to End Repression et al. v. City of Chicago et al.,* case nos. 74 C 3268 and 75 C 3295, U.S. District Court for the Northern District of Illinois, Eastern Division, September 21, 1992, p. 6.

9. For example, as James Dempsey and David Cole observed: "The Reagan Administration interpreted [the Freedom of Information Act] narrowly, especially as it applied to the FBI and the intelligence agencies, and the courts in many cases deferred to the Executive Branch" (*Terrorism and the Constitution: Sacrificing Civil Liberties in the Name of National Security* [Los Angeles: First Amendment Foundation, 1999], p. 76).

10. According to Dempsey and Cole, "Congressional oversight is inconsistent, often driven by partisan disputes rather than principle, and easily stymied by Executive Branch resistance. Indeed, the Congressional oversight committees just as often served as defenders and promoters of the agencies they are supposed to control" (ibid., p. 65).

11. In the thirteen-year lawsuit brought by the Socialist Workers Party against the FBI, the bureau concealed information from the plaintiffs and was, according to the judge in the case, "grossly deceptive"; in addition, the attorney general refused to comply with a court order to disclose information about bureau informants (ibid., pp. 92–93). Congressman Don Edwards, referring to the CISPES investigation, said, "It has taken us three years to get the full story." He pointed to examples of FBI denials made to his subcommittee that later turned out to be false. For example, "the FBI assured us that it was not investigating the sanctuary movement. It is now clear that the FBI surveilled sanctuary churches and investigated sanctuary activities" (ibid., p. 30).

12. Lefkow, "Report and Recommendations," *Alliance to End Repression et al. v. City of Chicago et al.,* February 4, 1991, p. 9.

13. Ann Claire Williams, *CISPES v. FBI,* U.S. District Court for the Northern District of Illinois, Eastern Division, case no. 74 C 3268, February 15, 1990.

14. Dempsey and Cole, *Terrorism and the Constitution,* pp. 165–166.

15. Ibid., p. 10; also see pp. 123, 160.

16. American Friends Service Committee, *The Police Threat to Political Liberty* (Philadelphia: AFSC, 1979), p. 52.

17. A lawsuit brought against Los Angeles Police Chief Edward Davis revealed that the Police Department Intelligence Division (PDID) kept files on the American Baptist Home Mission Society, the Methodist Church Board of National Missions, the United Presbyterian Church, the Catholic Committee for Ur-

ban Ministries, the Executive Council of the Episcopal Church, and the American Jewish Committee, among the wide range of political, educational, and social welfare groups it surveilled (Frank Donner, *Protectors of Privilege: Red Squads and Police Repression* [Berkeley: University of California Press, 1990], pp. 257–258). For information about PDID's sharing of its files, see Donner, *Protectors of Privilege*, pp. 283–286; and Ross Gelbspan, *Break-Ins, Death Threats, and the FBI: The Covert War Against the Central America Movement* (Boston: South End Press, 1991), pp. 169–171.

18. District Judge Susan Getzendanner, "Memorandum Opinion and Order," *Alliance to End Repression et al. v. City of Chicago et al.*, December 30, 1985, p. 1047.

19. Deposition of John Valkenburg, *Alliance to End Repression et al. v. City of Chicago et al.*, April 18, 1979.

20. Cook County Grand Jury, *Report on Improper Police Intelligence Activities*, March 1975, Cook County, Illinois, section I.

21. Senator Charles Percy is quoted in "Police Spy Report 'One-Sided'—Percy," *Chicago Sun-Times*, January 13, 1976.

22. Investigator 742 and 609, "Observation or Surveillance Report," Subject Matter of Investigation: The Black Strategy Center, Chicago Police Department, Intelligence Division, October 3, 1969, p. 1.

23. Editorial, *Chicago Sun-Times*, December 16, 1976.

24. Investigator's Report, Reporting Officers 397 and 548, Chicago Police Department, Intelligence Division, August 18, 1966, p. 1.

25. Memorandum from Patrolman Tom Braham, #12116, to Director Wm. J. Duffy, Subject: Spanish Action Committee of Chicago, Intelligence Division, Chicago Police Department, August 19, 1966, p. 1.

26. *El Puertorriqueño*, September 9–15, 1966, p. 1.

27. Investigator's Report, Reporting Officer 548, Chicago Police Department, Intelligence Division, July 9, 1966, pp. 1–2.

28. Investigator's Report, Reporting Officers 397 and 548, Chicago Police Department, Intelligence Division, August 18, 1966, p. 7.

29. Investigator's Report, Reporting Officers 397 and 548, Chicago Police Department, Intelligence Division, August 31, 1966, p. 1.

30. Excerpted from trial transcript, direct examination of Juan Díaz, *Spanish Action Committee of Chicago v. City of Chicago*, 1984, pp. B110–111.

31. "Memorandum of the City of Chicago in Support of Its Motion to Modify the 1982 *Alliance* Consent Decree," *Alliance to End Repression et al. and American Civil Liberties Union et al. v. City of Chicago*, case nos. 74 C 3268 and 75 C 3295, U.S. District Court for the Northern District of Illinois, Eastern Division, March 7, 1997, p. 3.

32. Edward A. Bobrick, "Report and Recommendation," to U.S. District Judge Ann C. Williams in the case of *Alliance to End Repression et al., Plaintiffs (case no. 74 C 3268), and American Civil Liberties Union et al., Plaintiffs (case no. 75 C 3295), v. City of Chicago et al., Defendants*, U.S. District Court for the Northern District of Illinois, Eastern Division, March 11, 1999, p. 24.

33. Ibid.

34. Ibid., p. 27.

35. "Corrected Memorandum of the City of Chicago in Support of Its Renewed Motion to Modify the 1982 *Alliance* Consent Decree," *Alliance to End Repression et al., v. City of Chicago et al.*, September 24, 1998, pp. 3, 33–34.

36. *Alliance to End Repression et al. v. City of Chicago et al.*, 561 F. Supp. 537, 564 (Northern District of Illinois, 1982).

37. "Motion of City of Chicago to Modify Consent Decree," *Alliance to End Repression et al. v. City of Chicago et al.*, March 7, 1997, Exhibit A, p. 3.

Index

Page numbers in **bold type** indicate interviews. Page numbers in *italic type* indicate photographs.

Compositor: Integrated Composition Systems
       Text: 10/13 Sabon
    Display: Sabon
Printer and Binder: Friesens Corporation
   Indexer: Ellen Davenport